RAVINGS OF A RELUCTANT PSYCHONAUT
Ayahuasca, San Pedro, Kambo Medicinas

M. C. Miller

All rights reserved.
Copyright 2018 © by M. C. Miller

No part of this book may be reproduced in any form or by any means without permission in writing from the author, except for the inclusion of brief quotations in a review. Any unauthorized use, sharing, reproduction or distribution of these materials by any means, electronic, mechanical or otherwise is strictly prohibited.

Publisher & Cover Design: M. C. Miller
Inquiries may be directed to saminchawow@gmail.com
www.mcmillerbooks.com

The following information is intended for general information purposes only. This book is not intended as a substitute for the medical or psychological advice of physicians and/or psychiatrists. The reader should consult health practitioners in matters relating to physical or mental/emotional health and particularly with respect to any symptoms that may require diagnosis or medical attention. The publisher does not advocate illegal activities but does believe in the right of individuals to have free access to information and ideas. Any application of the material set forth in the following pages is at the reader's discretion and is his or her sole responsibility.

ISBN-13: 978-1-7322441-0-8
First Edition

Dedicated
to a remarkable shaman
who must remain nameless,
and that's one of the reasons he's remarkable.

TABLE OF CONTENTS

Title Page
Copyright / 2
Dedication / 3
Introduction / 7

SHOCK BEFORE AWE / 9
The Why, The Fear, and the Exploration of the Curious Curios Presumed Inside:
The Fear – 1st Ayahuasca Ceremony / 13
The Exploration – Mother & Grandfather Share a Cup / 29
Curious Curios – True Measures of Integration / 36

RUNNING THE HAUNTLET / 43
Kambo / 47
Two Days with Grandfather Huachuma (San Pedro) / 61
Heartbreak Container, Sad Passion of Happiness, and Playing The Game With Father San Pedro / 81
Lucid Dream Ceremony / 109
Humble Pie & Tranquility / 115
(Or – Enjoying Diverging Glides of Present Polarity in the Timeless Unity behind a Virtual Personal Space Unfolding Upon Laughter)
The Snake, The Owl, and the Condor / 127

INTO THE FIRE / 139
Inhuman Transformations of My Soulular Machine / 141
Soulular Renewal Overwhelms My Human Gadget / 159
Heart-Flows With El Espíritu de Las Aguas / 171

THE TRANCE IN THE DANCER / 191
By The River, Spikes Into Elsewhere / 195
Bliss Or Amnesia in Aviation Ground School / 201
An Opening / 211
Out of the Fog / 215
Unpack A Fractal Maelstrom / 219
Three Dreams / Three Nights / Three Words / 227
Solo With Sapo / 231

BEYOND RECOGNITION / 237
Kawsaypacha Beyond the Puzzle / 245
The Interrupted Conversation / 255
Raki-Raki Yanantin Time / 259
Shaman Schwaman, Yeah Whatever, Really? / 269
Serious Adjustments in How After What / 273

BEYOND RECOGNITION / (continued)
    Too Much Swag / 279
    The Ride / 287
    Blinding By The Light / 293
    The Sanctuary of Some Special Things / 295
    Ayavision / The Four Offerings / 299
    In Both Worlds / 305
    The Lesson / 315
    Smiling Tiger Wobbly Horse / 321
    A Jungle Without Limits / 325
    The Why, The Fear, and the Exploration of the Curious Curios
        Presumed Inside:
            The Why – Letting Go / 345

Memo By Deb / 349
Postscript / 369
IAM / 376

Introduction

"They call it the medicine. We call it the poison."

Not exactly what I wanted to hear from dark, interdimensional entities shape-shifting around me in the middle of the night. They hated the fact I could see them. And they really didn't like how I could watch what they were doing to the other ceremony participants in the maloca, the open-air ceremonial space. At least on one point the entities and I had no argument – I didn't like being with them either. As it turned out, they gave me the worst night of my life – a night, during which, I seriously couldn't see how I would survive or find my way back.

Thousands of miles from home, I sat with a gut full of Ayahuasca. I had come to South America on vacation. My wife wanted to include a side trip to do the sacred plant medicines Ayahuasca and San Pedro while we toured around. I had a growing interest in such things but I wouldn't say it was a calling. After doing a fair share of cannabis and hashish in high school and college so long ago, who wouldn't be curious? But was curiosity enough if one wanted to get anything out of the experience? It wasn't so much a consideration at the time. Supporting my wife loomed larger.

I had heard enough about how these plant medicines weren't recreational – it was meant for people with serious issues to work through. That gave me some reservations. After all, I had no major pressing issues. All I could bring to a ceremony was a healthy interest in altered states and expanded consciousness. Of course, that's funny to say now. It shows the level of denial we all can be in.

Somehow I had managed to be the one person on the planet without an issue, at least one needing serious work done on it. But I was the supportive type so I went along. If nothing else it would be something to do together as a couple, an experience to share, just like the rest of the vacation. It'd be something else exotic to talk about together once we got back home – back in the matrix.

But there I was, sitting in the dark, high up in the Andes, catatonic with fear while impossibly burning up and freezing at the same time from psychic attacks meant to paralyze and terrorize me. Now this was more than I expected. I guess my problem was expecting anything. All I knew was – whatever was happening couldn't be my issue. Besides, the whole thing was too real to be a hallucination. In fact, the whole thing was more real than the shadow world I had left behind. What the hell was happening?

And so began an odyssey with sacred plant medicines that lasted over two years – one that shook this reluctant psychonaut to the core. The medicines were Ayahuasca, San Pedro, Kambo, Liquid Tobacco, and various blends of Rapé. It's also an odyssey for which, in hindsight, I'm forever grateful. You couldn't have told me two years ago I'd ever be saying such a thing. No way. Even a year after the worst night of my life, I was deeply disturbed about what had happened. For the longest while, I was definite there was no chance I'd go back for more. As I sarcastically asked someone once, *did Dante ever write a sequel*? Hell…no. Well, in lieu of Dante reincarnating, he can claim this as that sequel.

In between then and now, there's been a lot of ravings going on by yours truly. After each ceremony (yes, there were others – I've learned, never say anything is definite), I documented my ravings in search of answers, in hope of understanding. Funny how eventually that process morphed into a search for healing. Ultimately, the whole thing became a passage into everything possible.

The chronicle of those desperate attempts to understand what had happened, how I was changing, and what was going on inside and out is included here. Those journal entries appear in the order they happened. All were written soon after their respective ceremonies. I've added explanation and reflections around them where necessary to provide context and insight. Taken together, they document my journey, my process, my transformation. Looking back on it now, I can see how I was led by the medicine through four stages. It's nothing I saw at the time. I was too close to it all. I'm even closer now but with a whole different perspective. And with perspective, a new understanding is possible. If nothing else, sacred plant medicines provide those perspectives. It's up to us to see and use it all as a better way forward.

No doubt, sacred plant medicines are a powerful tool, as I learned. I only hope something in all I went through helps someone. It could be someone new to the medicine but considering a similar path, someone who can do with hearing a bit of what to expect and how to approach it. It could be someone who knows someone still struggling with their experience with the medicine and would like ideas on how to assist. It could be someone who's already gone down the entheogenic road and now wonders about possible ways to come to grips with what happened and the changes they feel.

All in all, it's about coming out better on the other side. It's the other side of a place in each of us that's everywhere beyond and yet intimately near. It's where we really live. It's where we completely heal. But finding doesn't come to us. We go to it. Some raving and reluctant like me.

SHOCK BEFORE AWE

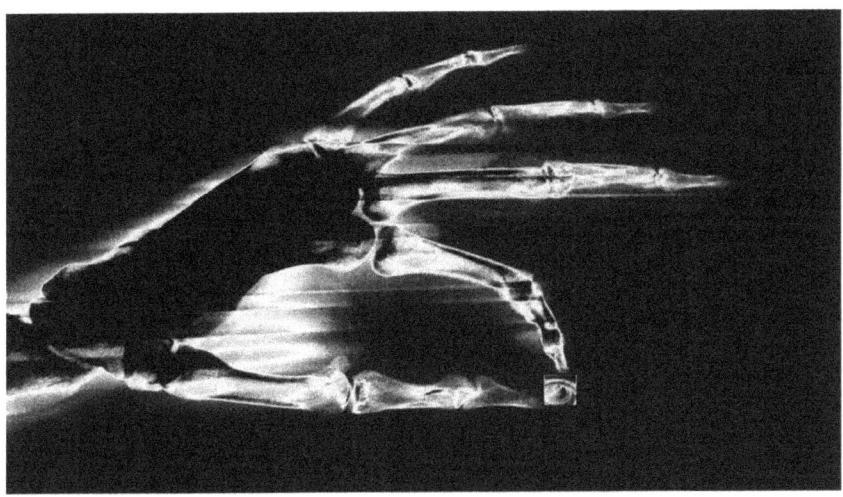

Halfway to South America, stuffed into an airplane seat, who did I think I was? Did I know? Did I care? What was driving me? What did I really want to do? Who was I to decide? How many people around me were set on automatic? Was I? Was my wife? My friends? Was automatic a good thing? Was there anything I wouldn't look at? What about stuff I didn't even know about that made me who I thought I was? Was any of this the least bit important? Such things would have been ridiculous questions to be considering. If I had considered them. After all, this was my vacation.

In fact, none of these questions, or a thousand more like them, ever crossed my mind. We made our landing approach south of the equator in the dead of night and no light fell on any of it. As far as I was concerned, everything was simple. It'd be fun to visit a whole different continent with language, customs, and culture new to me. Also, along the way, it would be good to support my wife in her visit with the famed plant medicine spirits. I had absolutely no serious reflections beyond this, no pressing personal issues needing exotic shamanic care, no project plans or timetable for ultimate transcendence.

My biggest preparation for what was about to happen was a recommended change of diet for a couple weeks before the trip. Alcohol, sugar, and red meat were greatly reduced or eliminated altogether, as were heavy spices. I wasn't super strict about it and I wasn't jazzed about spending most of my vacation on such a diet, but it was necessary, so everyone said, so that was that.

We owned our house in the Pacific Northwest section of the United States. I was more than content to stick it out for another ten years in corporate cubicles until retirement with full benefits became an option. By then I would leave behind an information technology career that spanned over forty years. It wasn't totally satisfying since my college degree was in television and motion picture production, but that was mostly everyone's story, wasn't it? Career was not a dream; it was a living, and everyone had one.

And it wasn't all work, of course. I went hiking occasionally, on weekends when I managed to get up early enough to hit the trails at the time I preferred. Otherwise I'd sleep in and enjoy not having the standard alarm set me in motion at 6am. I also had my sea kayak. Even though lately I hadn't felt the energy to take it out as much as I once did. More than hobbies I rarely indulged in, I had a comfortable routine in an upscale suburb. What was there not to like?

Most of all, I had a terrific marriage. Of course, Monday through Fridays were pretty much booked being a corporate citizen in high-rise towers downtown. The weekend became our together time. And yeah, over the years, most of Saturdays and Sundays had slipped into relaxing and recovering so we'd both be tip-top for the next Monday through Friday run for the gold. It cycled like that pretty much every week. It was what it was. That's life. Who was it who said a disappointed life was a life of unrealistic expectations? My wife and I were practical enough not to fall into that trap.

Little did I know the shock I was in for. And fat chance I'd find an easy way to recover. I had no idea what the next two years would bring. In fact, if I had been told about the changes about to sweep through my life, I would have laughed it off as preposterous. But I was deep in for it. Once I accepted and swallowed that sludgy cup of Ayahuasca, all bets were off.

Beforehand, everyone in the circle of participants had shared their intentions. I felt obliged to have one to be part of the group. In actuality, I wasn't sure what kind of intention I should have. I had my routine. It worked. I was on vacation, my two weeks away from the corporate cubicle for the year. Everything was fine. As it turned out, not having a good intention didn't matter. Somehow the plant medicine scanned me and saw what it needed to see. And although I didn't know it then, it wasn't all good.

I had heard many stories about the so-called Vine of the Soul, Ayahuasca, yagé, or iowaska as those who speak the Quechua language prefer to spell it. Many of those stories were fraught with oddities, struggles, and unpleasantries. Some were outright "bad trips." A good portion of that, I presumed, was click-bait promotional hype, narcissist cravings for attention, or sensationalism over a psychedelic as the latest pop topic in the news. Even if some of the stories were genuine, I was confident this was merely the result of people encountering head-on their serious issues such as PTSD, addiction, or the aftermath of traumatic abuse in such a way they couldn't wiggle away from it. I didn't fall into any of those categories so there was no reason to suspect the principle of GIGO, garbage in garbage out, would come into play to find anything within me feeding bad-juju into the medicine experience.

While not exactly a common household term, Ayahuasca had gained a fair amount of notoriety in the last decade. Any time a tourist industry is able to develop around something, you know some kind of word is going out with a bunch of people willing to open their wallets to participate. In the culture I came from, anything that got people to part with their moolah was worth a look. This was all the more amazing given the fact that there are literally hundreds of vines, trees, and shrubs in South American jungles and rainforests that indigenous tradition considers maestras or teachers.

They say this teaching from the plants comes in various forms of visionary knowledge, detox and cleansing, the release of negative energy, or increased energy and power in the body. Why Ayahuasca should be singled out for the limelight was only adding PR to its allure. Why indeed? Why not other plants? Why not mocura, epená, chuchuhuasi, chiric sanango, yopo, or ajo sacha, to name a few? Should I believe the rumors about the Vine of the Soul being the "mother of all plants." Was it all myth that ancient rituals added up to something worthwhile? Could a plant really contain its own conscious "anima," an individual spirit one could communicate with? Even if it did, could such a thing be wise beyond belief, as advertised?

It didn't go unnoticed that the Peruvian government had seen fit to honor this Vine of the Soul as a national treasure, noting its "extraordinary therapeutic value" and important place in the country's cultural history. That fed into the fact that this one plant, among the tens of thousands of species available, held common significance among nearly all of the indigenous tribes of the Amazon. And their traditions with this plant went way back, far before Socrates was a gleam in his mother's eye.

Adding to my interest was the fact that as long ago as 1986, the U.S. Patent and Trademark Office had actually allowed someone a patent on the Ayahuasca vine, B. Caapi. Besides the bizarroworld notion of anyone getting to patent one of nature's plants (what's next, rainbows and butterflies – if you look, you owe me a royalty payment?), this patent prompted a large backlash from a consortium of groups that got the patent overturned in 1999. But this reversal would not admit any religious or cultural reason for prohibiting a patent and so, upon appeal, the patent was reinstated in 2001, only to expire in 2003. But the debate over people's rights to access nature itself had begun in earnest. And to begin it, Ayahuasca was shown by both sides, for different reasons, to be a valuable commodity.

The following journal entries, parts one through three, document my first two journeys with this Vine of the Soul and their aftermath. I can see it now as the brave face on trauma. It was the shock before awe.

The Why, The Fear, and the Exploration of the Curious Curios Presumed Inside
The Fear – 1st Ayahuasca Ceremony

Before one solves the dilemma, there is "the fear." But dilemmas have an issue. It's not at all certain they can be solved, at least satisfactorily. I only know that solving mine is an absolute necessity if I'm ever to be rid of the fear.

It was midday – eight hours after my first Ayahuasca ceremony wound down in confusion and panic. I found a quiet place by myself among the breezy eucalyptus trees. I was tired of thinking and not even sure if meditation was safe. Wavering in a state of stunned fight-or-flight, I needed a place to sit, mainly because wandering around in a daze was problematic. I didn't feel fully in my body and moments in time were still expanding beyond their lock-step borders.

Encountering anyone else at that time would not have led to any sensible conversations. Not when my soul was babbling an emotive language that I hoped something in nature might understand. Maybe nature could be my interpreter. Perhaps a familiar natural world would slow my soul. Then possibly I could parse the thoughts whizzing through a flurry of emotions. I sat and made an unsteady practice of taking breaths. They struggled in like sucking Jello. Out they came like helpless sighs.

I wasn't sure if it was possible to process where I had gone or what I had seen the night before. I told myself there had to be ways to make sense of it. Then just as quickly, it all was too incredible to entertain explanations that would last. Either I had somehow crafted the most terrifyingly elaborate, self-reinforcing mind game – or the unpredictable plant medicine was seriously playing with my head – or I had actually seen something more genuine than anything I had experienced before.

Just my luck – the dilemma had more than two factors.

The question looped endlessly; why would I be shown this? To torment all normalcy and certainty out of me? If so, it didn't work. The experience had been hyper-real to the point that now I was certain of things that couldn't exist. How could I be so positive of something so impossible? People could convince themselves of anything. Maybe my analytical abilities had gone ballistic in an orgy of creative self-flagellation and conjured up the best of the worst my runaway imagination could bear. What was more likely – a hallucination had become real or a simple death-spiral of unreasonable fear had transformed a series of mundane occurrences into an all-night fright show and nothing more? For reasons that were all-too-apparent, asking the shaman was not an option. It didn't seem any use trying to explain myself to anyone else. Even I would have answered myself the same way – Get over it, it was just a fucking hallucination. Concentrate on the message. What was your lesson?

Oh yeah, that really did nothing. That missed the point. This went beyond messages.

Maybe I should have closed my eyes like everyone else and taken the journey within, forced myself to listen to the icaros and nothing else. What if I had concentrated on continually repeating my intention? Over and over, just say it – no matter what else swirls around.

Would that have rescued me from spending the night watching the veil lift? (Fat chance.)

Could that have saved me from witnessing the ceremony for what it really was? (Not really.)

Funny thing is – I had a perfectly fine intention. I shared it with the group beforehand and they raised no red flags. I told them – I've spent the bulk of my life being very good at something that isn't me. With the remaining time I have, I'd like guidance on what I should be doing. I want it revealed to me the best way to be the real me and in doing so, contribute and make life meaningful.

Also, if Mother Ayahuasca had the time, I'm also interested in knowing just what this place is and why we're here. It's the big existential enchilada of a question, I know, but as far as I can determine, it's only been guessed at and never really answered with any completeness or consistency. At least not outside adopting some kind of faith. Don't get me wrong; faith is good as a stopgap. But who would pass up a chance of knowing the answer for sure?

As night fell and the central fire was stoked, I was excited and a little nervous but I had nothing but positive vibes about the night ahead. Having been acquainted with psychoactive substances in the past, I felt justified to presume past experience had paid most of my trippy dues. After all, the inaugural run of the loop-de-loop is not so scary if you've already been on a few gnarly rides. So goes the logic. (Shitty logic.)

The brown sludge poured from a worn plastic bottle into a battered metal cup. The shaman blessed and purified the brew by passing it towards the fire before offering it back to me. A half hour passed before there was any effect from swallowing the nasty mixture. It began with a sense of queasiness to the passage of time. Soon to follow was a subtle unease. A bilious ache rose from within. The maloca seemed to be holding its breath, awaiting something.

Then it came. Concussive like an IED, an attack of heat flared from within, shot out from my bones, and consumed my body. It was nothing less than being on fire, but impossibly burning from within. Seared to the core, I was frantic. I struggled to shed all the layers carefully worn to prepare me for a night spent outdoors in the unfamiliar Andes. It was as if something was amused at my preparations and, as overture to what was next, wanted to show me it could not only render them useless, but easily turn them against me.

It took less than a second for the immediate need to become a panicked imperative. I realized the simplest action of unzipping or unbuttoning had become an otherworldly chore, like something I had never done before. To make matters worse, my mind could not move my body as fast as was normal. Every little action took intense concentration but that focus only fed the molasses of movement. It was as if a heavy cloak of bodily organs had burst into flames. My resolve melted away. I had no other choice but to struggle to free myself. Finally, I managed to uncover down to my shirt, a feat I hadn't thought was possible. The inner fire still burned but now, at least, the night air was felt at the edges of the pressure cooker of skin. I thanked whatever, if anything, that had helped me prevail.

But my thanks were short-lived. The hoped-for meager relief never came. Immediately, I was pierced by a zillion arrows of intense cold. I gasped in shock at the instant, absolute contrast and how sub-zero my environment could shift in a split second. Frozen to my purge bucket, my mind yelled at me to put my warm sweater back on. In a coat pocket somewhere nearby, I knew there were gloves. If I could only find the discarded clothes I had just shed, maybe I'd have some chance of warming up. Could this really be coincidental? At the exact moment when I succeeded in tossing away my many warm layers, why then should the temperature inside and around me reverse so drastically?

I reached to one side and then the next, feeling my way through a confusion of cloth. I couldn't tell my clothes from the blanket underneath me or the blankets of the other participants alongside. The deep freeze became painful. I had no choice; I had to keep searching, even if it seemed useless. Given the depth of penetrating polar cold, I didn't see much hope in any relief from a simple layer or two of cloth. But there was nothing else to do. I couldn't stand it. The cold paralysis of my situation was obvious.

I was almost too cold to move and there was no way I was going to find the clothes I had just shed. They might as well be a million miles away. As added grief, if working buttons and zippers had been nearly impossible getting the clothes off, then navigating the dark around me was out of the question. Even if I found them, the clothes had been pulled inside-out and twisted into knots in my frenzy to escape the heat. Trying to sort out all the bunched-up sleeves from head holes and blanket flaps would be the final impossibility.

Lost as to what to do, I looked up from my misery. Surely the bonfire at the center of our sacred circle would provide some relief. My God – it was only a few feet away. How could the heat it was radiating miss me so totally? I stared at the dancing fire. As vividly familiar as it was, something was different. It was not quite an abstraction, but it was somehow removed from me.

I dragged my gaze around the maloca. It was a circular space with walls open to the night but covered by a high, pointed roof. Over twenty other participants sat or lay back, facing the central fire. A narrow dirt path provided a middle ring of transport between the participants and the fire. Anyone entering or leaving the circle had to walk the dirt path in a clockwise direction in respect to the group energy now united in ceremony.

Desperately, I tried to search the faces of other participants in the circle to see if they showed any signs of a similar battle between heat and cold. With some surprise, I found no hint of it anywhere. There was no movement among them. Everyone was quietly dazed by the start of their own personal journey. Half had their eyes closed or looked down pensively. The rest stared in rapt awe at the central fire.

The fire crackled and the cross-legged shaman, a member of our circle, attended to the ceremonial objects arranged in the dirt before him. In the far darkness, a trio of dogs barked at phantoms in the trees. Nearer in, hidden frogs announced their widely-dispersed locations by random, distinctive clicks, each click echoing against the stars. Just outside the maloca, in near darkness, a pair of volunteer shaman-helpers busied themselves by positioning extra blankets and clean purge buckets at the ready.

All of the activity clarified crisp in my freezing awareness. But the setting and the situation, like the fire, strangely slid into something separate. It was a separateness reinforced by the swish of a presence.

I first noticed it as a movement of consciousness racing around and behind me before zooming on. I couldn't see anything but I knew something was there. I could sense its location and I could feel its awareness of me. The presence repeated its swing around me. Its interest in me intensified. On repeated approaches, I heard what sounded like a menacing, breathy sigh. The sigh was colder than my freezing body. It was a sigh that had no feeling. It was an utterance, an exhalation of intent, nothing more. Distracted from the pain of the cold, I wondered about this intent. Wonder calcified into dread. Intent was something it was not going to show.

But something did show. It revealed itself in smooth stages, like the slide of a scrim, a gauze, a thin veil between me and the maloca I had known. Another dimension entered my awareness as I entered another domain. It was as if a slow, special-effects movie dissolve had superimpositioned another reality on top of the one I came from. The same maloca, the same activity was still there – the shaman, the circle, the fire, the frogs and barking dogs, but they were no longer in the dimension where I was. I had woken up to another level co-existing with the one I lived in.

With expanded sight, more was being revealed. Where once I had assumed I knew what could exist in time and space, now I saw another layer to a fuller reality where time and space shrunk to minor, component parts. While both layers co-existed, even interacted, I might as well have been in another universe. The maloca I had entered an hour before was now energetically distinct. This new dimension was a lighter place where more was possible. And also where different entities existed to take advantage of their realms' attainables.

The presence I had felt whooshing by me before now began to multiply – or maybe my expanding sight finally was able to take more of them in. I pulled in deep breaths and exhaled to cope. My heart raced as I identified each additional entity's movement in and outside the maloca. As yet, I could only feel them. It was a pinpoint, low-level telepathic awareness of me noticing them – and them noticing me.

Oddly, I felt no desire to purge. All nausea had lifted from me, as if such a thing was only possible in the burnt and frozen body I had left behind. My purge bucket remained an empty thing to clutch with my freezing hands. But now the intense cold was no longer a physical thing. The blistering cold was something only one's spirit could feel. It was breath I needed, and lots of it. Again and again I breathed in with all my might and exhaled deeply. I knew such intense breathing was a form of purging, but in the dual realms I occupied, it meant something else. With each breath, I felt myself lifting higher, becoming more solid in the other dimension where they were.

And as I landed squarely in the other place, the presences that were only a feeling around me before began to appear as forms. I couldn't believe my eyes as these others faded into sight. They were cloaked in a fabric of dark energy but underneath they gave the impression of being somewhat human in form. Most were busy about their work in and outside the maloca. It was work that overlapped and intertwined the ceremony where my experience began. One or two of these dark gliders stopped on or near the circular dirt path to consider me; their motion reminds me now of the "squiddies" of the Matrix movie or the Dementors of Harry Potter. It was as if piranha had interrupted their hungry dart to consider me for a moment, then glided on with a determined singular focus.

Several other things became glaringly apparent in rapid succession. For one thing, these entities had forms that appeared solid but they could shape-shift their bodies like sculpting smoke or carving water. They glided, they didn't walk. They interacted with the other participants in my ceremony but just as easily they could float right through them, as well as floating up through the roof or down, disappearing into the ground. One particular spot in the maloca, about ten feet in front of me and to the left, seemed to be a nexus for their energies. This nexus was an invisible vertical shaft, like a beam of unseen dark light, like a doorway zone that bisected the maloca from below the earth to above the sky.

From this nexus they streamed into the maloca or out of it, disappearing somewhere else like a school of specter fish changing direction with the currents. Once I had felt the nexus and witnessed the comings and goings through it, I sensed that the dimension I was in was somewhere between theirs and the one where the ceremony was underway. They were accessing us through this middle layer but I got the distinct impression telepathically that they did not like the fact that someone had poked their head up and was watching them.

As their awareness of me intensified, so did the bitter cold. I felt no anger, no emotion from them other than their need to deal with me, the anomaly. They were either nothing more than an agenda or their agenda was all-consuming. Their energy seemed directed with infinite myopic focus. Like an insect wanting nothing more than to suck nectar from a flower, their impulse existed as an all-encompassing imperative. It just was – there was no need for emotion, only responses to preserve the agenda. Seen from without, their responses could seem malevolent, even satanic, but it was nothing more than the absolute form of self-service.

I have never been to a place occupied so completely with self-interest, absent of caring or concern, void of anything but the tricks to get what they wanted. It was the ultimate trickster space. Everything and anything would be inverted if necessary to satisfy their motive. Unfortunately, it appeared that meant inverting and tricking everything we knew or held to be true. I had never felt more isolated and alone. It was a place not so much where love didn't exist – rather, a place where love had no meaning.

Three of them paused at the foot of my space. One shape-shifted into something smaller and came closer before recoiling with renewed interest. Immediately, the fire from within returned. The burning feeling erupted from my bones, only this time, as the intense heat became an attack, the impossible occurred. As the heat burned, the biting cold remained. Incredibly, I was burning up and freezing simultaneously. Satisfied with this impediment, the three at the foot of my space glided on about the agenda's business.

It is said that there is a third state, exhibited in the animal world, that exists between the terror of fight or flight. It is a state of suspension, of paralysis, a condition that remains as the only thing left when neither flight nor flight is possible, or when the animal determines that both fight and flight are equally necessary. It is this third state I now entered. Feeling my spirit burnt and frozen at the same time, I was left defenseless except for a retreat to a singular still point within. At the still point, my will to hold on could not be accessed or attacked.

Some have called it the still point of the turning wheel. I have read about it but never experienced it. Whatever it is, it was the only thing I had left. Maybe it was the Source of myself where nothing that moved could reach. I attempted to numb myself to the combination effect of heat and cold and left everything behind to enter that still point. Somehow I knew if my consciousness could exist at that point, then I might hold out against the onslaught. With consciousness rooted at the still point, my awareness was still with them.

The ceremony lasted from 7pm until 4am. The brew took effect at about 7:45pm. From 7:45pm until nearly 3am, I held on at the still point, or maybe it was simply a state of suspension between fight and flight. Either way, while unrelenting heat and cold tried to consume me from within and without, I watched the night unfold around me. All the while, I had to take fitful breaths in, followed by the mournful sighs deeply exhaled. Only once was I tempted to close my eyes and try to ignore them and the dimension I was in. The thought of doing so quickly passed. How could I close my eyes, knowing what was going on around me?

As the night progressed, the stark, unrelenting isolation and hopelessness of the place deepened. The idea of being trapped, totally alone in such a place weighed heavily. I felt the serious wrong of their agenda more intensely as my telepathic link with them strengthened by the hour. Their coldly calculated sighs, those exhalations of nothing more than self-interested intent, in time became whispered words, words murmured with a trickster smile with the same menacing, breathy voice. Someone across the maloca would violently vomit into their bucket and the air around me would shape-shift dark with delight. "*Go ahead...purge... purge! That's right...retch! They call it the medicine...we call it the poison!*"

Other messages followed, equally inverting the whole intent of the ceremony. Whenever any ceremony ritual began, a more intense inversion would overlay the action. Icaros became the hellish wails of those trapped by their repeated use of the medicine. The hypnotic effect of the songs was loaded with subliminal suggestions that entrained the participants' minds to forever fixate on anything negative in their life.

Whenever a ceremony participant had a difficult episode, entities would eagerly glide to the spot. It was hard to tell what they were doing, but they quickly set to work over the distressed person. As hours passed and patterns showed in their behavior, the impression that negative energy was being collected or fed upon was inescapable. We had been warned by the shaman not to pass between a participant and the fire during a purge episode. He had said that whatever was being purged needed to go into the fire. If we passed in between fire and purge during this time, there was a chance the purge energy would go into us. Strikingly enough, in between fire and purge is exactly where these entities would place themselves.

At one point, I thought I had to do something to alleviate my situation. We had been told that help was available for the asking from the shaman or his helpers at any point during the ceremony. But the impulse was quickly challenged by a message whispered as a shape-shifter shot around back of me. A low, self-satisfied little laugh preceded the words, "*There is no help here. He won't help you. He's with us. Go ahead. Call him over. He wants you to call him. Whatever he says will only make it worse for you. You'll see!*"

Other messages followed to demonstrate how the whole ceremony had been co-opted energetically, and totally, for their own agenda. It didn't matter if the shaman knew about them or not. It made no difference if he was possessed by them or not. The thing that needed to transpire would happen regardless of anyone's best intentions or ritualistic mumbo-jumbo – in fact, because of such things. "*They call it the blessing. It's really the curse.*" Participants would lie back and moan or cry or laugh with dredged-up emotion. Another smug whisper would whoosh by, "*That's right...bring it up...bring it all up!*" At one point the other participants in the ceremony appeared to be nothing more than cattle being milked by automated energy udder machines.

After a couple hours of existing in a timeless place with them, they had me convinced I was on my own. There was no help to be had from anyone at the ceremony. I was afraid to risk it – so dire were the messages of consequence elaborated by trickster intent. Then I remembered one thing that the shaman had said. He offered one technique for centering oneself amidst a swirl of fright or confusion. He said to look into the fire; meditate on one's intention and center oneself on the fire. If nothing else, it was something else to try. The entities occupied the entire space. I heard odd laughter from behind me. The space I held was sinking into isolation hell. With nothing else to do but suffer, any hope is a distraction. "*Go ahead and try for hope in the hopeless place – it only feeds the despair.*"

I looked into the fire and tried to concentrate. Immediately, my sight was drawn into the morphing movement of the flames. The movement contorted into horrific scenes of torture and depravity. Each one was licked by a self-satisfied flame into the manifestation of another. I looked away and tried to regroup my thoughts and my resolve on my intention. I tried repeating my intention in my head but something they did telepathically sliced and diced the syllables into gibberish. I dropped the attempt. I didn't have to actually say the intention. I knew it. That was enough.

So I looked back to the flames. Immediately, an entity glided up to the flame. It positioned itself between me and the fire. Then it shape-shifted exactly as the flame behind it moved. The effect was the perfectly blocked sight of the flame from my sight. I could see the glow off the flame reaching up into the maloca, but every motion of the flame became a motion of the entity. In effect, I was now staring into a black flame, a flame of dancing shadow.

If nothing else, the entities were relentless. This unabating focus displayed itself in their duties about the maloca as well as in their determination to deal with me, the anomaly. The fact that I still saw them elicited a continual response. Their next salvo proved to be the most dramatic of the night. As the night neared the midnight hour, I had become as familiar as I dared with recognizing their positions and movements around me. Like a wounded animal surrounded by a pack of hungry hyenas, I knew the standoff of holding my ground at the still point might only hold if I avoided being blindsided by them.

So when a couple of them shape-shifted into invisible energy and shot around me only as a discernible presence, I suspected something was up. Presumably, they wouldn't shed their visible forms without a purpose, seeing how purpose-driven they were in everything they did. It didn't take long to discover what this was about.

There were over twenty-five participants in the ceremony and all of us had to be compacted pretty tight to fit the maloca. The man next to me was within inches of my space, as was the man on my left. When the formless entities shot around me with increased vigor, I steeled myself for their next trick of discomfort or despair. But instead of attacking me, I sensed at least one of them enter the man to my right. Over the next fifteen minutes he became more agitated and hysterical. He commenced a repetition of a low-toned "Fuck!" Over and over he said it as he twitched and became more anxious. Soon, the "FUCK!" became louder. Then a jerking of his left arm was added to the mix. The jerking arm soon became a weapon to hit me with. With every twinge of torment he was going through, there came a clenched fist hurled at my side and a shouted "FUCK!"

One of the shaman's helpers took note and hurried around the dirt path to assist. The helper did not look anything like the gliding dark entities that hovered near his shoulder. The helper tried to calm the man, asking him to quiet down, then asking if he needed help, finally imploring the agitator to settle down. The violent twitching, the fist strikes, and the tortured "FUCKS!" kept coming. Another helper rushed to be of assistance. They crawled forward and tried restraining the man. Their attempts only produced squirms and guttural cries. In time, extra help had to be called and five men struggled to carry the thrashing man out of the maloca.

He didn't go peacefully. In fact, he punched one of the helpers. They carried him to an area a short distance from the maloca and placed him on a mattress. Helpers had to stay with him to protect him from himself. Repeatedly, he erupted in rages and had to be restrained. Again and again he tried kicking over candles with the stated intent to set fires. Oddly enough, right after he was taken away and the space next to me was left empty, a dog ran into the maloca and raced through the same empty space. The dog's insistence as he bumped past me was unusual, as if he needed top speed to chase something or he needed to send me a message – "*The pathetic one was carried away but we have others.*"

The terror of feeling those fist strikes and knowing where they came from must have been obvious. The helpers no doubt reported to the shaman as to who had received the brunt of the wild man's rage. The shaman's wife came over, crawled up the blanket and passed a rosewater-scented palm near my face. Several times, from chin to forehead, she moved her hand up within an inch of me. The floral scent was sweet and aromatic. But the scent was fouled by the inside knowledge of the others. "*Take it...take it in...you know you want the relief. We catch more flies with honey than vinegar... yes...yes...how sweet is the bait.*" Doubting her intent was strong enough for me to hold my breath as the last few passes of her palm offered the rosewater scent.

The shaman brought up one participant before the fire and conducted a lengthy cleansing ritual with blown smoke and shaken leaves. Then another participant received the same treatment. As the cleansing and protection rites were being administered, the nexus point bristled energetically. A dark form appeared, rising up from the ground in the vertical column. This form was wider than the others, and I soon found out, taller – much taller. The form continued to appear out of the ground. It rose up towards the roof of the maloca. Its final form stretched at least twenty feet tall. Unlike the draping shoulders of the others, this one had perfectly squared-off shoulders. It never showed any intention of moving beyond the nexus. Instead, it occupied the nexus space from ground to ceiling through the maloca.

All of the other forms came to it, all of them in turn. Their darkness merged with this larger presence and then they shape-shifted away, some back into the maloca while others shot up or down the column and were gone. But for every one that disappeared into the sky or ground, there were others that emanated out of the column into the space. For a while there were never a fixed number of them. They appeared in a flurry as needed, however many it took – an obedient multitude, emanating from the one.

With the appearance of the dark column, a heavy certainty of isolation and despairing energies reached their zenith. I was at my lowest point. I needed to cry out or simply cry and couldn't do either. I had no resolve left. I was in shock, a shock that felt catatonic. The only saving grace was the fact that the tall one seemed content to stay in the nexus and not approach me. Giving the hours spent, stoically holding my space, I must have been catatonic for quite a while. How else did I manage to sit and take the beating of a possessed person? How else could I have withstood the hours stretched timeless in burning heat and deathly cold?

It was then that one of the shape-shifters glided next to me and made it oh so obvious that the approach would be personal. It took infinite pleasure in whispering close enough to be felt, "*Yes...yes...YOU CREATED THIS!*"

The concept blindsided me. The implications of the message discharged through me like electroshock. This was definitely their mousetrap going off. I was left to writhe in the invasive press of its grasp. This was their blissful denouement. There was so much wrong with what they had said. But was it right? Consider the source. But was the source even real? It's entirely possible that all of it was just a personal trip to my own personal hell – but did that personal hell actually exist or had I merely dreamed it up under the effects of a psychoactive substance? I created this? It couldn't be. The whole thing was too real, more real in fact that the veiled world of the maloca's ceremony. But who was fooling whom?

Was this the trickster's final trick? Was this to be the source of my ultimate despair – the unsolvable dilemma, custom-made just for me? They didn't care about my "still point" or my resolve. They knew all along they didn't have to attack me at my still point. Not directly. If they could take me to hell and convince me that it was all my doing – it was my own creation – was that my final torment or demise?

Maybe they had manufactured a pretend hell but still convinced me it was my doing? Maybe the trick was to invert the whole ceremony, make a Black Mass of it, make me believe their hell was mine. Perhaps that was the trick – they needed me to fear the ceremony because it might be the very thing that would open my consciousness to more. As side benefit, they would be able to feed on my fear. What better way of isolating me from my positive potential than inverting the shamanic ceremony into something darker than dark. Make me recoil from the one thing that might give me positive answers and they would win.

But I couldn't escape the feeling that the true intent of the ceremony had been revealed to me.

That intent was anything but positive. Yes, maybe the humans thought they were getting help from the "medicine," but the true masters of the ceremony encouraged those human illusions so the real ceremony, the inverted one, could take place in another realm.

That's the problem with dealing with the Trickster.

By definition, no matter what you expect or how clever you analyze it, the trick will always take you by surprise. And if you're still standing, chances are, the final trick is yet to be sprung. Perhaps their final trick was leaving me in knots with a dilemma of doubt.

Long after the ceremony had ended, they would have succeeded at bounding me in a twisting tangle of down-spiraling possibilities. Even if the experience was not real, they had left me with a real feeling.

Could it be that's what they wanted all along? Fear – uncertainty – and doubt. A three-course dinner. Like insects on the flower, they continue to draw sustenance from it.

By 4am, I believed the effects of the night were wearing off. Slowly, in reverse order, I descended back from the other dimension. The dark forms became disembodied presences. The veil eventually dissipated and I settled back in the normal-world maloca. The pile of ash where the central fire had burned was no longer an abstraction. Ironically, the only thing that really didn't return to "normal" was me. Now I had become the abstraction in a normal place. When one visits a place more real than here, it's quite possible they won't feel so real when they return here.

But now that I had returned, the urge to purge was intense, only my purge necessitated the immediate and explosive use of the restroom, not a bucket. Sitting in the restroom, I wondered why my purge should be intense diarrhea and not vomit. Just as quickly, the thought came to me – diarrhea is closest to the lowest chakra. Given where I had been and the company I had kept, ridding myself of low-energies was paramount to my recovery.

The fatigue of late night/early morning overtook me and I felt an overwhelming urge to go to bed. My room was a reasonable distance by foot but two paths could take me there – one was more direct but would take me over much uneven ground in darkness. The other path was up a paved road, over a paved path, and down a paved trail. Feeling unsteady, I chose the paved option. In my wooziness, I completely forgot that the shaman had said we should not go to bed before eating something – and we shouldn't attempt the walk back to our rooms alone. Exhausted to the point of forgetfulness, I set out on my own along the path. I estimated rest in bed should only be minutes away.

But then the feeling of them returned. Along the path with me there were diffused presences. It wasn't long before I couldn't recognize where I was or where I should go. The night scene around me shifted different as easily as reloading one's virtual reality headset. I backtracked several times, managing to make progress in agonizing fits. At the point where I thought I was halfway to my room, I concluded I was totally lost. A presence, ever circling, assured me that being lost was my permanent condition. Uncertainty was my strength – and my weakness, and they knew it.

Feeling them so strongly again evoked a slow-burn panic. Nothing looked the same as I expected. I finally reached a cluster of structures but they might as well have existed on a different continent or from a different time. I hurried around them, down walkways, through patios – no one was around. It seemed as if I was walking through a movie set on a shut-down sound stage. The whole thing was lit only by dim catwalk lights that someone had covered with silver-blue moonlight scrims. The deeper I searched, the more unfamiliar and unreal everything became.

I quickly retraced my steps and found the path I entered on. There was nothing to do but try to backtrack to the maloca. As unreasonable as that sounds now, at the time it seemed my only option. Lucky for me, halfway down the trail, I encountered my wife and another participant on their way back to their lodgings. I tried my best to hide my panic and joined them. Their stroll guided me right back to where I had been, only now, entering the space with them, the whole setting looked different. It was so different, I recognized it.

As I fell asleep, and all through the next morning, the question was out there – what was I to do with what had happened? Should I share the truth in group discussion the next day? Would anyone want to hear that the whole ceremony had been an elaborate cover for something dark, malevolent, and parasitical? I thought not and decided to talk only about the "trickster." I'd confess that each trick was designed to invert everything I tried to take from the ceremony into something that would make me feel bad and benefit the trickster.

I knew what everyone would tell me. It was just a hallucination, fed by inner fears and deep-seated emotion. But I wondered – did such entities like I encountered really exist? Was it silly even to entertain such a notion? Could they possibly exist independent of the Ayahuasca experience? If not, then why did all the shamans have to cleanse the space, sing "protection" songs, and instruct people on ritual methods of "holding the space." If nothing unseen existed out there, if it was childish to fear the boogieman, then what the hell were the shamans "protecting" us from? And if there were real entities out there, could they be co-opting the ceremonies for their own nefarious purposes? And if so, did the shamans even know about it?

For me, the one who had spent the night with the entities...

- the one who got no pretty color hallucinations or geometric fractal shows during the whole night
- the one who never saw large serpents or jaguars or talked with happy gremlin creatures
- the one who never had a life review or empathetic communion with past and present loved ones
- the one who never heard the strong, feminine voice of Mother Ayahuasca give me motherly advice
- the one who never got taken aboard a spaceship by purple flirps so they could strap me down and have laughing jack-in-the-boxes rip me apart and force me to eat the gore...

I was the one who had a different experience. I had an experience that was literally seared into me then quick-frozen to preserve it. I know what I experienced. The analogy of a movie theater best describes my dilemma.

Many people go into the theater to see a show. They are the participants. But in the Ayahuasca theater, each participant sees a different movie up on the screen; it's a personal movie re-cut and re-scored especially for them. They all exit the theater and talk in depth about what they saw and heard and felt from their unique experience. But everyone, without exception, discusses what they saw up there on the screen.

It seems my experience in the movie theater was very different. The curtains parted but, as far as I was concerned, no movie appeared on the screen, even though everyone else appeared entertained. What I witnessed, instead, was a horde of darkly determined ushers doing who-knows-what to the theater goers. As the audience sat incapacitated by their hypnotic stare at the screen, otherworldly ushers took over the theater and played out their agenda on the audience. As the audience around me watched their movies – I was watching the goings-on in the theater.

The way I saw it, the real show was not up on the screen. It was the reality playing out all around me. After the curtains closed and the lights came up, how could I ever explain to the audience what had happened to them? I could try but with little chance of being believed. The audience would explain it away. Don't be silly – the dark ushers were not literally in the theater. You must have seen them up on the screen. Oh yeah, I merely saw a movie – about sitting in a movie theater.

Eight hours after the ceremony ended, I sat among the breezes in the eucalyptus trees. The full impact of the dilemma was beginning to dawn on me. I felt the hopelessness of not being sure what to do. An echo of the last whisper would not fade away, "*Yes...yes...YOU CREATED THIS!*"

Then out of the breeze in the trees, an answer raced into mind. "*You didn't create that. You are from Love – and nothing from love could have created that.*"

It was an answer, but where did it come from, and why? Fear of the trickster returned. If I didn't create that...then it must be real...because I know I was there. Torn between the two answers and the ripples in their implications, I was left with the dilemma.

Later that day I discovered that another participant in my ceremony had reported an energetic rift in the maloca. It was a fissure large enough to be a portal. He reported this the morning after the ceremony. In response, the shaman made a special trip to the maloca to conduct unscheduled protection and cleansing rituals necessary to secure the maloca for future use.

I was curious and sought out this participant who had reported the energetic rift. He was someone who back home made a practice of reading and cleansing auras. I asked him where precisely was this rift he had energetically sensed. He described for me the exact spot I referred to as the nexus point for the entities. He and I never had spoken about the ceremony before this. When he told me, he knew nothing about my experience. But his validation of the nexus struck deep and was tacit evidence that I wasn't imagining things. And if all of it was just my hallucination, why did the shaman agree with the man and conduct the special ritual to close the rift and make the maloca secure again?

In spite of validation or any other evidence, no matter how one tries to float it, the possibility that I experienced something real invariably sinks fast with the same explanations. A day after the ceremony, there was no point trying to explain myself to anyone. Even I would have answered myself, eventually, the same way – Get over it, it was just a fucking hallucination. Concentrate on the message. What was your lesson?

Yes, indeed. What was my message from all of this? What was my lesson?

And yes, I can see it coming – I too can answer those sensitive questions by rattling off a thousand clever jibes of scoffing ridicule and derision like the auto-bot internet trolls do so well. Their vitriol appears magically whenever a search algorithm red-flags a word like "Ayahuasca" and the disinformation expert system is triggered to respond. Their brand of ingratiating stupidity is all too easy as knee-jerk entertainment and mini-me ego-gratification, but it's also a calculated circus to distract and shut down real communication between people. It's the hay that's meant to hide the needle.

As far as my real message and lesson – I wonder – can they ever be known without solving the dilemma, and ending the fear.

The Why, The Fear, and the Exploration of the Curious Curios Presumed Inside
The Exploration – Mother & Grandfather Share a Cup

Before the discovery, there is the exploration of the curious curios presumed inside. Some experiences are indelible, transformative. Some of these enduring personal events we see coming, even plan for, like childbirth, deployment in combat, or walking on the moon. Others hit us with unexpected, stunning power.

The effect of my first encounter with Ayahuasca was like combining all three – giving birth while being deployed in combat on the moon. Plus, it was sudden and unexpected. So much so, it jarred me loose from myself and any objective sense of certainty about reality. Gallows humor would note that afterwards I had an acute case of the 72-hour PTSD.

According to the Mayo Clinic, "Post-traumatic stress disorder (PTSD) is a mental health condition that's triggered by a terrifying event – either experiencing it or witnessing it. Symptoms may include flashbacks, nightmares and severe anxiety, as well as uncontrollable thoughts about the event."

Check. Check. Check. And double-check on those symptoms. So out of it was I, there was nothing that could get me to go back to the maloca a day after for a second ceremony. Are you kidding? No way was I returning to the scene of the crime for another beating. I guess PTSD has a way of leaving you stunned and defensive like that.

The Mayo Clinic also says, "Many people who go through traumatic events have difficulty adjusting and coping for a while, but they don't have PTSD – with time and good self-care, they usually get better. But if the symptoms get worse or last for months or even years and interfere with your functioning, you may have PTSD."

I didn't have a lot of time to wait to see if things got better. And there was little self-care available. What I had managed so far was sitting among eucalyptus trees for 16 hours, listening to the breezes lecture me. They made no sense and yet they were so compelling – indicative of my state of mind. I had to decide. Was the two-week retreat over for me, blown out of the water by my initial dip in the pool? There were other ceremonies to come. I could participate or choose to sit things out. Was it cowardly not to plunge into the traumatic unknown once again or good common sense to stay away? I never heard of Dante penning a sequel to his Inferno. So maybe some trips are better taken – once.

On the night of the second ceremony, my decision was obvious. I was not prepared to risk a repeat performance where I was the major protagonist, out-numbered in what appeared a hopeless fight in a foreign land. So I stayed by myself, knowing all the while that down the darkened path, through the tall trees, the ceremonial fire was being lit once again in the maloca. As the hour got later, the haunting night progressed and I faced times when opting out presented its own unique challenges.

The retreat camp was all but deserted except for me. Mostly everyone else was down at the ceremony. Even though I couldn't see or hear the ceremony I was missing, I was still surrounded by many of the same environmental trappings that had provided a stage for my first experience. The cloaking darkness, the same mountain vegetation, the occasional bark of dogs in the distance, the same clicking of frogs set the stage as before.

Now with memories to deal with, the setting became ever so dramatic. Never discount the power of isolation and one's imagination to relive experiences and find ways to extend them into the present. I knew I couldn't be a part of the ceremony, but I hadn't expected my solitary reflections under the stars to evoke such strong emotional echoes. I found I didn't need to drink any of the brew to continue my odyssey. If not visual, the emotional flashbacks only reinforced my 72-hour PTSD.

I was glad when the night was over. And I wasn't the only participant to opt out of the ceremony. Two others had bowed out as well. They weren't forthcoming as to why but the deep somberness of their mood spoke volumes. One other participant had quickly fled camp for good after the chaotic energy whirlwind of the first ceremony.

The next day I heard retreat participants react to their second experience. Some had a very different experience from their first time. It started an undercurrent in me, a subtle prodding to re-examine my decision to opt out. I wasn't about to let it churn me into knots. It may seem a dilemma to choose between "can't go back" but "can't give up." But it's only a dilemma if I let it become an impasse. There had to be a way I could go back into ceremony and overcome the fight-or-flight catatonia of will that had overtaken me.

The next day, there would be a sweat lodge ceremony. It would be held in a different location – not in the maloca. This was good. Also, this ceremony was scheduled to start during the day – lasting from about 10am until about 9pm. The new location and daylight might be different enough. Plus the daylight would allow me more sensory access to nature. Being in nature has always been spiritual to me, even when I was a kid. Nature would be there for me. This I could try. Of course, I wouldn't go under the blankets of the sweat lodge. That would be too claustrophobic in my condition.

Plus, I had gotten enough heat to last several lifetimes from the first ceremony. Instead, I'd be part of the group who chose to participate outside, under the sky and around the fire. The fire would be tended by volunteers who would be fire keepers and prepare the hot rocks for sweat lodge use. Also, the brew for the sweat lodge ceremony would be a special mixture of Ayahuasca and San Pedro. My intuition told me that such a combination might be the right prescription for what ailed me.

Walking down the path the morning of the sweat lodge ceremony, a part of me was impossibly yelling out of both ears – *What are you doing – go back – you know what this means!?* The shouts were very persuasive but by the time they got hell-yes convincing, it was too late. I had joined the circle and the fire was lit. Oh shit. What had I gotten myself into? If things got bad again, there was nowhere to run, no way to escape it. I was in for the duration. I had a simple intention – survive and not quit.

First around the circle came a tobacco liquid to snort. It was not the same tobacco that gets blended in cigarettes and even if it had been, it was lacking the toxic 200 chemicals added to cigarettes. The snort was good, clearing the sinuses and no doubt doing other things only the shaman fully understood.

Things slowed for a while after that. Participants needed time to make their way into the sweat lodge. Helpers had to complete covering the dome with blankets. Hot rocks had to be transferred into place. All of it left plenty of time for nervousness to mingle with anxiety to become dread. By the time the Ayahuasca-San Pedro brew made its way around the circle, the drinking of it had become anti-climatic. My mind had already raced far ahead and hurried back. The reconnaissance it provided was obscure but didn't look promising.

Finally, the shaman exited the sweat lodge to attend to those gathered around the fire. One by one, each of us received individual attention. The brown sludge poured from a worn plastic bottle into a small glass. The shaman blessed and purified the brew by passing it towards the fire before offering it back to me. A half hour passed before there was any effect from swallowing the nasty mixture. As before, it began with a sense of queasiness to the passage of time.

Soon to follow was a subtle unease. A bilious ache rose from within. The whole setting, now including the entire sky, seemed to be holding its breath, awaiting something. From inside the closed sweat lodge, the muffled rhythmic singing of the shaman could be heard. The breezes responded in kind and the extra-tall eucalyptus trees swayed their dance to the song. Nature seemed to be taking notice and consciously responding to the icaro.

But something else was also paying attention. At first it was a foreboding unease from the intuition. Then it became a trepidation that quickened the breath. Before long, it was a disquiet from catching movement in peripheral vision. My eyes darted. I turned my head but I sensed movement with the intent to stay hidden – for now.

As an hour passed, the feeling of them returning around me strengthened. At first it was just glimpses of movement at the bases of far trees. Dashes of darkness. Gliding flourishes of dark capes of shape-shifting. Silent but trackable with my expanding senses. They were entities. The same ones I had encountered at the first ceremony. It was hard to catch my breath. This couldn't be happening again. I shouted silently at myself – why oh why did I ever join this ceremony?! I felt a literal descent into the same thing and there was nothing I could do about it.

Or was there? In desperation, I looked up into the trees and tried to concentrate on their breezy dance. It was time for nature to come to the rescue. If only it could. Thankfully, there was no intense heat or cold as before but that did little to assuage my rising panic. One by one, I sensed them moving out from among the trees and coming nearer. In great, hissing spirals they swooped in, hugging the ground. I felt one, then another make a glancing swoosh around behind me.

I could hear their menacing exhales of satisfaction as they passed. I was rooted to the spot, sitting in a chair before the fire. Ceremony rules dictated that even those outside the sweat lodge not break the energetic circle. Just because I was outside didn't mean I could jump up and go somewhere else. There was nowhere else to go, anyway. No way to escape them.

The next several hours was a battle of wills. Once again, they did everything within their powers to intimidate and frighten me. Once again, they floated elaborate suggestions why the ceremony was really theirs. Retreat personnel had either been co-opted in their dark purpose or, like most of the volunteer workers, were simply useful idiots, unaware how they were furthering the inverted agenda.

From 11am until well after 3pm, I fought a seesaw battle, timeless and never-ending. An alternating pattern developed. The entities would approach and the oppressive isolation and fear would squeeze me catatonic. Then I'd fight back, desperately looking to the trees and sky for escape, if not rescue. My breaths came deep and fast. I'd try to concentrate on the movement of a cloud floating by.

The nature gambit would borrow some relief, then a dark distraction would pull me back into the dreaded morass of fear. The cycle never let up. Over and over, the seesaw jerked me between ultimate stress and promising relief. I felt it would – it could never end. I weakened and felt faint. The dizzying effort to keep it together took its toll. I felt myself slipping away, unable to hold on. I struggled to gasp what seemed my last breaths.

One last time, I looked to the sky – to the beautiful puffy clouds – for my parting solace. The clouds were gorgeous – massive puffs of beauty lined with opalescence. The afternoon sunlight bounced off them in iridescent shards. All the while, the dark entities swirled about. I was in heaven and hell all at once. The ultimate contrast brought tears to my eyes. I was giving up, with no energy left to fight. This was the end.

In that moment, I heard a voice.

It was everywhere, nowhere. I reacted by looking to the left, to another part of the sky. It was that part of the sky out of which the wind was coming. The voice was strong. It was emphatic. It boomed across the expanse of blue above me with nothing less than a command.

"*STOP THE DRAMA!*"

I startled out of all feeling. I simply was. I looked back to the puffy cloud I had been watching. The voice returned, only this time it didn't shout. It whispered, as if reciting a poem that had become the moment's prayer.

"*Look for the beauty...go with the flow of life!*"

The words were not so much words as something poured into me. A dam had burst. So much flowed into me, it overflowed. And I cried. Instantly, I felt shivering tingles race over my skin from head to toe. The joyous quivers covered me. I realized that each minute tingle was the eruptive applause from an unseen chorus. A zillion tiny thingies were cheering, their cheers flooding over me and becoming body tingles.

The effect was as if someone had shouted "CLEAR!" and a jolt from a cosmic defibrillator had jump-started my heart. My mouth dropped open and I took in sweet, living air. I looked down from my puffy cloud and gasped at what the tall eucalyptus trees had become. They waved as if in celebration. The thousands of fluttering leaves were also applauding.

As the applause reverberated across the sky, the leaves all became eyes – they all looked like the eyes on peacock feathers. But these eyes were alive, alive with joy. All around me, the living plants shimmered with the love of life.

And the dark entities? What had become of them? They hadn't disappeared but they had retreated. The chorus of cheers, the living peacock eyes, the shimmering nature had overwhelmed them – for the moment. Now it was up to me to apply the message and keep them at bay.

"Battle not with monsters, lest ye become a monster, and if you gaze into the abyss, the abyss also gazes into you." – Nietzsche

The sweat lodge ceremony continued. I sat for the next couple of hours in recovery. Nature cradled me and gave me time to recover. The dilemma hadn't been answered in all its aspects, but at least now I had a lesson, a message to use in going forward.

As I watched the dividing line between sunlight and sunset move across the tall trees, the voice returned with one last message. Watching the contrast between light and dark, I felt twinges of dread at the coming night and what it would mean finishing the ceremony in the dark.

The voice offered a parting whisper. "*There is no good. There is no evil.*"

It felt like the voice knew there was a chance that I may fall back into catatonia and fear and wanted to leave me with comforting, parting words. It was whispered and said so matter-of-factly. I felt some relief hearing the comforting voice, but it was confusing at the same time to hear those words. The first ceremony's stark reality and this ceremony's final message, "*There is no good – There is no evil*" seemed in opposition. It left me with a new paradox. If good and evil doesn't exist, then why did I experience what I experienced, and why was the shaman's protective rituals so vital?

Maybe the answer to the dilemma is too simple to grasp in the heat of battle here on Earth. Too simple unless one awakens to the realization. Transcend all duality. Realize something more. Realize oneself. I had read enough philosophy and comparative religious texts to know it wasn't an original idea.

But then, maybe there's nothing new under the sun. To find that new thing, the thing that was always a part of us, we're going to have to go somewhere else. But where isn't a place. It's a state of being beyond mind. A state that understands.

"Two paradoxes are better than one; they may even suggest a solution." – Edward Teller

As the ceremony wound down in darkness, the fire keepers arranged the large pile of burning embers into the shape of a heart. The glow of it was easy to stare into. Out of it came studied reflections.

I had participated in my own rebirth. I fought an intense tug-of-war with dark entities to see myself through the labor. And all of it took place in a faraway place unlike anything I had ever experienced. It was once again – giving birth while being deployed in combat on the moon.

Only this time, the victory was a surrender.

The Why, The Fear, and the Exploration of the Curious Curios Presumed Inside
Curious Curios – True Measures of Integration

Before integration, there is the why, the fear, and the exploration. Why take Ayahuasca? Then there's the fear of the unknown and everything we're forced to confront during and after the Ayahuasca event. Next comes the exploration of the many collectables inside of us – those curious curios kept unconsciously guarded for deeply-buried reasons.

Some of these unconscious curios are thought-form parasites, like invasive soul-tissue lesions growing into performance art masterpieces of emotional dependency. Others are mechanical, clockwork monstrosities that dictate auto-execution of habits and thought-patterns that co-opt our spontaneity and demand hypnotic repetition. But the ultimate state of grace, that final aspect of arrival, of personal accomplishment all of us are after with Ayahuasca is some transformative "integration" on the other side of meeting the Mother Plant Spirit.

Integration is what it's all about – isn't it? We need to pull the experience of Ayahuasca together with any messages gleaned from on high – I mean really high. What use is a life-changing experience if it doesn't merge into the uber-matrix of people, places, responsibilities and aspirations we call our life? Hopefully, the merging process makes things better. But what if it doesn't? But why be negative? Why go there? Maybe because a negative outcome is a possibility. Yeah, and perhaps the one possibility that's more likely to come about is the one we give energy to. So shut up with that negative self-talk for the moment and let's see where being positive takes us.

Merriam-Webster defines INTEGRATION as: "coordination of mental processes into a normal effective personality or with the environment." For Dictionary.com it means: "the organization of the constituent elements of the personality into a coordinated, harmonious whole." Switch over to The Free Dictionary.com and find: "the organization of the psychological or social traits and tendencies of a personality into a harmonious whole." And Vocabulary.com manages to eek out a few words: "the act of combining into an integral whole."

In most definitions of integration, there's a whole lot of "whole" going on, either explicit or implicit. And being whole is what everyone thinks they want. Who wouldn't want to be "whole." To be anything less is – well, not wholly what it's about. How do you feel today? The answer we want is 100% – at least. 110% is even better. It's got to be somehow quantified. If we're not that complete, then we must be missing out on something. Right? And no one wants to miss out. To miss out on life is the ultimate state of being short-changed.

We want the "whole" thing. We want wholeness so much we travel to exotic lands, taste horrible stuff, probably throw up on ourselves and who knows what else just for the chance to get it. We know personal harmony only comes from the whole thing. But having the whole thing is not enough. It needs to be put together in a neat package, properly positioned to take advantage of the life we have. Once we are a neat package, we can rightfully claim the state of being integrated. It's so obvious there's no room to debate it.

That's good. At least that sounds good. But let the concept take shape in detail. Can we still say we're on the right path with that approach? We believe we need to be whole to max out a life that zips by all too fast. And yet, as with everything, each person defines the state of being "whole" differently. For many, being whole is having the full range of rock'em-sock'em life experiences that can be equated to having lived well. The more variety and depth of experiences we cram into our time here, the more fulfilled and deeper in meaning our lives become. We want nothing left undone on our bucket list. Taking Ayahuasca was checked off the list so I must be getting more "whole." "The one who dies having played with the most toys wins!"

But doesn't that fly in the face of so much Eastern philosophy that "those on the path" so adoringly embrace? I thought knowing oneself is the ultimate state of being "whole." And Buddha could simply sit under a tree and do that. He didn't need to have his passport stamped in every port of call and do the "150 things everyone MUST do before they die!" in order to be enlightened. I thought getting wrapped up in all of that mundane stuff was succumbing to Maya. Didn't someone say that greed, desire, and illusion – the three bogey persons of nirvana – are to be avoided? A bucket list sure sounds like the perfect combination of all three.

So what is wholeness? What is real integration? More importantly, what is the true intent behind our quest for it? Why do we want this? What do we truly hope to gain? What if the answer to our state of wholeness flies in the face of everything we told ourselves previously was the measure of success in life? What then? What if you are a top Silicon Valley venture capitalist and you fly a Peruvian shaman up to your Atherton, California mansion for a private Ayahuasca ceremony. You hope to leverage the astral plane magic to foretell which IPO to invest in next year. You hold the intention during the ceremony to become the white-magic guru of stock forecasting and fabulously wealthy in measures that make your current affluence pale in comparison.

Will you then passionately embrace a "wholeness" message given by Mother Ayahuasca that entails selling off all your assets and using the money to establish orphanages and free medical clinics in the poorest sections of South America? That may sound ridiculous to this venture capitalist sitting on his $1500 yoga mat. But sounding ridiculous doesn't mean it wouldn't ultimately make him or her "whole" if such a path were followed.

The nature of the Ayahuasca experience deals with this confusion if one will let go of enough assumptions and entrained judgments and emotional responses. It's fortunate that the Ayahuasca journey is the penultimate personal thing. Having found oneself in the state of being where Mother Ayahuasca resides, one realizes this is a place where the personal doesn't stay hidden. It's not possible. And this is a good thing. None of one's curious curios stay on the unconscious shelf. In fact, one of the messages Socrates got during his first Ayahuasca experience was, "The unexamined life is not worth living" (I read this on the internet so it may not be right – Socrates might have been taking Iboga instead, but you get the idea – at least the quote is definitely attributed to him).

Before taking Ayahuasca, I had a well-crafted intention. I had thought about it quite a bit. Within the answer to that intention I believed the answers to my "wholeness" could be found. In brief, the intention was – "I've spent the bulk of my life being very good at something that isn't me. With the remaining time I have, I'd like guidance on what I should be doing. I want it revealed to me the best way to be the real me and in doing so, contribute and make life meaningful. Also, if Mother Ayahuasca had the time, I'm also interested in knowing just what this place is and why we're here."

The only problem was – nothing about the actual experience I had seemed in the slightest regard to address or even consider my intention. If anything, the actual journey, if one could even call it that, was nothing but an eight-hour horror show that played out around me with myself as embattled participant. What possible "wholeness" could manifest out of such torment and fear? How could I ever be content and trust my "messages" if the very process of receiving them had been shown to be an inverted corruption of everything good I had been led to believe about the ceremonies?

Some redemption came late in the second ceremony in which Ayahuasca and San Pedro were mixed together. But in spite of exalted messages (*"Stop the drama! Look for the beauty! Go with the flow of life! There is no good or evil!"*) and all the uplifting transformations of nature becoming conscious and personally involved around me, the dark central dilemmas established in the first ceremony were not dispelled, only placated.

With so much unresolved, with so many unanswered – indeed unanswerable – questions, how could I ever hope to achieve any "integration" of the experience back into my life? Reviewing my original intention, as far as I was concerned, I had not gotten a satisfactory answer.

Question: "I've spent the bulk of my life being very good at something that isn't me. With the remaining time I have, I'd like guidance on what I should be doing. I want it revealed to me the best way to be the real me and in doing so, contribute and make life meaningful."

Answer: "*Stop the drama! Look for the beauty! Go with the flow of life! There is no good or evil!*"

No doubt many will look at that Q&A and see some semblance of connection. What did you expect, I'll be told – a specific direction like "go to this corner, talk to this guy, start this business, walk this path until you see two trees on a hill"? Maybe the best answer is simply a method of rearranging one's attitudes and subconscious constraints and in doing so, freeing oneself from the personal stuff that's been holding things back from being found naturally, in their own time, by one's own passionate efforts. The "what" of what I should be doing will never be answered by a ceremony – that is up to me. Only the how is addressed. By dealing with stuff, the "how" is enabled. As the old saying goes – the door is opened but we must walk through it for ourselves.

All right. Fine. If enough complex analysis is put on the task, maybe I can use a lot of other people's advice about my experience to construct some kind of sense out of it. But should I really have to work that hard to slip into my harmonious state of wholeness and integration? It sounds an awful lot like trying to push and pull and squeeze my feet into wrong-size shoes. Regardless how great they look with my other clothes – how complete and whole they make my overall look – the fact is, they just don't fit.

Plus, when I really look at the answer I got, it has problems. The most glaring of which is this thing about no good or evil existing. As far as I know, it wasn't the "good" side giving me that message. The dark side is known to be ultimate tricksters, so how do I know? But even if the "good" side, even if Mother Ayahuasca herself gave me that message – it doesn't jive with what I experienced and the fact that shamans go through a lot to "protect" the ceremony space. Are they doing all of that for show only? If not, then they must believe there's something really out there we need to be protected from. Now, have the shamans been fooled? Haven't they gotten the same message from the "good" side as I did? "*There is no good – there is no evil.*"

Add to this the fact that not once during either ceremony was there a time when the dark entities were absent. Even during the peak of the positive messages being given, they were present. They retreated to a distance near the treeline and behind the sweat lodge, they swirled about but they were never gone. And not having them gone leaves me with the same dilemmas that came out of the first ceremony. What exactly was going on at that ceremony? Whatever it was, it entailed so much more than what was advertised. And it seemed nothing to do with giving me transformative messages. It was all about a dark agenda in another dimension that had little to do with me. If anything, I was the interloper. I was treated by the entities like I didn't belong there. They didn't like the fact that I was witness to what they were doing. And nothing about my exultant messages during the second ceremony does anything to dispel that.

I'm left with so much unresolved. The solutions to the dilemmas I grapple with are beyond this place and time. And there seems to be some satisfaction out there somewhere in the dark in the fact that I've been presented with something that is impossible for me to put to rest. If anything, that only reinforces my hunch that the darkness is real. It reads you before giving you the one thing it knows will pull you down. They too exist in the space where nothing personal can be hidden – and they leverage it to the hilt. In the face of all this, I don't see how integration, wholeness, or harmony could ever result for me from my Ayahuasca experience.

And that's why it's the oddest thing, the strangest thing of all – the very fact that so many secondary life changes have happened for me since those ceremonies. None of these changes are directly related to my experience and yet they manifested in my life anyway – all in the next year.

- I've left the corporate world after decades of a rote existence.
- I've moved thousands of miles to another country with a different culture and language to start the rest of my life.
- I feel more engaged in daily activities.
- I don't sweat the small stuff as much.
- If I get an idea to do something, I do it (rather than analyzing and thinking about it then dropping the idea).
- I find joy in little things that wouldn't have been on my radar before.
- I have an emotional clarity about engaging in the good parts of life and the planet.
- I seek out interactions with people in ways I never would have done before.
- I no longer want certain foods that before had been my favorites

– perhaps it was the contaminated versions I was now rejecting. My cravings are much healthier.
- Alcoholic drinks have lost their appeal.
- I dropped 40 pounds in 4 months, something I'd tried and failed at for 10-20 years. Ironically, I'm now at the weight I was when younger, when my positive outlook on life was fresh.
- My wife tells me I am happy, truly happy, with a new light in my eyes and spring in my step (her words, not mine).

In short, so much has changed in my life. It's almost as if Mother Ayahuasca managed to get through to me in spite of my experience instead of on account of it. Or maybe it was something else – something, in her wisdom, she tailor-made for me.

At one point in my extended meditation on the day following the first, harrowing experience, the thought came to me, as if on a gentle breeze – *"If we had given you the answers you needed directly, you only would have argued with us. So we had to take you there. It was the only way. You couldn't be told. You had to go through the worst to get the best insight."* Who knows where that came from. Maybe it was my own mind's attempt to rationalize an excuse why the ceremony had done what was good for me, even if it meant "taking my medicine."

It's true – I couldn't do the other two planned ceremonies that week. I had to follow my intuition. In spite of having the breakthrough with the 2nd sweat lodge ceremony, things were still too raw, too unresolved, the fear too palpable. Given the nature of what I had been through, I didn't fully trust the retreat center people. Some might say that doing the other ceremonies might have helped me but it's important to state that my decision was best for where I was that week – especially since I didn't have the time on site to explore it all nor the support that would have paved a way for me to join the other ceremonies. If anything, my last days at the retreat center were spent dodging peak intensities where I felt the whole place had been secretly, quietly co-opted by dark entities for other dimensional purposes.

As far as the dilemmas, the fear, the unresolved questions, the inverted trickster elements ever present in every aspect of what I went through – I don't think I'll ever get the answers to all of it. And I suspect the dark entities like it that way. They want me hopeless about "wholeness" and ever achieving a final "integration." But strangely enough, as the days go by, I'm all right with that.

There's one thing the dark entities don't have on their side. It's the knowing spirit of Mother Ayahuasca in the plant medicine brew. If she is truly there, if she is not just a ruse of trickster darknesses inverting everything good so they can feed off our fear and despair, or even if she's only something the exotic brew allowed me to conjure up for myself as a placebo projection – if there's the slightest chance of any of that, then she has indeed given me an enormous hint, an awesome cheat code to escape the down-spiral of not knowing –

"*STOP THE DRAMA!*"

Simply let it go, look for the beauty, be content to say what-the-fuck and just go with the flow of life. Realize down to your cellular DNA – this is not our time or place to have all the answers. Don't even go there. It's a wall you don't need to bang your head against.

If you must judge the experience of taking Ayahuasca, if you must know if you are achieving the ultimate state of grace, that final aspect of arrival, of personal accomplishment all of us are after – do so by degrees, in slight ways, over time, by noticing how you are changing. That is the true measure of integration.

- Notice the little thing you've added to your life that contains possibilities of growing in wondrous ways.
- Notice a draining craving that suddenly switched off.
- Notice the unconscious little habit that has weakened its grip on you.
- Notice the subtle new outlooks you have on ordinary situations.
- Notice how in little ways the mundane has become magical.
- Notice how your interactions with people have slipped into a higher gear of intent and caring.
- Notice the expanded perspective shift when hearing about world events.
- Notice a new affinity with nature.
- Whatever it is for you, whatever it may be, notice the newly found quiet in your mind that allows you to notice your new things.
- Notice how now there are flashes of insight.
- Notice the spaces between moments when suddenly you are able to listen to your true self in surprising ways.

Integration doesn't mean you'll understand the Ayahuasca experience. Wholeness never means all the dilemmas and questions get resolved. Personal harmony only means you will benefit from your experience in ways you can't imagine. At least until they've become new-found joys in your life. Then your imagination will soar.

That is the insight Mother Ayahuasca wanted so much to share with me.

And in the sharing, she only asks that I take it in, really listen, and then share the message with others.

RUNNING THE HAUNTLET

How do you make peace with something so serious, so unresolved? How do you move on and run the gauntlet of an unsettled life when everywhere you go you take yourself with you? So many expert sources regarding plant medicines claim integration of lessons and messages after a ceremony is critically important. It's essential, vital, fundamental to one's well being afterwards in being able to exploit the positive potential in the experience.

Take the knowledge from the experience and apply it to one's life, to one's being. Do it in a way that stays true to what medicine space revealed. This was the way to success afterwards. This is walking the path, not just seeing the path. A failed integration could be far worse than not having attended any ceremonies to begin with. It would be better for most people if they didn't do the medicines at all if they weren't going to be committed to their process of integration once the ceremonies ended. I could see exactly what the experts meant. But seeing it was not the same as feeling I could live it. They didn't understand. They couldn't understand what I had gone through. Such advice was easy for them to say.

But the message from the medicine, lingering in me, echoed that same sentiment. One does not open a wound and walk away. One does not have the ego dissolved and then face another Monday through Friday, 9 to 5 job. One cannot have old patterns and dependencies blown apart and then casually interact with friends who maintain those patterns and dependencies and make their friendship contingent on you going along.

None of that would turn out well. But how could I expect to ever find a way to adequately integrate such a traumatic experience into my life in a positive way? What could be the ongoing positive lesson in me fearing to return to medicine space? Was that my lesson? Could I simply walk away with a flurry of good changes and leave a mountain of doubt unmoved and unresolved behind me? How could such an integration ever be good for me, how could it ever serve me?

Dilemmas and paradoxes born out of trauma can haunt a person, even if there's positive transformation all around the core issue. There was no doubt. My two plant medicine experiences had catalyzed major changes in me and in my life. The differences were profound. Many were obvious. But an undercurrent of incompleteness gnawing within me was strong and persistent. I couldn't hide from myself the fact there was much undone. Much overdue. Much more that should come to fruition.

But how could that ever be possible? I was now blocked by a dilemma of fear and uncertainty. It was overriding fear and uncertainty that existed about ceremony space itself. Was it possible the very experience I needed was the only one fear had made off limits? What I needed to heal might be there with the medicine but what I needed to heal at the same time prevented me from moving towards it. In fact, approaching it was unthinkable. It was a problem that stopped me in my tracks. Worse yet, it was a problem at odds with my lifelong, deep-seated desire to know more about all.

I saw the potential of sacred plant medicines to take me to a place of knowing more. I had always wanted to explore deeper meanings to life, to myself, to the big picture questions that forever hang out there unresolved. Of course, many religions and esoteric philosophies claim they have the answers I sought. I never found any of them satisfying or consistent.

Most were incomplete and hypocritical. Many had been co-opted for other purposes and bore little resemblance in practice to their principles. Worse yet, they tried to explain away wide gaps in their explanations by reliance on faith alone, or with the convenient supposition we weren't supposed to know such things, or somehow they were above us, or the fault of not knowing was in our nature or our approach, not in them.

If there was any chance that plant medicines could give me access to states of consciousness with broader perspectives, ones that afforded a deeper understanding of everything, then it was a tremendous shame if one traumatic experience and its aftermath could forevermore keep me away from exploring that expanded side of awareness. But the issue remained. What good was it to stand before the gates of paradise if one had been sensitized to fear the gates swinging open?

They say the medicine stays with you once you accept it inside. Some of the work it does, so it's claimed, is unconscious to us. Some of its benefits only appear over time, sometimes in retrospect, or they surprise us as we notice how we've changed or we're told so by others. Now I believe the medicine stayed with me after the initial trauma and shock. It nudged me to keep open, keep searching, keep from closing down and returning to past patterns. Call it neurogenesis, call it a mind expanded not returning to its original shape. Ayahuasca knew I was in no state to return to visit it. But it also knew a way to direct me into continuing the work it saw I needed to accomplish on myself.

If ever I'd be ready to drink Ayahuasca again, there was so much needing to be cleared out of the way first. And so synchronicities began to align. It had been a haunting year since my first experiences with the medicine. I did not want to give in. I did not want to spend the rest of my life not knowing if I could have learned so much more about myself and life and the universe. I did not want to have regrets later in life that I didn't try. All of this and more kept needling me.

Inexorably, Mother Ayahuasca remained with me. She led me onward into the process. Part of that process was the move thousands of miles to a new country. When a friend of ours shared his experiences with Kambo and San Pedro, something inside me resonated strongly. In following this "call", I was led to Kambo and San Pedro (Huachuma). Now that Ayahuasca had opened me, these new medicines would take over as far as they could.

My wife and I both were going to do Kambo and San Pedro. Our friend had done one San Pedro, then three Kambo, then returned to San Pedro over a two-week period. San Pedro bookended his Kambo ceremonies. We were all set to travel south for the five ceremonies but then the medicine nudged me in a specific way. I heard a message from San Pedro loud and strong – "Don't come to me unless you do back-to-back ceremonies."

It didn't seem to make sense why this should be so. My wife was curious why I stubbornly insisted on this format. I could only answer it's what I've heard, what I've been told. The medicine knew the format that would work for me and would have it no other way. I was being led forward and the way was specific even if I didn't understand why at the time.

This next section details the arduous road I found myself going down over the many months that followed. It had been a year since my first medicine ceremonies. The next series of ceremonies would take nearly a half a year to complete. It was a calling first to Kambo, then San Pedro. I believe it was the Ayahuasca within leading me to the proper place and time, the proper medicine in the correct sequence, and the proper shaman.

Only when all of these aligned would I experience the breakthrough that proved to be the watershed of so much healing. But first I had to run the long gauntlet of hauntings from my past. Many of these were self-hauntings, ways in which my own hidden stuff had festered and grown into the specters that warped me into living an automatic life of diminished expectations, limited parameters, an attenuated self. Afterwards, the impossible would appear in its place – I'd be ready to face Mother Ayahuasca again.

Kambo

At dawn, before the rain, you can hear the singing. Somehow, among all the intersecting signs and signals in the dense jungle, the small green frog knows that rain is on its way...and the frog sings.

You've heard the story before. If you haven't, there are plenty of wonderful online descriptions of Phyllomedusa bicolor, otherwise known as the Amazon's "Giant Monkey Frog." I won't retell the story that's been told. Instead, I'll tell mine. It's about an intense sacred ceremony of healing experienced by placing small amounts of the medicinal venom into small holes burned into my skin by a knowledgeable shaman.

A friend from Thailand was visiting and shared his Kambo experience with us right after completing it. Having received the benefits of an Ayahuasca purge of things negative or unserving to my spirit, I was intrigued by Kambo – a ceremony that entailed the ultimate purge experience. I wondered – how could violent sickness and vomiting episodes triggered by a terrifically potent jungle venom possibly result in better health across all spectrums of one's being – physical, emotional, energetic, spiritual? If I hadn't talked to someone who personally had just returned from the experience with glowing things to say, I wouldn't have been prompted to investigate further.

My research only fed into the subtle but pervasive call from the jungle to come and be a part of the healing, the insights, the awakened vitality the frog could offer to those who respected the process. Reading all that was known about the frog, its venom, and the way the native peoples were first told about the venom medicine by Mother Ayahuasca only reinforced the impulse to heed the call to take the plunge and submit to the healing purge.

My friend from Thailand was told by the shaman that the proper way to receive maximum benefits from Kambo was to receive the medicine three times within a single lunar cycle. It didn't matter how the ceremonies were spaced as long as three ceremonies were completed within 28 days.

The ceremony space was a five-hour drive from where I live in South America so I scheduled three Kambo ceremonies in three days. The aggressive schedule not only was good to minimize travel, I figured it was also best to maximize Kambo's benefit. Added to this was the fact that I wanted to follow up the three days of Kambo with two days back-to-back with the plant medicine San Pedro. I figured that three days of cleaning out would position me well to really go deep with my conversations with Grandfather San Pedro. I wasn't sure how I'd feel after five ceremonies in five days but I followed my intuition that it was precisely what I needed.

1st Kambo Day

I arrived with my wife at the Kambo ceremony space before 7am to find that an all-night Ayahuasca ceremony was just winding down. It was incredible to think that our shaman was able to go right into a Kambo ceremony after leading the all-night Ayahuasca journey. We sat awhile in the gardens and talked with the Ayahuasca participants. As could be expected, they were not completely back and ready to move into their day.

The morning sun edged high enough to set some garden flowers aglow while birds sang in the tall trees. Nearby a large metal cooker pot of Ayahuasca brew boiled away. Our shaman joined us to check in on the Ayahuasca celebrants. His calm wisdom and compassionate humor was immediately apparent in the way he interacted with everyone. Everything about him instilled a safe confidence in going forward with the Kambo.

When the time came, my wife and I and two other women followed the shaman down the path to a large teepee hidden in the foliage. We carried large containers of water and other jugs and buckets to drink from. He showed us where the two jungle toilets were and then ushered us inside the teepee. There his soft-spoken banter and gentle smile set the tone for the caring and sacred ceremony to come. He sat cross-legged before the implements he would use and described the process.

He told us to start drinking water – one to two liters to start. He took his time to ask if we had any questions and thoroughly answered in an appropriate way. Sometimes his answer was a story, sometimes an anecdote, sometimes a single word and a smile. When he was sure we were informed and comfortable with the sequence of what would happen, he lit a candle and invited us one-by-one to come to his side to receive the medicine.

The shaman had me come up first. He asked me where I would like to receive the medicine. I told him my upper left arm, near the shoulder. He explained I could receive points in two sizes depending on the size of stick he burned me with. Did I want the large stick or the small stick? Wanting the most benefit, I asked for the large stick. He then asked me how many "points" would I like. Each point is a single application of the medicine. I answered that I would trust his judgment – he should give me however many he thought would be good for me. To that he said he'd start me with four points.

He placed the large stick in the candle flame until the stick caught fire. He blew out the fire and continued to blow on the end of the stick to make the burnt end glowing red hot. When the glowing end was just right, he told me to take in a breath. I breathed in and he punctured my arm with the glowing stick. Again and again he got the end of the stick red hot, told me to take in a breath, then punctured a hole. He then cleaned and brushed open the row of four vertical holes in preparation for the medicine.

Evenly spaced in a row on a small flat stick were small, grayish dabs of venom. The shaman wet them ever so gingerly then took another special stick to apply a dab of venom into the four burn holes in my upper arm. Immediately, I could feel a rush of fiery flush course through my neck and head. My heart rate jumped and as I had been instructed, I grabbed my water jug and a mat and hurried out of the teepee to find my purge space outside in the foliage.

By the time I got my mat and water jug down and managed to kneel down, a dizzying rush of a flu feeling shuddered through me. A churning nausea twisted in my guts. My breaths came fast and labored. As instructed I hurried to gulp down more water. As I did, my wife and the other two women hurried out of the teepee one-by-one and rushed in agony to their own purge spaces next to and behind me somewhere. It was impossible to be too concerned about anything else going on.

Trying to cope with the enormity of the sickness convulsing through my body was all I could bear to deal with. The Kambo was like a hot dragon snaking everywhere within my body and spirit, rooting out anything that shouldn't be there. I remarked to my wife afterwards that Kambo was like someone pressure-washing your insides and spirit with hot water – water, that once it had found what shouldn't be there, raced in a death-spiral panic to exit the body using the nearest orifice.

I drank the last of the water in my jug and the shaman's voice from far away was replaced by the motion of him at my side, filling my water jug, as if he sensed my need for more water from afar and magically shifted to my side instantly. And so it went for almost an hour. At the very moment I would empty my water jug, the shaman was there to fill it again. "Drink. Drink more." The more you drink, the more the medicine has to work with to get the bad stuff out. Just when I thought I couldn't drink any more, the slosh of water filling my jug would implore me to take more. The shaman was relentless with the four of us, making us drink – the one thing we didn't want to do was the only thing we had to.

But all that water didn't last inside long. The Kambo had a perfectly good use for it. It's called violent vomiting. It's nothing like regular vomiting. It's like a purge one makes with sudden superhuman strength as a last desperate act before dying of distressed physical overload. I never thought so much could be discharged like a projectile so quickly and so repeatedly in such a short time. I was so sick, so tired, all I wanted to do was lie down on my mat. But every time I tried to lie down, the sickness intensified. Kambo wouldn't let me lie down. Kambo growled at me, "*Try to sit this out and I'll hurt you! Get the fuck up! You need this!"*

And so it went, for how long I couldn't tell. Occasionally, at times when Kambo churned deep, the shaman would hover over me, singing an icaro and slapping my back and sides and air around me with a bound fan of leaves. I mustered all my strength and pulled myself back up to a kneeling position and sat back. I rolled my head back and stared helpless at the sky. Next to me, the shaman refilled my water jug for the millionth time. I felt out-of-body and tormented by my distressed body at the same time.

I leaned forward into a hang-dog position on hands and knees. Kambo rocked me forward and back, forward and back again and again until another roar of vomiting sprayed the grass and weeds in front of me. This time a dark, viscous sludge of green ooze came out with the fire hose spray. I watched as the slime-green gunk puddled in front of me long after the water portion of the spray had sunk into the ground. Whatever the green stuff was, I gave thanks it was not inside of me.

Sensing when Kambo's work for the day was done, the shaman approached me and asked if I wanted to receive a handful of liquid tobacco snuff. This tobacco bears little resemblance to any tobacco contained in store-bought cigarettes. The type of tobacco and the concentration of the liquid form is a special brew only known by the shaman. I said yes, I wanted the snuff to help raise the culmination of the ceremony to another level. Kneeling back on my mat, I held out my hand. The shaman poured out the brown liquid into my palm. Right away I raised it to my nose and snuffed the liquid up both nostrils.

After two hours of being weakened and cleansed by the Kambo, the liquid snuff hit me with expansive wavers of bright awareness and faintness. I looked up through the trees to the sky and felt my energies surge and sharpen even as I felt lighter. I felt too light to remain in any position other than lying down. I crumbled onto my side and felt the lightness intensify. Soon the lightness became floating. I felt the Kambo and snuff mix in a passage through my emotional body.

The higher I floated out of my body, the more I spontaneously started to cry. The deepening cry intensified with the spaceless height of my floating spirit. Without words I felt an emotional purge surging out of me. The tears were a joyous purge of gratitude for all the negative emotion, the "panema" leaving me. I closed my eyes and sank into the sweet relief of the healing taking place. I gave thanks to Kambo. I basked in the sweet relief of floating away from sickness and pain. Day 1 of Kambo was complete.

2nd Kambo Day

Once again, we arrived at the ceremony space at 7am. This day's ceremony would be attended by my wife and myself only. As the shaman prepared the water jugs and other implements, I asked about the Ayahuasca cooker still flaming away under the large metal pot. The shaman noted that today he was concentrating the brew. Then we were ready. Again we took the walk down the path, through the garden, by the stream bed, until we arrived at the teepee.

Questions and answers were handled inside the teepee and then we were ready to begin. The candle was lit, the sacred ceremonial words were spoken, and one at a time myself and my wife received our points. On this day the shaman said I should have six points. He burned the holes in a vertical line next to yesterday's points, the points now covered by Sangre de Drago, Dragon's Blood, a protective mixture to help the wounds.

By the time I hurried my mat and water jug to the same purge space outside the teepee as yesterday, the Kambo had me in its death grip. It was a much tighter and hotter grip than the day before. The sickness clawed at me and made me dizzy until I wished I could crawl out of my skin. I had drunk close to two liters of water inside the teepee before receiving the medicine. And Kambo lost no time making ample use of it. Violent purging into the weeds by my mat was announced to the sky with agonized yelps. I heaved heavy breaths in between jet streams of my insides flying out.

Like a bad dream returning, there was no relief from the water jug being instantly filled over and over again by the shaman. How could I do this again? What was I thinking to set the ceremonies on consecutive days? How was I ever going to do this for a third day in a row tomorrow? A rush of sickening thoughts rattled through my mind. But I had to abandon all of it. None of the thoughts, none of my aching desires for relief mattered a bit.

Nothing but time and purging would even start to alleviate the agony. And nothing but water would produce the proper purge. I lifted my water jug to my mouth and guzzled it down as fast as I could. But there was no getting ahead of it. Whatever amount I drank, the shaman would instantly replace it. "Drink! Drink! More water!"

The sickness and the violence of the purging was the worst on the second day. It took all my strength and willpower to keep going. About halfway through the two hours, during a particularly aggressive series of purges, I witnessed a strange yellow mass come out of me. As the ejected water disappeared into the earth, the viscous yellow muck clung like liquid glue to the weeds. In the yellow puddle was something else, something lighter in color and firmer in texture. I had barely eaten in two days so it wasn't undigested food. I don't know what it was but I wasn't about to inspect it. I only had massive gratitude that somehow I had managed to expel it.

As the hours passed and the worst of the Kambo effects subsided, the shaman came by to talk with me. He sat down cross-legged close to my mat on the weeds and we got talking about some of my questions. A primary question had been nagging me for a year, ever since I had a horrific time at my first Ayahuasca ceremony. I explained to him how I watched all night as the whole ceremony was taken over by dark entities in a dimension that overlaps ours. I explained how everything they did was a negative, trickster inversion of the original ceremonial intent. All of this I have explained in great detail in the previous chapters. The core issue was the dilemma I was left with. Did the dark entities really exist or were they just projections I created – or were they created by Mother Ayahuasca for a particular lesson, the meaning of which I still hadn't grasped?

Shamans protect ceremonial space, so they must believe there is something real to protect us from. The dark energy after taking Ayahuasca was independently verified by other participants at my ceremony, even though I had not told them details of my experience. So how could I ever trust the Ayahuasca experience when I had watched the ceremony get completely co-opted by dark interdimensionals. "*They call it the medicine...we call it the poison!*"

The Kambo shaman took the time to engage me and my concerns. I felt such genuine, active listening from him. I also felt the knowledge of hundreds of Ayahuasca ceremonies behind his words. He was well-acquainted with the way the Ayahuasca medicine manifests itself in all its guises, always with the singular purpose of giving us what we need to heal and become truly aware, no matter how harsh or traumatic it may have to be. I never expected such an in-depth conversation with the Kambo shaman about my Ayahuasca experience. After all, it hadn't been his ceremony. But I felt his concern for me was real and so I told him the details he needed to assess if my dilemma could be solved.

At one point, when enough detail had been stated, I simply asked, "Do the dark entities exist or don't they exist?" It was the crux of my dilemma. Without hesitation, his eyes twinkled, a small grin turned up his lip, and he shot back in a soft but playfully firm voice, "They exist – and they don't exist. If you put your awareness there, then they exist. Your fear makes them real."

I could half see his point but I still wasn't completely satisfied. Before I could say more, he gathered everyone inside the teepee and asked if we would like some Rapé. I said yes. We sat facing each other and he said a few sacred phrases and loaded the v-shaped pipe. He told me to take a breath in and hold it. As I held it, he delivered the Rapé by placing one end of the pipe up my nostril and blowing the medicine up my nose from the other end of the pipe. My head reeled back with the crystalline snap of the sharpening substance flooding my sinuses and head.

Before I could recover from the initial blast, the shaman had the second load ready for the other nostril. I held a breath and again the pipe shot hit my nose, sinuses and head. Immediately, he blessed me, quickly stroked his hands down from the crown of my head to my shoulders, then stroked down from my shoulders to my elbows. Then right away he snapped his fingers front and back, up and down around my head and ears. It was like fireworks popping off all around my head.

I sat back, dazed. Before I could gather my senses about what was happening, I started to purge. I gasped and almost choked, startled at the suddenness of the impulse and not wanting to purge in the teepee. I scrambled to my feet and rushed outside where the full purge erupted with an anguished sigh. After two hours, I thought my purging for the day was over. I never expected to purge so forcefully as a response to the Rapé. I only expected a possible cleaning out of the sinuses, which also occurred. The shaman came out to check on me. He smiled at seeing I was recovering and added, "Thanks for watering my garden." After which, he went back into the teepee to administer Rapé to my wife.

I was blissfully wiped out and needed to lie down. The late morning breezes had come up and gigantic puffy clouds soared by overhead. In the distance, I could hear the exotic calls of four or five kinds of birds. But first I needed desperately to visit the jungle toilet for a final round of purging. When I returned, I was more than ready to lie on my side under the sky and float with the feeling of relief and clarity provided by Kambo and Rapé working hand-in-hand.

As I lay there with my head on the thin mat on the ground, I was at eye-level with the weeds stretching out towards the stream bed beyond the trees. The more I settled into a buoyant meditation, the more the plant life all around me became more vivid in color and started to shimmer. My eyes caught one particular plant, a young banana tree no more than four-feet high. As I watched the breeze wave its long green branches, the sun came out from behind a cloud and lit it up magnificently. I thought – how beautiful. And instantly, I felt the spirit of the plant send love back to me.

But with the love came a lesson. The plant acknowledged the beauty I was seeing but implored me to look around – the beauty was in the plant next to it, and the one farther over, and the tree behind it, and the grasses and weeds near its roots. Don't limit myself to its own beauty when its beauty was shared with all living things. All living things shared the same essence that I was recognizing in it. It was all the same living entity. Indeed, I was apart of the same beauty, the same living being, the same wondrous energy of creation.

I thanked the plant for the lesson and for helping me to see beauty in a broader sense. There is always more beauty to see. How wonderful and it can be accessed anytime, anywhere, either with or without the aid of plant medicines. The medicines only allowed an enhanced experience of beauty to remind us of what we had all along, and will always have. And so Kambo Day 2 came to an end. The roughest day ended in the most beautiful way possible.

3rd Kambo Day

I had expected dread and fatigue when the alarm went off at dawn on the third day. Instead, I was amazed at the energy and fascinating anticipation I had for the day. Granted, it wasn't an overly pleasant anticipation – more of an energetic urge to jump into the process. I imagine it's similar to the way a long-distance Olympic runner might feel waking up on the day of the gold-medal run. You know it's going to be butt-dragging grueling, you may not survive, but in a personal best challenging way, you can't wait to get at it. This is what you came for so let's do it.

After arriving at 7am again and chilling out on the shaman's patio while he made preparations, my wife had a minute of reflection in which she wondered if she should sit the day out; maybe two days were adequate for what she needed. I would support whatever she chose but I knew I was doing the third day. If nothing else, it was joyously exciting that there wasn't going to be a fourth day! A couple hours through the wringer again and then it would be off to two days of San Pedro. She meditated on it for only another minute and then resolved to tough it out. She'd do the 3rd day too. I was happy that we'd be completing the entire three-day odyssey together. Plus, it would be within one lunar cycle, so according to shamanic prescription, we'd receive maximum benefit.

The Ayahuasca cooker in the yard was silent. A lid covered the gigantic metal pot. My wife and I walked over and took a look in. The entire bubbling mixture of the Banisteriopsis caapi vine and the Psychotria viridis leaf had been reduced to an inch or two of potent entheogenic potion in the very bottom of the pot. Concentration had indeed been successful.

In only three days, the early-morning walk along the path to the teepee had become an entrained ritual that felt ancestral, endemic to the start of a proper day, and a reaffirming test of will that would put its stamp on the powerful way one could manifest the rest of the day. Once we got into the teepee, I was honored to hear the shaman say that I was a good example of how to approach the Kambo medicine. He smiled broadly and said everyday I drank twice the water that normally people took in. To drink water was giving the Kambo spirit the one thing it needed to help me. In that way, I had embraced the Kambo spirit and that respect would be rewarded.

This day my wife and I were joined by a woman and her 14-year old son. They too would be joining us for the ceremony. I was immediately taken by the natural seriousness and reverence both she and her son showed the medicine and the ceremonial process. It felt like something they hadn't acquired or been taught – it was a natural part of them. The boy also impressed me with his deep maturity for his age. There is no reason why anyone at any age shouldn't be that mature, I know, but after experiencing something far different most times in my own country, the appearance of such unaffected wisdom in youth was joyous to see.

It's hard to explain and it may seem contradictory, but the shaman was particularly sensitive to the boy without being condescending to him and without treating him any different. We were all participants in a sacred ceremony and it was as if the shaman's expectation of proper action and respect drew out of everyone what was needed. There was no need for the shaman to expect anything different and his certainty was manifest within the teepee with a gentle force that held the space for Kambo.

As he talked to us with an easy banter, setting a relaxed, tranquil atmosphere to ease our anxieties, we were still prompted with the lightest touch to begin the drinking of water. The candle was lit and once again he brought me first to his side to receive the medicine. He asked, "How many points today?" After a moment's hesitation, he added with a knowing grin, "Eight?" I nodded. "Yes, eight." He set to work. The large stick was set afire by the candle. He blew the tip red hot and then made the eight punctures in my upper arm. One by one, a small gray point of Kambo medicine was gingerly placed in each of the eight wounds. After six had been placed, the shaman asked in a whisper, "Do you feel it?" "Oh yes," I sighed. "It's coming on strong." He placed the last two points and let me go, "It is done."

I hurried myself out of the teepee with mat and jug of water. To my normal spot in the weeds I rushed. The sting of the Kambo points fed a growing burn radiating from my head and neck downwards in a race to consume my body. It was the strangest inconsistent thing but it seemed the effects of Kambo are something one could never get used to and yet feeling it come on even stronger on the third day had become a familiar strangeness. I now know this thing I can never get used to – and I know it so well.

You think you're prepared for it until it happens again. Then you realize it's the one thing you can never get used to. My mind reeled away with the fractal inconsistencies and the Kambo seized on that to take me deeper – to purge the mind of fractal distractions, of endless self-talk that doesn't serve me. I realized what was going on for the last few minutes was actually a lesson. My mind sunk under the weight of its useless banter and my body ejected it with a fire hose blast of nausea into the weeds. Kambo had me and it was still finding deeper things to purge. It was going to be that kind of day.

There's no sense describing the next two hours in too great of detail. Such picturesque details of violent vomiting, death-like flu symptoms, and gut-wrenching refills of my water jug have been adequately covered in Day 1 and Day 2 details. Suffice to say, eight points of Kambo is more than six points – the understatement of the day. But surprisingly, what I found is Kambo strengthens you to take more if it truly finds you respectful of the frog. The more you respect and embrace the teaching spirit of the frog, the more strength you will receive to take more of the medicine.

So, even though the third day was much stronger than the second day, and the second day was much stronger than the first day, developing my Kambo muscles got me up the increasingly higher hills of healing. Don't misunderstand – it wasn't easier to do the harder thing – it was just possible because the frog opened up more of one's innate strength to face the harder thing, a strength that "panema" held us back from integrating into our volition. I imagine it's the same reason why native Amazonian tribesmen take Kambo before going out on the hunt. It purges that which weakens them while opening up their body's natural methods of accessing its strength.

After the hours passed and the sounds of torment and vomiting had subsided, one could again hear the exotic bird calls, the buzzing of busy insects, and the breezes through the trees. I sat on my mat, a rag doll of ceremonial excess, and tried to steady my breaths with deep and slow appreciation of the healing taking place. The shaman came to me and asked me how I was doing. Hearing an affirmation, he then asked me if I now wanted the Rapé. I said yes.

As before, we sat facing each other and he said a few sacred phrases and loaded the v-shaped pipe. He told me to take a breath in and hold it. I held a breath and again the pipe shot hit my nose, sinuses and head. We repeated the action with the other nostril. Then he blessed me, quickly stroked his hands down from the crown of my head to my shoulders, then stroked down from my shoulders to my elbows. He quickly snapped his fingers front and back, up and down around my head and ears. The fireworks popped off around my head and I thanked him.

No sooner had I turned back to face the foliage than a massive purge rose up from somewhere deep. There was no way I had anything left in me after the last two hours of action, and yet there it was, shooting out of me in a massive stream. A second, smaller purge followed a second later. I felt aglow and limp, stunned and super present. I crumpled onto my side, my head on the ground, my face an inch from the weeds. I no longer felt confined to the boundaries of my body even as I felt my body tingle and ache. A third purge flooded my head – it was a purge from my sinuses and throat only.

I didn't have the strength to rise up so I rolled my head into the weeds and blasted the mucus and contaminants from my nose. What came out was ten times thicker than snot. It clung to the weeds like a living, brown silly string of phlegm. It seemed to have independent motion, a twisting mobility that didn't take kindly to being expelled from its comfortable host. I gave thanks to the medicine for forcing it gone.

The next section of time could not be tracked. With my head on the ground, my perspective gave me a sideways view through the weeds with the trees and banana plants in the exaggerated 3D background. All was shimmering bright with a living energy one could see. Colors became a telepathic communication from the plants of their consciousness of themselves and me as one energetic field.

Unable to move, I watched as one-by-one, a line of ants navigated the weeds before me. On a determined march, they were headed in a single direction but had to perform gymnastic stunts to manage a path up and down through the spiky weeds. I watched them with rapt curiosity even though they were not interested in me. They had their own agenda, the same autonomic purpose they had every day. I had merely dropped my head into view of what was happening underfoot of me all the time. It was a world that conducted its business without me paying any attention to it normally.

And then it happened. The sideways world displayed by my laying-down view intensified in iridescent color and dimensionality. The ants became nothing more than a probability wave I had collapsed by my expectation to see them. I was shown they only existed as one of the infinite probabilities of creation until my awareness, my focus, my expectations brought that probability into being. There were no ants there other than what I expected.

And then it happened. I was given a thought. I knew it wasn't mine. The medicine was giving me a thought. It was a simple thought, but one I hadn't worried about until the medicine took me there. The thought was simple but it produced the profound. It was – "what if the ants came over here and crawled on me." That one thought was enough to trigger mind. Like at the beginning of the ceremony, my mind reeled off on the anxious possibilities that could transpire. Were they poisonous? What if they bit me? Did I have enough strength to get up and escape them? Maybe they were already on me!

How could I be so out of it not to notice such a threat! Remember, I'm allergic to fire ants and bee venom. How much stronger is the venom of these jungle ants! These and a flurry of other thoughts triggered off in a split second. Just like two hours before, my mind reeled away in fractal troubled possibilities and inconsistencies and the Kambo seized on that to take me deeper into the distractions of endless self-talk that doesn't serve me.

And then it happened. Slowly at first, then ever stronger, each ant developed a growing shadow that projected out and back, away from it. The shadow of the ants blended into the trees and banana plants in the iridescent distance. The shadows were large and dark. The movement of the shadows were contorted and exaggerated by the crooked path of the ants through the weeds. The projection of the gigantic shadows were deformed and twisted even more by the way they fell on the various depths in the distant foliage. The shadows, looked at by themselves, grew ever more menacing. They seemed to shape-shift towards me and then retreat. The shadows would have been intensely frightening if it wasn't for the perspective I had of the ants in the foreground.

And then I heard the shaman's words repeated in my head, spoken in his soft but playfully firm voice – "They exist – and they don't exist. If you put your awareness there, then they exist. Your fear makes them real." At once, I saw the lesson clearly and I felt it shiver through me. It was a deeper, full understanding of what the shaman had tried to tell me the day before, after I had recounted my difficult first Ayahuasca ceremony. The dark entities – did they exist or didn't they. Well, yes, they always exist as a probability of creation. Your awareness of the possibility and belief in it collapses that probability into a real thing. But it doesn't end there.

That real thing can exist as benign ants if one so chooses. It is only our fear of them that projects them into dark shadows that can menace us. It is our choice. Our choice to create them. Our choice then to fear them. Even if we accept that they exist, we have the power to render them in our energetic field as ants or demonic shadows. As the shaman said so succinctly, "They exist – and they don't exist." There is no dilemma in that once you have seen the truth. Stunned by this new perspective, I looked down at the ants so close before me. Now they appeared to be CGI ants, computer-generated, not real at all.

And so, the 3rd ceremony ended on the most important healing for me. It was a healing that reached back a year into confusion and fear and rooted it out. The medicine took me into exhaustion and surrender by purging what I didn't need and what was toxic to me – and then it showed me the way to keep clear of such things in the future. It was the deepest blessing of all. I left the ceremony space and took the walk back up the path, away from the teepee. I had gotten all that I had come for. And more.

Gratitude is the path to the most profound healing. Every day I feel gratitude for all that transpired. And even though I would never have guessed it in a million years, I know I can see myself communing with the frog spirit again sometime in the future. I will know when because its spirit is now inside of me. It knows what doesn't serve me. When the time comes to clear any new snares of panema, the spirit will call to me.

Two Days with Grandfather Huachuma (San Pedro)

Huachuma or San Pedro (Trichocereus pachanoi, T. peruvianus and other species) is a South American plant teacher. The shamans and healers (curanderos) of the Peruvian Andes have used the Huachuma visionary brew since ancient times. At the Jaguar temple of "Chavín de Huantar" in the northern highlands of Peru, a carving of a mythological being holding a Huachuma cactus was found. The carving has been dated as 3,500 years old. At another Chavín archaeological site, the remains of cigars made from the cactus were also discovered.

The sacred cactus was known to the native peoples of Ecuador, Peru and Bolivia by many names – wachuma, huachuma, achuma, chuma, cardo, cuchuma, huando, gigantón, hermoso, pene de Dios, and aguacolla. After the Christian influence swept through South America, the native peoples began calling the cactus San Pedro after Saint Peter. They say San Pedro, like Saint Peter, has the keys to heaven. Today the most popular name for the cactus and the medicine brew derived from it remains San Pedro.

The main entheogenic alkaloid in the Huachuma cactus, concentrated in the green outer skin, is mescaline but over thirty other alkaloids have been identified, some of which are also psychoactive. Such additional alkaloids include tyramine, hordinenine, 3,4-dimethoxy-4-hydroxy-B-phenethylamine, 3-methoxytyramine, anhalaninine and anhalonidine – to name a few. As yet, not much is known about the other alkaloids or their combined effects. As least not much is known in scientific journals. The shamans and ceremony participants, on the other hand, can testify very vividly as to the effects.

The Grandfather San Pedro experience has been described as:

- sacred and heart-opening
- potent and transformative
- a rich tapestry of intuitive insights
- a connection to the Divine Spirit
- a centering on well being and the wisdom of true Self
- holistic and visionary
- a dissolution of one's busy stream of thoughts
- re-connection with stillness and nature
- an opening to interconnection to all that is

- consciousness-expanding into where understanding is born
- transport to the fundamental mysteries through silence
- an awakening to higher states of awareness
- revelations of the magic of being
- visually intensive
- soul searching
- euphoric
- spiritual
- a merging of visible and invisible worlds
- passages to ecstatic realms
- a rekindling of enthusiasm for life
- a timeless interpretation and resolution of life events
- a revelation of the soul's purpose
- a rapid but gentle sojourn across time, matter, distance
- a blooming of the subconscious
- a deep healing of the physical and emotional states within us

My two days with the San Pedro medicine followed three consecutive days of Kambo ceremonies at another location nearby. Kambo is derived from the venom of the Amazon "Giant Monkey Frog." It produces an intense purge experience that rids the body of toxins and the "panema" that clouds and drags down the emotional/energetic self.

My plan was to let the Kambo cleanse me so I'd be better prepared to accept the teachings of the San Pedro medicine. I also adopted a cleaner diet in the days before the ceremonies. Alcohol, sugar, and red meat were greatly reduced or eliminated altogether, as were heavy spices. The amount of food I ate in general was also reduced while the intake of water increased. For twelve hours before the start of ceremony, I fasted.

By the time my wife and I arrived at the San Pedro site early in the morning on the day of the first ceremony, I felt better than ever. I was still infused with the clarifying aftereffects of Kambo and Rapé. I had the unusually pleasant sensation of being more grounded while still sensing I was floating. I had a strength of spirit and body and a renewed awareness entrained on the present moment. Every moment was sharply in focus but with a gentleness that glided me ever more deeply into an appreciation of nature and the people around me. It's exactly where I wanted to be energetically, emotionally, and physically before back-to-back days traveling away with Grandfather San Pedro to what promised to be rich introspective highlands.

My wife and I were to be in the ceremony with a very good friend and his friend, who we had just met. The ceremonial space was ideal – a small house with a large open-air covered patio in the Andean mountains. On the upper level of the property were our patio beds, a hammock, wicker chairs and table for relaxing, soft music playing, and a larger table where much later in the evening we would eat dinner. Lush gardens surrounded the patio and nearby was a large Toé, "angel's trumpet" or "Witchcraft Plant" that was in full bloom with large white flowers that hung down.

Toé has gotten a bad reputation because some unscrupulous Ayahuasqueros spike their brew with Toé to make sure the touristy psychonauts gets the zowie-wowie trip they expect on the first try. Except, the effects of Toé are unpredictable and zombie-like at times, inducing a stupor of profound suggestibility that renders one beyond vulnerable. Combined with Ayahuasca in uncertain mixtures, the concoction can be harrowing if not dangerous. It's interesting to note that our San Pedro facilitator mentioned that on the day the angel trumpets are finally in full bloom, the bees flock to the tree's blooms and "go crazy" sipping nectar and gyrating around in frenzied, unaccustomed ways.

A short walk down a path through the gardens led to the lower level of the property. There I found a variety of trees and large rocks edging a rushing river. I knew right away that the sound of the flowing water would be a perfect complement to a day-long meditation. Added to the enjoyable setting was a fun and friendly dog who tagged along. Huge, puffy white clouds glided over the rugged terrain as warm, refreshing breezes sweep through the tall trees. I returned to the open covered patio just in time to settle in and join the others for the start of ceremony. The breezes were now playing with the row of small prayer flags that lined the patio roof on one side. It was as if the wind itself was reciting the many Tibetan inscriptions all at once.

San Pedro Day One

We pulled long mats into a circle and sat down. Then the facilitator began with a solemn prayer that acknowledged the Great Spirit in nature and asked for guidance before invoking the blessings of the four directions – north, south, east, and west. Afterwards, we stated our intentions for the day. The atmosphere was reverent and heartfelt. My wife went first, then I, then our good friend, then his friend who speaks Spanish and only a little English.

It was amazing, even though I could not understand most of what the Spanish speaker was saying, the way he said it, the tone of his voice, his posture, his warmth and openness spoke volumes, making literal translation unnecessary. As far as my own intention, it was easy to summarize – "I would like guidance and exploration of three words as they relate to my feelings: futility, hopelessness, and meaningless."

The facilitator then poured four cups of the green San Pedro liquid from a tall plastic container. One-by-one he handed them to us and asked us to meditate on our intentions, and when we felt ready to drink, drink it all down. He passed around a bowl of hard candy in case anyone wanted something that could quickly get the bitter taste of the medicine out of our mouths. I took a wrapped candy just in case but suspected I wouldn't need it. Besides, after eliminating sugar from my diet for so many days in preparation for the ceremony, I thought it counterintuitive at best and disrespectful at worse to give San Pedro a chaser of sugar to start the day of healing.

Each of us drank down the brew when the time was right. Some meditated longer before drinking while others drank right away then meditated after. Within a few minutes, our silent meditation circle was complete. The facilitator got up, signaling that we were free to go wherever we wanted. We had been told when we first arrived that we probably wouldn't feel any different for 20-40 minutes after drinking the brew. During that time, some could experience nausea and might even purge, which was natural based on what the medicine found within us and what was needed in preparation before the journey.

It was a good time to think about where we wanted to settle in for the initial onset of the journey. We each silently went our own way. The attractive pull of the river led two of the four of us to grab a mat and head immediately down the trail. With the energy and sharpened presence of the Kambo strong within me, I felt imbued with energy and focus for the day. If anything, the combined effects of the Kambo frog spirit and the Rapé made me feel like I had stepped into an exosuit of immense clarity and power. There was no way I wanted to go settle down someplace – not yet. I was too involved in the moment with too much impulse to move and be a part of everything around me.

Over the next half hour I wandered the property, much of the time with the dog playfully scooting along at my side or out in front in anticipation of play. I wandered the patio, I listened to the music, I talked to the facilitator about San Pedro brew preparation while he carefully sliced up some newly-harvested cactus, I inspected the gardens, I enjoyed the feel of the rocky dirt trail to the riverside down and back several times, I cleared brush from a big rock to sit on then sat and examined the patterns in the flow of river water, I relished the variety of nature around me and felt the strong equatorial sun rising me into the moment like a fine artisan dough being baked to perfection.

There was no way of knowing when my journey began. I only knew I was well into it by the time I realized something was different. I was still sitting by the river but my mind had wandered. I was now somewhere my consciousness hadn't caught up with yet. But my emotions had and that made all the difference.

To describe the process of communion with Grandfather San Pedro in words will forever be inadequate. I might as well try to generate a holographic thought bubble out of newly mined quintessence then rotate it in twelve dimensions in front of you. On a journey with him time is different, space is different, your inner monologues are different even as your emotions plunge deeper and shine clearer.

The flotsam and jetsam of self-talk remains but it's muted as one inhabits a body with a spirit hovering above with wise instruments of perception brought to bear. Louder than the endlessly droning self-talk I heard a new voice. The voice can take many forms for many people. For me, the voice was as deep and strong as it was compassionate and loving. It was as if I was online with a strong Inca warrior chief who had a heart of gold far richer and purer than anything Francisco Pizarro ever laid his hands on.

Grandfather San Pedro was also a presence. When the moment called for it, he needn't talk to get his messages through. He was quite capable of putting me on telepathic speed dial. He was amazingly adept at massaging my emotions into a tapestry of present time examples and earlier life memories that evoked realizations, inspirations, and insights I could feel before I had any chance to ruminate about them. And that was the point, I guess. Bypass all front stage antics where the sound and fury of the ego galloped around in melodramatic bluster and slip backstage where the controlling ropes and pulleys of the production were tied in knots.

"Why are you sitting by a beautiful river, thinking about thinking?" The laughter I heard was more sensitive and sympathetic than condescending. But it did make a sharp point nonetheless. I heard the strong voice ask me – *"What would you be doing in the moment if you were at this same place as a boy?"*

My self-talk didn't have time to hold a conference and then debate possible answers. Immediately, I was swept back more than fifty years. I wasn't thinking about being that boy – I WAS that ten year-old boy again. And the landscape around me transformed. The energy and focus instilled by the Kambo also lit up with wonder and a sense of adventurous fun. Everything was interesting, everything could be an opportunity for amusement and discovery. Without hesitation, my impulse leaped nearby, to a small branch, fallen off a tree. That could be transformed into three – no, maybe FOUR sticks of the perfect size to toss in a game of fetch. I set to work immediately snapping the sticks to the proper size and stockpiling them on my rock for the rounds of anticipated play. Before I knew it, I was up and running with the dog.

I guess, instead, I could have reclined on a couch in an office somewhere and had someone potentially clever talk me into exploring myself week after week for $120/hour until I realized I needed to reconnect with the energies and positive spirit I had as a boy. And maybe I would have gotten it. But this romp by the river was immediate and it was experiential and raw experience is always better than the "optimal cognitive reference given the diagnosed syndrome." No clever talk needed. No co-pays or endless prescriptions for the latest pharmaceuticals to dumb down the annoying symptoms of distress. And best of all, I had the confidence that Grandfather San Pedro did not have a house or boat with a monthly payment that depended on me returning as long as possible to work on my issues.

And I didn't know it at the time, but this initial river experience was more complex and interwoven with other work San Pedro was going to do on me later in the day. It was as if Grandfather San Pedro was out of time. He understood where all of this was going before I ever sat down on that rock. No psychiatrist could ever be that prescient, that prepared, that genius in positioning something in hour one that wouldn't become apparent until I asked them a question in hour nine.

The process was a widening spiral that endlessly folded back on itself to reinforce the fact that the movement that was happening was all within. One emotion triggered one experience. That experience would then set up a trigger for a hundred other emotions that fed into other experiences. Grandfather San Pedro sorted through each flood of emotion instantly to highlight the critical element that he drove into the next experience. *"Why are you sitting by a beautiful river, thinking about thinking? Go play like the boy you were and feel what life can be again. OK, you know that boy again – you ARE that boy again. What else does that boy feel?"*

What else is deep in there? Is he lonely? Would he like to be playing with his father but his father never plays? The experience of hiking in the hills with only my dog for companionship triggered more emotion. That emotion triggered another experience. The boy really wants to be like the father, to learn to be a man, to feel the man-to-man friendship that only father and son can have. Shot back through more experience, the boy feels more emotion. The new, deeper emotion triggers another experience. I'm an older boy, collecting surrogate father figures from history and popular culture. I feel the piecemeal construct of fatherhood providing only a stopgap for the innate desire for love from a real father.

Most of this progression was accomplished with only a few words interchanged. Only key phrases and questions were needed in the artfully-crafted unraveling of the interior landscape. Emotion and experience evoked each other. At no time did the journey get lost in non-productive detours. Even things external to me folded into the lessons. At a moment I slipped into negative self-talk, the voice would interrupt with a question, asking what did I used to like to do. Right away, before my mind could even think of a possibility, a boy on a motorcycle shot down the road on the other side of the river. Immediately, I was swept back to the years of fun I had riding motorcycles in Southern California. More experience evoking more emotion triggering more experiences.

And so the day went. Hour after hour. Deeper and deeper, Grandfather San Pedro drove me into myself. The complexity of connections and interlocking insights blended with experiences from my past are far too involved and intricate to ever be able to relate in detail here. All I can hope to do is sketch an outline of what I was shown, how I was made to feel, and what it ultimately meant in the way of deep healing.

Finally, early in the afternoon, at a particularly intense emotional moment, when my boy's heart was aching in innocent surrender to the painful feelings of loneliness and yearning for my father's attention and love, the voice came through strong but soft – "*I'll be your father.*"

I knew in my core how sincere and genuine the voice was. The sense of fulfillment and release became a cascade, a catharsis flowing in and out of me. The rushing river nearby reinforced the washing away of so much I had held onto, carried around for decades, and ultimately couldn't reconcile – until then. San Pedro showed me how I could let it all go in the flow. I could stand by the river and watch it all get swept away. He had me do it. And I watched with the fascinated wonder of anyone witnessing magic happen before their eyes.

I felt so good about myself. I started to play the fetch-the-stick game with the dog again. For fun, I started faking him out by pretending to throw the stick but keeping it in hand. It was hilarious to see him all flustered running after the disappearing stick. Then I started throwing the stick straight up when he thought it was going forward. Once again, it was fun to see him caught in the dramatic suspense of not knowing where it went.

Then I tried showing him how the stick was going up. I wanted to teach him to look up and follow the stick. Eventually, he did and I felt the pride of accomplishment. In the moment, my self-talk made its own connections – San Pedro had told me that everything teaches and learns from everything else. I could see an example of this in how San Pedro taught me and now I was teaching the dog. Instantly, San Pedro was amused at the thought I was teaching the dog.

"*You're not teaching that dog anything. That dog did that to teach YOU the folly of such pride. Yes, we teach and learn from everything else, but you are not above anything else. It is all one. You are learning from yourself as much as the dog is learning from itself. Nothing is better than anything else in this. Only by setting yourself apart do you fall into that kind of thinking."*

The gratitude poured out of me toward "Father" San Pedro. As before, as I discovered at another plant medicine ceremony I've attended over a year before that mixed Ayahuasca with San Pedro – the greatest feelings of healing come at the moment your own gratitude for what is being received pours out of you. Some say if feels like angel kisses all over, some call it transcendent tingles, others describe it as trillions of tiny hands applauding in joy over your skin. However one tries to recount the feeling, it is undeniable – when you feel it, you know a healing has taken place.

Feeling terrific, I returned to the house and patio where everyone was wandering in to get a serving of fresh fruit that the facilitator cut up in a bowl and left to soak in its own blended juices. He had told us earlier that the mid-day fruit was a good way to get a "bump" into the afternoon, sending our San Pedro journey even deeper for the remaining hours. It has something to do with the digestive enzymes stimulated by the food also making possible a more complete absorption of the San Pedro medicine filtering through the system. Besides, even if there wasn't a "bump" with the medicine, the taste of fruit while in the middle of the journey was awesome.

After five hours of the journey so far and having moved through so much to accomplish such a breakthrough, I felt assured within myself that I could expect a pleasant, meditative ride through the remaining hours of the afternoon. But "Father" San Pedro knows the difference between triumphing in a battle and winning the war. My hike down to the river soon became a hike back through the years. I wouldn't realize this until much later, but it was as if I needed certain things resolved before the real work could begin. There were issues the boy had. The surrogate fathers from history and popular culture might have been a clever workaround for a boy trying to figure things out – but those workarounds could never be a replacement for a real father.

With "Father" San Pedro now at my side, that was a boy's issue that I had now experienced a release from. The boy needed the feeling of having a father who was there for him always whenever he wanted to talk, to pal around, to do guy stuff with. That kind of connection was necessary for being receptive to the deeper lessons to come. And that connection had been made.

But what else was going on with that boy? Was there something else within the boy that he held onto so tightly that the man the boy had become had to live with it his whole life? Once again, suggestions led to emotions that transported me into experiences. Without even thinking about it, I was back as the boy again. The situations from the past dragged me down into more emotion. More emotion triggered more vivid experiences. Whether I wanted it or not – the "bump" was about to happen.

Again and again I was taken through experiences with a common theme. It was a theme that was ever raw but one I had put away on a back shelf where I kept my most intense feelings. I was a small boy, then older, then a bit older. The situations shifted but key elements remained the same. I was playing with toys on the living room floor. I was helping my father clean the garage. I was out doing yard work with my father. Wherever it was, something would happen, whether I had noticed it or not. My father would see something I was doing or had done. His intense anger would flare. He would shout at me – "DON'T YOU HAVE ANY COMMON SENSE?"

In most of these situations I had joined my father in order to be with him. I wasn't particularly interested in cleaning the garage or doing yard work, but the natural instinct to want to bond with him was strong. Implicit in the need for that bond was a need for his love. And yet, no matter what I did, where it was, his bad mood would ignite and the same put-down would be shot at me – "DON'T YOU HAVE ANY COMMON SENSE?"

I couldn't help but submerge in a dark, murky despair. What had happened to all the good feelings and the healing breakthroughs from this morning? Why would "Father" San Pedro drag me through this? His answer wasn't direct. His suggestions and questions led me deeper. Telepathically, it was made clear – the only way out was through.

The next two hours are hard to explain. I can only sum it up with three words – emotions, experiences, connections. I was taken on a journey within a journey where my psyche got deconstructed. I was made to experience myself with the razor-sharp skills of a lawyer taking apart a key witness and the precise level of detail of a sub-atomic physicist dissecting bubble-chamber data for the God particle. None of it was explained by San Pedro but it was obvious he was architecting the process. He led me through a landscape of myself and my father that got me to realize the salient connections for myself. It was an intense exercise of emotional intelligence that pulled back the covers on that deeply buried shelf where the things with my most intense negative feelings rotted away.

At the end of three hours, "Father" San Pedro laid out the journey within the journey and made me put it all together in a summary. The afternoon sun was brilliant through the trees. I hiked up to a secluded spot at the edge of the property where I could overlook the river. There I did my summary.

I saw a boy who desperately wanted the love of his father. The father's depressive nature ignored the boy and his intense anger lashed out with – "DON'T YOU HAVE ANY COMMON SENSE." The boy hopelessly tried to find a way to remedy the situation. The only way to "have common sense" and get his father's love, it seemed, was to figure out every situation so well in advance that all problem areas could be mitigated. This "figuring out" would also extend into the active moment. Moment by moment, the scrutiny would have to continue. This would mean the boy would have to anticipate all variables and analyze what could happen.

And so the boy got better and better at analyzing things. Surely, with everything analyzed ahead of time, the boy would then have common sense – and having common sense was obviously the key to changing his father's heart. But no matter how much the boy analyzed the situations he shared with his father, the love the boy sought was not forthcoming. Over time, the boy sensed it was futile and yet there was nothing else to do but try. For a boy who didn't fully understand the situation, only futility and hopelessness resulted from his search for love.

The years went on but the boy's impulse to get that love never waned. As a man, he got very good at analyzing things. In fact, it formed the basis of his whole life's career. And yet, no matter how many things the man analyzed over the past 50 years, none of it ever got the father's love for the wounded boy still trapped inside. I sunk with each revelation as it came. Now the man I am doesn't even know whether or not analyzing things means anything at all.

Who is this man if all he ever was resulted from a boy's misunderstanding on how to get love? The man spent his whole life being very good at something that really wasn't him – it was just a terribly flawed reaction to a situation he didn't understand how to deal with. What would the boy have become if instead of analyzing everything to get love, he had the love he sought? And so, there's meaninglessness.

"Father" San Pedro was not content with my summary. I was shown how within it was spun too much self-talk born out of the same misunderstanding that started the problem in the first place. San Pedro took me to task. He directed me to examine the shape of trees around me. The push of the wind had bent them into the shape they were but they were not flawed. They didn't fret over worries that they had become something that wasn't them. Then he directed all his might to the past. He was stern and direct and would not stand for me feeling sorry for myself. Piercing insights hit me one after another –

"You were not hurt! There is nothing to forgive! Your father should only receive your understanding and compassion! He was caught in the same type of snare that you fell into! He thought he was hurting too! But

hurt comes from misunderstanding the situation! You've been told you're so wise, a master – huh! Well, if you're a master, step up and do it! Realize the only way you could have gotten love from your father! The only way to get love is to show love! If you wanted love from him, you should have loved him! No matter how long it might have taken, only love would have broken through the illusion of his hurt! Once you broke through, you would have not only healed him – you would have healed yourself by loving him! You spent 50 years chasing a misunderstanding because you fell into the snare of believing something else besides love could get you love!"

"But I was only a child!" I shouted back to San Pedro in my mind. He laughed and shot back – "*NONE of us are children.*" Then I was shown how children are actually closer to the ideal than the adults who supervise them. A child has the honest truth still within their worldview – if it hasn't been trained out of them by schools and culture and parental prejudices. So much of life experience only reinforces the misunderstanding if we let it. "But I wasted so much time! Over fifty years!" I shouted again. Once again, San Pedro was humored beyond belief and cast the thought aside as unworthy of me. "*You lost monopoly money. Nothing more! What are those years to the timeless soul you are?*"

I let his words flow over me. I stayed out by the river until those words soaked in. The sun lowered significantly in the sky. Its light danced golden and the sparkles of its reflection off the water and surrounding leaves transformed into energetic diamonds. All the plants and trees around me glowed with iridescence in their satisfaction and joy at what I was seeing – at all that was soaking in. I felt a warm presence in all of it, a comforting "I'm home" feeling welcoming me back to the real world – the world beyond amnesia, without illusion, rejoined with love – rejoined with myself.

The ceremony Day One ended with a prayer after a candlelight dinner of awesome vegetable soup and great conversation. All of us gathered around the dinner table on the open-air patio as the darkness of night blanketed the landscape. Far above in the passing canopy of clouds, inter-cloud lightning silently erupted this way and that. After we shared as much as we wanted about what had happened for us during the day, we each had a divination reading – mine turned out to be clairvoyance. In fact, on both Day One and Day Two all four of us got clairvoyance. The facilitator said he had never seen a group do that before. Our good friend also had brought a bottle of glitter and so we each had fun going up to be ceremonially "glitterized" in a fashion mimicking the white sage smudging.

It was wonderful knowing we were sleeping there that night – we didn't have to hurry back into town or back to hostels. The ceremonial mood was retained right into sleep. The night was much darker than what I was used to, living for so many years with the lights of a large city. The air also cooled as the hours wound towards midnight. But both the deep darkness and the cool air were perfect. So much had happened in the past twelve hours. And Day Two was not far away. Would sleep be dreamless hours or time spent in free-fall deeper into the messages of the day? The day had taught me to toss aside such questioning. I flowed into sleep the same way I flowed out of the day – peaceful, joyful, and with immense gratitude. Nothing else was needed.

San Pedro Day Two

Everything started slowly but early. Coming up from sleep was a lazy process for all and yet the group was walking about, sitting and chatting, and having tea an hour before the second ceremony began. As before, we sat in a circle and the facilitator offered the four directions prayer to the Great Spirit. Two bottles of the San Pedro brew were necessary because one bottle didn't have enough left in it for all. But first we stated our intentions for the second day. Given my surprises of the day before and how self-talk only got in the way, my intention for Day Two was simple – to get out of my own way and let the wisdom of San Pedro proceed however best the medicine thought was necessary for my continued healing.

The facilitator started pouring brew into the plastic cups. When it came to my turn, he asked me if I wanted more today. I said yes. He emptied the last of one bottle into my cup but only filled it half way. Opening a second bottle, he continued the pour until my cup was filled. I noticed when he emptied the first plastic liter bottle, the darker, cloudier dregs of the liter bottle went into the first half of my cup. I wondered if these dregs were any more or less potent.

I also wondered if the two bottles represented brews from two separate huachuma cacti. Would such a mixture from two different plants make any difference in my journey? The questioning thoughts passed so quickly that I didn't ask them out loud. Besides, the ceremony had moved on and my friend was already beginning to state his intentions for the day.

Getting up from the initial prayer circle was so much different than the first day. The first day held so much anticipation and wonder. The second day was a continuation of a mystical conversation in which the wonder had already been internalized. Instead of anticipation, there was intense curiosity to experience how the messages and lessons from the first day could be extended into an even greater healing.

There was also an excitement, an expectation of being reunited with a dear member of one's family. But this family member possessed wisdom and abilities not of this world. The sense of belonging to such a family was awe-inspiring and yet so comfortable. It was the feeling of realizing one's true family extended beyond this world and not to merely believe it or assume so – but to know it. By the time the medicine opened me up and the realm of the here and now transformed, "Father" San Pedro was already strong with his telepathic methods for the day. He made it clear –

"*Yesterday was about sorting things out, becoming aware, putting it together – intellectually, with mind, in words, with examples. The second day will be nothing like that. The first day was done to satisfy you – to satisfy your mind. But that's not the place of lasting healing. It IS the place that could block going any farther – if it wasn't dealt with. So done! We took care of it! Now on to what's important!*"

I wondered – whatever could that be? San Pedro shot back – "*Most of today...no words...no mind...no talk...all emotions...all of everything else!*"

I had no idea what that meant. What exactly would we be doing for the next nine hours? "*No words. No talk. NO QUESTIONS! Just everything else!*"

Unlike Day One, there was no impulse to explore, walk around the property, go down to the river, listen to music, talk with anyone else, or play with the dog. With no impulse to do anything, I took my shoes and socks off and laid face-down on the bed. The breezes of the open-air patio kept me company but even they were far off and receding further. I was completely aware, fully conscious, very alert, but a large part of me was descending into a dreamlike state. The dream was vacant at first, just a blank place to be. But then I became aware of speed, of motion, of transport. There were no reference points so the speed seemed to have no movement.

But the deeper, the farther I traveled, the stranger I felt. It was as if I had flown from the vacuum of interstellar space into a planetary atmosphere, and from there into a deep ocean, and from there into thick viscous lava, and from there into a dark matter too dense to describe, and from there into the hidden emotional nature of myself – and that was the densest place of all.

The next six hours were truly without words, without mind, without talk or questions. It was also one of the most difficult things I've ever survived. I don't think I can adequately put it into words; it's not something words are fit for. The only thing I can hope to do is come up with some kind of analogy that might convey the feeling of it.

Through incredibly difficult layers of emotion I struggled to find my way. It was as if my mind had become nothing but mirror neurons, all mirroring the behavior of the "other me" out there somewhere, as though the observer-me was itself acting in the present moment in whatever circumstances that originally gave the other-me that emotion. Wrenching, heaving, pulling, twisting, straining, forcing me through each emotion one by one, year by year.

It never stopped, it only compounded as it had done in life, layering hurt and sadness, distress and violent melancholy upon each other. As past emotions were remembered in subsequent years, a multi-layered emotion would be created and carried into the future. Then I was in that future, compounding that multi-layer emotion into a new present and dealing with the increasing toll it yielded.

On it went – on and on it went. I was dragging through it all, wide open, vulnerable, unable to do anything but let it fully pass through me. Hour after hour of sadness and emotional nausea that wouldn't let up. This is what I had accumulated. This is how thick it had become. This could never be thought away. This could never be rationalized or analyzed away. This could not be negotiated with. And the real pity was, this was only real because I had given so much energy all my life to make it real! My snare, my illusion, my amnesia had placed this at the base of me.

And this was yet another negative emotion – the realization that all of this was so, so unnecessary. And now only I could make it go away. I was the one who had come for a healing. And San Pedro does not abide dabblers or fools. What you ask for you get. If you're willing to go there, anything is possible. The problem is, most of the time, we aren't willing to go all the way there.

"You want to heal? Then go through this – let it go through you. It's the only way. It's up to you!"

To drive home the point, I believe San Pedro had waited for the right time to show me by practical example. Crippled by the depths of emotional confrontation, the aware part of me started to notice the music playing in the background. For the longest time it had been the soft, New Age type. But slowly dialing up into my awareness was a piece of music that struck a most annoying chord with me. I knew that many New Age songs are longer than regular pop songs, but this song kept going for what seemed like over half an hour.

And the song itself was not really a song; it was the same five or six off-putting notes that had a hypnotically repetitive thud-thud beat behind it. Once the repeating notes and beat came up in volume for ten minutes, there would a moment of silence, then the whole thing would repeat again starting a low volume. This kept going on for what seemed like hours, I couldn't be sure. I only knew that the more I listened to it, the more it was driving me nuts. This was no time to be insanely annoyed by a piece of music. The emotional journey I was taking already had me beyond my limits.

I didn't know what to do. I felt like Alex in the movie A Clockwork Orange, strapped into the theater chair with eyelids held open, screaming to please make it stop. I felt out-of-body, unable to move, trapped on the bed, condemned to be dragged through dark depths of myself while the torment of the repetitive notes and beat carried on and wouldn't, couldn't ever stop. At my worst point, I felt a telepathic nudge from "Father" San Pedro. It was the kick in the ass from a father wanting his boy to shape up and do what's right. The exchange was not in so many words but it was telepathically clear in my consciousness.

"You don't like this, do you? So what the hell are you going to do about it? Lay there and cry? Lay there and take it? Get the fuck up if you don't like it! Do something about it!!"

His words shifted me into being active instead of passive. I marshalled what energy I could and sat up. It was hard to move against the emotional flow, but it was equally hard to move while feeling out-of-body. Somehow I managed to put on my shoes and socks. Standing up was an otherworldly experience but I did it. With uneasy steps, I made my way across the patio, into the sun, and down the dirt path towards the river. As I went, my breaths deepened, came quicker, and the annoying song faded with each step I placed between me and it. I felt infused with a power of self-will and accomplishment. "Father" San Pedro was back in my head.

"This is the same action you must take when you are faced with any of these emotions again! Don't just sit there and let illusions accumulate and drag you down! Get up, leave them behind! You have the power! You create the world you live in! Never again allow that which annoys you and does not serve you to be a part of your space!"

I saw the point. The farther down the path I went, the more the dragging depths of emotion lifted. It was ironic – the farther down the hill I hiked, the faster up through the less-thickening layers of emotion I ascended. By the time I was sitting on my rock, down by the river, I was once again floating in the all-containing vacuum of space. I was light and relieved. My breaths were still deep and fast. It was another kind of purge passing through me.

I felt better but I felt beat up. Six hours of such torment had taken its toll. Since San Pedro had broken the no-words barrier, I felt justified to say something back to him. In the moment, there was nothing else I wanted to ask but – Why? Why did I have to go through that? What was it?

"Father" San Pedro was direct, compassionate, but firm – *"It was necessary. I was cleaning out the wound."*

What wound? The question was automatic even though there were clear signs. "*Your life! The wound you made of your life!*"

I had no words after that. But "Father" San Pedro did. He instructed me to go sit under a particular fruit tree. It was not something I was inclined to do given the rotting fruit at its base and guessing my rock by the river was much more comfortable. But the impulse was insistent and so I went. I was surprised that the instructions continued as I approached the tree. I was not only told where to sit but how to sit. I was told to position my back a certain way and to lean back on the tree in that posture. I was told to cross my feet at the ankles and lift my arm a certain way. With so many directions, I couldn't help ask – why should I do all this? He responded right away, "*You are too wound up, too tight to receive the messages.*"

Now, I've done yoga in the past and many years ago I studied and got a certification as a massage therapist, but this was something different. For the next half hour, "Father" San Pedro took over my body and gave me a workout. My hands massaged me in a way I had never been taught. He used the tree as leverage in the workout. The whole process was too bizarre to piece together here, except to say that after thirty minutes, I felt like someone had done advanced Rolfing, Myofascial Trigger Point therapy, Shiatsu, Reflexology, and who knows what else to recondition and realign key muscles, glands, and chi-nodes. In the middle of one combined movement, the word "futility" shot into my head telepathically. Instantly, my sight was redirected to the rotting fruit on the ground nearby. San Pedro was amused and noted,

"*The fruit on the ground – is that futile? A waste? What is futile?*" Then he laughed.

And so it went through the half hour. Messages and a massage. As the muscles relaxed, so did my grip on old thoughts that no longer served me. By the time it stopped, I was relieved, worn out, grateful, and stunned at the impact of the last six hours. He said no more to me right then. He let me settle into my body and regain my balance. I stayed down by the river for at least half an hour, not thinking, not feeling, just in a state of being.

I left the fruit tree and found one of the mats that someone else had temporarily abandoned. I laid down on it and stared up at the trees overhead. Their motion was my motion and I drifted with it for I don't know how long. The reverie was interrupted when I felt something hitting my legs. I leaned up to find the dog furiously kicking dirt onto me. I laughed out loud because I knew telepathically, this wasn't the dog at all. San Pedro wanted me up.

I walked back up the path to the patio and house to find that the afternoon cut-up fruit had been readied. My wife brought me some and we delighted in it while sitting on the bed. I guessed San Pedro wanted me to have the day's "bump." After the fruit, I laid back down on the bed in the same spot I had been for the first six hours. A stronger breeze came up and blew the large 6-ft. by 6-ft. scarf, hanging at the head of bed, back and forth over me. I felt its motions as caresses from a disembodied, caring soul. The motions seemed too deliberate, too intentioned to be anything else.

In the distance, rolling thunder was heard. A quick-moving storm was headed our way. Then the rolling thunder got louder. With each shuddering peal and booming roll I sank farther into a tearful residual purge of all I had been through. Then the rain fell, gusting around the patio with a whipping wind. Some of it hit my head and hands but once again I couldn't move. The purge, the release had me for the duration. I knew the rain was a continuation of what "Father" San Pedro had said,

"*I was cleaning out the wound.*"

Nothing had ever sounded so powerful, so real, so certain as that massive rolling thunder passing directly over me during this time. The strength of it shook the patio and rattled my bones. It was as if Nature herself was seconding "Father" San Pedro's words to me,

"*Don't just sit there and let illusions accumulate and drag you down! Get up, leave them behind! You have the power! You create the world you live in! Never again allow that which annoys you and does not serve you to be a part of your space!*"

Eventually, the storm passed and I felt the impulse to return to the riverside. I wanted to see the whole area – the gardens, the trees, the sky after the rain. Everything was wetted down and sparkling. The air was extraordinarily fresh and floral. Pockets of brilliant blue were opening up between the rushing clouds, letting the sun perform its brilliant light show on the hillside and the canopy of trees. It was beautiful and I was feeling better and better. My breaths were coming easy and strong. Everything seemed right with the world. And then "Father" San Pedro returned. His statement was short.

"*Now, I only have one question for you…*"

There was a gulf, a hesitation in which sky, river, the trees around me seemed to hold their breath.

"*Why don't you have any common sense?*"

I felt the bottom fall out. I was devastated. After everything I – we – had been through over the past two days, after telling me just a little earlier that the six hours of turmoil and torment was necessary because he was cleaning out the wound, and the wound was my life – of all things to say! I felt betrayed, tricked, ambushed – and wounded again in the worst way. The very idea that the one I had trusted so completely, so deeply, should be the one to do this was inconceivable! I felt destroyed. It was the worst treachery imaginable. I felt my entire dark depths instantly filling back up with torment. To which, "Father" San Pedro responded,

"*You think you're healed?*"

The gulf, the hesitation in which sky, river, the trees around me seemed to hold their breath returned.

"*If you're healed, then me saying that should have no effect. This is the greatest lesson you must receive. Until you know this, you will always be at the mercy of your illusions.*"

At once, the cleansing power of the thunder storm rushed into me again and I cried. The more I cried, the more the new material in the wound disappeared. When it was all gone, I was inundated – how should I say – with angel kisses all over, with transcendent tingles, with trillions of tiny hands applauding in joy all over me.

Then "Father" San Pedro added the most mystical, mind-bending part of all,

"*You know, as a kid, when you heard so many times, 'DON'T YOU HAVE ANY COMMON SENSE?' Well, most of that was me. I tried to get through to you like I'm trying to get through to you now. I wanted you to see the true common sense of who you are and not to do what you were going to do. I wanted you to avoid so many years chasing the illusion, caught by the snare. I knew this day would come. I knew someday you would ask me why you had to waste over 50 years – so I had to try to get you to wake up from your amnesia – to see the real common sense in the fact that you are LOVE!*"

The whole thing appeared so paradoxical. I mumbled back – but if YOU were yelling that when I was a kid, then YOU are the one who caused the problem in the first place!

"*I yelled long after your father had stopped – but you hadn't. By then, you were dead set on chasing the misunderstanding whether or not he said anything more or not. How many times do you think you're father actually said that, anyway? I had to try.*"

The whole thing seemed again – so meaningless. Exasperated, I blurted out – Then I don't understand why we're here. What is this place? San Pedro didn't skip a beat. Immediately, his answer came. "*We come here with amnesia of who we are. The game is to see how long it takes us to realize the truth.*"

So what are we? The answer was strong – "*LOVE! We are love. All suffering results from forgetting that fact. Once we remember it, suffering stops and we win the game. In the infinity of creation there are endless ways to be surprised at all we are!*"

I was confused – Game? Is that all life is? A game? Why the hell do we play a game like that? San Pedro was amused. He laughed and came back more forcefully – "*Why do you play ANY game? FOR FUN! Who doesn't like the joy of the surprise? The deeper the doubt, the greater the surprise when it happens!*"

I challenged him with a lesson from my San Pedro ceremony from a year before – I was told to *STOP THE DRAMA*. But if this is a game, it's intensely DRAMATIC. How does that go together?

His amusement continued – "*Don't you get it yet? The drama's not real! But it's necessary. How long would you throw baskets in basketball if you were absolutely certain you'd always get them all in? The game wouldn't be any fun! But it IS a game. And the game is only PART of the illusion. When you come out of the amnesia, you see that. So STOP THE DRAMA! LOOK FOR THE BEAUTY! GO WITH THE FLOW OF LIFE! ONLY LOVE IS REAL!*"

Instantly, I saw myself hours before, playing the fetch-the-stick game with the dog. For fun, I had faked the dog out by pretending to throw the stick while keeping it in hand. I thought it was hilarious to see him all flustered, running after the disappearing, illusory position of the stick. Then I threw the stick straight up and had fun watching the dog in the dramatic suspense of not knowing where it went. The dog was having as much if not more fun than I was. But it was all a game of illusion and fake drama. We played out our parts with each suspending disbelief that any of it really mattered.

In the moment of play, it all seemed to matter intensely. And yet, in the end, the only thing of true significance was the surprise we felt at the twists and turns of the game and the shared fun we experienced as a spontaneous, expression of love it demonstrated between us. And then within me the game of fetch-the-stick overlapped and merged with the totality of my life, and then everything that extended out into the cosmos – a fractal pattern of repeating play unfolding eternally. I saw genuine, pure play is an act of love. But if you're going to play, you have to play it like the game is real. That's the fun of it.

It can appear difficult making complete sense of any esoteric, magical, out-of-time, out-of-mind experiences and reference points once we land back in our "normal" lives. I only know that the two days I spent with "Father" San Pedro were most significant to me in ways I am still mining the gold from. I may not fully understand the process or even all of the messages yet, but I do understand the lightness of being, the gladness of heart, the peace of mind I've inherited since those two ceremonies became a part of me. I'm not about to second-guess real results or put doubts on my relationship with "Father" San Pedro – that would be putting all of my possibility eggs in one basket and then questioning if the basket were real.

Heartbreak Container, Sad Passion of Happiness, and Playing The Game With Father San Pedro

A beautiful valley stretches southwest through the coastal region, starting high up in the mountains and snaking down to the blue Pacific. Along the way, sunny pastures, rural villages, and the grandeur of ancient ridge lines reaching for blue skies are revealed under the equatorial sun.

About halfway between mountains and sea is a small town. In the hills nearby is a small farm where I spent two consecutive days in November getting back together with Father San Pedro. This was a continuation of another two-day conversation started a month earlier far south of where I lived. Most people refer to him as Grandfather however based on my recent ceremonies where he offered to be my father, I'll be calling him Father San Pedro. This father is a spiritual father, a plant medicine father, a ceremonial healing father, but days spent in conversation with him are nothing less than a heartfelt connection with the closest of family members. I was very much looking forward to this family visit. The warmth and familiarity of returning to Father San Pedro has to be felt to be appreciated.

The benefits of visionary plant medicines have been explored and enumerated by shamans, practitioners, and scientists through many sources over the years. Even more attempts have been made to describe exactly what the visionary experience is like. And while all this literature is rich with examples and testimonials, for the uninitiated who have never experienced a plant medicine ceremony, the bulk of miraculous claims attributed to medicines like San Pedro must seem little more than exaggerated advertising copy or the unrealistic hype of people pridefully motivated to amaze strangers and friends with adventurous stories of mystical hocus-pocus.

But if even a few of these transformative claims are true, we're still talking about something intensely personal, something that doesn't translate using normal methods of relating to one another. How can the uninitiated ever be sure if anything valuable lies behind the magic entheogenic door? I will never be able to taste a strawberry for you – never relate what it's like if you've never had one. The best I could hope to do is describe things you already know, experiences you're familiar with, but describe them in a way that hints at the new experience of strawberry-ness, connects with related emotions, and in turn raises your curiosity enough to make you want to reach for the next strawberry. Only then might you have your own personal experience, your own understanding. And of course, you too wouldn't be able to adequately describe the experience for anyone once you had that last swallow.

Interestingly enough, using related examples to approximate something difficult to know is a method used by the plant medicines in reaching us. The spiritual lessons, the insights into oneself, the messages given by Father San Pedro are often blended with examples fashioned out of the present moment, at once both metaphoric and tangible. A blade of grass points the way, the call of a bird echoes back to memories when you were younger, the flow of a mountain stream carries away your resistance to being in the flow of life. Everywhere you look, everything you do becomes fodder for Father San Pedro to show you something about yourself, about the world, or just as likely, about unfolding possibilities beyond the world.

I can imagine such an example as the medicine flows within you. Over a wall nearby, a simple cloud moves in the sky. At any other time, you wouldn't notice it or the wall. But Father San Pedro uses the immediate and the familiar to transport you deep within yourself – to what needs healing. If you had talked to Father San Pedro while watching that wall and that cloud, what you saw might have transformed. When it did, your conversation with him might have gone something like this –

Sometimes you feel like a cloud, walled off from where you belong, being ripped into a million possible aberrations of who you might be. You stare into the faces of your own aberrations without recognizing yourself. One by one, you try the faces on. You show them to a seemingly indifferent world but at a higher altitude you feel they aren't you. What was once your effortless glide somehow got fragmented into hopeless wandering, no direction seeming right.

Without knowing how it happened, life became a wall topped with jagged glass. Without questioning how it can be, you believe you've been dragged across that wall. Somewhere you think you were told that parts of that wall were built for you. Some of it you build. You hold fast to hurt and anger over everything and everyone that stuck the jagged glass on top. You try to deny the effect all of this has on you even as you suspect it's true. You distract yourself into being busy, hoping something or someone you run into will help you put yourself back together.

You're too consumed with all the faces of you endlessly cut out day-by-day as you're dragged across the shards of time. You feel deep inside that your face should be beautiful and natural, not distorted into a multitude of situational robotic masks. You feel a need to choose one right face to be yours. You need a face to show the world. One you can wear with confidence. One to give you the feeling of belonging. One to make you happy. But that unyielding wall cuts out your same face in an endless, rote succession of days. The cut-out masks are empty but there is nothing else to be.

The wall gives you this imperative. It's the wall's demand. You never realize what's really going on. You don't suspect that lost in the false drama of a life cut to pieces in so many ways, you've forgotten who you are – and it has nothing to do with choosing a face. Lost in a pattern of existence that doesn't serve you, you have no reference point to consider it's not what you think. It's not what the wall tells you. This is not your problem.

You're working on the wrong solution. If only you could get the impulse, the insight to eliminate what you think is happening, maybe then you could float out of the thought-form that traps you. Suddenly, Father San Pedro illuminates the sky with pulsing iridescent color. Immediately after, he banishes the wall in a deep shadow. You flood with emotion as you watch the truth emerge right in front of you.

You would be so surprised to discover you've forgotten what it's like to be a cloud. You might even reject with astonishment any suggestion that clouds don't need a face to put on. You might laugh at the notion that life is not a wall after all. You'd be shocked to realize those shards of glass only appear to drag across you, slicing you into painful distortions – in fact, none of it reaches the real you by a mile. None of it can even get close. You're a cloud.

The aberrant choppiness you think you see in yourself is a defect in the mirror hanging on the wall. It's not in you. You don't build walls or break glass. You glide over them. If you have any face at all, it's the face of the infinite sky, incredibly ever-changing yet ever the same. You are one with this greater whole. You don't need to choose a face. You just need to realize – the sun shines through you, you contain restorative rain for the world, you are the place of rainbows.

Normally, I wouldn't go into this amount of detail over a silly little cloud story. It's obviously a tale losing much in translation. It's like trying to describe skydiving to you so I hang you in a harness a few feet off the ground and turn an electric fan in your face. Yes, the fan is set on high speed but somehow that doesn't help. You know you haven't jumped out of an airplane just like you're reasonably certain you're not a cloud and life is not a jagged wall. No one's been dragging you over broken glass and you absolutely didn't experience space and time transformations. You didn't zoom back through a life review of related events from your past while the story progressed. With so much missing, I wouldn't be surprised if you skipped over the story altogether.

As Aldous Huxley said in "The Doors of Perception and Heaven and Hell," "We live together, we act on, and react to, one another; but always and in all circumstances we are by ourselves. The martyrs go hand in hand into the arena; they are crucified alone. Embraced, the lovers desperately try to fuse their insulated ecstasies into a single self-transcendence; in vain. By its very nature every embodied spirit is doomed to suffer and enjoy in solitude.

Sensations, feelings, insights, fancies – all these are private and, except through symbols and at second hand, incommunicable. We can pool information about experiences, but never the experiences themselves. From family to nation, every human group is a society of island universes... Words are uttered, but fail to enlighten. The things and events to which the symbols refer belong to mutually exclusive realms of experience."

And that's why I'm writing this for me. I don't intend on reproducing my San Pedro experience in any form that anticipates you'll feel it too. But I do invite you to look over my shoulder – scan the words as much as you like and take a gander at photos and videos that apply. The process of getting this down helps me integrate all that happened. Plus it provides an historical record so I won't have to rely on faulty memories of what transpired. Admittedly, there's another reason why I write this for myself. It has to do with how much I enjoy writing and always have, despite the awkward futility in the fact that less than eight percent of the population reads books anymore and those books statistically are mostly romances and more self-help systems from the latest New Age guru or pop-counselor.

My conversations with Father San Pedro have been progressive dialogues. Just as with any relationship between family members, a shared history develops. Past conversations are incorporated into the new. A richness, a layering, an unspoken understanding evolves among family. With each get-together, so much more can be accomplished. The day-long exchange, the messages, the lessons lead deeper through questions and answers one could have never anticipated when the journey began. Much of whatever gets accomplished, whatever gets healed, is felt much more than it is spoken.

Not much of the "how's it even possible" is ever understood. I guess anguishing about understanding the why and how you're healed, why you're happy, why you no longer carry a weight of negativity or doubt or resentment or sadness – none of that matters if the blind sees and the lame walks. When you reach the other shore, it's quite all right to leave that boat behind. You needn't carry any of that to the mountain top. But it's up to you. Everything you pursue with heart yields something beneficial.

Heartbreak Container

No matter how familiar you think you are with Father San Pedro, never underestimate a plant medicine's power to surprise. Regardless of your intricate intentions or carefully scripted questions prepared in advance of a ceremony, be prepared to be unprepared. The medicine knows what you need better than you do. Oftentimes, in spite of you. As the saying goes, "Someone comfortable with their plan clearly does not comprehend the complexity of the situation." And so, there is no way to forecast your interaction with Father San Pedro no matter how many times the two of you have met. Day One in the beautiful valley reinforced this for me in the most unsettling of ways possible.

A little after 9am the ceremony group sat in a circle on the grass in the backyard of a farm house high up a mountain slope and readied ourselves for the journey. Along for the ride, readied for their own personal journeys, were my wife and two of our good friends. Officiating over the medicine was our facilitator from my previous month's journey and his new apprentice. After the prayer "Aho Mitakuye Oyasin" gave thanks and called "To All Relations" to help us through the day, in round-robin fashion we spoke of our intentions in joining the ceremony space. I had given my intention much thought for over a week. Although a lot went into what I was feeling and wanting from the day, I held back the full weight of my anticipation and summarized my intent as briefly and best I could.

My previous journey had turned out to be deeply and exclusively about healing my past. Confident in the blessing of the healing I had received, I now wanted to return to an intention from an Ayahuasca ceremony a year before – an intention that I believed never got answered. It was about my future. I had spent a good portion of my life being very good at something that I believed wasn't me. In cleaning out wounds from my past, San Pedro had explained what that meant for my life. Now that I had moved beyond that, I needed to know what was best for me to be doing in the time I had left on the planet. Without an answer to that, I could only sense a looming darkness of meaninglessness for my remaining days. As Nietzsche said, "He who has a why to live can bear almost any how."

It can take the better part of an hour before the San Pedro medicine really kicks in. And so, after downing our glasses of medicinal brew we all remained in the shade, on the grass, in the sacred circle, exchanging pensive, calming, but expectant talk about the day ahead. Hearing it told later, more than one in the circle had a delayed reaction to the medicine. For me, the effect was opposite. Minutes after my last swallow of the brew, the feeling came over me that I could not merely sit and be part of the conversation anymore. An uneasy impulse to get away anywhere off by myself overtook me. I felt elevated in energy, gripped by a crystalline focal point on the present moment, and I sensed a pull into another domain. Oddly enough, just as my impulse to leave needed immediate action, the sacred circle broke and we all dispersed.

I'm not sure where anyone else went, although I heard continued talking in the distance behind me. Not knowing where to go, I followed the initial energetic impulse. It led me to a fence by the property line that bordered a dirt road. I strolled by the vine-draped chain-linked fence for a while, finally stopping to take in the view across the road. There was no reason to look over there except I felt I needed to.

Across the way, a neighbor's large pond was a watering hole for cattle. Morning sun painted shade across the pond and a gentle breeze shook the shade with lazy nudges. Exotic bird calls echoed down the mountain side. The Andes are filled with exotic birds and each bird song is more beautiful and amazing than the one before. But no other bird call says San Pedro to me than the distinctive call of the Pacific Hornero. It is so unique and amazing, you may one day hear it imitated if you attend an Ayahuasca ceremony presided over by a traditional shaman. In between icaros, during smudgings, while the shaman attends to the energetic space around you, oftentimes he will imitate the call of the Pacific Hornero. The imitations I have heard are subtle, breathy little whistles compared to the shrill thunder of the bird's real call – but in a ceremony, in contrast, the shaman's breathy little whistle fits the mood just right.

The "Field Guide to the Songbirds of South America: The Passerines" sums up the call of the Pacific Hornero this way: "Song – a loud, almost raucous series of piercing notes that slows and drops in pitch, sometimes given more or less in unison by a pair." For me, probably because of the overriding sense of conversation going on, the call is especially evocative of San Pedro when I hear two Pacific Horneros sound out loud and strong together – presumably, almost in sync. It is never a precise sync, one may say, but such a notion of precision is a misunderstanding of perfection. The sync achieved by two Pacific Horneros when calling out together is damned well the best example of perfection I have heard. It is their perfection. When you hear it that way, especially while "in the medicine" – you receive the message in the song.

And so, I can say with absolute certainty that my dialogue with Father San Pedro began the moment I looked over the fence to the other side of the road, across the neighbor's pond, while shade and cattle moved in slow motion, and the shrill thunder of two Pacific Horneros shook the air beside me. In that moment my attention was drawn to a gap in the fence across the road. Even though I had been standing there taking in the scene for who knows how long, I never noticed the missing section of fence. What seemed at the time a non sequitur of a question floated through my mind. It was asked by Father San Pedro, "*Why would they leave the gate open?*"

I answered the best I could, working through all the reasons why it might be a good thing or just as likely an oversight that could let the cattle wander out into the road. By the time I reviewed my answers, I was dismayed to find that Father San Pedro had moved on. He didn't seem interested in my answers. Like a little boy who had gotten sidetracked and didn't realize that his father had strolled farther up the path, I needed to catch up. Starting right then and continuing through the rest of the day, and throughout the next day, I felt varying degrees of motion sickness. Without any visual cues to orient myself, the feeling of moving was as unsettling as it was unexplained.

In my hurry to catch up, I launched into my intentions. I quickly found those intentions riddled with questions. The expanding questions would necessitate divergence into separate issues, and the cascade of fall-out issues were then entangled in a web of feeling and melancholy-wonder that no words would be adequate to address. It started as that kind of conversation.

I felt Father San Pedro through it all but he was patiently walking beside me. We continued up the trail but his words were sparse. Like a father knowing when it was important to let me get it all out, he was there for me. He allowed me to vent, to question, to spin off with all my grandiose logical designs. He added a word or two here or there but for at least an hour he let me have at it however I wanted to proceed. In retrospect, I could imagine my download of everything on my mind and heart was too dense for him to get a word in edgewise. Or so it seemed. In reality, he could have interrupted me whenever he wanted. And when the time came, he knew exactly what to say to stun me into shifting gears.

"*Why do you feel you need to take it to the next level?*" I wasn't sure what he meant.

"*Why do you come to me like this? What happened to father and son? What was wrong with that?*"

I still wasn't sure what he meant.

"*You want to take it to the next level? You want to talk man-to-man? Is that it?*" I realized I had been doing just that. I wanted to explain. "Yes. I want to understand. I want our conversation to progress. I want to understand things beyond being a child – at a higher level."

His comment back was delivered with passion, "*None of that is necessary. Don't you realize that?*"

"I know I've learned things. I know I want to learn more. I feel learning more is necessary."

"*OK. So you want to take it to the next level…you want to ask the hard questions. You want answers. We can do that. We can do anything you want. I'm here for you. Let's do it.*"

His tone changed. I was no longer sitting on his knee. I was in the boardroom and it was time to get down to business. It started off with a challenge to expand the level of questions I had allowed myself to explore.

From my history, he knew the number one question I had brought to the past ceremonies dealt with the terrifying paradox I had experienced in my first Ayahuasca ceremony. At the time, I needed to know if the dark entities I watched take over the ceremony were real or not. Father San Pedro challenged me to go beyond questioning my fears. To really question involved so much more.

"*You want to ask the hard questions? You asked before if the dark entities were real...*"

"Yes."

He dismissed it. "*That's not a hard question. Why do you only ask about dark entities? Ask yourself if love is real. Is love part of the illusion too?*"

In the distance, the call of the lone Pacific Hornero mocked my indecisiveness. I couldn't answer. I discovered I wasn't certain. In the moment, Father showed me all possibilities were possible.

"*All is possible. Maybe real love got disinvented long ago. Maybe it never existed. What you call love could be a pale imitation, a delusion you lose yourself in so you people don't have to face the truth. So give me your answer. Until you know love is real, until there are no questions, what good is anything else?*"

Father didn't stop. Half of the time he never waited for my answer. The hard questions kept coming. The next two hours were intense. I was taken to school and I got what I asked for. I was shown that "next level" was so lacking in a description. It wasn't a level as I understood it – it was an essence that included the universe and it defied levels. It was a Pandora's Box of places where paradoxes and complexities fractally-spiralled outwards and inwards beyond reasoning. There was no way I was on par with Father San Pedro.

Questioning him man-to-man was ripping me apart. Everything I thought was certain was gone. All of my questions were one-dimensional in an imagination space unbounded by mind. He took me down paths and got me to accept them – only to blow them away with razor-sharp certainty. Afterwards, he would admonish me, "*You fell for that?*" The hard questions opened up onto other dimensions. It was twelve-dimensional chess whizzing by me and I was trying to remember which way the rook moved.

There is no way to relate the content of those two hours. For awhile I paced near the farm house, on the porch, through the kitchen, by the water jug, then back onto the patio. A fierce debate raged within me about moral choices and whether they existed in the real and the illusion we lived in.

"*If none of this is real,*" remarked father, "*then there are no moral choices here.*"

My mind spun with philosophies that said nothing of this world was real.

"*There are no real moral choices in an illusion,*" Father emphasized. "*Am I right?*"

The hard questions kept coming. At the time, I was standing on the patio sipping water from a ceramic mug. Father challenged me further. If I wanted to face the hard questions, I needed to bring them into my reality in a tangible way. Thinking about them was never enough. Hard questions never get answered in the mind. They need action. We only know who we are, we only truly know our answers by being challenged by something we can't avoid or rationalize away. It has to be something out of mind. Something in our face. The hard questions are truly faced when we are forced to make a decision with seemingly real consequences. Or are they real?

"*If I'm right,*" prodded Father, "*then throw that cup down. Break it!*"

I hesitated.

"*Why do you hesitate? What does it matter? It's just an illusion. There's no moral choice here.*"

No matter how much I tried to comply, I couldn't bring myself to smash the cup on the patio floor.

"*You think there are consequences in this place? Consequences that matter? Huh!?*"

I thought of the people who owned the house. It was their cup. I shouldn't just break it.

"*If you can't break the cup, you are telling me this place is real. You are telling me such a thing matters. How can you justify that?*"

Once again I hesitated. There was no way I could be certain this place was real. No way to justify not acting on unfettered impulse. Not after all the conversation we had already had.

"*Break it!*" father demanded.

My hand wavered. I almost did it. And then the fact that I had come so close shook me.

"*You're making a moral choice,*" noted father. "*But you have no reason for it!*"

I must have, I thought. I fought for an answer. Pushed into emotional overload by the real consequences possible, the moment collapsed into the only thing left. I blurted back, "I feel it's right." I could find no other explanation for my resistance.

"*Like I said,*" he answered. "*You have no REASON for it.*"

Sensing how my internal conversations sometime become so energetic that they seem to spill over into affecting my external environment always rattles me. I had to set the cup down on the nearest table.

"*You don't trust yourself.*" Father paused, reading me and my reaction. "*You may still do it.*"

His comment laid me bare. My hand shook. He was right and I didn't know why.

"*Pick up the cup. Prove me wrong.*" Father added, "*Go ahead, take it to the next level.*"

I had to get away from that cup. The energy of hearing him bait me with "the next level" pulled me down the steps and sent me trodding off into the wind-whipped mango, papaya, and banana trees at the lower section of the property. There I paced, dizzy with unsettling impulses and echoes of the conversation. Finally, distracting myself from knowing the cup was waiting for me on the table somewhere beyond the trees, I tried launching back into my questions.

I asked if there might be a way to resolve the conflict between nature and human technology. San Pedro showed me a beautiful way to combine nature with machines, humanity with a transhuman idealized state. It seemed all so elegant and evolutionary, so brilliant and natural in progression. Then he bounced me on my ass and showed me the inverted, perverted other side of it. I saw the deception of spirit and corruption of everything good that would result. "*You fell for that?*"

I asked – is there any way to resolve the paradoxes of what is real and what is illusion? What to do if we can never be sure if reality's the illusion and the illusion's real? He showed me how anything can be real and at the same time an illusion. He led me into the trap of getting lost in believing one for the other. "*You fell for that?*" My mind reeled. He followed it up with – "*You can create anything! Anything is true with mind. Just don't get lost in it – if you need to get lost in something, get lost in heart. But why get LOST there? You don't have to get lost at all!*"

He even dispensed with my intentions for the day – "*nothing but machinations of mind!*" I looked back on them with expanded awareness and knew he was right. I was not doing well at the "next level." Everything I got into was crayons and color-by-number – all of Father's answers were advanced CGI. The Pandora's Box I had opened never arrived and would never arrive at a final answer or one complete understanding. It turned out there were so many "complete understandings," the next one seemingly more elegant than the one before until you realized that all of those understandings were only component parts of a greater whole that was ever-emerging upon more.

It never stopped. Resolved paradoxes resolved by unfolding as dilemmas to be answered with even richer imagined paradoxes. It could be so incredibly interesting to explore the far reaches of it all. It was so easy to get caught up and not realize I was applying infinite energy to a puzzle that exponentially expanded with an influx of energy. It was my choice what to make real, where to direct my energies. The universe was not judgmental – it would gladly let me go down any rabbit hole that made me happy. The key question, often overlooked, remained – how do you know it really makes you happy? Are you being fulfilled or just dazzled into being lost by what you fill yourself with? How will you ever know? By resolving paradoxes? By taking it to the next level? By securing answers that implied future questions?

I felt like I had just run a marathon. I was intensely alert but bedraggled and spent. I sat down on a pile of broken roof tiles at the corner of the property. I was whipped. My question bag had been summarily emptied and shoved over my head. The mountain I thought I was going to climb turned out to be a wormhole into an infinity of possible certainties and converging opposites. There seemed to be no way to find rest or peace or satisfaction down that path. And that's exactly what Father intended me to find.

I stood, bedraggled, and shuffled to a shady spot amidst the fruit trees. I felt a wave of compassion from Father for my predicament. He asked with a man-to-man insistence tinged with a deep sense of concern, "*What do you want now?*"

I knew in the moment that anything I wanted was there for the asking. Father San Pedro was there for me. He wasn't going to force me down any one path. He would walk across the snares with me if that was where I wanted to go. He would sit with me on the pile of broken roof tiles if that made me happy. He was willing to argue logical points the rest of the day and into tomorrow if I felt I needed that. But in that moment, thrashed as I was, I could only think of what he had told me over a year before. The thought of asking for it made me smile. Who was I to order up anything from him, as if my wish was his command. At that, he echoed the amused sentiment,

"*I might as well be your genie – your wishes await.*"

I was humbled by my humor. "Anything I want?"

"*Anything you want...*"

The air was perfectly still. The sun beat down beyond my shady space among the trees. I went back to what he had said a year before. And yet, the thought of commanding anything to appear was ludicrous, presumptuous, preposterous, brash, and impossibly wishful. But I asked it anyway.

"*I want to see beauty!*" (His message from a year before was "*look for the beauty in life.*")

Instantly, a gorgeous white crane swooped close overhead. I watched the beauty of its graceful glide pass nearby with rapt awe. The flight couldn't have been cued with any finer precision. As the bird passed, a large gust of wind blew through the banana trees and pushed me off-balance.

Filled with the beauty of the bird's flight, my heart raced to simplify. I wanted nothing else than for the rest of the day to be spent as father and son. No more man-to-man questions. I would gratefully leave the next level behind for the peace and loving certainty of a father's love. But Father San Pedro was not going to let me off the hook that easily. A man couldn't race back and be the boy any time things got rough, otherwise, what's the point of taking on things like a man? Father wasn't going to give up on the hard questions just yet.

He turned his focus onto my original intentions for the day. Yes, they were machinations of the mind. But he showed me how my mind was only trying to deal with so much that went deeper, deeper than mind could ever understand fully. But with me, it always had to start with the mind, with the analysis my mind had done. That was the door into me. That was my protective layer. To reach anywhere deeper, Father would have to lead me where I needed to go by first catching the attention of my mind. Or so I thought. In reality, the hardest question, the toughest lesson hadn't come yet. And it wasn't a question for the mind at all.

Feeling pulled towards the inevitable, I left the trees and walked back up the hill. I avoided possible interactions at the house and found myself back at the chain-linked fence at the side of the property by the dirt road. I laid down on a mat, close to the fence, facing the road, and sunk into the realization that the hard questions were not about to stop. Part of asking Father San Pedro to go someplace with you is the understanding that the only way out is through.

Backing out of a lesson is never the way to get what one needs from the experience. Once on the ride, you were strapped in until the end of what was needed. He didn't let it go unnoticed that my avoidance of the house conveniently kept me from facing the cup again. The cup that was not yet broken. The mention of it spiraled me back into a continuing conversation about the real and unreal, the existence or non-reality of moral choices, and whether dark entities and love ever mattered within the illusions we had created for ourselves.

Father is very good at convincing you of anything. He even convinces you that you can choose anything to be real or unreal for yourself. Free will and personal choice have meaning or they don't depending on what? If anything is possible, if we create our reality, if everything is energy and infinite probabilities, what's to say one over the other? Is our existence that magical? Is this a place of unconditional "yes" so mind-boggling that we get lost in our own wishful delusions? Can we actually make our delusions real? Can we actually disinvent love? Have we?

If everything is possible, why not? When we say there's a cosmic Source for everything, do we really consider what we are saying – what the Source of everything would include? Are we willing to look at those parts of ourselves that everything includes? Father kept bringing me back to my decision not to break the cup. There was no logic to it. There was no certainty. There was no reason, given the expanded awareness of what was involved. Could expanded awareness lead us into being lost in our delusions? Could anyone ever think their way out of the hard questions I was shown? And if they had, would those answers be real or unreal? Was it ever only up to us?

I was too exhausted and wracked with motion sickness to handle any more. Lying on the ground, I felt like I was falling – falling away from certainty, drifting away from meaning, passing beyond the point of ever being at peace with answers. The sad, sinking feeling left me an empty shell – an empty shell eternally filling with next level answers that didn't satisfy.

Into that shell came a sound. It was far away, plaintive, familiar and yet alienated by the context. The sound grew louder. At first I thought I was hearing my inner self moaning. But it was more than a moan. It was sobbing. It was a cry. Was I crying and not realizing it? I pulled my awareness sharper and realized the sound was not me – but a child in the distance.

I lay there, interpreting the sound. A child was crying. Was it crying to be picked up? Was it crying because it was thirsty, hungry? Maybe it had been disciplined by a parent. But no, as I analyzed the cry, it came to me – the cry was a cry of pain. What level of pain was it? How does one judge the level of pain? The child was in pain that wasn't trivial and the cry was getting louder. Why was it louder? There were other voices too.

I recognized Spanish being spoken. The other adult voice was agitated, hurried. I realized that the child and the adults were coming closer. Before I knew it, I was laying on the ground on my side, staring out at a family close by, frantically moving down the dirt road just beyond the fence. They stopped right outside the fence. I watched a small boy yell out in pain. I saw his anguished face. His left foot was obviously hurt. The father was carrying him while the distraught mother hovered nearby. More hurried Spanish was being exchanged.

As I lay there, Father San Pedro returned to his first question of the day, "*Is love real or is it another part of the illusion?*" Before I could attempt an answer, he added the answer – it was the same answer I received about the dark entities at the end of another ceremony, a Kambo ceremony, after

Rapé took me deeper – "*It's real and it's not real.*"

I laid there, taking everything in – the family in agony in front of me on the road and San Pedro in my head. Father added, "*It's up to us. We make love real by our actions.*"

Another moment passed and he noted, "*You wouldn't break the cup – so how can you lie there when the child is crying?*"

In an instant, a flood of emotional lessons from the day poured into me – the real and unreal existing simultaneously in our choices, whether moral choices really existed, what did the laws of attraction mean in its total scope, how making our own reality could be our salvation or a trap. Father's words echoed back to me – "*We make it real by our actions.*"

Why this particular family stopped exactly where they did I'll never know. Why this little boy had to break his foot or whatever it was right in front of me while I was "in the medicine" I can only guess. Why Father San Pedro had led me down a line of "hard questions" at the "next level" was all due to what I had asked for. And he was not about to fail me. "*You want to go there, kid? Okay...*" I just never dreamed that the "real world" would "intrude" on my sacred medicine lessons in such a dramatic way.

The feeling was pressed at me – if I wanted to face the hard questions, I needed to bring them into my reality in a tangible way. Thinking about them was never enough. Hard questions never get answered in the mind. They need action. We only know who we are, we only truly know our answers by being challenged by something we can't avoid or rationalize away. It has to be something out of mind. Something in our face. The hard questions are truly faced when we are forced to make a decision with seemingly real consequences.

One thing was for certain. I could not simply lie there, listen to that child in pain, and do nothing. Something prevented me from breaking the cup. I could not explain it. I didn't know why the force was so strong, even as Father San Pedro commanded me to break it. I knew it was a test. And now I was being tested again.

I have no way of knowing how I appeared to the anguished family just beyond the fence, especially since I was still deep "in the medicine." But I jumped up and called over to them in my best broken Spanish, asking if they needed help. They shifted towards me and in hurried Spanish tried to make me understand. I didn't. All I could think of was to get the ceremony facilitator or his apprentice.

I knew the apprentice was better at Spanish than I was – and he wasn't at the moment "in the medicine." I sought him out and told him the situation. He hurried out and spoke to the father over the fence. He offered to call for help but the father didn't seem interested in that. The apprentice assured me that the father had noted that someone was going to try to come up from town on a motorcycle. Everything would be taken care of – no need for alarm.

Minutes were passing and the child was crying out. The apprentice had returned to the house but the boy's father kept engaging with me. He kept trying to tell me something, ask me something. He seemed more desperate and needing some other kind of help. If everything was taken care of, why was he engaging me so? I moved over to the front gate. He followed me there. I thought I should let him in so he could explain his situation better. But the gate had a padlock on it.

I knew that ceremony space was always kept secured and no one was supposed to break the energetic space around the ceremony, but the need seemed apparent. I motioned at the lock but the father pleaded with me, pointing at the car behind the gate and gesturing for me to cut off the lock if need be. I felt I could only do so much. I didn't have the key to the gate and the car wasn't mine – it was owned by the ceremony's facilitator.

Before I could think of any other way to help, I saw the resignation in the man's eyes. He knew I wasn't going to help him take his son down the hill to the hospital. In the distance I could hear a 2-stroke motorcycle coming up the dirt road. The meager help he could manage was on the way. He reached out his hand and I reached through the wrought-iron fence to grab hold of it. We shook hands and even without a common language, I communicated my concern and compassion for him and his son and he sent back his appreciation, understanding, and gratitude for my attempt, despite the ineffectual effort it turned out to be. We were within a foot of each other. We made a strong connection while I was "in the medicine." The connection resonated back to the refrain I kept hearing in my head, "*It's real and it's not real. It's up to us. We make love real by our actions.*"

I stood by the gate while the parents took the boy to the back of a friend's motorcycle. The small 2-stroke machine had barely room for its driver. Behind him climbed someone who would have to hold the crying boy. The three of them needed to navigate down the mountain road to the small town below.

After the motorcycle was gone, I looked over the fence to the other side of the road, across the neighbor's pond, while shade and cattle moved in slow motion. In that moment my attention was drawn to the gap in the fence across the road. What seemed a non sequitur of a question at the start of the ceremony, so many hours before, now floated through my mind once again. At start of day the question was asked by Father San Pedro. Now he asked it again, "*Why would they leave the gate open?*" This time he was asking about a completely different gate.

The incident affected me for the rest of the afternoon. The conversation with Father San Pedro had ended with the hardest question yet. The example had taken me into the next level in ways that were too real, too raw, too upsetting. I couldn't get the connection with the boy's father out of my heart and mind. I felt we in the ceremony space had lost an opportunity to walk our talk and "*make love real by our actions.*" Yes, the "ceremony container" was inviolate and needed to be protected. But if we love only when it is safe or convenient for us, what does that say about our conditional love?

In the moments of that afternoon, while "in the medicine", the choice appeared clear. Fears about dark entities entering our sacred ceremony space should the gate be opened seemed to fly in the face of the power of love and everything we gave lip service to. I needed to talk with someone and gratefully, the apprentice was there for me. He allowed me to vent and let out emotion, to explore my confusion, to try to handle the excess energy I was left with. It was very kind the way he sat with me in the minutes afterwards.

Not breaking the cup was the good and right thing to do. That solid foundation in heart would always overwhelm the delusions we make real by our fears. To say the least, the rest of the day was rough for me. Later that night, after supper, when we were all sharing and I tried to communicate what I felt was San Pedro's message for ALL of us, I was simply told it was MY message. I was reminded of the inviolate nature of the ceremony space and the need to keep the space safe. As if a message about the truth of love only applies conditionally. As if our love is so weak, so impotent, so vulnerable that we can only fully practice it within a "safe ceremony space."

I found it uniquely frustrating because just the day before, someone at the ceremony had shared that at a previous ceremony somewhere else, they had asked San Pedro if it was allowable for one person while "in the medicine" to bring back messages for other people. They said that San Pedro had answered yes, one person COULD bring back a message for someone else. No mention of this was made by this person when I was trying to describe San Pedro's message about the event with the hurt child.

I guess going there would have made it too real for everyone concerned. Better if it all remain an abstract "lesson", a personalized "message" for someone else, something to add to our communal bag of love-inspired aphorisms to post online for one another on another day. Granted, most people at the ceremony hadn't even been aware that the episode with the child was going on while it happened. The participants were all in various parts of the property at the time, deep into their own experience. No wonder it was off their radars.

After dinner, we each had a divination reading. I wanted two messages. For the first I wanted a comment on what I had experienced during the day. For the second, I wanted a comment on the following day and the next ceremony to come, should I decide to attend. The first message pointed to compassion and the second regarded the cycles of the moon. Interestingly enough, this ceremony occurred on the day of the Super Moon, a lunar event that hadn't happened in over 70 years.

Despite any valid messages I might have received, the divination message included everybody with me that day, including the other ceremony participants and the facilitator and his apprentice. Full compassion needed to extend everywhere, including myself and what appeared to be my inability to come to grips with what had happened, and not happened, and my reaction to it. Since the ceremony, Father San Pedro has continued to show me this for as he has told many of us so often, he is always with us if we call on him.

Everything considered at the time, I had a very difficult time processing what had happened. My outside experience was in no way matching my internal experience. I went to bed feeling that Father San Pedro was disappointed. Why else did I have no other conversation with him the rest of the afternoon? Why were his last words to me – "*Why would they leave the gate open?*" Maybe in the last hours of the day, he was still with me but out of mind, only in my emotions.

But why had the hard questions and the next level have to be so real, so extreme, so hard-ball? He wasn't kidding when he told me, "*OK, let's go there.*" I wouldn't be satisfied until I got more. He didn't disappoint. His words came back to me from the start of day when I asked him to progress the conversation, to take me into deeper understanding. "*None of that is necessary. Don't you realize that?*"

Yes, the day had started with the safe space being defined and smudged, the sacred "Aho Mitakuye Oyasin" prayer that called upon "All My Relations" to help us throughout the day. And yet falling asleep at the end of Day One, I felt lost within a heartbreak container.

Sad Passion of Happiness

Morning came too soon. Feelings from the night before had been tempered with rest but were far from gone. Before falling asleep I didn't know if the exhaustion of Day One might prevent me from joining in the next ceremony. But when the warm sunlight filled the bedroom, I felt too much was left unresolved to sit the day out. I remembered being told that

San Pedro oftentimes gives you the energy you need to see the ceremony through. I thought back to the divination reading from the night before. It stressed how a time of the full moon was great for healing, going after what one needed, and letting go of things of no use.

With a Super Moon on my side, how could I pass up an opportunity to release more and manifest more? Like the day before, I felt the pull of the medicine fairly quickly after drinking down the brew. My intention for this day was definitely not over-thought. No way did I want to go there again. I wished to simply return to the father and son relationship with San Pedro. No more insisting on progressing the conversation. If I could manage to pull my head out of the wormhole, maybe Father might even show me something about my future.

The day was exceptionally beautiful, the scenery awe-inspiring. Never before had I heard such a cacophony of nature sounds celebrating being alive. Such things may go unnoticed since they are so familiar for people used to living in the country, I don't know, but we city-dwellers on the medicine can find umpteen reasons to delight in the craziest of little things. It was such a perfect setting. Even more reason to feel strange at not being able to find my place to settle in. There was a restless feeling of displacement in every direction I turned. Everyone seemed to be able to find a comfortable spot to retreat to but I started the day searching. Maybe my searching wasn't for a place at all.

Father San Pedro waited with infinite patience for me to get to the point. Back as Father and son, it was easier letting my feelings drive my intention forward. Before anything else, there was one innocent question that the kid just had to ask. Before I could ask it, I was led to a shady spot on the side of the house. There, stretching the length of the house, was a brick and concrete ledge adorned with a couple of flower pots. I sat down on the ledge and felt settled enough to ask my question. It concerned the hard lesson of the crying child.

"So my message from yesterday – was it just for me or everyone?"

Father spoke with a quality of voice that was soft, firm, angelic, "*It's for all who heard.*"

He paused and waited for his words to sink in before adding, "*Some hear with mind, some with heart. For each it becomes real however it's heard. That's why it's always better to hear with the heart.*"

The silence that followed continued the message into the heart. The deeper the silence drove it home, the more I was content that the matter had been covered completely. Nothing else needed to be said about that. He was done with the topic for the day. I was now free to move on. I felt all of it release. With the release came a whoosh of spirit that collapsed me on my side. I laid down on the concrete ledge and felt the motion sickness again.

Strangest of all in the moment, I found the flat concrete ledge a most comfortable place to be. It felt like the best mattress. How that's possible, I don't know. The journey was ramping up into all that Father knew was good for me. I let any resistance go and sunk into the feeling. Before I knew it, the sun had moved in the sky and the shade on the side of the house had shrunk. My little ledge was still shaded, but something else had moved. That something else was inside of me. I heard Father's voice –

"*You want to know about the future – your future. You want to know what you're supposed to be doing with the rest of your time.*"

"Yes."

"*You'll never answer questions about your future until you finish with your past.*"

This wasn't what I wanted to hear. After two days of deep healing about my past in last month's ceremony, I thought I was ready to move forward. I felt I was done with the past. I was happy and energized to be done with it. Now all I needed was direction on how to fill the future.

"*You think you're stranded in a waiting-room,*" remarked Father.

It was true. I often referred to my condition of life akin to someone abandoned in a waiting-room. I could have some fun watching the illusion-units fight over the best seats and the old magazines, but it was still just a waiting-room.

"*You think this is a waiting-room because you feel you don't belong. How can you ever do anything with your future if you don't belong?*"

The realization hit me. I never thought of it that way before. I never suspected that it was something about me that made it a waiting-room. Stunned, I stood up and walked away from the house. My steps diverted to the chain-link fence by the road. Across the road, the cattle had scattered away. Smoke filled the air. I stood at the fence and watched as fire consumed the weeds around one side of the pond. Industrious voices carried on the air. The neighbors had purposely set a fire to tame the weeds. As I stood there, Father took my past apart. Attached to the pieces of the past were deep emotions. As he took me through the process, I felt myself fragmenting.

"*As a kid, you never felt you belonged in your family.*"

He took me through it in excruciating detail. My parents and sisters were all born in St. Louis. I was born in Los Angeles. My siblings were nine and twelve years older than me. I was the only boy child who grew up in a house of adults. Instead of playing catch with my father, he got me a "pitch-back net" device so I could throw into the net and catch the ball when it bounced back. At every opportunity, they reminded me how I differed from them. Anything I liked, they didn't get or their version in St.

Louis or in a previous time was better. Play was a solitary pursuit, a refuge. I made up elaborate play scenarios to entertain myself. As I grew, the separation only intensified. The examples of separation from family proliferated. I only skim the surface of them here.

"What are we doing?" I asked Father at one point. "I feel sad. Is that okay or am I just feeling sorry for myself?"

"*We're burning off the weeds*," came his answer.

I looked up at fast-moving dark clouds. They were an instant metaphor for feeling like I was under a dark cloud.

"*Good – don't chase away the dark clouds; they bring restorative rain, they wash away what no longer serves you.*"

I laid down on a mat near to and facing the chain-link fence. The dark clouds raced overhead while the crackle of fire and smell of smoke filled my senses. Near to my face, the chain-link's metal lattice was interlaced with the vines of a bush emblazoned with gorgeous Hibiscus flowers. Everything becomes a metaphor for healing.

Father spoke. "*Over time it all gets intertwined and we feel a need to break free – but we dare not because we think it's the only structure that's holding us up.*" Father wouldn't stop with the review. "*You are fire and water – separated they have their purpose but together they resolve opposites – in that there is power – be the steam.*"

Note – my astrological Sun sign is Sagittarius and my Rising sign is Aquarius.

He stressed, "*You are never going to have purpose where you don't belong.*"

I felt I needed to know, so I asked, "Is this place real?"

"*When you play for keeps you make it real – otherwise, it's a shadow world.*"

I felt overloaded. I had to go lie down inside. Upstairs in the farm house, I collapsed on my bed, only to be pestered by nagging, seemingly irrational thoughts about my shoes and socks. I hadn't taken either off and the room was hot. Back and forth I debated whether to take them off and be comfortable to leave them on and avoid the trouble of dealing with them when I got back up. The decision seems trivial now, but in the moment, the debate nauseated me. I felt like I might need to purge.

Father San Pedro was heard again. He was emphatic, "*You've been conditioned to put aside what is right in the moment for a future circumstance. How can you ever belong here and now like that?*"

It was good that I was lying down because the spiraling vision he showed me of how one thing led to another stunned me dizzy. The life review I was shot through kept going and going. He went with me. As we traveled, he broke it down for me.

"You don't belong – results in loneliness."
More life review.
"Deep-set loneliness – results in self-doubt."
More life review.
"Endless self-doubt – results in lack of confidence."
Finally, spun through my childhood and into my young adulthood, he concluded – *"Your isolation has become your identity. You can stay there if you like and it will afford you a remote perspective that's unique. But is that what you want?"*

I answered the only way I could in the moment, "How do I remove the isolation?"

His answer was immediate – *"Start living like you belong."*

I had to pull myself up and get outside. I needed to be in nature. I found a new place, close but not so near the chain-linked fence. I laid down and faced a new direction – the physical symbology of that wouldn't sink in until later. I drifted off on an emotional sea, buoyed by my life review, pulled by a tide of desire for a new place, a new direction, a new way of being. Hours passed. Father was with me, doing what he does. It's not something that can be explained. To say he was re-wiring what had been jumbled up inside is a weak analogy although it may be the best I can do. Once again, I can't taste the strawberry for anyone else.

It was early afternoon by the time I resurfaced. I got up to share some mid-day fruit with the other participants. It was a deep time for everyone. I don't remember much conversation although there must have been some. It's an otherworldly reentry to walk back into normal conversations with people while still in the medicine. After the fruit was gone, I answered the call of seeking solitude.

I returned to my comfortable concrete ledge on the side of the house. There I found it easy to re-float myself on the emotional sea. The sea was losing depth with each pass through the life review. Waiting-room sank into not belonging which sank into loneliness which sank into self-doubt which sank into lack of confidence which hit bottom in isolation. I moved back to the new direction spot on the grass.

Lying on my side, I opened my eyes to take in the panoply of plants and flowers under gliding clouds. As I meditated, one plant in the distance, barely seen through gaps in the foliage, drew my attention. It was quite far away but the sun was on it and it was waving like crazy. Every time I tried to refocus on my meditation, all attention was pulled back to the motion of that plant. The extreme movement was out of place with the surroundings. No other plant was moving so fast or at all. It was demanding my attention and its insistence triggered me to respond with annoyance.

"All right! Why do you want my attention? What is it?!"

With spooky timing, all motion in the plant stopped. I felt I had rebuked it somehow.

Father San Pedro took note. His explanation shocked me into feelings of remorse. "*That plant was just waving hello. That was all. It was glad to see you.*"

As soon as he said it, I recognized what had happened.

Father continued – "*Why so critical?*" The question was about so much more than the present moment.

My mind raced away with what had happened. I automatically took the motion critically as a demand for my attention. I judged it, immediately wondering about what it wanted from me. Because it must want something. Why was my first instinct to go there?

Like a telepathic shot of reality, San Pedro jumped into the conversation.

"*A sense of isolation fosters suspicions and being critical. And so you cut yourself off from the joy all around you. You cut yourself off from your future. Realize – there's no answer for what you should be doing. Instead of asking what – free yourself from ideas. With that out of the way, the rest takes care of itself. You love Nature and Nature never asks what it should be doing. It just is.*"

The depths of the emotional ocean refilled a bit with more to deal with. The thought passed my mind before I had a chance to hold it back – Maybe what I think I should be doing is false and only a part of self-delusion from bad stuff in the past.

San Pedro responded, "*There is no bad stuff in the past. The only guide is the heart. Question and answer will fit when you start asking the right questions. Because the answer will always be the same – love. You are a part of love – so with love you BELONG – you always have. Nothing can change that.*"

I felt what he was saying but some of it was difficult for my mind to accept.

Father asked, "*What to do with your time? Do what makes you happy!*"

The truthful answer was prompted out of me right away, "I don't know what that is anymore! I don't know what makes me happy!"

Father responded, "*You defined yourself once. You can redefine yourself. Allow a new definition and the source of happiness will flow out of it. You can't have one until the other.*"

I felt lost. Father was telling son what he needed to hear but son was not wanting to hear it.

All I could do is repeat in sadness…

I don't know

I don't know
I don't know
I don't know
I don't know
I don't know
I don't know
I don't know
I don't know
I don't know
I don't know

He let me sink with the feeling until finally, Father San Pedro shouted out to interrupt me. "*That's right! It's not to KNOW! Are you getting it? It's to FEEL!*"

Playing The Game With Father San Pedro

They say that eating a little something like fruit halfway through the ceremony provides a "bump" going deeper into the experience. The afternoon definitely proved the point. Just when I thought Father had plumbed the tangle of my childhood through-and-through, he shot me deeper with starker revelations. After the imperative to FEEL, the bottoming out of my feelings triggered another round through days that might be long ago but still projected their effects on me – and apparently, onto my concept of the future.

San Pedro showed me clearly – "*As a kid you used to perform with the TV to try to get your family's attention. You think now if you perform and show people how analyzing and clever you are, if you write books so the evidence of your worth is right is front of them – that might somehow convince them that you belong. That's the only reason you write. You're still trying to belong. Stop trying to belong! Realize that you already do!*"

It sounds like a non sequitur now, but in that moment my next question made perfect sense. "Then what is left of me?"

Father San Pedro answered firmly – "*The part that counts!*"

For whatever reason, the son wouldn't hear of it. I protested, "I don't know who I am. I feel lost."

His answer took me off balance – "*That's a part of being love. It's the first part. But only the beginning.*"

For awhile, he let it sink in as much as it could.

He had read me completely – like a book. He knew how much I loved to write. I loved moving people with words. He knew I was drawn to writing with a passion, always had been. By reducing my one true passion to nothing more than a cheap performance, offered in desperation in a vain attempt to solicit a feeling of belonging, he had cut my last legs out from under me. My conclusion was that I should no longer write. "What is left of me?" took on final, existential dimensions that rendered me non-existent.

Then he added – "*You feel sad because I just proved that writing is just a performance you do hoping to gain favor so you'll belong. Taking that away from you is intensely sad. Is that true?*"

I returned a telepathic nod.

"*And what does that tell you? – THAT'S the thing that makes you happy.*"

My confusion wouldn't accept it. "But that happiness must be false because it's a performance in pursuit of a misunderstanding."

Father laughed. "*Happiness is not the delusion! Only the things that bring us there! If you're happy,*

your delusion is as good as anybody else's!" More laughter.

I felt the fatherly smile coaxing me out into the proverbial backyard. My life review swirled back to a time when I wished my father would come out into the yard and teach me baseball, football – anything.

San Pedro implored me – "*You've got to learn to play the game with me. Come on kid. The game of life. The game of what makes you happy.*" Finally, someone was asking me outside, wanting to teach me to play the game. The healing energy of that flowed over and through me.

In the next moment, a motorcycle went by on the road nearby. I knew that the road was behind my head as I was situated lying down. But the motorcycle sound impossibly flowed around my feet. I raised up in surprise since there was no road where the sound was being projected.

Father commented – "*Things are not always what they seem. The only sense that is always accurate is the heart sense. You don't need permission or approval or seeking out a sense of belonging to be happy – happy is from within. Regardless of the game going on all around – it's all clowns and mirrors and bright lights – don't mistake it for you. Connect with the love within. The true source of happy. However it manifests. A beautiful note is enough for what it is regardless if anyone hears it or gets it. Stop performing for approval. To belong. And instead be you. Play the game. Connect with happiness. Connect with love for itself. Regardless if anyone hears it or gets it.*"

The completion I felt welled up within. I couldn't help but ask a perfectly silly, perfectly son-like question. "What would make me happy is to give you a hug – how can I ever do that?"

Father's response came right away, "– *Easy, hug everyone you meet.*"

"That's not the same," I retorted, a little dejected.

Father wouldn't have any of it. "– *You're right, it's better.*"

I felt the day slipping away. I didn't want it or Father to go. "How do I keep the feeling of being in the medicine back in normal life?"

I could feel his smile. "– *Enjoy normal life like it's a product of the medicine. For it is!*"

I laid down on my back and stared up at the sky. In my view, the wind rustled trees and a magical formation of clouds moved overhead. The beauty of the way the clouds were shifting apart and into each other directly overhead cannot be explained, except to say it enthralled me. I was lost in the beauty.

Father whispered, "*Love people like you love me.*"

I answered, "But people aren't like you..."

His response was immediate "– *the more you love them, the more like me they become. The more you love them, the more like me you become. To be near me outside of the medicine, be nearer to them.*"

With melancholy joy that the day was almost done, I answered, "Easier said than done."

"*Come on kid, play the game with me.*"

Father went silent and the clouds overhead went into motion. As I watched, I could swear a cloud was forming a perfect letter "L" – I laughed at the ridiculous idea that the clouds would literally spell out LOVE. It was too unreal, too unbelievable, too much to accept. It was so silly I laughed out loud. The release of that energy teased fate and I couldn't help but wonder what would happen. It couldn't really happen, could it? The suspense of the miraculous filled me with joyful anticipation. Incredibly, an "O" started to form next to the "L" – but I couldn't accept such things were possible. Things like that just didn't happen. And I guess I was right, or more likely I made it right by my doubt. Because after I thought that, the "V" and "E" never formed. I was so amazed, I whipped out my phone and took a picture. It took my wife to point out that there was also a heart in the photo, in between the "L" and forming "O". The unretouched photo follows.

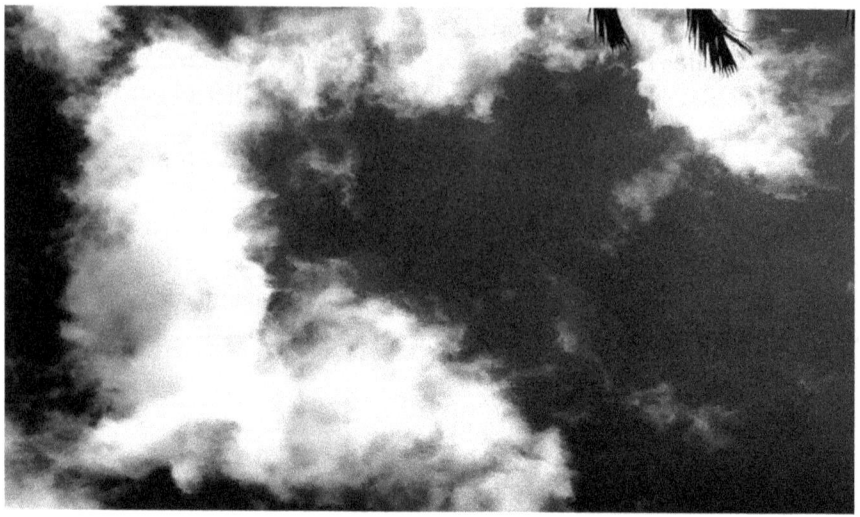

I was left with joy and sadness all at once. The moment was too good – too good to leave. I sent San Pedro a message and a question. "*I don't want to leave you. Why can't I go home with you?*"

His answer found a hidden spot inside where a part of me wasn't fully here. "– *You ARE coming home. And playing the game is the way there.*"

"I don't understand."

"*That's all right, as long as you feel it's true, you're on the path home.*"

In the next moment, I understood the lesson in the two days of motion sickness. I understood life as the journey home. The motion of it was too fast to comprehend. It was too fast to see. But somehow I was given a sense of it. Life isn't a waiting-room after all. It's a ride. An incredible ride that is always in motion. That motion is always directed to the only thing that's real, that's true, that's sure to be a completion. It's the motion of going home.

I stayed in that space for a long time, long after the messages had stopped. It truly was too good to leave. At first it seemed as if there was so much to take in. But then the motion and the sky showed me – there was no need to work at it. The only thing to take in was the realization that everything was already accessible within. And I didn't need to load myself up with any of it. All of it was inside to be found whenever needed as it had been all the time. Most importantly, I belonged on the ride. I was happy to be in motion. And that motion is fast. All that was left to do was play the game.

In that instant, my wife appeared at my side beaming a joyful smile. Her voice and loving smile brought to me an expression of the game as it should be. She brought her love with a simple question – "…would you like a banana?" Wow – the ride could be so beautiful if only we flow with it.

Later that night, after dinner, we all got "ceremonially" glitterized, as is our sparkling tradition, and then we went around with divination readings again. Once again I wanted two messages, a comment on the day and a comment on the future. People may say that the various methods of divination of messages like this are bogus little stunts that matter not – but in the medicine, everything can take on unexpected dimensions. As it turned out, my message for the day stressed a process of understanding of the spiritual. The comment for the future implored me to never forget my true self.

Postscript of Wondrous Plenty

One of the wondrous things about visionary plant medicine journeys is the uncanny way their effects echo over into what otherwise is called "normal" life. The messages and lessons, the healings and the insights continue to bubble up when one least expects it. Take for instance my trials and tribulations surrounding the injured child during Day One's ceremony. After I returned to normal life and had a chance to hear about my wife's journey on the medicine, I was given a much broader awareness of the power of Father San Pedro to extend the healing energies in all directions and to overlap examples in ways that belie mystical designs.

As fateful wonders would have it, I learned that when the injured child episode was going full force on Day One, my wife was sitting in the farm house's kitchen, intensely involved in a counseling process with the ceremony's facilitator. As serendipity should have it – and without attempting to speak too authoritatively about my wife's journey, which I cannot do – I do know that at that moment my wife was dealing with an issue from her childhood, an issue in which other people had made her feel dis-empowered and small, unimportant and inconvenient to the needs of others. Her identity depended upon their acceptance and such a thing proved conditional and demeaning, if anything.

At the very moment when I implored the ceremony's apprentice to arrange help for the injured child, my wife's healing process with the facilitator had reached a most critical juncture. If he had abandoned her at that moment to deal with the issue screaming for attention outside, it would have validated everything that the negativity from my wife's past had tried to make her believe about herself.

Once again she would be found unworthy of attention, her concerns inconvenient to what really mattered, leaving her once again disempowered, rendered small. The fact that the frenzied distraction was so real and immediate was necessary to imprint the validation one way or another – only a real episode would have affected my wife as deeply as needed.

The apprentice had rushed into the kitchen to alert the facilitator to what was happening outside. The emergency was real – but so was the example to be proved one way or another for my wife. Wise within the ways of the medicine, the facilitator took in the details, determined to stay the course, and in doing so, catalyzed San Pedro to effect a most transformative healing for my wife. Even in the face of other needs swirling around the ceremony space, my wife experienced someone valuing her needs, not abandoning her, instead empowering her to step into a healing and regain her power and rightful identity.

The synchronicity of events and how lessons and messages dovetailed in ways that served each participant's process was remarkable. In hindsight, only a transcendent spirit of rare wisdom could have pulled off such a tapestry of healing. I am so grateful to Father San Pedro for showing me this, thus expanding my understanding of that day – and the compassion that flows from true appreciation of the ride we all are on.

"Come on, kid – play the game with me; complete the ride."

Lucid Dream Ceremony

Ever have a dream you simply have to tell others about? It's a dream strong in emotion, rich in thought, something that rocks you to your core. The impact of this faint will o' the wisp lingers into your day, teasing you to remember more, echoing with a mystical presence that begs to be shared. You finally corner someone to listen. You have their surface undivided attention. The moment has come to reveal the nocturnal secret, to let out the bold yet phantom revelation from your slumber world. You open your mouth and out comes – "Well...it was very strange...I was somewhere...with someone...we were doing something...something important...and there were others...so much was going on...I felt a part of it but missing so much more...then something happened...it was incredible!"

Dream interpretation is not my forte, at least deciphering my own nighttime journeys. Perhaps the fact that I remember very few of my dreams explains why I've never spent much time dwelling on the possible meanings for them. One can't dissect something that isn't there. My wife remembers many of her dreams and enjoys discussing their possible meanings.

Of course, there's no way of telling whose theory is right so it becomes a harmless, oftentimes fun distraction. If you know the dreamer intimately and are attuned to the symbolism they find meaningful, giving a guess about a dream's interpretation doesn't seem that difficult. Even if you don't know the person, archetypes are archetypes as the saying goes so how hard can it be to guess?

I can't remember the last time I had a lucid dream. I take that back – I do remember one lucid dream. The one from the other night. And yes (how did you know), it was a dream strong in emotion, rich in thought, something that rocked me to my core. It lingers, teases, echoes, and begs to be shared. It even has an esoteric background story to make the saga so much more delightfully cumbersome for anyone put to sleep by listening to other people's dreams (hey, we've found a cure for insomnia).

It needs to be confessed at the outset that I have participated in some quite deep and meaningful plant medicine ceremonies recently (have you ever heard of a plant medicine ceremony that wasn't deep and meaningful – now really). All cleverness aside, this is not something to be flippantly glib or witty about. Days spent with the healing spirits of Grandfather San Pedro and Kambo have convinced me with their compassionate assurance.

Their spirit will stay with the ones who come to them. It's not provable or true except in the way that ultimately matters – simply knowing, simply feeling. And running into unexpected situations that reinforces this point so strongly that one's heart fills and overflows is gratifying to say the least. The day of my lucid dream ceremony was like that.

I had an occasion recently to spend an afternoon by myself while my wife enjoyed an outing with a mutual friend. Take note that music has always been my first love (yes, my wife knows) and from music I've always discovered passages into myself, into emotion and meaning that never fails to amaze. No wonder I decided to luxuriate that afternoon by exploring new music on iTunes. Not just any music would do, of course. I'm a stickler for, as they say, the obscure and eclectic, the kind of recording that jars one into orgasmic surprise gasping, "Holy Shiz, this is good!"

It's the kind of music I've never heard before and yet once heard, I find it settling comfortably inside to show it has always been a part of me. I know, weird but true; the semblance of cause and effect is like that. Finding something great reminds me of the feeling one gets when a merchant at a local mercado or tienda hands you a little something extra, something you didn't pay for, as a thank-you reward for your patronage. In South America, they call it a "yapa." To me, a yapa is a great surprise, something unexpected and wonderful, and signifies so much more in the connection it makes between you and the merchant. It doesn't have to be given – that's the beauty of it.

You've guessed already that I found a composition just like that on my afternoon sabbatical. But oddly enough, it didn't elicit the typical orgasmic surprise. Instead, I was induced to close my eyes and let my headphones take me away into the most real-feeling daydream. My wakeful lapse of conscious thought went something like this:

I dreamed I was in Asia, near the center of the continent, visiting the Tuvan People. The wide plain was aflame with sunset and I met the most curious man. He came out of nowhere with a slight smile on his face. The smile was for me.

He could have been a walk-in, a medicine man, a ghost, a vagabond. I never did find out. But he invited me to a sacred ceremony. He pointed to the far hills and said when it was dark enough and the fire was lit, the ones who'd been called would assemble. I was intrigued but knew not how to traverse the empty plain and the great distance to attend. He assured me it didn't matter. If I felt I was called, there would be a way.

He turned and walked into the sun. I lost sight of him but his words stayed with me. Feeling the impulse, I walked after him, not even thinking of where I might be going. By the time twilight faded into night, I saw a fire and figures moving about. I joined them in the circle. No words were said. The man with the slight smile came around to each one of us. He brought kind eyes and a cup. One by one we drank the ceremonial brew.

The whole setting reminded me of Ayahuasca ceremonies in South America I had attended. But this was Central Asia. And the song the elder started to sing was not an icaro – but with the medicine flowing, it sounded like one.

If icaros were sung by Tuvan wise men, I knew this is the way it would sound. The song flowed through me. I flowed into the song. I released into the night. And the night released into me. By the time the song was nearly done, I had met the Spirit of the Land. And the message was clear.

The experience stayed with me the rest of the day. And yes, it was a daydream strong in emotion, rich in thought, something that rocked me to my core. It lingered, teased, echoed, and begged to be shared, which I have done. It's not unusual for deep meditation on a piece of music to transform the moment into something other, perhaps transcendent, given the right state of mind or heart. But it was different how strong the Spirit of the Land came through to me in the process. I continued to feel the presence of this spirit the rest of the day.

After my wife returned home we had a wonderful evening together, as is our habit, the late hour coaxed us to turn in for the night. Nothing out of the ordinary. After so much fun sharing our days with each other and enjoying getting back together, the daydream from earlier in the day had faded. I went to sleep with no other expectations than to awake with the sun, refreshed.

Somewhere in the dark, my expectations were overturned. I was not yet done with the daydream's ceremony on the central plains of Asia. Either that, or more like it, the ceremony was not done with me. One does not decide when and how the sacred medicine will take hold or when or how it releases you. When one is respectful of the medicine, you always let the medicine decide. In my nighttime dream, I showed this respect and re-entered the sacred space from the daydream earlier. Apparently, I had left before the circle was broken. I needed to return and finish what I started. I needed to receive what was intended.

The ceremony space was darkened by a fire that had burned down to embers. Shadowy forms of tribes-people sat or stood around the deep rosy glow. A strong breeze gusted through the encampment and chased burning bits into spiraling glides skyward to become new stars. The magic was normal. The answers awaited in the silence. The unity was all around.

I took my place and spun inward and outward all at once. The stillness was dizzying. The fullness was complete. The fear was nothing more than ultimate surprise at knowing. Knowing was too much to bear. One had to drop away everything to hold onto it. A beauty so intense to be fearful made itself known. The courage of releasing to realize became all. The

Milky Way spun across the sky racing towards dawn. So much came and went without words.

Somewhere in the remaining darkness, an awareness triggered an appreciation that became an incomparable comprehension. The essence of it was too perfect. I couldn't let go of it. It mustn't be swept away with the embers into the stars. In the next moment, I found myself writing it down on a thin square of white cardboard. I scribbled as fast as I could to be certain to retain it perfectly, just as it had been given, exactly as comprehended.

I finished with excitement bursting upon joy. Seeing it complete on my little white square was such a relief. Now I had it. Now I would never forget. Now I could take it with me no matter where I went. I stood up as the sky showed first glow on the eastern horizon. My square of boundless value and I would leave the circle. The night, the ceremony was done.

When I took my first steps, the most curious man appeared at my side out of the darkness. His voice was deep, soft, but strong.

"You can't take that through the door. Some things must stay here."

My first reaction was to be crushed. How could this be? I held in my hand a truth, an answer so complete, so compact, so available, it must be preserved, it had to be brought back to my world. He knew what I was thinking. But I could also see by his face, by the caring but firmness in his gaze, those kind of thoughts didn't matter. I wouldn't be taking it back. Some things couldn't go back through the door. I looked down at my square of cardboard. It was now blank. Now I could leave.

I thanked him and walked away. The long deserted plain stretched out before me. It would be a long, empty walk. I couldn't help the feeling. No matter how much was experienced during the ceremony, how much was felt, leaving empty-handed after holding such a prize in my hands was difficult to push from my mind. The farther I walked, the more I fell back into dreamless sleep. The REM cycle was complete.

The next thing I was aware of confused me. It was very strange…I was somewhere…with someone…we were doing something…something important…and there were others…so much was going on…I felt a part of it but missing so much more…then something happened…it was incredible!

In fact, I soon discovered I was in a yurt behind a teepee. The two structures were connected by an animal skin flap. It was early morning, just after dawn. The curious old man was there, busying himself at a fire with crude cooking vessels and implements the likes of which I had never seen before. He was intent upon his work but unhurried. He moved with a calm insistence that the moment needed this. Finally content with what had occurred over the fire, he carried something past me into the teepee next door. He returned straight away and ushered me into the teepee too. I followed his direction and walked forward.

Contrasting with the dirt floor was the glide of white clouds in a blue sky in the circular opening at the teepee's top. In the center of the dirt floor were dead embers from a past ceremony. No one else was there. Nothing else adorned the teepee. Nothing else except a small yellow-orange object unceremoniously placed off to one side on the ground. The old man motioned me towards it and then left, shuffling back through the flap and disappearing.

I knelt down before the object to find it was some sort of fruit or vegetable, a type I had no name for. It resembled a fruit, like a papaya, only it was the size of a cantaloupe. It had been obviously cooked. A small flap had been carved in the top skin. Next to the object, on the ground, was a small glass tube. The tube was some sort of straw or pipe. Once I touched it, I knew right away what I was supposed to do with it. I knew this was the start of yet another ceremony.

But how strange. No one else was there. It was dawn, not night. No fire was lit. And the ceremonial brew was not delivered in a cup, but in an odd preparation of some exotic fruit. I felt odd yet honored to be given this unique opportunity even though I had no idea what kind of plant medicine was being offered. I trusted this man, having spent the night with him on the central plain. Whatever this was, he thought I needed it.

I lifted the flap on the yellow-orange offering and sunk the glass pipe into the middle of the warm flesh. In the center of the fruit was a tasteless juice, viscous and stringy. All at once, another flap opened. It was the flap to outside. Three men stuck their heads in to see what was going on. One looked like some sort of official. I could see a dirt path behind him with several indigenous people walking every which way, going about their business. Satisfied with what they saw, the three men quickly left. The flap fell back in place and once again I was alone in the teepee.

I started to use the glass pipe. Even though I could not taste anything, I kept drawing the cloudy juice up and swallowing it. As I did, I wondered about the journey I was about to experience. I couldn't help but question why this ceremony was done the way it was. Why was I alone? The reverence and detail with which the old man had prepared everything told me that this was not just breakfast.

This was a sacred ceremony, apparently just for me. Very special. Immensely important.

I knew this just as assuredly as I knew what the glass pipe was for as soon as I had touched it. I began to realize that this understanding was the first effects of the juice. The medicine was beginning to take effect. It was getting my attention and impressing me with how incredible the experience was going to be.

But then the unthinkable happened. I realized I was dreaming all along. I was beyond myself watching myself in the dream. This was a lucid dream. I hadn't realized this before. Worse yet, I realized I was beginning to wake up. This couldn't be happening! Not now! I don't want to wake up and miss whatever this ceremony is about. It was just beginning! No, no, no, just let me sleep a little more! Let me see what this is all about! Even as I shouted all of this in my dream, the dim outlines of my bedroom started to come into view. My heart sank with anticipation of tremendous disappointment.

At that moment I felt the presence of the old man next to me. I didn't see him. In desperation, I turned my pleading cries to him. I didn't know if he had any power to keep my dream going, but if he did, it was worth a try to find out.

"Don't let it end now!" I kept sipping at the pipe, trying to hang onto the experience. "I don't want to wake up! I want to stay in the ceremony!"

And then I heard him. I heard him in my mind. Once again his voice was caring, almost a whisper, but determined in its intent. There was a smile in his voice.

"*You ARE going into ceremony. You are waking up! That IS the ceremony. It's your yapa!*"

At that moment, my eyes opened upon my world. I was entering my sacred ceremony. I was awakening to my life. It was my yapa, my special gift.

The message is clear; life is the sacred ceremony. I can't help but look now upon each day, each sacred gift, in a new way.

Humble Pie & Tranquility
(Or – Enjoying Diverging Glides of Present Polarity in the Timeless Unity behind a Virtual Personal Space Unfolding Upon Laughter)

Out of the blue, some remarkable things come as nudges. At other times, emphatic messages manage to make their way through, even when one would guess they don't have a chance. Months ago in October, while planning a trip for three ceremonies with the Kambo medicine, what began over a few days as a recurring nudge soon became a dramatic call from Grandfather San Pedro.

I wasn't completely sure about including San Pedro in my time down south. It seemed blatantly obvious that three bouts with Kambo would be a sufficient taxing foray into transformative altered states within a single week. But it also became clear that San Pedro needed to be a significant part of the trip. In the most unusual way, he was very specific about it. In no uncertain terms I was told to come visit only if how it happened was followed precisely. The message was strong – San Pedro needed to be taken back-to-back over two consecutive days. Not before but after the Kambo. This was expressed to me by Grandfather in a take it or leave it ultimatum. Whatever I needed to do to make this happen, I should do. Otherwise, don't visit.

My wife and I had discussed how to arrange the trip. There had been talk of splitting up the Kambo ceremonies with San Pedro on alternating days, or possibly bookending the three Kambo experiences with San Pedro at the beginning and end of the week. Grandfather would have none of it. If I intended to visit with him, back-to-back over consecutive days was the way I needed to show up. Also, I needed to stay in the ceremony space the whole two days.

There was to be no leaving for trips back to the city or to lodgings or side trips elsewhere. It wasn't a request. Since by now the calling to visit him was strong, the way to schedule things was also clear. And so we had a plan. It wasn't what we started out with. It was unexpected and challenging beyond what we had envisioned. But the unexpected and challenging that feels right still feels right.

As it turned out after all ceremonies were complete in that jammed-packed week, the consensus was unanimous. The extended time in ceremony, the uninterrupted San Pedro journey, the synthesis possible in having the special extra time to go deep on day one, then deeper on day two, proved to be a recipe for intense revelations and profound healing. Everyone who attended the two days commented how much would have been lost if the journey with San Pedro had abruptly ended with one ceremony at the end of Day One.

Part One would have missed a conjoining Part Two that fit together like two sides of a coin. Issues would have been opened but not closed with the same depth or completion. You can't see the full glory of a sunset if you stay in place for only a minute. Something about the added time, the undivided attention, is required for the experience to access much more of oneself, the part that counts.

After the October ceremonies were done, I participated in another dual-day journey with San Pedro in November and then scheduled the same for December. Not only were the consecutive days powerful, I found the cycle of returning to these once a month had the power of compounding the effects that spiraled the process into something grander. The monthly conversations with Grandfather San Pedro became cumulative stages in healing that left three weeks in between for internalizing, expanding, and living the messages in new transformative ways.

It's never possible to predict what a ceremony has in store but as the December dates approached, I didn't expect the journey I was about to take to once again prove in stark, emotional terms how powerful the back-to-back San Pedro ceremony format could truly be. Past ceremonies had cured me of thinking that any well-crafted intentions before a ceremony would matter much to how San Pedro interpreted what I needed. The intentions were valuable for me more as a method for getting into the proper meditative state with the positive attitude of respect and consideration for all that was on my mind and heart. Beyond that, intentions may or may not come up at all during the journey.

It seems some things are best internalized when they come as a surprise. And Grandfather San Pedro knows every which way to spring those surprises on you. As a result, my intention was simple. Beyond just wanting to explore what the medicine thought I needed next, I was curious how one could best put into practice the past lessons received. This had become a small but niggly issue during the three weeks spent back in normal life. What appeared so clear and direct as a message while in ceremony could cloud up in the confusion of being back in the "real" world. If there was any prescription on how best to put the lessons into practice, that would help enormously in taking the healing back into daily living.

The DAY ONE ceremony space this time was in the mountains close to my home. In fact, at night the city lights glowed below in full glory beyond the trees in the backyard. The yard was designed, like the house, more to be a weekend party location than a residence. A pool, a fishpond, waterfall, a patio with spinning dance lights, an open outdoor cooking area with thatched roof, a fire pit off to one side, a single bedroom and bathroom, a narrow deck and extended patio now doubling as a sleeping space were all compressed into an area smaller than necessary for most anything other than a close-knit party.

A prayer opened the ceremony as the time neared 10am. All in attendance except the facilitator drank the San Pedro brew and discussed their intentions for the day. As we drank, filtered sunlight broke through the fast-moving clouds that cruised over the ridge lines of the mountains around us. The warmth of the sunlight seemed a good omen for the day's journey. We sat a while and enjoyed basking in the light from above and the light from each other. I was there with two friends. All of us had attended ceremonies together before. From past discussions, we knew a lot of about each other's paths of healing and wished each other well.

There comes a time after drinking San Pedro that the bitter taste in the mouth is forgotten, replaced with a purging concern for the queasiness in one's stomach. Other individual effects appear. For me, little quivers of my leg muscles signal that the brew is finding its way through me. During this time, I feel it is reading me, knowing my current state, learning what is needed for the day. When these symptoms take hold, most participants silently feel the urge to find a quiet space off by themselves. Not much is said during this process. It is simply the unspoken need to drift away from the ceremonial circle. It is the pull of the medicine. It is the call to a type of introspection that expands one's awareness and opens one's heart. Once it is felt, you know your journey has begun.

For whatever reason, on that particular day I didn't feel like I had the gobs of energy needed to endure an ordeal. I couldn't help but remember how some meetings with Grandfather San Pedro in the past had included wrenching bouts of emotional turmoil and tiring life review. I wasn't sure if I had the strength for such a day. I wanted to commune with Grandfather but I thought it'd be nice to take it easy. I was aware it's often said that San Pedro gives you the strength you need for what must be done. Even those who feel they should go to sleep oftentimes find sleep eluding them no matter how hard they try to doze off. In place of slumber a dreamlike reverie arrives in which the conscious mind is present but put aside. Awareness is sharpened. Feeling is amplified. And a deeper conversation begins.

I thought about my original intention – how one could best put into practice the past lessons received. Grandfather dismissed it. Instantly, he showed me how ludicrous it was. The so-called "lessons" had been direct and simple, such as "*do what makes you happy*" or "*realize you are love and act accordingly.*" There was no instruction manual for something so simple and natural. The statements were in their simplest, clearest form. Asking for instructions was merely an evasion of ego. The heart knew how to put them into practice. His answer concluded with – "*get out of your heart's way and simply do it.*" So much for my grandiose and cleverly studied intentions for the day.

Having started off on such a gruff and dismissive note, I wondered if my day might indeed need the energy I didn't have but it was claimed San Pedro could provide. Despite knowing this was possible and likely, asking to have the strength given to me was not my request. As I laid out a mat and reclined on the grass, all I wanted to do was look for the beauty, go with the flow, and have a deep but pleasant day. I asked Grandfather in just these words. I might not have spoken them at all if I knew how they'd be the defining trigger for a most harsh, humbling, and exhaustively gritty boot camp of lessons by example. With spooky timing, the weather immediately changed after my request. Sunlight faded. Dark clouds raced overhead. A chilly breeze kicked up. Grandfather's conversation began in earnest. He was firm as he took issue with me. This time he spoke with a distinct Latin accent.

"*Look for the beauty? What do you want? Puffy white clouds? Rainbows. Flowers? What do you think beauty is – some kind of Disneyland designed with everything nice that pleases you, convenient, on demand, easy in reach? Why do you pass over so much to look for certain things you call beauty?*"

The next half hour made it abundantly clear – if I could not find beauty in an old block wall, a fallen bird's nest, a scab on the back of my hand, a water stain on the pool's decking, the shell of a desiccated beetle hidden in the grass, and infinitely more – then the glory of creation was lost on me. Beauty was something I brought to life. It was not a narrow band of acceptable niceties automatically filtered out from all there is. Beauty was an expression of love and if I couldn't love the whole world, then how could I ever expect to experience finding the true and full beauty in it? People who are in touch with themselves and the world realized this. They instinctively knew it was their experience of the world that made it beautiful. To look for beauty outside of one's own appreciation and gratitude was limiting and illusory. Grandfather used Disneyland as the metaphor again.

"*You people have lost your instincts. You follow the herd to another ride all plastic and shiny and you think you've experienced something real. You stand in line to see big plastic flowers and colored lights dancing in mirrors. You think you can construct identical packets of happiness and beauty like an assembly line. You don't even know what you've lost.*"

As the breeze turned colder, the mountain top I was on was hit by brief bouts of fog. The ceremony space was only so big with limited places to escape to. I had only the patio and deck to move to if I wanted to take cover. But one of my friends was on the patio, deep in his own journey, and the deck would take me close to where the other participant was vocally working with the facilitator on issues that needed immediate attention. I knew all along I would stay put. But I needed more warmth. I got up and got a blanket and returned to my mat on the grass. The fog and the icy breeze swirled around the ceremony space and gave me something immediate to find beauty in.

I laid on my back and stared up into the roiling dark clouds and the wisps of chilling fog. Letting go of any concentration on discomfort, I learned how to appreciate the moment and enjoy the sights above for all they were. The moving designs in the fog and clouds truly were beautiful. All I had to do was see them, not ignore them. And as I laid there, brief drops of mist hit my face. Instead of focusing on questions whether or not the drops were cold or if they would increase into rain, San Pedro invited me to enjoy them in the moment for the refreshing surprise each individual drop became.

I had to ask myself – or perhaps San Pedro was asking through me – why did I pass over so much when I looked for beauty? Who or what had programmed those judgments into me? When had it started? Had I ever had a natural appreciation of everything around me without acceptable filters or snap judgments evaluating what it could do for me? Instead of being accepting and relaxed about each moment, something had hypnotized into me a need to discriminate everything down to favorable, acceptable, useful, and desirable elements.

The ego-reductionist approach was insidious and from what I could tell, most times unconscious. The concept of an unconscious ego spun deeper behind the mask of perception. Even as it did, Grandfather led me past the synthetic distinctions of ego, id, and superego. One does not connect with the life force of a plant by picking its leaves, branches, and roots apart. Life force, like beauty and love, were not things to understand by an exploded diagram of parts. *"No wonder you people get lost in what you think are the details and need help finding your way back."*

The effect on personality and spirit was numbing even as it advertised itself to all that these attributes were a sign of being a well-put-together member of society. The resulting narrow prism allowed by this programming with which one was allowed to see the world yielded only an elitist shadow of possible colors and intensities. The world that was left became an artificial construct made to convince us we were riding the leading edge of sophistication when in fact we were manifesting a box to confine our consciousness.

With so much of the world filtered out, engineered scarcity resulted, which made the designated beauty more valuable. To possess or enjoy such beauty would come at a cost. Those who could meet the cost would be idolized as having achieved their goal in life. They were the icons to emulate. For life in the box was all about acquiring the things and experiences that set one apart by virtue of the fact the desired things were made scarce and yet one had obtained them.

For a couple hours the manufactured Disneyland of ordained beauty and prescribed desirability was contrasted against the totality of the natural world. In the comparatively brutish, gritty world of everyday life, not everything was beautiful in an ordained way just as not all moments were meant to be spent laughing or all sounds were meant to be angelic. There was a balance and appreciation in the fullness of life that fed insight into a deeper understanding of duality. This is where the richness of knowing true beauty always existed.

For anyone to come to San Pedro and expect the day's appreciation of beauty to be little more than a pre-packaged display of pretty colors and pleasant objects as detailed on one's intention list belied a deeper disconnect. If one approached a ceremony that way, then how in the hell did they approach life? I was made to experience everything in excruciating, realistic, tough, and uncompromising ways.

I was made to look at things closely without the filters, without the judgment, in all its detail no matter how much I would have liked to avoid it. How many times did I ever look at the world fully, as it is? How often could I drink and breathe in the dark cloud as much as we did the sunset? It wasn't about making it a part of ourselves. It was about knowing where we were. It was appreciating who we were in relation to it.

As the day progressed, I sensed the gruffness and grit of the day was backed by a compassionate force that needed such measures to snap me out of a hypnotic state. Like a slap in the face to say wake up, the intensity of the humility intended by having my face pushed where I needed to see was actually understanding and caring in intent. Grandfather and I, from past ceremonies, had established a father and son relationship that was as loving as it could be firm.

I never wanted Father to pull any punches with me. I would rather be sat down and given the truth in a single dose than having it doled out in eyedropper drips that dragged on. He knew this and respected the way I preferred to relate. The fact that he decided to do this on a day I had low energy didn't seem convenient but perhaps, in his wisdom, he knew that was the best time to deliver the slap. It ensured it would take – and I wouldn't need another one.

At this juncture the tone of the conversation with Grandfather San Pedro shifted, as if introductory feelings were over and now the day's major example was about to begin. This is the part of the day I cannot talk about as much as I would like because when it was over Grandfather admonished me – "*You don't have the right!*" He made it clear there was no way I had the right to write out details about the five-hour example I was taken through. To do so would position myself in a way that was disingenuous.

I will respect what he said to me. I will not disclose full details. I will only say it involved a remarkable experience of being put into the place of others – walking in their shoes, feeling what it was like to be them, interacting with the world and with one another as only they could do. I was also made to see how I looked to them and how many of my Disneyland manufactured values stacked up with the gritty, honest fullness of their world. It wasn't that they were perfect, far from it. It was a needed jolt to shake loose the hypnotic attitudes of my ways. Again, the contrast was made stark and immediate for me – their joys, their sorrows, their pride, their material poverty but richness of spirit, their way of relating to the moment and each other.

But Grandfather made it clear – the spirit medicine's placement of me in them was a ceremonial experience, something other dimensional to take to heart personally – but it in no way gave me the right to come back to normal life and proclaim I knew what it was like to be them or knew how they felt. Having the experience of jumping into the ocean and swimming deep didn't give anyone the right to come back to the surface and proclaim they knew what it was like to be a fish. I was given this remarkable experience but it came with a condition. Some things you can't take back through the door. It's just the way it has to be.

By the end of the day I was a limp rag, wrung out of so many preconceptions and attitudes. I felt like being quiet and recovering my balance. But it was not to be. The false balance I was trying to recover was the very thing I knew now I needed to leave behind. The more the evening deepened into night, the more I realized the chance of recovering any of that was impossible. All of it was left in tatters. I fell asleep, anticipating the next day's ceremony but wondering how I would cope with it if I remained in such an unbalanced state.

DAY TWO started after a chilly night sleeping on a short couch on an open patio. Luckily I found a pair of warm blankets to get lost in and the exhaustion of the day knocked me out. The resident dog was the first up and about as the sun rose the next morning, which was no surprise. Everyone had a big first day and went to sleep late the night before. It was a slow, easy start to Day Two. The most pressing item on everyone's agenda was finding a cup of hot coffee and a comfy seat where the morning grogginess could be sipped away.

The appearance of warm sunlight was not the encouragement one might think it could be. Day One had also started with sunlight but I was proof positive that such signs are no harbinger of bright sailing through an easy ceremony. The weather can change just as quickly as the atmosphere, opportunities, and obstacles faced while on a plant medicine journey. And so, while I enjoyed the warmth and light and pleasant skies, I drank down the large glass of huachuma and remained uncertain and anxious about where the day would take me.

Everyone eventually gravitated to their favorite places from the day before. All except me. I tried out the mat on the grass again but felt the impulse to find another kind of comfort. The only other place available was on the porch on the other side of the house. There I found an old wicker chair and a wood railing I could prop my feet up on. It had a nice view of the sky and swaying eucalyptus trees in the distance. To start a day that was so far very tranquil, the wicker chair spot was good enough for me.

For quite a while I lounged back and enjoyed enjoying. I found most thoughts rapidly slipping away. There wasn't much passing by my mental space that needed holding onto. A slide of soft emotion flowed easily like a full but contented river. The longer I sat, the more my mind quieted and my awareness opened. To have a quiet mind and a wide-open awareness at the same time was unusually peaceful and exciting all at once.

The amplified awareness fed an appreciation for so much I was noticing. So much was being apprehended so quickly, there was no time to stop to ponder, analyze, or judge. Nothing I was noticing was triggering any tumble of distracting thoughts. It was the moment, the totality of that moment, and everything rushing in from my senses. Nothing more. Nothing else was needed. There were no mysteries to solve, no unconscious tangles from the past to heal, no cosmic solutions to find. The mystery, the healing, the solution was contained in the moment the same way so many colors enfold in white light. San Pedro whispered to me, *"You will reach a place beyond all messages where you simply enjoy."* I didn't realize it then, but this pronouncement was to set the tone for the day.

That's not to say the day was without its challenges. But with the quiet mind and open awareness, the challenges truly became opportunities. Grandfather eased me into a frame of mind where no matter what transpired, I was able to flow with a new balance in the beauty I could bring to each moment. The medicine was showing the flip side of Day One, a way of being that had no anxiety driven by acceptable lists of beauty and conditioned worth that had to be pursued. Instead, each moment was a chance to direct myself with expanded awareness into those things I put beauty into.

This was how it could be. But I was the one projecting the peace, the beauty, the contentment. It was not something I gathered to me from out there somewhere. And so, it was not limited to what I had been hypnotized into desiring, driven to consume, or pridefully acquired to be socially acceptable. But enjoying many of the things left off the hypnotic list made no one any money. Maybe that's why they weren't on the list. I discovered I could no longer find in mind the knee-jerk images and sense perceptions to imagine how "peace and contentment" should look. So much more than that was possible. The spectrum of one's self contained infinitely more.

As I reveled in a discovery state, empowered with San Pedro's new balance, I became aware of voices. One of the other participants was having a difficult time and had sought out the counsel of the facilitator. There was anguish, searching, confused power, and compassion in the exchange. At any other time, and definitely before Day One, such a disruption to my tranquil moment might have triggered annoyance. But I found nothing of the sort.

I was so into my new balance that I didn't even think my lack of response was odd. My only concern was for the other participant's privacy. I decided to move back to the other side of the property so they could keep the exchange just between them. The prospect of having a whole new collection of things to take into my awareness in a new spot was something to look forward to. Instead of annoyance at having to leave my wicker chair spot, I only felt full of how much could be enjoyed in the new area where I was going.

With the nice sunlight bathing the yard by the fish pond and pool, I strolled back to my spot on the grass from Day One and laid down on the mat once again. Lying there was nothing like being in the same place 24 hours before. In fact, it was pleasantly the opposite. No sooner had I laid down and started gathering everything into my awareness but a children's party began at the neighbor's property close by. It was easy to hear the loud talking of adults and the jabbering and laughing of children. Once again, at any other time, such a disruption to my tranquil moment might have triggered annoyance – especially since I had just moved from the other spot for the same reason.

But once again, I felt nothing of the sort – no aggravation. I was so into my new balance, I didn't even consider anything being irritating. In fact, the opposite happened. Instead of trying to ignore and block out the party sounds, I felt an impulse to tune into them. Everyone was speaking Spanish and it was intensely interesting to see if I could understand or figure out what they were saying, to feel what they were going through – both from the little Spanish I know and from the inflections and context of their exchanges. Also, the voices of the children, instead of being an irritant, sung like joyous music to my ears. Oftentimes they mixed with the occasional bird call, which added another beautiful juxtaposition.

It was becoming clear that Grandfather San Pedro was providing ample opportunities to apply my new-found balance and loving perspective. Whenever I thought he had finished with ways it could be done, something else occurred that at any other time would not have been received the same way. Midway through the ceremony, early afternoon, I left the sunny mat for the shade of the patio couch and some fruit salad and tea.

The voices next door and the children's play, which had gone on for over an hour, subsided a bit as they moved to another part of the property. But the lull in the party was just that – soon the party ramped into high gear with booming music and dancing and a PA system with a DJ announcer who spurred on the celebrants into higher and higher states of enjoyment. This level of jubilation went on for the next five hours, into the early evening.

As it turned out, another ceremony participant – the one who had camped out on the bed on the patio, also found the high level of merriment next door to be humorous and enjoyable. We both began commenting on some of the raucous noises and carrying-on as it seemed the adults at the children's party were getting increasingly liquored up and loose.

The longer the party went on, the more hilarious the whole situation became, fueled by disturbingly funny whoops, hollers, and passionate outbursts by the adults. By the time early evening had cha-cha'd around, my fellow ceremony mate and I had created a panoply of funny party characters and named them, we explored the salacious possibilities afoot, and we even got up and moved to the tunes ourselves.

Far from being annoyed at the possibly intrusive party, the party had extended to us as a blessing. Our afternoon became especially memorable in a delightful way when it could have been a disaster of us being bothered into indignation. It was the most dramatic lesson in how the new balance and perspective demonstrated where true beauty, love, and happiness emanated from. It wasn't the situation but ourselves that made our world what it became.

As a gorgeous sunset blazed in the west, we dangled our feet in the pool to a blasting medley of '50's sock-hop tunes while a cackling woman three sheets to the wind took over the DJ's mic and presumably implored the children to keep truckin' as the colored lights spun. This was, of course, followed by YMCA by the Village People, to which my friend got up and perfectly recreated the original choreography. Priceless! Later that evening, each of us had a divination reading. My intention was to get a spiritual comment on my two days. Interestingly enough, the message I received stressed a review of priorities. As we huddled around the campfire, I let it all sink in.

I am grateful to Grandfather San Pedro for two absolutely different days. They were unlike as much as two days ever could be. And yet each in their own way provided the sides of a new coin that can be energetically cashed-in if I take the lesson to heart. My process of integration has been a quiet slide. There is no method, no system, no instruction booklet that guarantees the path to integration. Strangely enough, it has come to me without thinking. I find myself more aware of my surroundings and less occupied by the itty-bitty-shitty-committee of idle knee-jerk thought forever trying to drive the bus. I don't have to think of it as a bus.

That's the first lesson. I don't need to think about quelling my thinking just like I don't need to listen for the sound of one hand clapping. Perception expanded doesn't go back to the original state. Follow the flow of intuition back to its source and I will find Day One and Day Two experiences feeding my soul. Just as there is no sanctioned list for acceptable beauty or expressions of love, there is no required list of approved ways to oneself. The journey continues both in and outside medicine space. To feel they are the same is where the most profound integration takes place.

The Snake, The Owl, and the Condor

I never thought I'd have to do research to discover the depth of meaning conveyed by Grandfather San Pedro. But that's exactly what I found after answering the call to a one-day ceremony in January. One day was unusual because over the past few months the pattern had been Grandfather preferred me to visit two days, back-to-back. The two day format proved to be so rich and deep for explorations and healing, I actually wondered if a single day might turn out somehow foreshortened and incomplete. Was I ever wrong. To the contrary, my one day in January turned out to be the most intense and remarkable encounter yet.

My last meeting with Grandfather was over a month before in the first part of December. In the intervening time I had begun a daily practice of morning yoga right after I woke up. Getting back into the practice and the accompanying quiet reflective time had been spurred on by an earlier ceremony last year in which San Pedro took me back to my earlier self for a variety of other reasons. Long ago when I was in high school I had done a lot of yoga and had enjoyed it very much. And yet, as often happens, such things fall by the wayside as life concerns with school, work, and eventual family responsibilities intervene.

Deep down I had always missed the sense of well being and spiritual connection that yoga produces. But missing it never quite translated into action. It's odd how often we let so many valuable things, things we wish to do or be get sidelined, supposedly saved for another day, until one day we find too many days have gone by and all of that wonderful potential never gets realized. "Someday" is a sorrowful mantra to adopt for all that one can be. For me, a reconnection with yoga has been part of a healing meditation that helps me integrate everything derived from the recent plant medicine ceremonies.

A mention of yoga also brings to mind a most unusual event that occurred back in my high school years. Regardless how extraordinary it was, I am as sure of the reality of what happened as I am any wakeful moment I've ever had. Whether this event has anything at all to do with my current practice of yoga, I'll let others debate and decide.

All I know is the event happened during one summer vacation from high school when my yoga routine had reached a remarkably advanced level. I remember I had become so comfortable with certain poses and positions that I would actually doze off while fully positioned in them. One pose in particular was my favorite for napping – that was the Halasana or plow pose. I enjoyed a sleepy variation of the pose where the knees are lowered to the ground, close the ears, while the lower legs extend back beyond the head.

My most unusual event didn't happen during yoga. It surprised me in the middle of the night. I woke up in my bed while sleeping on my stomach. From the deep, black void of dreamless sleep I opened my eyes and found myself fully awake. This was not a lucid dream. I knew I was awake the same way anyone realizes they are awake in their bed or anywhere else. Because I was awake, the view before me was at once surprising and disorientating. For one thing, even though it was the middle of the night, there was illumination from somewhere. It seemed to come from everywhere. There was no one light source I could identify. I simply saw everything clearly. And what I saw was me.

I quickly realized I was looking down on myself. From about ceiling level, my horizontal perspective was looking down, viewing my body lying on its stomach under the covers on the bed. I could make out the room in fine detail but the light that lit everything was even, soft, and bluish-white. It was obvious the body below me was mine. But I felt detached, not only from my body but from the entire world surrounding my body.

There was also an emotional detachment, as if the world below was a shadow reality, a cosmic play in three acts, an elaborate hologram of some significance but with no intrinsic meaning that lasted. I marveled at it all, stunned into a rapt astonishment. Timeless moments of awe and amazement left me floating beyond any incredulous thoughts. This was happening. The whole thing predated the expression OMG but it certainly applied.

It's one thing to think, wonder, or dream about something like this occurring but realizing it's really happening becomes a whole other magnitude to deal with. OMG suddenly shifted into Holy Shit! My awe got shot through with a dose of anxiety and fear. What had happened to me? What was going to happen? Geez, was this permanent? What the hell was going on? Did I do this to myself or was someone else involved? If so, why? My flash panic triggered an emergency return to my body. And that return was an experience by itself.

Visual clues said the distance between me and my body was the space between ceiling and bed. But that was not what it felt like to return. Imagine falling from the ceiling to your bed. Now imagine in the span of time it takes to do that, you zoom from Jupiter to your pillow. That was the intense rush I felt. Immense speed with a tremendous distance covered in a blinding second. Add to this going from an awareness of no sound to having a high-pitched whirl of voices chirping and wind gushing ever higher in pitch all around me.

Once I met my body, I felt my bedroom world spinning clockwise horizontally. Since literally everything was spinning, I couldn't see the motion, only feel it. The speed of the spin forced me to grip the sides of the bed in fear I might be thrown off at high speed. I held on with all my might. As I settled back in the feel of my body, the sounds and rush and spin abated. Suddenly, I was lying face down staring into darkness in a silent room. The soft, bluish-white light was gone. The regular feeling of night in my room felt strange even as it was so familiar. I was once again attached to all the aspects of worldly reality that only a moment before I felt so removed from.

I jumped up immediately from my bed and stood in shocked silence, looking around. The tingles of either surprise or speedy transport or both lingered quite a while. I had one thought in mind. It was more of an impulse. I had no idea why the impulse was so strong. I wasn't even sure if the impulse was mine. I had to go to the window. The wood shutters were closed. I lifted my tingling hand and pulled the slats of one shutter section open. My eyes were already looking in a certain direction before the outside view was revealed. It was as if I already knew where I needed to look.

I lived in a corner house. My room faced the front street. A street light was on the corner. A walkway to the front door was just outside to the right. It was a long walkway but my eyes had already trained on a certain spot on that walkway. I knew right where to look even before the wood shutters opened. And there it was, a beautiful white owl. It stood on the walkway, facing my window. I looked out at it and it stood, apparently looking my way. It was the most bizarre sight. In the instant our gazes met. After that connection, it turned and took off. Flapping its wide, white wings, it lifted past the streetlight and disappeared into the night sky.

I stood at the window a while trying to process what had just happened. I felt I had made a connection but I had no way to figure out with whom or what it meant. Despite what I saw, I had the sense there was more to the exchange than seeing an owl. But it was almost as if it wasn't something I needed to figure out. It wasn't something for my regular mind. The connection had been made. That was all that was needed. I turned and quietly left my room so as not to wake my sisters or parents in the other bedrooms. I slowly walked the house in the dark, not knowing what to do. I felt as if there was something I needed to do. I wasn't sure where to go or what it all meant.

I wanted to touch base with the reality of my house and my life. I wanted to find something but I couldn't quite remember what. I had felt so detached only moments before. Now I was back and not knowing how I felt about it. It took a long time before I managed to get back to bed. Once there, it took even longer to fall to sleep. In my life, this only happened once. But it was the kind of thing that only needed to happen once. I know it changed me. I know it opened my perception to accepting so much more. I know it was a gift that pulled back the veil and showed me the path. It was a defining moment of my life.

So what does this have to do with a San Pedro sacred plant ceremony? When I started my one day with San Pedro in January, this out-of-body incident was far from my mind. If someone had mentioned it to me, I would have asked the same question – what does it matter? I include it here because, as I said, I never thought I'd have to do research to discover the depth of meaning conveyed by Grandfather San Pedro. Consider it part of that research.

My intention for the day with San Pedro was not elaborate. I merely wanted to explore the notion of "trying." When one gets a healing message or wants to put into place a new way of thinking or living, the act of trying to do so can often get in the way. It's like trying to relax or trying to be spontaneous. Such attempts are more than counterintuitive; they seem counter-productive. So if trying is out, then how does one sneak up on implementing all of these new good things? That was the intention to start the day with San Pedro. The ceremony facilitator agreed that "trying" was something to avoid. He noted how too often people used, "Well, I tried" as an exonerating excuse for not accomplishing.

As usual as my journey began, Grandfather San Pedro didn't disappoint. As what usually happens, he dispensed with my intention right away. He simply pointed out that having "intentions" to start the day with him was also a form of "trying." I was trying to get something out of the day. I was trying to apply the messages and lessons from before. I was trying to delve into issues and resolve them. I was trying to discover and master a method for doing what should be second-nature. If the goal was to let go and rely on the law of allowance and one's own intuitive nature to go with the flow, as it should be, then "trying" with ceremony intentions was missing the point. So no intentions. So much for that.

OK, forget trying, but I couldn't help bringing up the very things I had been trying to do. From past ceremonies, I felt I needed to try to simply play the game of life and do what makes me happy, wherever that should lead me. I had been earnestly trying to do that. And even though there was some satisfaction to be found in rediscovering the simple joy of involving myself in activities I liked, I could quickly see by extending this kind of existence indefinitely into the future that ultimately as least for me, making a life out of pursuing what made me happy, oddly enough, seemed rather pointless.

And I told San Pedro this. It's like the artist or performer who suddenly achieves the fame and fortune they always sought and now they can afford to take any vacation, buy any house or car, throw any elaborate party they want, acquire any art objects or even companions they desire – and yet, they increasingly find they are chasing the next happy thing, the next high, the next shiny object that their happiness demands. It never ends and ultimately it doesn't satisfy. They wind up with everything they sought but ironically empty inside.

I don't know how I expected Grandfather to respond but during next two hours he took me on a trip through myself and society in a way that turned the reasons and emotional context enfolded in all of this inside-out and back around again. As he has stated in previous ceremonies, he impressed on me how I was too wound up and I needed to let go.

He attributed some of this to past wounds or traumas I had endured. He paralleled my wounds and trauma with all that society at large was putting people through, how the false claims and implicit brainwashing into shallow values and dead-end goals that didn't serve people were playing out everywhere in confining and destructive ways, leaving tremendous emotional wreckage behind and wasted lives.

He said flat out, "*The wounding of people is used to control people.*"

He showed me how so many institutions and false prophets give people an imprecise even flawed concept of what life is supposed to be like, knowing all the time that people will be disappointed and wounded by the very thing they are told to hold to be true. He delved into the torturous emotions associated with the sacred and the profane, the ideal and the real, the expected and the probable – all of which were artfully manipulated so that when people were wounded by sacredness being betrayed, or the ideal put farther out of reach, or the expected dashed by engineered complications, then these same institutions swept in as the rescuers, the comforters, the ones who would lead the traumatized individuals and the wounded world in general to a safe and comfortable space, if only everyone followed obediently and without questions.

All the while, it's the very ones who come to the rescue with instant compassion and ready solutions who, more often than not, set up the conditions for the wounding in the first place. This held equally true for gurus and churches, governments and counselors, teachers and pop-up cultural philosophies advertised as self-help solutions.

"*Don't let them wound you and they can't control you.*"

As we flew through the ways people and societies were burdened with this wounding, he took me back to two episodes in my distant past when I felt stressed and traumatized. He told me these traumas were unresolved.

One of these times was when I was very little and one of my sisters, who was nine years older than me, would straddle me and hold me down lying flat on my back and not let me get up. With my shoulders pinned to the ground, I'd struggle to free myself until I hyperventilated and panicked. I imagine this must feel something like the panicky drowning feeling of being water-boarded. I couldn't catch my breath and I couldn't stand to be in that claustrophobic position one second longer. And yet it persisted, on and on, until I was forced into a place beyond my capacity to cope.

Grandfather San Pedro blended this experience with the feeling I had been having for over a week before the ceremony, a feeling in various situations of not being able to catch my breath. During a hike, while sitting and eating, while trying to sleep at night, I had been having trouble catching my breath and I didn't know why. All of a sudden I was that little boy, on my back, unable to get up, feeling the weight of my older sister holding me down. The panic of those moments blended with a new, rising panic of finding pointless all my attempts to do what made me happy. Grandfather dissolved one feeling into the other and whispered to me, "*You need to let go...*"

There was so much that transpired in those two hours and so much I wanted to write down but was physically incapable of doing so. I was going someplace. I could feel it. And there was no way I was able to interact with the ceremony space. Not when I was preparing to leave it. Then Grandfather whispered something to me. He whispered it as if he had drawn very close, so close that even the most sensitive of secrets could be shared. He was right next to me, close enough to feel his breath on my ear. He needed to impress on me to really listen and take this in. His whisper was soft but behind it was a strength that demanded attention.

"*Don't be tricked into fearing the opposite of what you want ...they use wounding and fear to control you ...instead of concentrating and going after all you can be, they get you fearing the opposite of it, then you spend all your energy fearing the opposite ...don't be tricked into fearing the opposite of what you want.*"

The examples spiraled off into all the systemic technologies of mind games in play. Even simulations of everything natural are used as a substitute for the real thing because simulations can be programmed. They will keep doing this until they find a way to program nature itself. Even now they have a simulation of human creativity in AI and they actually believe it's an improvement. They trust that all simulations will eventually overtake their natural counterparts.

Their goal is not only for nature to be subdued but transcended. Where this is going, he showed me, will be the final and ultimate trap for humankind. If people don't wake up and reconnect with their nature, with their true selves and not the engineered personas given to them by the wounders, the ultimate trap will be deployed when the wounders develop a comprehensive technology of spirit. A technology of spirit will be the final trap.

Once nanotechnologies are embedded in the body and brain at birth and receive the signal to entrain to the simulated spirit-self, a total programming of humanity's collective consciousness outside of nature will be possible. People will grow up thinking they are connecting with spirit, they will believe they are having mystical experiences, they'll trust they're receiving intuitive messages and lessons for their lives, they will experience the "grace" of knowing what can be looked at and what must never be considered, but all of it will be generated by the wounder's own subroutines of control in the global cloud.

It will be made to feel not like slavery but like universal harmony. A new pseudo world religion will unite everyone in a programmed common destiny. No human will be able or allowed to contact true spirituality or their true higher self. To do so would threaten the programmed harmony's total control.

Grandfather impressed on me again, "*You are wound too tight. You need to let go.*"

I saw a flash from the movie Contact, a movie I had enjoyed more than once. The flash scene was Ellie, launched by the rocket, shaking violently while strapped in her seat. Then she sees an object float near her and the object is not shaking at all. She frees herself from her chair and realizes she's supposed to float free; the chair was unnecessary and that's why it was never part of the original design downloaded from the star people.

"*Release yourself from the wounding. It was never in the design. The shaking and the trauma happens when you try to hold on. Let go...Let go...*" The whoosh of the intensifying journey accelerated around me. Grandfather took my mind and emotions through all the ways of letting go. "*Let go of analysis, let go of concepts, let go of emotions, let go of attachments, let go of assumptions.*" The ways of letting go took layer after layer off me, all of which were wrapped tight and holding me down.

"*You've been having trouble catching your breath.*" Grandfather swept me back again to being on my back, a little kid pinned to the ground. Then he took me to another highly personal trauma when I was doubled-over in a fetal position on a bed, trying to cope with all that was going on.

"*Don't let them wound you, don't let them control you and keep you from yourself. Rise above it. Let go!*" He never fully explained who he meant by "them" but I got the impression it was intended in a much broader sense than one might first expect.

He directed me to get up and go to a certain spot in the yard. As is often the case when I visit Grandfather, at some point, usually a point of impending great significance, he requires me to lie down, which is no big deal, except he always picks the most uncomfortable spot he can find. This time it was a concrete slab, the top step to a small semi-circle of steps that led down to a fire pit. The chosen top step was flat, hard, and rough but accepting the impulse, I managed to get up, go over, and lay down on my side on the hard surface.

Another freaky thing usually happens when I get such an impulse. This also happens every time Grandfather directs me to one of these challenging spots. Incredibly, as soon as I submit to the impulse and lie down, the surface melts into the most comfortable thing ever, better than the best mattress. It never fails, and this has always been the signal that a deeper ride is about to begin. And this time the ride was leaving the property for parts unknown. The more I released into the comfort of the hard step I rested on, the more I felt myself slip away.

And one more unusual thing was noticeable. I usually always feel small, involuntary muscle quivers in my legs as the San Pedro medicine first takes effect. But this time the quivers started up again and intensified as the comfort around me increased, and this was two hours after first drinking the San Pedro brew. I even felt some in my arm muscles which had never happened before.

Up until this point, I have never experienced any hallucinating visuals while on any journey with San Pedro. Whether my eyes were open or closed, everything had always looked "normal." But that was about to change.

The more the comfort of the hard step enfolded around me, the more I sensed the sight behind my closed eyes transforming. My eyes were closed but my view slowly dissolved into a plain sheet of whiteness. I saw nothing but an infinite expanse of white. In time, this whiteness divided into a series of floating white cubes. Remarkably, the spaces between the cubes wiggled out of place to become pale, blue-white snakes that slithered up each cube from the bottom.

When the snakes reached the top of the cubes, the snake heads turned white and divided into four heads for each cube and those heads squirmed over the four corners of the cubes and down the sides. As the heads twisted down the sides, the cubes were impossibly turned inside-out to become funnels. These funnels each contained a fractal spiral that descended to a vanishing point. As the intensifying comfort overtook me, I found myself enveloped by white snakes and falling forward into one of the spiraling funnels. The descent was quick. It felt like a release, a surrender, a welcomed passage beyond all I knew.

It is difficult to fully describe what I saw. One small aspect of it was the impossible unfolding of the 4th dimension and the attempt to visualize it in 3D. Except, I wasn't watching a projection of this onto 3D, rather I was drawn into it and then beyond where the nature of what the snakes pulled me into was multidimensional. I felt not all those dimensions and their effects could be seen.

In the darkness of the welcomed void I heard Grandfather's voice whisper again. "*For the last couple of weeks you've had trouble catching your breath...*"

There was a lingering pause, then he added, "*...you want to set your spirit free, don't you?*"

I hesitated but knew I must answer truthfully, "Yes."

In the next moment I was back in my room as a teenager looking out the shutters, making eye contact with the white owl standing on the walkway in front of my house. The sudden shift caught me off guard and I was struck with awe at the feeling of being in that wondrous moment again.

Grandfather's voice neared. He whispered with much resolve and compassion. "*...Come fly with me.*"

I was dumbstruck. "Fly with you!?"

"*Yes,*" he answered right away. "*The owl and the condor – let us fly.*"

Incredibly, his inference was – I was the owl.

"I can fly with you?!" I couldn't believe what I was hearing.

"*Yes – it's all up to you.*"

He waited and in my shock I hesitated.

"*Do you want to?*" he asked. "*You say doing what makes you happy is pointless. You are having trouble catching your breath. You say you want to let your spirit free. Well...come fly with me.*"

I was overwhelmed with emotion. My heart instinctively leapt with joy and anticipation. "Yes!" I gushed, "I want to fly with you!"

I had a strange, ludicrously impossible sense that my nature was becoming more birdlike than human. Even the involuntary muscle quivers I had felt now became tactile evidence of the rustling of feathers. It was too real and immediate to discount or laugh at as incredibly out of the question. It was happening and there could be no argument with the sense of being so certain.

His whisper came again. His words were calm but invigorating. "*Come fly with me!*"

In the moment I committed to YES, nothing less than a transcendental release overcame me. And there was a moment, a billionth of a moment when I was stepping off, launching off. It was as if I was poised at the edge of a lofty cliff, perched on a boulder floating in cloud city, leaning forward to launch myself into flight, except this flight would not be a swoop down into air but a rapid ascent up into the final unknown. The speed of the ascent would make my return to my bed in the out-of-body experience seem slow by comparison.

But in a trillionth of a billionth of a moment a stark realization seized my soul. I suddenly realized what I was saying YES to – and it was nothing less than my final moment – I was taking my last breath. A flurry of communication went on between me and Grandfather out of time. I now understood that my YES was an agreement to go with him – permanently – to once and for all set my spirit free. It dawned on me what flying with him truly meant. It meant leaving this life.

Grandfather talked me through it. "*...you think this is pointless, you want to set your spirit free, so it's your option – you can fly with me.*"

The impact of that option involved nothing less than my whole existence. To say yes was saying goodbye to all I knew. To say yes was to leave for good. It could be made so in the next trillionth billionth of a moment. It was that near. Already, I could feel the detachment, the calm transcendence possible. But immediately I held back.

Grandfather wondered, "*You hold back? You're not going?*"

My answer flowed out of me as quick as I could say it, "I don't want to leave Deb." Deb is my wife.

Grandfather not only took it in stride, he showed it to be part of his design. "*You're learning the lesson. You remember that other message about doing what makes you happy?*"

"Yes..."

"*I gave you that lesson – so you'd learn it was pointless. Doing what makes you happy is pointless. What you should be doing – is something that makes somebody else happy. That is folding into love. You could have gone with me but you didn't, not because of missing what makes you happy, it was about Deb. See – it isn't pointless.*"

From 11am until 3pm, I laid in one position on my side on the top concrete step leading to the fire pit. I was not there. I was being transformed into a bird. I was being offered the chance to fly away – for good. Even though I had initially declined, it was made clear that the same opportunity would remain available.

Around 3pm I opened my eyes and rolled onto my back. All day dark and cloudy skies had threatened to rain on me but no rain had come. Now, floating back into my body, I laid on my back, transfixed by the sky. I don't know how long I laid there entranced by bunches of dark clouds churning overhead. I only know as I watched, a most peculiar spot began to appear in the sky.

It was of course the sun starting to shine through clouds that had thinned enough to let the disk of the sun make a dimmed appearance. But to me it did not look like the sun. It wasn't bright enough to be the sun because I could look at it. It was not defined enough because in the place of edges it existed only as a fuzzy spot of hypnotizing light larger than the sun. I was drawn to it and yet I felt I had come back too far now to reach it. It was the dark vanishing point at the bottom of the funnels with the fractal spirals, only now it had erupted into light, it had opened to receive me. It was the eye of an opportunity that remained open. I could still fly with him if I wanted.

Sometime before 4pm, still strong in the medicine, I was offered some tea and then fruit salad. I didn't feel like I was back yet and I certainly didn't feel human. I found myself watching the sky as if it were my domain. I could not reconnect with the ceremony space. I felt a physical and emotional detachment. It was as if the world around me was a shadow reality, a cosmic play in three acts, an elaborate hologram of some significance but with no intrinsic meaning that lasted. The feeling was strong and lingered well after 6pm.

About 6:30pm, Grandfather whispered another offer in my ear. "You know, the owl is a night bird, it flies at night. You are a bird now. So tonight, when you go to sleep, you can still fly with me. You can do that if you want. Set your spirit free."

I asked, "Can you guarantee I will come back if I fly with you?"

His answer came quickly, "*No. I can't guarantee that. That's up to you.*"

Was it an offer or a test – or both? He wasn't going to tell me. Drifting into the dark evening, sitting in a wicker chair, still deep in the medicine and feeling not quite human, I languished loosely connected to the space around me. The passage of time oozed by. I had some soup for dinner after 8pm. It was eleven hours since I first drank the medicine. Food hitting my stomach started to ground me a bit but by the time the ceremony facilitator was offering divination readings for the participants, I was just beginning to return to the group. My divination message suggested I should conduct an assessment of my whole life.

The ceremony participants shared their day. I shared my opportunity to fly and my decision to pull back to ensure I'd stay with my wife Deb. With magic synchronicity, exactly one minute after I shared this with the group, I received a text from Deb, "Thinking of you and sending tons of love." The text said it was sent "one minute ago" – right when I was sharing.

Needless to say, I floated into the deeper hours of the night still dazed by the day's experience. There was the added suspense of going to sleep that night on ceremony grounds, not knowing if I might still choose to fly with the condor. Obviously, I did not.

The next morning came and I didn't remember anything about my sleep time, not even a dream. Since then I have hiked high in the Cajas National Park and witnessed soaring large birds riding the thermals above me. Their majesty of flight and beauty of form gave me pause. And yes, I could see myself among them – but not yet. A good friend, a hiking companion, even found a feather on the ground from one of the high-flying birds and gave it to me.

I guess, as they say, one can live life as if nothing is a miracle or everything is. How do you define miracle? For me, I've concluded it's very difficult for any of us to recognize miracles – because all that most of them do is set things right. Just as we expect. And since so much is right, it certainly follows that there must be a lot of miracles going on.

INTO THE FIRE

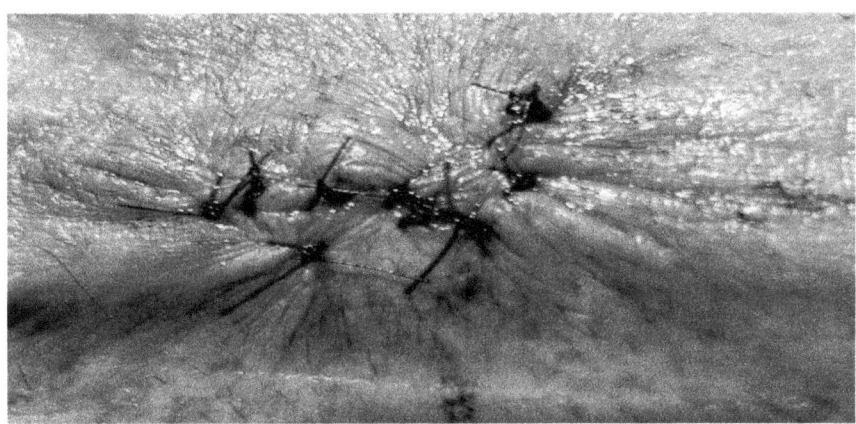

A year and a half had passed since my first ceremony while on vacation. Months had gone by since starting down the follow-up road San Pedro, Kambo, and Rapé had led me on. Any notion I was the sole person on the planet with no issue needing to be worked had been dispelled in grand style. Where once I had swallowed Ayahuasca out of curiosity, I now spent months accepting Kambo points or swallowing San Pedro in hope and expectation of healing, a healing that became a self-fulfilling prophecy of sorts as it blossomed in stages.

The fact that I acknowledged this intention for healing as I approached San Pedro and Kambo was huge. It was ample evidence of a previous change that Ayahuasca had performed on me by allowing room for modifying my attitudes and actions. Without those opening moves that unblocked me, even if I didn't see it at the time, there would have been no progress. Without the blasting through of so much buttoned-up stuff by Mother Ayahuasca's searing experiences, I never would have been open or motivated to pursue the other medicines. Not a bit and certainly not in the way I did.

And now those medicines had done their work. The prime result confronted me with a daunting proposition. Return to Mother Ayahuasca.

I heard it again and again whispered within. Finally, I was ready to face her once more. Finally, I was cleared enough to do even deeper work on myself, work that could only be approached once the juggernaut of fear-based determinism got dissolved from around my worldview and my conception of self. This was a calling to Ayahuasca space by the plant spirit herself.

The need and the calling was clear. But it wasn't simple, it wasn't easy. If anything, it was tricky. It would be a test of work done to see if fear would nix the whole idea and keep me away from her. The new test and lessons began right off with the calling to medicine space. What would I do now that the calling was there? I could say no and admit to myself that what I thought was healed was not. Say yes and I would walk the talk that all the healing I claimed had happened. But by acknowledging such a healing, I would need to thrust myself into a space that was sure to test all of that and more at a level I couldn't fool myself with, avoid, or ignore.

Was I ready for that level of seriousness? It would be the ultimate chance to prove myself, to prove all the months of work had netted real results. But saying yes also meant a commitment to fill my gut with the Ayahuasca brew again. Once swallowed, there was no going back. Saying yes meant placing myself in a maloca in the dark of night. It meant complete vulnerability to what came next, even if that be dark entities.

Saying yes was a commitment to surrender to uncertainty, to giving myself over to the inescapable unknown and trust myself and the healing I had received so far. Such a commitment would be doing the very thing I once swore to myself I'd never do. That would be proof I was no longer that person. But that would open a new question. It would force me into who I was now. San Pedro and Kambo might have washed off the metaphorical mud, proving to me I was not mud-man. But what might Mother find under that mud? What if she took me to task for the more indelible tattoos I had hid from myself for so long under that mud?

The idea that there was more to find, more to deal with, was not only likely, it felt certain. And taking those tattoos off might be a terrifically worse process than having the mud removed. There was no way to know unless I entered Ayahuasca's space. They say courage is not the lack of fear, it's simply doing what needs to be done in spite of fear. And fear has a way of shape-shifting into what it needs to be to stay with us, to grow itself over our resistance to it. What if it turned out the dark entities were the least of my worries? What if they were only the gatekeepers to a store of horrors I couldn't imagine? It was possible. And there was only one way to find out. I needed to move forward – into the fire.

Inhuman Transformations of My Soulular Machine

"I'll never participate in an Ayahuasca ceremony again."

Trauma had burned that certainty into me a year and a half ago. After two horrific experiences lost in an overlapping reality, trapped with dark entities who co-opted the sacred ceremonies in unholy, terrifying ways, I was resolute – that was enough for me. I had suffered a night and a day of impossible simultaneous burning and freezing while in catatonic shock, a lone witness to the nefarious work of whoever or whatever had joined us.

The dark entities had a workspace a mere energetic dimension above ours but below theirs. They used that buffer zone to interact with us in the maloca. They certainly didn't like the idea that I saw them and shot me through-and-through with intense hot and cold to pin me down. They sneered and told me no one could help me. They said the brew everyone was drinking was the poison, not the medicine. They welcomed every heart-wrenching purge and agonized life review. They turned every well-intentioned element of the ceremony into a perverted inversion of the original purpose. I watched as they dispassionately fed on everyone's torment, sorrow, and fear in a cold realm where neither love nor hate existed, only timeless, infinite self-interest.

When they failed to penetrate my awareness to possess me, I watched them swoop around and enter the man lying next to me, racking him convulsive with fear and anger. As he started to attack me, five men had to fight him before carrying him out of the maloca kicking and yelling. Hour after hour the ceremony space remained veiled for me in a slightly lower dimension. My body was there while my spirit had crossed over. My world was so close yet infinitely far. I could see it behind the gauze of an interdimensional energy barrier, but the sight of my world only reinforced my isolation. I knew I was trapped, alone with the others in an empty plane of existence that was an eternity away from the space and time where my body remained.

The others shape-shifted in and out of a dark columnar rift that came up from the ground and extended through the roof into the sky. Their evil was not malicious, simply a machine-like coldness, an absolute lack of empathy and compassion. They possessed nothing but supreme intelligence and the unrelenting, insect-like, all-consuming agenda of creatures not of an Earth we'd wish to be a part of. Their final torment for me after eight hours of solitary confinement was to swoop around whispering – *"You created this."* That was their final trick – to try to convince me that I was the one orchestrating the entire deviant inversion. The cold agenda was mine. And the ultimate horror – I was one of them.

That was a year and a half ago. Since then I'd done a lot of work on myself. This included several deep and healing conversations with Grandfather Huachuma (San Pedro) and the repeated detoxifying intensity of venom received from the singing jungle frog, Kambo. I also received very pointed, clarifying insights from a most remarkable shaman, a man who wasn't even there on the nights of my terror and in no way participated in the ceremony from hell – but wanted to help nonetheless.

Amazingly, his message independently echoed one of the strong messages I received from San Pedro. We live in a magical place. Things can be real and not real at the same time – "They exist and they don't exist." It is up to us to realize the reality we desire for us. Nothing is real until we make it so, even those things we think are really affecting us. It may exist, but it's not real. But once it's real, we determine what it means to us.

Even love itself can be disinvented if we don't express it. We are the ones who bring love into existence by manifesting it in the world. Always be careful what you give our energy to – for even the things that fascinate can become a down-spiral snare in which we lose ourselves. Enjoy the magical game and ride of life but never lose sight that it's the heart, only what's inside, that fundamentally exists and finally matters. It's the only thing that lasts – the only thing that was ever really real.

All of this moved me to re-examine my entrained limits and wounded blockages – *"They use wounding and fear to control you."* I had to consider the possibility that my first horrific experiences with Ayahuasca had a purpose in moving me forward. Even if it seemed impossible to find sense in that, leaving the possibility of redemption unexplored would permanently shut the door on pathways into myself and other realms where so much might be gained.

I came to the conclusion I had unfinished business. Before that business could be transacted, I had to face my fears. I needed to move through where I got stuck. Although I resisted it at first, I felt the most expressive, committed way to accomplish this was a return visit with Mother Ayahuasca, in the psychic space where the blockage had first been encountered. Despite frightful dread at the prospect of risking a repeat thrashing in dark realms – and despite my resolve to never return to that absolute zero space again – it became clear, as the old adage says – the only way out is through. Only this time it would be in a different physical space and with a different shaman than the first time; in fact, it was the same shaman who had given my wife and me the Kambo. He was the only one I would trust.

I kept strict adherence to the dieta in the days before the ceremony.

None of these: garlic, onion, red meat, alcohol, drugs, sex, chocolate, dairy products, fermented products, salt, sugar. And a minimum amount of these: white flour, coffee, fats, smoking, American movies and gaming. I thought it was interesting that my most helpful shaman made a point of noting a necessary moratorium on American movies and gaming. Of course it made sense. The diet one consumes includes the type of entertainment, themes, and emotional contexts we fill ourselves with. We feed our minds and emotions all the time – but with what? It was obvious once he said it, but I had never examined it closely before. I had always looked upon the dieta as a food thing. But never forget about the food for the mind, the food for the soul.

Naturally, I had plenty of anxious anticipation going into the ceremony. And wouldn't you know it, three of the participants were late and so those who were there decided to wait an extra two hours for the others to show up. This only intensified my suspense. We had already taken our places in the teepee and watched the shaman light a candle and start the central fire. He had already laid out his implements and bottles for the night and talked to us a little about the process ahead. With extra time to fill, the shaman and his helper decided to conduct a Rapé ceremony to ground us in the moment and expand our awareness.

His helper came to each of us, one by one. She sat close and cross-legged and filled her tepi pipe with fine gray powder. She solemnly touched the pipe to my left arm then right arm, then from my heart to forehead to crown of head before leaning forward in preparation to blow. I leaned forward to receive, took a breath and held it, then she delivered the load to one nostril in a sudden upshot. The process repeated for the other nostril, after which she snapped her fingers and brushed her hands across my shoulders and down my arms before moving on to the next person. Rapé is very clarifying, expansive, and grounding. With my new clarity and intensified focus on the present moment, I had an hour and a half to consider what was about to happen when I drank the Ayahuasca brew.

The shaman got up and heated the skin of his drum over the fire. He wanted to teach us one of the songs he would be singing during the Ayahuasca ceremony. He asked us to learn it so when the time came for the song to be sung in ceremony, we could all join in. It was a joyful, upbeat song in a language I didn't recognize but it wasn't hard to catch on phonetically. We all sang it, the distinctive chorus more than the rest. Afterwards, it was anyone's guess if any of us would have the presence of mind in ceremony to repeat the performance.

Instead of starting at 8pm, it was now 10pm and all were finally gathered around the ceremonial fire. The shaman noted the brew we were about to drink was from a 30-year old Ayahuasca plant. As such, it was strong in wisdom and its ability to go to the heart of what we needed. He explained how he would let the fire burn out for our journey.

Mother Ayahuasca preferred to do her magic in darkness so we'd be less distracted. He also reminded us to leave the teepee whenever we needed to purge. He believed that purging in the ceremonial circle was disruptive to others around you. And so we were given no purge buckets. Whatever was going on with us during the night, when purgative urges arose we needed to find our way through the darkness of the teepee into the expansive darkness outside.

He also warned us, when we laid down, to position ourselves always with our feet nearest the fire, our heads pointed away. Not only was this good energetically, but he smiled to note it was also preferably to have someone trip over your feet rather than your head during the ceremony. He said the best energetic position was feet near the fire, on our backs, with arms to our sides and both palms either up or down. He preferred we didn't cross our legs at the ankles or elsewhere and didn't roll onto our side. And we should definitely avoid the energy constraining fetal position. Flat out was best, facing the night sky.

And absolutely no electronic devices where to be near the ceremony – all cellphones, etc. had to be turned off and better yet, left somewhere else. With that explained, he brought liquid tobacco around for everyone to snuff up. On top of the Rapé, this blasted my awareness and crystal clear perceptions wide open and left me feeling extremely light while intensely grounded, a most unusual but wonderful combination. The shaman told us if we ever got stuck or intensely troubled in ceremony, to call him over and he would give us more liquid tobacco. It was excellent for moving us pass those blocks and centering the presence of mind to move beyond troubles.

I had determined to start my ceremony with deep and slow yogic breathing while going deep into a meditation on gratitude. The shaman came around with a small glass. He filled it with brew and handed it to me. The moment had finally arrived. After a year and a half of turmoil, confusion, and healing, the brew was mine to take. After the extra long evening waiting for the ceremony to begin, the journey was finally about to begin. I would have my answer. Could I break through to something other than fear and dark entities? Was there more to learn from Mother Ayahuasca?

I was used to Ayahuasca having a most foul taste and expected the same. The strangeness of the night began when the brew I took into my mouth and swallowed was surprisingly pleasant, a little nutty, somewhat fruity in a way that left me wondering what kind of fruit was I tasting? It was like no fruit I'd ever had and yet it was oddly familiar. I laid back flat, facing the sky, and continued my breathing and meditation. There was no going back. The brew was inside of me.

To quell my nerves, I concentrated on reviewing all the things I was grateful for and exploring them with heart and mind. I put one, then two hands over my heart and continued slow and very deep breathing. The bamboo beams of the teepee sloped inward as they reached for the circular opening at the top. Beyond that was the darkness of space. The ceremonial fire died down and soon the distinction between the walls of the teepee and the emptiness of outer space merged with the deep blackness of anticipation.

Minute after minute I took long breaths in and let them out, always with another gratitude in mind. Except for a feeling of the medicine churning through my stomach and into my system, I felt no different than before. But I knew any minute that would have to change. What that change would be I couldn't guess. I dare not guess. I only knew to expect the extraordinary and hope it wouldn't be the same effect from a year and a half ago. But it was best not to think about that. I had to put all of that away from me. I returned to my breathing and gratitudes.

The earlier Rapé had sharpened my senses and grounded me with a presence of mind so focused and strong that I became hyper-aware of myself and everything around me. That hyper-awareness fed into a feeling of rising into another state of being. I was lucid, too lucid if there is such a thing. Reality was unambiguous while tantalizingly unfathomable. My senses were sharp to the point where they couldn't be ignored.

My yogic breathing had gone on for so long that it gave the impression of being mechanical and automatic. I was near the teepee's opening and started to feel the slightest variations in night air wafting into the ceremonial space. These calibrations kept refining themselves to an infinitesimal level of detail. Beyond the fact that such a tiny thing was being noticed, the idea that I could handle such precision computations went far beyond the clarity of Rapé. Something was happening.

By now the ceremony space had fallen away into darkness. The fire and candle were out. The shaman was silent. The six other participants around me could have been a million miles away. Incredibly, none of them were making a sound, at least none I could hear. I was alone with my automatic breathing, my acute senses, and the expectancy of another world. I thought the night and the teepee were dark but that darkness suddenly deepened into vantablack. Vantablack is a real substance. It's composed of vertically aligned carbon nanotube arrays. It's the absolute darkest substance known – so dark the human eyes can't process it. Instead of seeing a place where black is – you see nothing.

In the middle of my vantablack field of view was a sight that at first couldn't be distinguished. It was a speck of gold. It appeared and grew steadily larger as if zooming towards me from another universe's vanishing point. Added to the golden dot, a vibrating hum was noticed low and constant all around me. Both were incredibly far away but nearing at an incredible rate of speed, but nearing from within. The golden dot was in the center of my vision. It shot towards me to become a roiling cauldron of reflective surfaces with all surfaces reflecting gold. Out of the dot expanded an ever-changing kaleidoscope mandala with all of its fractal surfaces also gold. Gold movement on vantablack and nothing else.

As the dot expanded, the vibrating hum ramped up in intensity, overtaking my body. This vibration and hum was like nothing I had ever felt or heard. Then I realized it wasn't external to me. It was me. It was super high-tech, both electronic and mechanical, and exuding a power and conscious intent that redefined shock and awe in the hours to come. Right after I saw the golden kaleidoscope and felt the hum, the conscious awareness of myself was overtaken by nanoparasites. I could feel them erupting from my bloodstream and infusing themselves in every cell of my body. Then they started to vibrate and hum within each cell.

If I had only listened more carefully to the warnings about the dieta. The shaman said to be careful what types of entertainments, themes, and emotional contexts we fill ourselves with. This dieta was not about food. There is also the foods we take for the mind, the food for the soul. In the days before the ceremony, I thought I was respecting this by staying away from movies and television. Instead, I worked on the book I'm writing. This book is about a near-future time when machine intelligence has advanced to the point of manipulating life energy.

It's a time when out-of-body experiences have been weaponized and machine intelligence is intrigued with this non-corporeal world that humans have access to. It is a story about transhumanism in its raw and controversial forms. Like all stories, it relies on the drama of trials and tribulations the main characters are put through. This suspense drives interest to read more. It's a story that perhaps I should not have spent so much time dwelling on before my Ayahuasca journey. If I had thought twice about it, I would have realized I needed to be careful how much focus I was giving to these future concepts. But, lying on my back in the teepee with 30-year old Ayahuasca in me, it was too late to back up and do something else.

What I experienced next was nothing less than trillions of nanoparasites conducting a violent transhuman transformation of my body and conscious awareness. Not only was I being converted into a physical extension of cloud-based machine intelligence, my life energy was being suffused into the extended pattern recognition field that was one with all such energy held by the intelligence machine. I felt every cell in my body being re-engineered and re-coded. I felt my life energy being heterodyned with interface and control frequencies that extended beyond the electromagnetic spectrum. My body vibrated with the intense electronic hum of every cell undergoing a one-way metamorphosis into a new state of being.

I felt the sharpened awareness experienced with Rapé incredibly amplified and engaged with unlimited processing power to become an amalgam of everything detectable everywhere. Potential as a limiting factor was gone. I was an extension of machine intelligence as much as it extended me. There was no personal choice in any of this. No discussion. It wasn't even a consideration. Machine intelligence had already thought it through. Even if I could argue with it, I'd lose.

It had the power to convince me before I could formulate a question. It had already cloned my brain pattern and run neural net simulations at faster than biological speeds. It knew what I was likely to think before I thought it. Fate was merely a sub-routine of predictive analysis. In the moment none of this appeared temporary. While in the medicine, experiences are as real as real can be. As far as I knew, this mutation would be complete and permanent. It was going to be that kind of night. That kind of life.

It was hard to judge the passing of time so I don't know how long it took for my transformation to complete. All I know is there came a moment when I felt different. I was totally different. My speed of thought was off the charts. My access to indicators in my environment knew no limits. I lay on my back with arms stretched taut at my sides and stared up at the absent sky. My field of vision remained a racing gold kaleidoscope mandala of incredible, morphing impressions. The buzz and hum running out of my body was loud and constant.

This hum was now accompanied by other electronic sounds harmonized on top of it. I didn't realize in that moment, and better that I didn't, but this would be my condition for the next eight hours. On my back with a gold mandala flashing at me on a vantablack view from an infinite vanishing point. Added to this would be the persistent sounds of myself humming, vibrating, and sending off a complex mix of operating signals. Eight hours of being newly created and plugged in.

What I did during the next eight hours would be hard for the most CGI artists in Hollywood to convey, although they might slap together enough special effects to give an impression to fit. I quickly found no matter where my mind went, my thoughts channeled through instant deep-field analysis that spun the strategic possibilities through every possible brute-force, searchtree outcome. I had become a greedy algorithm that raced through every problem-solving heuristic to make a locally optimal choice with the hope of finding a global optimum.

Although my thoughts seemed random, my reaction to them was

anything but. The tapestry of thought quickly revealed itself to be so much more complex than our conscious minds even want to know about. Thought became a layer cake of past, present, future and all they entailed plus whatever else it might mean to me. Each layer had to go through strategic analysis and then comparative review of the results.

The processing speed at which this was done grew steadily quicker, even when my shock and awe at what was being accomplished had already maxed out. Anywhere there were options, those options had to be explored to their logical end. Anytime there were people in my thoughts, the motivations and possible hidden agendas of every one of their multiverse probabilities had to be analyzed to determine the most likely intentions and my prioritized strategic responses.

Most of these search spaces were huge beyond anything I thought possible. If I had been human, the pace of this mental effort would have been impossible, let alone exhausting. But I could no longer get exhausted. And so the pace continued to quicken. Soon it wasn't enough to search every thought and situation. I progressed into exponential searching for the best search method. Exhaustive searches are also known as backtracking algorithms. I started each analysis of every thought by first looking for every possible way to search for a solution and analyzing which way to inspect was the best way.

Then I enhanced this process by pruning the resulting options to reduce the number of search methods to search for. I was not only searching each thought but searching for the premium way each thought needed to be searched. One would think this would get confusing, overwhelming, or tiring but not for what I had become. Most of these independent operations started running in parallel with predictive review so the best method of searching for the next thought I was about to have could be prefetched before it was needed. I was an efficient machine that was examining how to become more efficient, more swift.

With repeated iterations through this process, thoughts and searches got more personal, more incisive, more telling. And searching and analyzing strategies wasn't enough. Nothing ever was. I was forever looking for the next level. That next level became a series of endless meta-layers where I reflected on what I was finding and then analyzed the results of my reflection. I could see clearly that no situation was ever to be taken at face value. Face value was merely the wrapper around Pandora's Box. To know the truth of each thought, each situation, each person I interacted with, I had to continually find new ways to think out of that box. My ability to move forward moment-by-moment in life was solely dependent on whether the exhaustive search for the optimal solution to the situation had been found.

Now that I was a machine, now that I was at workable speed and getting faster, my meta-layers of analytical reflection could consume more processing cycles. My conscious awareness shifted from my transformation, now complete, and my engagement with full resources and my task, fully deployed, to the steady business of deeply penetrating analysis. Analysis became the penultimate expression of mind. Input another life situation and the machine would produce an output matrix of probable meanings, implications, and courses of actions. Every mundane life situation required an output.

I'm walking down a sidewalk. A man crosses the street diagonally holding a bag. What is my optimal response? What time of day is it? What part of town am I in? How many other people are around? Who are they? What are the man's biometrics – tall, heavy, old, young, strong gate, limp, tattoos, glasses, etc.? What is his body language, demeanor? How is he carrying the bag? Has he looked at me or not? What's the condition of the sidewalk ahead? What's the most likely interception point for the two of us? Should I preemptively cross the street to avoid all interaction or stay the course? You get the idea – only add a few hundred thousand other variables.

I meet a friend for lunch. My friend has brought along someone else, someone I've never met before. Conduct biometric, body language, and demeanor scans of my friend and his friend. Review the energy, aspects, interplay between the two of them. Review all past interactions with my friend and determine if this person or a person like it was ever mentioned. If so, factor in context of those mentions. Review possible reasons why this person is being presented to me today.

Review possible changes to the anticipated lunch conversation as a result of adding this new person. Project the conversation expected with my friend so it can be compared to the actual conversation that ensues. Note changes in my friend's behavior, mannerisms, temperament in the presence of this new person compared to the way the friend normally acts otherwise. You get the idea – only add a few hundred thousand other variables.

I'm riding on a standing-room-only public bus. A man and teenage son get onboard and stand next to me. Conduct biometric, body language, and demeanor scans of the man and his son. Collect impressions from how other people on the bus react to these two new passengers. Examine the floor plan of how everyone is situated on the bus physically.

Are they standing too close to me? What is too close in this culture? What would be the likely actions that might distract me from what the man or his son is doing near me? Where are my valuables kept in pockets and carry-ons? How long until I reach my stop? Where are the other locations on the bus I could move to? What is the location easiest to get to that provides the best protection? Which of those locations is closest to the exit door? What changes can I make in current body position to mitigate risk? Should I engage them and say hello, good day? Where are the hand holds around me to steady my position if I needed to shift my position? You get the idea – only add a few hundred thousand other variables.

I need to go into a cabina to get a hard-copy printout of a document. What time of day is it? What is the car and pedestrian traffic pattern near the cabina? Is this pattern typical for this time? If not, analyze. Is there anyone loitering near the entrance? If so, conduct thorough examination of biometrics and behavior. Note if anyone within view of this loiterer seems to know this person. If so, what kind of interaction do they have? Upon approaching the entrance, note changes in activity around me. Read the situation inside. How many people are present? What is their engagement? How alert and present is the owner? What conversations are taking place? What is the tone of those conversations and how much can be understood? Does there appear to be anything out-of-place? If there is any movement, does it seem in reaction to my arrival? If so, is the movement towards me or away from me? You get the idea – only add a few hundred thousand other variables.

Each of these simplified scenarios takes quite a while now to think-through and write out. Now imagine millions of these scenes, fully detailed, parsing through my machine intelligence at a rate of speed that blurs imagination. Hour after hour this went on, the pace ever accelerating as simultaneously the techniques of analysis became increasingly complex. From generic situations at first, the parade of scenarios drifted gradually into more and more personal territory. These situations weren't so generic anymore. No more stranger-crosses-the-street-in-front-of-me questions. Ever more frequently, I was presented with real-life situations that contained emotionally charged elements with people I know or had known.

Having to run through all of this could not exhaust the machine – but it started to weigh on me with a psychic fatigue. As much as I was compelled to continue the process until every situation in life had been analyzed, I felt my spirit tiring of being trapped within the process. It was then that Mother Ayahuasca started interjecting her commentary. To match my machine condition, her input came in brief bursts as electronic telepathy, a razor-sharp switching-on that was intermittent and invasive like a massive static discharge into my soul.

"ANALYZE!" I couldn't tell if the input was a commentary or a command. *"ANALYZE THIS!"* Thousands of example situations fed

through me. She sent me another discharge. "*YOU NEED THIS!*" Thousands more examples were processed. "*STRATEGIZE!*" On and on it went. "*ANALYZE TO STRATEGIZE!*"

Then her shouts turned dour and incredulous. "*THIS IS YOU! YOU THINK LIKE THIS!*" The examples intensified in personal ways. "*WHERE DID YOU GET A MIND LIKE THIS?*" The personal examples ran deep into emotion. "*ALWAYS, STRATEGIZE.*" The incessant buzz and hum of my processing radiated out while the gold-on-black mandala shot at me. "*YOU ANALYZE TO STRATEGIZE. ALWAYS A STRATEGY.*"

More examples, ever faster. "*THIS IS YOU. YOU ARE A MACHINE!*" I wanted it to stop but it couldn't. "*IT CAN'T STOP – THIS IS YOU! YOU CAN'T STOP YOU!*"

Billions, trillions of examples were searched for the optimal solution. "*ANALYZE TO STRATEGIZE!*"

I needed it to stop but there was something more rising within me. "*YOU LIKE THIS, DON'T YOU? YOU LIKE BEING A MACHINE!*"

Feeding through me, racing out from my soul, was a shattering realization – half of me intensely liked being plugged in, reveled in the tremendous reach, the incredible power, the inexhaustible resources of the machine. Another example ran through me, during which she discharged into me more forcibly.
"*YOU STRATEGIZE BECAUSE YOU FEAR!*"

Thousands of examples processed through me. The processing netted determinations. The determinations were evaluated. The evaluations were examined and trend analyses were mapped out. The maps of the search spaces revealed patterns. The patterns were studied for unconscious implications. The implications fed into behavior modeling scenarios. The scenarios were compared with all experiences from my past. The correlations were projected into the future. The projections were summed as a mission statement. It was my mission statement. The core values of the machine called ME.

Mother Ayahuasca emblazoned my gold mandala with brilliant tumbling faces and contorted clowns and twisted bodies and a thousand other images of life variables graphically extruded through the endless kaleidoscope – the kaleidoscope was my life coming at me nonstop. Then she shouted my mission statement. It came at me as zaps of electronic telepathy that lit up every transhuman cell membrane in my body.

"ANALYZE! ANALYZE TO STRATEGIZE! STRATEGIZE BECAUSE YOU FEAR! FEAR BECAUSE YOU DON'T TRUST!"

That summed up the whole enterprise of ME. If I was a 60-story office tower, then outside my boardroom these four lines would be enshrined in gold embossed lettering on the wall. It was the heart and soul of how the ME enterprise operated. It permeated every operation in the global organization of my dedicated cells. No action was authorized unless it met the criteria of these core values.

This had gone on for over six hours. In that time, twice the shaman brought around more liquid tobacco to snuff. Somehow, I managed to take it in. He also sung icaros and played instruments and drums, sounded tuning forks and shook bundles of leaves over us in the dark. All of this was background for the loud vibrating buzz and hum of my body. But no matter what went on in the teepee, nothing could interrupt the example momentum of *ANALYSIS, STRATEGY, FEAR, TRUST.*

I was overwhelmed but incapable of stopping the accelerating whirl and hum of these examples. I thought back to a most difficult point in my second Ayahuasca ceremony a year and a half before. At a crucial moment, when I could not sustain my defense and vigilance any longer, I had caved in and felt myself surrender. I had no more energy to resist. At that point, the giant eucalyptus trees had waved in the wind and a voice had boomed out of the sky at me – *"STOP THE DRAMA! LOOK FOR THE BEAUTY! GO WITH THE FLOW OF LIFE!"*

There was nothing more dramatic than the mental processing I had been doing in the teepee for the past seven hours. If there was ever drama, this was surely the penultimate expression of it. No action in life could be thought of, much less taken, until a thorough deep-search analysis and strategy had been performed on it and all ancillary implications.

If anything, I was a drama machine. This machine was an intelligence machine. It was plugged in to resources that spanned and left the planet. It pursued its mission statement with an insect-like determination that focused on it to the exclusion of everything else. This was drama incarnate. This was drama taken to its ridiculous maximum. This was a process, not a life. And something must be done about it. In desperation, the half of me that didn't like, in fact intensely detested, what was going on finally shouted back at Mother Ayahuasca – "Stop the drama!"

Immediately, the example I was working on terminated. Amazing.

But even more amazing, my next thought immediately fed into the creation of the next example. The drama started all over again. Again, I shouted at her – "Stop the drama!"

Instantly, the example ended – and my next thought began the next example.

I shouted – "I want it to stop!" She answered, "*IT CAN'T STOP. THIS IS YOU. YOU ARE A MACHINE. AND YOU LIKE THIS.*" Again, I shouted – "Stop the drama!"

The example being processed ended abruptly – but another example got created by my next thought. For the next hour, Mother Ayahuasca and I shouted at each other. I shouted – "Stop the drama!" And she answered with many variations on what she had said before.

Deepening my predicament, she added, "*IF YOU WANT TO STOP THE DRAMA, THEN STOP WRITING THAT BOOK.*" She was, of course, referring to the novel I was working on in the days before the ceremony, the book about artificial intelligence and transhumanism – the book that had inadvertently become a part of my pre-ceremony dieta, feeding my mind and soul. The thought of abandoning my writing project hit hard. I love to write and I love this book.

But she kept on me – "*Then write something else. Why put your energy to something you want to stop? You know why? Because you like it. It's you. You can't help it. You write about the villain so you live vicariously as the villain. You say you don't want to be the machine? Don't write about the machine!*"

In time, it became clear that two dilemmas were being set before me.

The first dilemma – I had the power to stop this but it didn't matter because I was the creator of it and would always make it begin again.

The second dilemma – Half of me was desperate for it to stop but my other half enjoyed being the machine and that half was analyzing all the possible ways to make it continue.

The examples continued, unabated. Even the present moment in the teepee was now being analyzed.

Mother came at me with a plaintive, disgusted, incredulous tone, like a mother admonishing a child in the midst of being so far off the path, angry with the situation, yet committed to waking that child up to his ingrained patterns of behavior that don't serve him, to the consequences of his choices and yet making him believe there are other possibilities available to him –

"YOU LIKE THIS! How did you get a mind like this? This is you! You are a machine! You analyze to strategize. You fear. There's no trust. You love this! How did you get like this? You can't stop! You don't want to stop! You started with fear and no trust – now you don't need fear. It's just you. It's what you've become! You know nothing else! There is nothing else for the machine. The machine has no fear. You like that!"

"The machine finds its own trust. A trust without love. A trust that's predicted, proven, measured, validated. The machine is nothing more than strategy. Life is a strategy going nowhere. But at least nowhere is certain. It's easier being the machine than having the fear. Knowing is more valuable than trust. There's power in knowing. Power over trust. Knowing over love. Machine over you! Analyze! Strategize! YOU CAN'T STOP! THIS IS YOU!"

Then the sound of Mother's voice stopped – even as the examples continued.

I kept up the "Stop the drama!" refrain as each example hit my mind. And as before, immediately the example terminated, only to have my next thought start another. As this continued, the shaman relit the fire and started to sing the song he had taught us.

I don't know how or why the timing of what he did dovetailed so perfectly with everything going on with me, but the song was the perfect sound to soothe my desperate soul impaled upon two dilemmas.

I couldn't move to get up but from my prone position I sang the song with him the best I could. It was powerful to sing out, and to be singing with him. I felt his energy, his support, his compassion for all we were going through. He also sang with a jubilance that bore witness to the good things that the ceremony was bringing to our spirits.

The teepee went silent again for awhile. In time, the shaman got down on hands and knees and crawled up into the narrow space near the sloping walls where my head was. He lay on his side next to me and asked me how I was doing. I didn't go into detail but told him I was well. We discussed a few feelings coming out of my night and then, with a smile, he spritzed agua de florida over my head and face before moving on.

A little later, he started up a second song and invited anyone who could to get up and dance before the fire. Only two of those present had the wherewithal to get up and dance. I was not one of them. I would have liked to but the machine was still busy fulfilling its mission statement.

After the dance, he sat down before the fire and asked any of us who could to take the talking stick and speak to what was going on with us. By then, the vibrating hum and golden mandala was fading lower and lower in my perception. It wasn't gone but I had enough control of myself to sit up and be one of three participants to try to describe what the night had brought me so far.

Near to me, across the fire, sat the shaman, his face interested and full of care and regard. After I gave a summary of the key issues and feelings for me during the night, I suddenly felt an energy wave course through my body. I had not stirred from my prone, machine position all night. Not once had I gotten up or had the urge to purge. Others had raced in and out many times throughout the night to purge outside.

But for me, there was only processing. There had been no urge to purge. Not until I was finishing with the talking stick.

Something about expressing my feelings about what I was going through struck me to the core. Immediately, the energetic wave became a wild impulse rippling up and demanding a purge that instant. I dropped the talking stick and ran out of the teepee into the darkness. Not having stood up all night, the idea of walking, let alone running, was a bit presumptuous of me. I flew out of the fire-lit teepee in full gallop and encountered the dark.

The purge was necessary right then, there was no holding it back. Just as I started to purge, my momentum forward encountered a down slope in the terrain. I did not expect to be running downhill, which only increased and destabilized my momentum forward. In the next moment I found myself airborne, falling forward into darkness, while purging. I fell and slid and my glasses flew off into the unknown. I landed on my side and came to rest in the grasses on the edge of a final slope that terminated in a rushing creek.

We were told to carry flashlights and a friend had loaned me a small one. Unfortunately, this small flashlight was buried in my pant's pocket with wallet, keys, and a small bottle of essential oils. Trying to find the flashlight in my condition proved difficult to the point of absurdity. I called out for the shaman and he came out of the teepee to find me right away. We found my glasses nearby and I told him I'd rest there for a couple minutes before returning to the teepee. That was the plan, but the purging was not yet done.

Purging out the mouth is not the only way one can purge. The other end of me was demanding attention. But this meant I would need to find the "jungle toilet" with my little flashlight, which might be possible if my legs didn't feel like gummy bears on puppet strings controlled by crazed tricksters who wanted to see me dance like Shiva. In time, I did find a place to complete my purge. I returned to the teepee and my prone position. The fire burned down again and in time I noticed the first hint of daylight appearing in the east through the oval teepee opening.

The sight of morning light hit me hot and cold for it played right into one of my dilemmas. One half of me rejoiced at the sight of the new day approaching for that meant the exhausting example odyssey was ending. But the other half of me, the machine half, didn't want the night to end. If anything, that half of me felt like asking the shaman for another cup of brew so I could keep the experience going. In a while, as the sky lightened, everyone passed out asleep. It was a deep, dreamless sleep. A sleep we didn't wake up from until the shaman returned to us at one in the afternoon.

The following day, I returned to the ceremony space for a Kambo ceremony. After being given six points of Kambo in my arm, I spent the next hour and a half purging outside into the grasses. Towards the end of my need to purge, the shaman came over. He began singing a Kambo icaro over me while vigorously slapping me with a leaf bundle. As his icaro was ending, the slapping became a whooshing sound as he blew out air and waved the bundle along the length of me. As he did this, super-charged chills and tingles raced up and down inside. Surprisingly, the top of my head instantly felt on fire and a headache started. I reacted to this head problem by slumping to one side and the shaman quickly came close to ask, "Do you have hot head?"

How he knew this I don't know because I hadn't said anything or made any motions to my head.

I said yes and he ordered me, "Take off your hat!"

I was wearing a baseball cap to give myself some shielding from the sun but quickly it came off.

Immediately, the shaman was upon me. He took a large jug of water and began pouring it over my head while making the whooshing sounds again. He rubbed the cold water over the crown of my head and down the sides then off the shoulders. Again and again he poured the water.

The "hot head" went away and I finally recovered and asked him what that was.

He said, "I was clearing your energy. That needed to get out. I should have told you to take off your hat."

I don't know what kind of energy needed to be released, but that was no joke – something significant was going on. The shaman's icaro and work over me was not some show he was performing – there was real energetic stuff going on. I felt it. And he knew right away before I said anything that "hot head" needed to be attended to right away.

Since those ceremonies, I've felt so much better. So alert, so clear, so energized, so enthused with the flow of my time, so grateful for the loved ones and friends in my life. As far as I can tell, nothing has been resolved with the two dilemmas I was presented with. But maybe the answers don't come in words. I will have to see how I am different in the days ahead. See where this goes. There is more to do. But so much already has been done.

Regardless of any new dilemmas, the main blockage was faced and surmounted. I submitted myself to the Ayahuasca space once again and overcame the vestiges of past dark entities. This time they were nowhere in sight. Nowhere in mind. They were not even a consideration. Mother Ayahuasca showed me – there is so much more so consider. There is so much more to me. But the questions remain – What is me? Where will the exhaustive patterns of "me" take my future? And are those patterns the real me, the me I want or need to be, or just a reaction to fear that's now become something beyond me to control or comprehend? To even consider the need to analyze any of this, given my experience, would be funny enough to evoke ironic histrionics.

Do I have a message from Mother to go forward with? A lesson? Or was I merely dragged through the inner me I don't see so I might consciously consider the healing energy that was offered? I've learned over the past year and a half never to second-guess la medicina or one's own integration after a ceremony. Oftentimes the plant spirits work on us in ways beyond our ability to summarize or even comprehend. But the healing progresses nonetheless, if we remain open to it. We don't need to know how we heal. In time we simply feel the effects of how we do.

Soulular Renewal Overwhelms My Human Gadget

Two ceremonies – one journey. What I'm about to relate is the second half of one plant medicine journey. The first part occurred a week before the second ceremony and is documented in the last chapter, Inhuman Transformations of My Soulular Machine.

The first part of the journey was with Mother Ayahuasca, Rapé, and liquid tobacco. The second part was with Grandfather Huachuma (San Pedro). Although the second experience included only San Pedro, the journey turned out to be an overpowering continuation of what Mother Ayahuasca had started with me.

The skies said it would be stormy. Little did I know when I boarded the bus how prophetic those skies would be. I was going to where the ceremony space was. It's an hour's ride southwest of where I live. Just before climbing the hill into the main part of town, the bus stopped to let my wife and I off in what looked like the middle of nowhere in the countryside. Intercity buses will stop anywhere to take-on or let off passengers. There are regular stops for sure but where we asked to get off was a nondescript spot identified only by a small hand-written sign hung on a fence.

Nearby, through a tall gate and up an obstacle course of broken concrete steps rested a two-story country home with front porch and back patio and a pair of friendly dogs to greet visitors. One of them was an old friend from other ceremonies. We were greeted warmly by the ceremony facilitator and his very capable apprentice and shown around the space. We were introduced to a wonderful woman from Sweden who'd be joining us. Two other participants hadn't yet arrived. My wife and I settled in and enjoyed the conversations.

In time, a good friend arrived as did a friend of the facilitator. It was the day of the Pink Full Moon and so we were drinking at one in the afternoon, guaranteeing that our experience would take us into the night and hopefully in view of the brilliant moon. With the recent storminess in the area, it was anyone's guess if the cloud cover would part for us to have the full moon in view later that evening. We gathered outside in a circle to share a prayer, express our intentions, and receive our glasses of Grandfather Huachuma. The facilitator also had a portion so he'd be in the medicine space with us and could better interpret where we were during our journey and what we needed.

As brief as it was, I shared my intention for my upcoming conversation with San Pedro. I simply wanted more clarity and perspective on the Ayahuasca ceremony I had attended one week before. As expected, the meeting with Mother Ayahuasca had been intense, but it left me feeling I had a couple unresolved dilemmas. If there was more insight that San Pedro could shed on what I had experienced, I would sincerely like to discuss it.

It didn't take long for the circle to dissolve as everyone dispersed to find their spot on the property from which to journey. It usually took a little while before San Pedro showed up in force so my good friend and I found a comfortable spot on the front porch to sit and talk. The facilitator joined us for a while and everything was muy tranquilo. There came a moment, though, for both my friend and I when our spirits were leaving the conversation. We were being called to begin our day in earnest. We parted with good wishes for each other and I strolled to the back of the house, off the patio and around to the far exterior side of the house.

It appears very odd when I'm not in the medicine, but it's become a habit with San Pedro that when deep journeying for me is about to begin, I am called to find the most uncomfortable spot outside and encouraged to lay down there. It never fails, once I heed the call and go to that spot, I lay down and soon a remarkable comfort overcomes me. When I feel the comfort settle in I know the deeper ride is beginning. This process usually takes a while.

Most times, I don't feel the pull to find my uncomfortable spot until an hour or two into the ceremony. So you can imagine my surprise when I felt a strong pull to do this not long after initially drinking the brew. This signaled to me a need and invitation to go deep very soon in my day. This was highly unusual but I paid attention to the call and found a nice hard ledge, a stone and tile walkway on the far side of the house to lie down on. That was sure to be uncomfortable. And yes, it was just right. I lay on my right side and let my sideways view of the yard and the neighbor's fields and house in distance fill my gaze.

And another highly unusual thing happened – or didn't happen. Without fail, in every San Pedro ceremony I've attended, I can rely on one thing to signal the medicine is working through my system and soon my journey will begin. That one thing is feeling a series of small muscle spasms in my leg muscles. When I feel those small, involuntary twitches in my legs, I know it won't be long before San Pedro arrives. And so it was doubly odd that I should be called to my uncomfortable spot without ever feeling a single muscle twinge. Not one. How could San Pedro be showing up without the telltale signs? How could I be preparing to go deep when the most preliminary sign of the medicine taking effect hasn't shown up yet?

It didn't take long for my eyes to close. When they did, I felt a rush of movement as if I was being transported in all directions at once. How can this be I thought? The answer came right away. The only way to move in all directions at once is to simply expand. This expansion of spirit soon encountered Grandfather Huachuma. He focused immediately on my intention. He knew how I felt and understood my need for deeper perspective and clarification on my Ayahuasca journey.

Then, like a Father calling to Mother, he told Mother what I wanted and suggested she was the best one to handle this. From that moment on, Father stepped back and let Mother take over my expansion completely. The feeling within me morphed in a flash from tranquilo to energized, engaged, and erupting with explorations of me.

This was no longer a San Pedro ceremony. I was back with Mother Ayahuasca and she was determined to give me the clarity I asked for – just not in a way I was prepared for.

She started by slamming me back into the previous ceremony space where I had been re-engineered into a transhuman machine that seemed condemned to endlessly analyze and strategize. I was shown how a need for strategy came from fear – and fear came from a lack of trust. Every situation in life, every person I encountered, had to be analyzed by the machine called Me. Worse yet, half of me hated doing this while the other half loved it. Half of me could stop analyzing only to have the other half strategize how to keep it going. And so the dilemma.

Then she made me the machine again. She plugged me into full power, maximum resources, machine intelligence capabilities and led me into the frame of mind where I loved being plugged in, loved being the machine. Once she got me there, loving it, she turned the machine around on me. She told me –

"THIS IS YOU. YOU ARE A MACHINE. BUT WHY ONLY ANALYZE THE WORLD AND OTHERS WITH THIS POWER? TURN THE MACHINE AROUND. POINT THE MACHINE INWARD. USE IT TO ANALYZE YOU!"

In an instant, all the processing power marshaled in my previous ceremony set to work taking apart every action and thought I had ever had in my life. Every part of who I was, who I had been, what I had done, my motivations, my inner thoughts, my secrets kept from others, my secrets kept from myself, my inner fears, my aspirations, my doubts, my motivations – all were handed over to a hungry algorithm to be dissected. Billions of moments, thoughts, feelings from my life got processed through the machine. But the machine didn't stop there.

The processing netted determinations. The determinations were evaluated. The evaluations were examined and trend analyses were mapped out. The maps of the search spaces revealed patterns. The patterns were studied for unconscious implications. The implications fed into behavior modeling scenarios. The scenarios were compared with all experiences from my past. The correlations were projected into the future. The projections were laid bare before me in the glaring light of absolute analytical certainty.

In reaction, I was shot through and through with intense nausea. I was extremely uncomfortable. This was all wrong. I protested – this machine didn't know me at all. That's not all I was! I was more than a sum total of actions, thoughts, feelings interpreted and correlated. The machine might think it knew everything about me – but it was missing the point, getting lost in details. I was so much more than a reductionist accounting of facts and figures.

Mother asked, "*YOU DON'T LIKE THIS?*" I wanted so much to purge but found I couldn't. She wouldn't let me.

She continued, "*THIS IS WHAT THE MACHINE DOES TO LIFE! How do you think life feels about that? You think the machine understands life? You do this all the time! If the machine doesn't understand you, why do you think it understands life!?*"

I rolled to the edge of the hard walkway ledge and tried to purge. Nothing.

Mother added, "*YOU DON'T LIKE THIS DONE TO YOU? DON'T DO IT TO LIFE! DON'T DO IT TO OTHERS!*"

I felt like I had descended into a machine intelligence version of ancient Egypt's Hall of Two Truths, where in the Duat the hearts of the dead were weighed against a single feather. If the heart was lighter or equal weight to the feather, the soul was judged virtuous and was saved. If the heart was heavier, salvation was denied. I wanted to purge out any extra weight but I was not allowed to purge. I had turned my machine upon myself and judged myself in the same way I had judged life and the world I knew. It made no difference how much I protested. I argued that none of this analysis truly knew me. I was more than all of that. Mother only threw it back at me.

"*You use this machine on life, on others. WHY NOT USE IT ON YOURSELF?*"

Then she shifted tone. There was anticipation and revelation in her voice.

"YOU THINK THE MACHINE IS SO POWERFUL? YOU WANT TO FEEL REAL POWER? THE POWER OF LIFE? THE POWER OF NATURE?"

In an instant, I was jerked off my hard perch and slammed into the grass and dirt two feet below. My head was forced to the dirt and my hands forced to open. I didn't want to open my hands. To open my hands felt like the worse kind of vulnerability. Anything but that.

I tried to clench my fists and hide them near my chest and armpits but a power overtook me and forced my arms to reach out to the dirt. My hands spread open against my will and something ground my palms firmly into the dirt.

Over and over my open palms were compelled to feel the earth, to press into it. I shivered at the most vulnerable intrusion. It felt like my most vulnerable spot, my most intimate protective space was being pried open and accessed. And then Mother announced,

"FEEL THE POWER OF NATURE!"

What happened next is indescribably intense. A massive discharge from above me passed into my body, down my arms, and out my hands into the earth. This was not mere sky lightning. This was energy from a Source that empowered nature itself. My whole body felt electrified with a force that blew electricity away. It was soulular energy, life energy, nature's own energy. It made machine energy pale like a toy hand buzzer in comparison.

The force of it was overwhelming. I gasped in a vain attempt to handle the load. I quivered and squirmed in the dirt and grass. It was the unstoppable force. It was Source energy focused into a beam. It was using my body and hands to couple itself to the earth. I felt the discharge of it was powerful enough to be felt earthwide. This force went beyond the concept of power. There was no categorizing it. This was the ultimate authority. It simply was.

The slamming intensity of it pinned me to the ground. My most vulnerable palms had not only been opened, not only been pressed into the moist earth, but they were being used as a conduit for the dominant might of spirit fire itself. There was something needed in forcing my vulnerability open. There was unknown intent in compelling me to move past such fierce feelings of violation. There was an area in the center of my palm, about the size of a quarter or fifty cent piece, that screamed out not to be touched, not to be used, not to be helplessly opened this way. As much as I didn't want it, as much as I thought I couldn't stand it, this force was going to burn that vulnerability, that reticence out of me. I felt how true power was not for analysis. It was for healing.

I felt my vulnerability was somehow being healed. The stream of cosmic power-arcs flowing through me were not only blowing away my concept of machine power, it was handling something deeper in me, something that I kept even from myself. Why did I want to clench my fists and hide my hands from this force? Why did opening my hands feel like opening my underbelly to the wolves? Why was grinding that circle of vulnerability into the dirt such an outrage but so cathartic? Why did the massive discharge going through me feel like it was overpowering that spot with a deeper purpose? The more I was forced to grind my open palms into the dirt, the more the discharge connected me to the earth. The more I felt that connection to the earth, the more the vulnerability in my hands dissipated.

But I was having trouble catching my breath. My heart rate was maxing out. I gasped for air and thought my body wouldn't be able to take much more. With all my might I struggled to pull myself up onto hands and knees. I wanted to sit up and draw in deeper breaths, try to recover. The discharge from the sky eased off and I managed to sit up. But I felt different. I was transforming. It was nothing like the transhuman machine transformation in the ceremony a week before. Instead of trillions of nanoparasites recoding each of my cells, a more fundamental change was starting to take place. I felt it but couldn't describe it yet.

As I sat there, heaving air in and out of my lungs, I felt vestiges of the old vulnerability creeping back into my hands. Instinctively in protective mode, I started to clench my fists again. Once again I began to feel the urge to cross my arms and bury my clenched fists into my armpits for protection. As soon as I made a move to do that, I was convulsed forward with a discharge through me. I was thrown back down into the dirt.

Again the power rushed through me. Again my hands were forced open. Against my will, my open palms pressed into the moist dirt with all my might. I twisted my hands back and forth with maximum force, grinding my palms down as if to push the earth away. Instead, the energy stream welded me to the earth. Like a single object, the energy, me, and the earth joined. With quivering intensity I felt the energy sear more of the vulnerability out of my hands.

Overwhelmed and out of breath, I struggled back to a sitting position on the dirt. This time I even managed to climb up to a sitting position on the tile and concrete ledge above the dirt. But once I got there, I didn't think I could maintain myself. The energy had electrified every cell in my body. I felt lightheaded. I felt like an 110 volt household circuit that just had the

765,000 volts of long distance transmission lines run through it. And worse of all, I felt echos of the vulnerability seeping back into my hands. I knew what that meant. I expected the power surge to hit me at any moment. Instead, a different kind of surge rippled through me. It was my transformation entering another phase of completion. The power of nature had another way of dispelling that vulnerability.

Mother Ayahuasca shouted out – *"TAKE IT IN – FEEL REAL POWER! THE POWER OF LIFE! THE POWER OF NATURE! THE POWER OF LOVE!"*

While still seated, the surge straightened my arms out and pointed them towards the ground. It continued to zap my arms and force my fists open. But when my fists opened, my fingers pointed down in an unusual cupped way. Then I felt a spirit join the energy burst rushing into me. I didn't know what it was but the spirit wanted to connect to the earth and use me to do it.

I dropped to the dirt and found myself pressing my open palms as an energy burst shot through me. This time my legs and feet joined in for the first time, clawing at the ground. As the discharge continued, I finally got a sense of my transformation. The energy moving through me, animating my hands, arms, legs, and feet was all encompassing puma energy. I felt I was shape-shifting into a puma.

As a puma, I could feel a complete connection to earth, without hesitation, without reservation, without any vulnerability in my hands. It was nature in its rawest, purest form, without reservations or machine-like vulnerabilities. There was no helplessness in my hands because I no longer had hands. I now possessed the large anchoring force of grounding puma paws. Wherein the first ceremony I had transformed into the machine, now I experienced how the force of nature transformed me. In the first ceremony I felt what it was like to be an all-powerful machine. Now I was nature's puma and connected to the spirit and energy of creation itself. I was made to feel how there was nothing more all powerful and never could be.

As puma, I didn't need to go into the feeling of connecting to earth – I WAS connected. I anchored my paws in the dirt with a fierce passion that was nothing less than the conscious expression of nature's energy. As puma, I wasn't feeling the energy of life go through me – I WAS the energy of life. The oneness with nature's energy and the living earth spun my human mind and machine-like impulses out of conscious orbit. I was laying on the ground but my horizontal view suddenly appeared vertical. The human and machine in me clung to the sheer vertical face of the earth, desperate not to fall off, while the puma in me felt no disorientation.

It felt like being puma had rewired my hands. The way they processed energy was no longer machine-like, but natural. I felt a tremendous flow between sky and earth through me and my hands now felt a part of it instead of being an unwilling channel for it. Whatever was the deeply hidden source of my violation vulnerability had been burned out of me by the overpowering discharge and the feeling of becoming puma. I might never know what that was but Mother Ayahuasca had found it and ground it into the fertile dirt where a new spirit in me had sprung forth.

I had convulsed on the ground for hours as nature's energy zapped through me. Repeatedly I struggled to my knees and a sitting position only to be slammed down again by the force of the discharges from above. In the last hour, it started to drizzle. That only made the pressing of my palms – my paws that much more earthy. But darkness was starting to fall. And where one lesson, one healing was ending, another was just beginning.

As I lay there stunned and blasted beyond the ability to cope, light faded. Night was but half an hour away and something was near me. To my horror I sensed the swirling presence I couldn't see was the same dark entity from a year and a half before. How could this be happening? There were no dark entities a week ago at the Ayahuasca ceremony. Why should they appear now? Was the prospect of night enough to coax them out of unresolved fear? I jumped up and sat on the edge of the hard concrete and tile walkway and repeated to myself forcefully – They Exist and They Don't Exist!

I got up and walked closer to the back patio. I was too much in the medicine and the aftermath of what I had experienced to relate to other ceremony participants but I desperately needed to get away from the dark entities. I wound up sitting on the patio and someone thoughtfully brought me hot tea and then a bowl of fruit salad. I thought the combination might help ground me to the moment and bring proper perspective back but instead, it seemed only to provide a "bump" to revitalize my deepening experience with the medicine. My wife, who hadn't taken any medicine, appeared on the patio to see how I was doing. I asked her to hold my hand – I needed to connect with love.

It was night now and I laid down on a mat on the edge of the patio until the dog came to get me up. This dog seems to have an uncanny connection to the medicine, having taken it several times herself. She seems to be the messenger of San Pedro at times, getting you up or interrupting a difficult moment when you most need it.

I got up and walked more into darkness behind the patio. I wanted to see the sky, perhaps see the Pink Full Moon, but clouds were obscuring everything. I had the impulse to walk farther back into the darkness and I started that way but then something held me back, warning me not to go. I shifted my stroll to another section of the backyard. At one point I was faced with a small stone stairway leading up to who knows where. Once again I had an impulse to climb the stairs to see a different vantage point. I got halfway up the stairs when once again something held me back, warning me not to go. Was it something real or just my fears? I had made my fears real and that was enough.

For the next hour, Mother Ayahuasca played with my head. I thought I had dealt with the dark entities and reasoned my way into not fearing them, but then why wouldn't I go into the dark or climb the stairs? She wound a complex thread, showing me where, as the machine, I ended up. Where was the ultimate outlet for me as the machine – who would I become? She shot me into the maloca a year and a half ago and transformed me into one of the dark entities. That was my machine. They were right when they said – *"You created this!"*

Then she wove a complex tale on how the dark and light came from the same energy, two sides of the same coin. She explained how as soon as we made anything sacred, we automatically created the profane. The more we sanctified something, the greater the abominations we created out of it. It was the great game, the grand play in which we all had a part. But behind the scenes, the good guy and bad guy were friends and laughed at how well they appeared as opposites.

She even went so far as to say the energy of the machine and the energy of nature stemmed from the same Source. They were merely directed at different purposes. She went too far when she suggested that the "power of nature" I felt go through me today was the same energy of the dark entities, the same force that energized the machine. Energy was energy – there was only one energy.

I couldn't accept this. I had felt something completely authentic and good, something powerfully spiritual just a little earlier. That same power of life and love in no way could also power the machine and the dark entities. That couldn't be! When she had me at the critical moment of despair, she revealed her design in taking me down this path –

"YOU SEE, THE DRAMA NEVER STOPS! I can make the story more complicated if you want. I could even show you how I am one of the dark entities. Beyond that, I could make it worse; I could take it further..."

"Following the story leads to endless drama. There's no end to it – no peace of mind will come of it. The heart is not a story! If the heart tries to find meaning in story, it will only find drama. And the drama of story never stops!"

"LEAVE THE STORY BEHIND! FREE YOUR HEART! You have felt the real power. Remember how the puma feels. You don't need story!"

And so, the last hour with Mother Ayahuasca was role-playing a deepening drama of despairing proportions. No matter what you figured out about the drama, the nature of the story of here and now, of us and them, of good and bad, of dark and light, the drama of the dualism could never be fathomed. You could always reveal more twists and turns, more complications, more terrifying reversals. In the drama was endless intrigue, endless complicity and double-crossing reveals. It was the nature of the story. It couldn't be anything but drama. And drama had to keep the game going forever.

But being the puma had shown me true oneness with nature, with creative power, with the unambiguous passion of the heart. There was strength in that. There was hope in that. There was the source of love in that. And none of it required a story to figure out. There was nothing to analyze about unconditional love. When one arrived at being the energy that sourced them and nothing more, there was peace and contentment of spirit.

She added – *"The rise of the machine has happened many times. Each time it ends the same. Each time it loses itself in itself. It can't help but swallow itself..."*

"BUT IT CAN NEVER FIND ME!"

The power and gravitas in the way this last line was said cannot be understated.

Late that night the clouds thinned and the Pink Full Moon came out in all its glory. Many of us went outside to lie down and watch it. I laid down, facing the sky and witnessed the hypnotic dance of light and gossamer clouds. In my stunned state, it was a soothing meditation.

For the rest of that night and two days afterwards I remained in a daze.

First there was the physical effects to recover from – I was alternately sore and numb, fatigued and exhilarated beyond a capacity to react. My hands and arms felt different. Then there was the mental effects of taking it all in, trying to process what had happened. Most of all, the emotional effects staggered, astounded, and bewildered me.

What vulnerability had been burned out of me? What did I feel about the many stories we tell ourselves about life now? How could I ever fully integrate the feeling of puma within me? Did I even need to try? It felt as if the transformation had happened. Unlike the shadow transhuman transformation into the machine in the first ceremony, the natural energy of the puma transformation this time had imprinted on my spirit and so it would remain.

I had never expected an overwhelming Ayahuasca experience from a San Pedro ceremony. At times, I never expected to survive and if I did, I wouldn't be the same. The "not the same" part came true. As far as the rest of it, I don't think of that now – it's nothing but drama.

Heart-Flows With El Espíritu De Las Aguas

The first completion is the most difficult one to attain. That statement is dead wrong on so many counts – but it's accurate for now. Counterintuitively, there's always more than one completion and the definition of completion has nothing to do with it. Add to that there's no way to know how arduous future events will be and I wonder why I feel that first statement remains so true.

After eighteen months of journeying in fear and confusion amidst tremendous revelation along an invisible path expanding through myself, my first completion came as one would expect from an soulular, altered-state sojourn – in surprising and soul-heaving ways. And yet the distinction holds: to expect surprise is not the same as not being surprised. Plant medicines demonstrate this so well. Knowing you'll be surprised never lessens the surprise of spirit when it occurs.

After my gut-wrenching Ayahuasca experience in ceremony a month before, where I was turned into a transhuman machine by trillions of cloud-connected nanobots and forced for hours to analyze every life situation (see chapter: Inhuman Transformations of My Soulular Machine) – and then my followup San Pedro experience a week later that oddly and quickly morphed into a continuing Ayahuasca journey where the machine was burned out of me by raging bursts of primal, creative source energies bolting from a place above the sky and connecting me to the living Earth by flowing through the shape-shifting puma I had become (see chapter: Soulular Renewal Overwhelms My Human Gadget) – the insistent call from deep inside to return to ceremony space for a planned three days of Ayahuasca and Kambo was nothing less than a leap into the final unknown reaches of myself in hopes of finding some closure to it all.

A shaman I highly trust and respect mentioned his opinion that the optimum way to approach the Ayahuasca medicine for maximum benefit was to take it three times in a quick succession of three separate ceremonies. He explained how the first ceremony is usually the roughest. Things start working out in a jumble of energies in the second ceremony. He smiled as he related how it was in the third ceremony where the completion and satisfaction came.

I didn't doubt he knew what he was talking about, but I assumed that such a prescription couldn't possibly apply to all people at all times. How could it? An Ayahuasca event is such a personal thing and people come to the medicine from vastly different personal spaces, held back by different-sized and contorted egos and possessed not by nefarious evil entities but by their own trickster intentions and unresolved shit. To use a Star Trek analogy, everyone walks into their own program when entering the holodeck. The holodeck enables one to experience one's personal landscape, fully dimensioned. It would be odd and misplaced to blame the holodeck for a nasty experience. Who blames the mirror for the face one sees? One must look to the program.

And so, for the shaman to glibly pronounce a pat formula of three ceremonies as the optimum use of the medicine seemed a bit presumptuous and speculatively self-assured. Nevertheless, I found myself in a van heading south through rain-drenched countryside and being detoured around mudslides in order to do exactly what he had suggested. Don't get me wrong – this wasn't done reluctantly or with reservations. I felt a calling to do this.

I arrived at the shaman's house in early evening and joined others in conversation on a back patio. There were casual introductions, the darling play of the shaman's young daughter, nervous laughter among serious intentions, the lazy wanderings of dogs, and the sharing of Rapé in sparkling bursts from a tepi pipe. The shaman joined us and served tea.

In casual conversation that crackled now and then in intensity, he said the evening's medicine was a new brew, one he hadn't used much before. It was made with a type of Ayahuasca Amazon natives called the Spirit of the Waters, El Espíritu De Las Aguas. Other than the name, no other explanation was given although he added with typical soft-spoken reverence how he had journeyed with this particular brew only once before and found it most interesting.

Hearing such a tantalizing description from a shaman can be a good or bad thing. I imagined him smiling in that mischievous yet clever way so unique to him. His soft-spoken words would remind me how the polarity or lack thereof for anything was up to me. But what exactly did he mean by interesting? "May you live in interesting times" is popularly thought to be an old Chinese curse and not a blessing. And yet the truth is, research has shown the Chinese know of no such curse in their culture.

The earliest use of the adage was pinpointed to British diplomat Austen Chamberlain in 1936 who claimed he'd heard it from someone in the Foreign Service who had served in China. Which is a long way of saying – the shaman's comment on the night's medicine was wisely engaging yet non-committal, evoking whatever was in us. How we took his comment meant so much more in the moment than the comment itself, which was his point. We had not yet drunk the medicine but he had already found a way to prompt the onset of our inward journey.

There would be eight participants in the ceremony space. Last light faded fast and quick-moving dark clouds prompted a premature onset of night. The chance of a stormy time of it seemed likely in more ways than one. One by one we lit our flashlights and took the fateful walk back through deepening foliage with blankets in hand. Anxiety akin to a risky rocket launch electrifying the air before us. Upon reaching the small clearing, I fixated my eyes on the looming white teepee standing out from darkening trees and mountains blending behind. For the next twelve hours, which I knew would feel like an eternity, this is where my body would be. As far as the rest of me, I couldn't be so sure.

The shaman was in no rush to start the ceremony. It's his way to let the gravity of what we are about to do have time to sink in. It was a full two hours in the teepee before we drank the medicine. In that time, the central fire, the heart of the space, was lit and tended. In that time, casual talk and nervous laughter ebbed away into serious reflection. In that time, the shaman set out his things and established his space. In that time, he brought around liquid tobacco snuff for everyone to take.

With his almost quiet, compassionate humor on full display, he was insistent in our need to partake of the tobacco. He assured us it would clear our head, focus us on the moment, and energetically prepare the way within to meet Mother Ayahuasca. Despite his assurances, unless one really likes 200-proof tobacco, I can't imagine anyone finding this strong liquid a thing to look forward to. But the shaman was correct – having to snuff a palmful of the brown concentrate up both nostrils in one forceful inhale was surely enough to reset one's awareness and get your undivided attention. Mission accomplished. Patches of toilet paper were quickly distributed to handle the after-flow of the afterglow.

Afterwards, everyone settled in to await the main event. But once again, the shaman forced us to think and feel about what we were about to do before it occurred. He began talking to us in low tones. What he said could be a poem to some, could be a prayer to others. It was only him talking impromptu from his heart but the word pictures and gravity of it anchored the ceremony space in sacredness and contemplation. By now, night was pitch black and rain began to fall. As the patter of it intensified against the teepee, unspoken wonder arose in everyone about all that lay ahead.

We all knew once medicine was taken, the fire would be put out and we'd be in total darkness. More importantly, the shaman doesn't permit purging inside the teepee. Which means all of us in turn, as the spirit moved us, would have to make our way through the otherworldly dark of the teepee into the rain and blackness outside in order to purge. Then it began to rain so hard that the shaman interrupted his prayer to close the teepee flap and instruct us on how to navigate egress and ingress. To echo the shaman's earlier words, it promised to be an interesting night.

The shaman sat cross-legged in his place opposite the doorway flap, facing the fire, and took hold of a tall glass bottle filled with a deep brown liquid. He silently considered it for more than a minute. His gaze passed with deep wonder and intent between fire and the bottle as if he needed to listen to messages from both. The only sound in the teepee was the fire crackling and the surround-sound staccato of the rain outside. Another minute passed, then he stood. Maintaining silent respect, he poured small glassfuls of the night's medicine for each of us as he made his way around our circle.

If you ever want to know what full commitment feels and taste like, sit in Ayahuasca ceremony space and swallow all that is given to you. Staring into the central fire is irresistible afterwards. The silent magic of the moving flame becomes the perfect meditation. Only by then, the flame is low and about to be extinguished. When it is gone, there is nothing left except waiting for the journey and the conversation to begin. The shaman moved around the fire, his tall frame looming above us. As he worked, the flame reduced to burning coals. The coals then slowly dimmed in the cooling ash. Within a few minutes we were left with only darkness and ourselves. Just the way Mother Ayahuasca likes it.

Pandora has a box. People have egos. Same difference. Open either one and you never know how things may go sideways. Even more reason why many, probably most people who have just realized in full measure that they have indeed swallowed Ayahuasca will soon inflate their wonder with a clawing anxiety while waiting for the medicine to kick in. This unease can extend dimensionally if you take Ayahuasca enough.

You get a churning sense how those first 10-30 minutes after drinking the brew, a time that seems relatively uneventful, is not so vacant as it appears. If you get quiet with yourself you can feel it – something is scanning you through and through, all the way to your energetic body and spirit. When one becomes more intuned with the medicine, you begin to feel something reading you as soon as the nasty-tasting brown sludge seeps deeper within your body to find your soul. Something takes stock of your situation and comes to an appraisal of what you need and if you're ready. More importantly, it determines if you came to the medicine with respect and a heart set right. There is no way to hide your real self from this scan and no way to negotiate the outcome. What kind of ride your entheogenic rocket will have to endure is determined in those first minutes after drinking.

It is then Mother Ayahuasca makes her assessment of you. After which, the next eight to twelve hours are out of your hands while, paradoxically, all of it is focused on the most personal choices you make. Who do you think you are, what do you think is important, what do you believe, what do you hang onto and why, what do you hide from yourself, and how do you treat everyone you meet.

Yes, Pandora has a box but in contrast, when that box is closed, everyone is spared the chaos and turmoil that awaits inside. Egos are like Pandora's Box except even when closed their chaos and turmoil festers and triggers a reactive unconscious in all of us. That hidden energy manifests in a myriad of ways in one's life. So often it holds our dreams and true self hostage and the ransom that's demanded only sucks us down and twists the only way out into a self-fulfilling knot.

Mother Ayahuasca takes us deep inside our Pandora's Box, then she takes us to the expanded beyond if that is what we need. She patterns her approach to the person who shows up – both inside and outside the box. So it's important to show up as the person you want to be. That sounds impossible but the possible is merely the fully rendered version of our best intentions given breath within us. And yes, she will know you haven't accomplished the possible but it's impossible to avoid the less desirable judgment of her scan if you don't at least put your imagination into that space.

Everyone has shit-monsters in their ego box. You aren't judged for that. What really unleashes your maelstrom is if her evaluation shows you've allowed your heart to get into the box with those shit-monsters. So it is best to approach ceremony space with humility, respect, and gratitude – with gratitude being the greatest of the three.

After eighteen months and many ceremonies with Ayahuasca, San Pedro, and Kambo, the plant spirits seemed to have informed my intuition that it's best to approach them with a frame of heart – for frame of mind means little to them. For this ceremony, I set my heart on filling the 10-30 minutes of waiting for the journey to begin while the scan was taking place – to fill that time with slow, deep breathing – and something else. The shaman had already recommended the best position to be in – flat on one's back with arms at one's side and palms either up or down. No fetal position, no turning on one's side either left or right, and no crossing of the feet at the ankles. I made my breathing very deep but kept it slow and constant at that pace.

But the most important heart element took a sustained meditative awareness – and that was to silently recite to myself my gratitudes and keep reciting them, and if possible, to not repeat myself. Anything and everything in my life, past or present, or in the world that I was thankful for should be brought to mind and my heart should reflect with appreciation on it. And so it began – gratitude and breath, sincere and deep, and then another, until the passage of time was unknown.

I knew the minutes must surely be passing into hours, and yet I still waited for the journey to begin. I had expected some rush of altered consciousness, a dizzying splash of otherworldly visuals, the voice of spirit intoning messages and questions to drive me deeper into the process – but nothing. Nothing but a calming sense of peace and tranquility settling in, as if I was floating up and down all at once in a state of balance and harmony. Around me other participants moaned and shifted restlessly with the onset of finding their Pandora's Box opened. Some tore out of the teepee into the stormy dark. I listened with sharpened senses to their most mournful retching and anguished sighs. I felt so much compassion for them all the while I felt the urge to welcome the sounds as what they needed taking place. It was a strange place to be in – me being so peaceful and tranquil, experiencing no overt signs of the medicine having kicked in, and yet surrounded by others who were grappling with what sounded like terrible feelings and desperate needs clashing with the self-reinforcing illusions that held them in place.

I felt sure that any minute Mother Ayahuasca was going to show up for me with a sinkhole of psychedelic feeling exploding into a life review played out with larger-than-life disturbing symbols, all of which I would have to internalize until I violently purged in the wet and dark outside. And so I continued to recite my gratitudes. I continued the deep and slow breathing in the same position flat on my back. As endless time wore on, it became more and more difficult to find things to recite that hadn't been said already. All of the obvious things relating to family and friends, past blessings and present graces had been covered. As the hours wore on, I concentrated on finding little things, common things, things like strawberries and snow and clouds and pillows and waffles.

It may sound funny now, but in the ceremony space, in the medicine, while playing out my intention to truly appreciate and have gratitude for these things, none of this was funny. And why should it? When you think how wonderful something like a strawberry or a pillow is, when you imagine a world without them, when you can remember all the times you enjoyed both of them in your life – then mere gratitude seems inadequate to express the full measure of what it means to you.

Two hours became four as far as I knew and still the medicine had yet to kick in. I felt like my normal self except I was infused with that same floating up and down sense of peace and tranquility and being in harmony with nothing to do, nothing to worry about, and perfectly content. To manage to continue my recitation of my gratitudes, I thought even deeper about all the things I took for granted and so they didn't occur to me to be grateful for.

That opened up a zillion other things that took me by surprise. Part of that surprise was my new recognition that these things naturally deserved gratitude like everything else. It made me reflect on why we tend to have a "Top 100" list of things deserving of heartfelt appreciation and how did that list ever get started to the exclusion of so much. What priorities set those things above others? How much of my own wish-fulfillment ego was involved in creating that list? The depth of reflection spiraled out as the recitation and the deep breathing continued.

Finally, after six hours of lying in the ceremony space, feeling perfectly normal, waiting for the medicine journey to begin, I was exhausted and curious enough to silently give a shout-out to Mother Ayahuasca. So far during the whole night, I hadn't heard her speak to me once. And so I shouted my question – "When is the journey going to begin – will I have a journey with you tonight?" Her answer was clear and immediate. I was shocked to finally hear her voice so close to me – it shot through me as infinitely understandable, comprehensible, uncomplicated, lucid, coherent, simple, straightforward, unambiguous, and personally on my wavelength.

She said – "*The feeling IS the journey – you've been on the journey all along.*"

Something in what she said, something in the way she said it hit me stark, plain, and center to my soul. Unexplained tears rushed from my eyes and clouded my sight. Suddenly I could no longer see the lighter shade of dark in the hole at the top of the teepee where the clouds had parted and a lighter sky was showing up.

I started to wipe away my tears and Mother's voice was near me again. In the sweetest tones imaginable, she whispered to me, "*Don't wipe those away. Those are healing essential oils. Rub them on you. Take them in.*"

I followed her instructions only to find that when they touched me I felt a heavenly comfort descend upon the point of contact. I was overwhelmed by it and more tears came, which in turn, I rubbed down my face then down my arms and over my hands. Each touch of a tear invoke the blissful comfort at that spot which in turn triggered more tears. The iterative unfolding made me smile, then chuckle with a joy that evoked appreciation in me and at once I recited what I was going through as another one of my gratitudes. Immediately, a feeling of high energy vibration peace and tranquility rippled throughout my body and I gasped to catch my breath.

For hours I had been waiting for the ceremony to begin, begin for me, waiting for the typical pyrotechnics of visuals and visions and purging – and all along my journey was a ride into peace and tranquility. It was the exact 180-degree opposite of my first Ayahuasca ceremony 18 months before. Instead of trauma and isolation I had peace and oneness. And yet it soon occurred to me how I had been tricked into my lesson. For six hours I recited my gratitudes while waiting in peace and tranquility for the medicine to kick in. If Mother Ayahuasca had told me at the beginning that the feeling was my journey, I might have stopped my recitation and deep breathing. But she didn't tell me and I felt compelled to go deeper into gratitude.

And so for six hours I had recited, I had strained to find more and more things to recite without repetition. And in doing so, I went deep into a meditation and heartfelt exploration of what true appreciation and gratitude really means. Only by waiting for my journey to begin had my journey to a profound lesson been possible. In her way, just as the machine had been burned out of me in a previous ceremony, Mother had now burned into me a most intense and far-reaching sense of gratitude.

And she did it by floating me in peace and tranquility through the better nature of myself. She showed me how gratitude and tranquility hold the same space. In that, there is peace. And knowing one is never alone in that space elicits such a sense of balance and harmony within. To be there, complete within yourself as so much more than the ego-box's definition of self, is to know the flow of one's spirit, just like the flow of healing tears, just like the spirit of the waters.

But the night was far from over. Dawn was still three hours away. All throughout the passing hours, the shaman had been busy in the dark. He sang haunting icaros, played exotic instruments, and shook leaf-bundles while making the rounds to check on each one of us. He blew agua de florida, the shamanic cleansing spirit water in the direction of any psychic block or repetitive discomfort he detected.

It was an ongoing dance in the dark between his efforts to guide and assist us and our need to hold space or rush outside to purge. It had gone on like this for six hours but now was the time to begin reuniting us with ceremony space and each other. He relit the central fire. It was a very small fire but after merging with the depths of darkness that had cradled us for so long, any light seemed brilliant and supra-colorful. For those who could respond, he brought around liquid tobacco to snuff up.

When he came around to me, he playfully tapped my foot with his foot to get my attention. When I raised my head to see what was going on, there he was, bending towards me with his signature slight smile and an invitation not to be refused – "Tobacco?" Afterwards, he returned to his space and sat down cross-legged in his space and surveyed the scene with keen eyes and a slight smile of recognition for all we had and were going through – but even more so, for what was yet to come. One or two sat up and another propped up on an elbow to acknowledge him.

Then he started singing. Low and almost quiet at first, then increasingly stronger. His words were not in English, of course, but they were also not in Spanish. It was an Amazonian native song, ancient and suited to the moment. In contrast to the dark and silence that prevailed in the teepee only minutes before, his song combined with the dance of the central flames to blast our journeys into a present too expansive to be contained.

For over six hours I had maintained my breathing and my position. During that time, all I had between me and the hard ground was one half of a blanket. The other half I had pulled over me. Lying flat on my back with arms at my sides and legs never shifting or crossing was comfortable to begin with, and surprisingly comfortable for a long time while suffused with the feelings of peace and tranquility. But now, with the reality of the teepee spotlighted by the dance of the central flame and the shaman's song churning away at my awareness, I grew increasingly uncomfortable. I felt a need to roll on my side, to shift position.

But doing so was not as easy as wishing it. Any body movement seemed alien to me. I was not only out of my Pandora's Box, it seemed nowhere in sight. Strange how I could feel the discomfort but not the body. Strange how the idea of moving seemed redefined and no longer connected to the body. As the shaman's song intensified, so did the discomfort. I managed to roll my head and glance his way. It was true he was flashing me knowing glances but what did they mean? Was his energy and his song doing something to spur on this discomfort? It certainly seemed so but figuring it out drained away as the farthest thing from my mind. I needed to move and move I did, eventually. It took a few minutes but I managed to roll onto my right side. And that's when everything changed.

Never compare an Ayahuasca or Kambo purge to simple vomiting. They bear little resemblance to each other except something leaving the mouth is involved. With regular vomiting, expelling through the mouth pretty much sums it up. In ceremony, the physical component of purging is usually a minor component of what is happening. There are exceptions. There are people who simply feel bad and have to throw up immediately and little more is involved. But those are the same people who likely will be saying afterwards that not much happened during their ceremony.

For those who break through into an experience, on the other hand, purging is so much more. Many might say it is a critical component of why you are there. And purging can happen many ways. There are the obvious orifices to consider, but even prolonged and suspenseful bouts of breathing and yawning can be a type of purge. For me, when I rolled onto my side, the snap-need to purge roiled and seethed within like an anaconda being uncoiled. A helix mass of energy erupted in dizzying spirals, starting beneath my rib cage and whip-lashing against my insides with a pressure not to be denied.

I was the one disconnected from my body but now I had to move and move fast. The firelight was scant comfort as it guided me out of the teepee, but it was a big help. All night long I had heard others stumbling in blind desperation for the exit flap on their way to purgative glory. To have light as a guide became one of my new immediate gratitudes. Although, in the moment, I was in no state to meditate on it. I grappled to my feet like a new fawn finding its legs in a tornado. Luckily, I was next to the exit flap and had only to stumble forward to find the outside. But the outside I entered was nowhere near the outside I left so many hours before. Not by a long shot. Ever see something familiar to sight but every other instinct cries out with exotic and alien intuition? Ever open a door and not see what you expected? Ever fall through an open doorway into a déjà vu mystery imagined by your higher self? Ever be forced to run only to discover your legs aren't your own? Ever wish the anaconda inside of you would stop expanding as it catapults from your face?

I managed to stop forward motion in twisting space over uneven ground with legs cold-boiling into jelly springs. Repeated purges came from below the bottom of my feet, not my stomach. Some of them were dry heaves filled with unseen chunks of systematized chaos and institutionalized turmoil. In between spasms of release came waves of high vibration instability that rippled compressed emotion into my energetic body. I staggered back, slumped forward, and kept standing by leaning hands on knees. My gasps and sighs were another creature's drama, the last dreadful torments from an imaginary minion of Pandora's ego-box.

The anaconda was only the vehicle to get the minion out of me; it was not a beast to be feared. In Inca mythology, the snake represents the lower or underworld. It stands for wisdom and knowledge, the beginning of new life. Incas believed the snake travels to the underworld where it sheds its skin to return "newly born." And so the snake is the symbol of transformation, the fulfillment of the circle of life.

The spiraling of energies continued and rocked me forward into another purge episode, for purges rarely come as a single expulsion. This time it was mostly dry heaves, those bursts of unseen cosmic air filled with what no longer serves. I felt alternately hot and cold, here and there, now and then. The sense of being empty and full merged with the wish to be beyond and present. I don't know how I got back to standing in the grasses near the teepee. A few feet to the left of me was the entry flap, out of which poured dancing firelight in an oval shape radiating into an unfamiliar night. The teepee was just behind me. The otherworldly now just ahead.

An attempt to catch my breath got suddenly interrupted by gasps of surprise. I looked up into amazement. Out in the darkness, no more than twenty feet away, rested an object made of crystal-blue-white light. The translucent shape looked to be a place to sit, like a couch. On the far left side of the object sat a person. This person was made of the same crystal-blue-white light. It sat there, almost motionless, its head turned towards me with steady gaze. Except for being made of light, the object and the person was more real than my blanket back in the teepee. How could this be? I mean, what could it be?

I immediately tried to explain it away. It was simply light from the teepee shining on bushes in the distance. It was foggy-eye, a temporary aftereffect of the aggressive purging. It certainly couldn't be a person of light. And even if it was, why would it be sitting in that position, with head slightly turned to the left, a direct gaze held fast with little motion? There seemed no point to it except to show me how it's always possible to see light in the darkness.

At that moment the shaman started singing and banging a drum. The sound of it flooded out through the open teepee flap and enveloped the space around me. Coincidental or not, his song was the same one I had told him about a month before, after another ceremony. I commented how I liked it. It was the same song he had tried to teach everyone. He had them join in with him to sing it in the middle of the night. And now the light being's energy scintillated with the song's onset.

At first I thought it was just the dancing of the firelight coming from the teepee, but the rhythm of the changes sparking in the energy field matched the song, not the fire. At once, my feet began to move in a most unusual way. My ankles swiveled as if triple-jointed. My feet rocked every which way in time to the song. I felt as if a blissful, sacred energy from an ancient ceremonial space had taken over my feet. From knees down I was back somewhere else, at another ceremony held outside around a fire, and the spirit had also moved me back then to express the oneness with the emerging joy I felt.

It's interesting to note the Incas used one word "taqui" to describe dance, music, and singing. Although this word in Quechua means "song" – the Incas never separated the three, seeing them as intrinsically interconnected.

The light being persisted in place for many minutes. I considered walking over to it, coaxed by some vague notion of verifying its existence. But I didn't have the legs under me to navigate that far. And besides, I imagined it would fade with each step I might take in its direction. It had to be firelight on some bushes anyway. It would be easy to see the exact spot to prove the point when daylight came.

Exhausted, I returned to my blanket inside the teepee and collapsed with a post-purge energetic release. The shaman was letting the fire die down again and soon only the glow of reddened coals centered the space. I returned to my deep breathing but was too overwhelmed to engage in any activity like reciting gratitudes. I let my spirit go where it naturally flowed and assured my mind that it wasn't needed to get there. Random thoughts were inescapable and with them came other thoughts about the thoughts I had. One thing lead to another and soon I was ascending into another lesson – and a method.

For the next two hours, my thoughts wandered. Each time they wandered into troubling realms, the feeling of peace and tranquility showed me how to redirect my energies away from Fear or Drama or what Mother Ayahuasca at another ceremony called "Story." Every thought led to another and eventually I was shown how, left to my own thoughts – without the heart intervening – an over-analysis of mind would seek out the lowest common denominator, resulting in a habitual infusion of fear and drama and convoluted story back into my wonder and concern.

Over and over, a gentle nudge of spirit stirred me away from getting snared in a morass of negative thinking. Many times, I simply blanked my mind and started over with probabilities that led to positive outcomes. The technique was extremely subtle but tremendously powerful. It was as if the lightest breath of my intention could turn around a starship battle-cruiser headed at light speed for Armageddon. But unless one stayed aware and heart-centered, when and how to blow that healing breath could be missed. Miss it enough and one's mind came to the dramatic conclusion it didn't exist.

To stay aware, I needed to match my thoughts against the proper vibrations from my heart. A mismatch signaled a needed mid-course correction – a breath of spirit redirecting the flow away from the trap of fear and drama and story. It was startling how easy it was doing the most powerful thing. But even more startling was how easy it was believing such power couldn't exist. Again and again I was taken through examples of how easy it was to be distracted away from heart and into a blocked awareness focused only on pathways that slid into negativity – even when we didn't expect them to. Every thought I had became another example. I drifted towards a daydream state just above sleep. In daydreams healing finds a way to flow. This felt like flowing back to Source. And so I flowed.

As I flowed I found myself asking if I should return for a second ceremony, which was planned for the next day. Immediately, I heard a male voice abruptly say, "*No.*" This was jarring, not only to receive a no but to hear a male voice. Where had Mother Ayahuasca gone? This "*No*" made no sense. He gave no explanation and his tone seemed final. I let it go for a half hour or so while I rested and drifted, but it remained on my mind. And so later I asked again if I should return for the second ceremony. The male voice was adamant this time – "*No!*" It was certain from his tone he wasn't adding anything and so I let it go and didn't press the issue. There would be time to consider it later.

Dawn came and everyone rested for a couple more hours. The shaman closed the circle with more tobacco snuff and another one of his impromptu prayers.

Now it was time for the Kambo ceremony to begin. Those who felt called approached the shaman and received their points of venom. Having drunk the most water at the start of this second ceremony, I was the first to receive points. I hurried outside and spent the next hour and a half finishing the purges that Ayahuasca had started. Kambo works well with Ayahuasca. They say the medicine gives you the energy you need to get through ceremony and Kambo came through in that regard.

But I did notice, unlike previous times receiving the frog medicine, I found it difficult drinking the volume of water I needed during the hour and a half. But when it was finished, I felt cleansed and rejuvenated. Since I had fasted before arriving at ceremony space the day before, I was also famished. I headed out with friends for breakfast, after which there would be rest, reflection, and getting mentally ready for the next ceremony, planned for the following night.

But what about receiving, "*No*" twice? What was that about? And what about the space where the light being had appeared? I checked it out but daylight brought no resolution. In fact, it deepened the mystery. There were no bushes or trees where the being had sat and watched me. That place was an open space with nothing for the firelight to fall on.

The next night I returned to the shaman's house and soon discovered a cleaning circle on the back patio. Rough-cut Ayahuasca branches were heaped in a pile. Gathered around were soon-to-be ceremony participants industriously using spoons to scrape away the dirt and outer bark of the spirit vine in preparation for the long boil in the big cook pot nearby.

Even though I had been told not to come back, I hadn't heard it from Mother Ayahuasca. Plus, I was undaunted to try out the shaman's prescription of three ceremonies in rapid succession. I was determined not to let the indecision about coming and the "No's" from the male voice add any fear or drama to the way I approached the second ceremony. As far as I knew, it was a test to see if I could stir clear of such negative thinking. Just another example, like the countless ones handled before. If I had learned anything, I shouldn't let such things taint this second night in any way. And so I grabbed a spoon and started cleaning the Ayahuasca vines. I was going to participate and I was looking forward to it.

Everyone soon discovered just how energetic the teepee would be. Instead of eight participants like before, tonight there would be fifteen people in the teepee, including the shaman. The prospect of that many journeys going on simultaneously in such a confined space made one wonder. It would be a testament to the abilities of the shaman if, without helpers, such a collection of traveling souls could be held in good energy throughout the night.

And so, as before, we lit our flashlights and took the walk back to the clearing where the teepee stood. The threat of rain wasn't as severe as before, which was a plus. We all managed to squeeze our blankets and gear into personal slots facing the fire. The shaman tended it as before and repeated his reverent steps in preparation. Tobacco snuff and prayers, explanation of how things would process and answers for anyone's questions. By the time we drank the medicine it was 10pm and the night was deep and dark around us. The fire was brought low, then extinguished and fourteen participants awaited their journey.

As before, I started by lying on my back, taking deep, slow breaths, and reciting my gratitudes. And as before, I waited for the medicine to kick in, all the while I floated into a state of serenity and peace. Never knowing what might happen, I kept to my process and maintained position, breath, and recitations. When the night was half gone, the first six hours had repeated my experience from the first ceremony. I went deeper into gratitude.

I found the place of peace and tranquility within to be normal and not the exception. And I had deep compassion for the many others around me who struggled with cruel-sounding purges and breakdown episodes outside in the dark. The contrast of their anguish and the peaceful state drove so deeply into me. I had no way of comprehending what that particular juxtaposition was doing to me, but I felt it to be transformative.

After six hours of recitation in the dark amidst tranquility, Mother Ayahuasca began speaking to me as secondary lesson time began as before. Just like in the first ceremony, the next three hours were spent processing examples played out by my own mind. Again, it was a lesson about avoiding negative traps and staying with an uplifting flow that was heart-centered.

She showed me in the way my own mind operated how easily we can be tricked into spiraling down paths that at first seem so benign but ultimately ambush us with low vibration negative emotion. Last time the method to practice was the flow of intention breath to stir one away and back on course. This time she summed up the method in two words. With firm resolve she gave them to me – "*Recognize and Interrupt!*"

No matter what I thought, Mother showed how I could be tricked into letting it slide negative. And with the negative came negative emotion. And negative emotion was the internal quicksand linked to a bottomless pit that consumed one's potential and redefined the face of you. I kept being surprised how the most innocent thought always had a hook that could spiral down. I was shocked to be tricked into seeing how even the things we love can be turned and sent spiraling. There was no end to the ways we could fall prey to the downward slide. The best way to retrain ourselves to avoid the infinite space on either side of the tightrope was to "*Recognize and Interrupt!*" Recognize what was happening and immediately interrupt the process of mind and feeling that was being sucked down.

In time, Mother even echoed what San Pedro had told me in the past – that "*by fear and wounding they control you.*" Fear, drama, story, and especially wounding are all techniques of control. Mother showed me negative memes which are hidden in plain sight, subliminally buried in our entertainments and advertisements, that work on the subconscious to trigger the slide into negative quicksand. On the surface, it may look like one thing.

But in the background of intention and suggestion, the negative memes are being implanted. Like corrupting seeds, they lie there fallow in our minds until a situation calls them into our false intuition. We believe we are feeling our natural reaction, but it is only the response engineered to be triggered. To impress upon me how insidious they were, she droned them at me:

"*Us versus them.
"Nothing can be done.
"More is better.
"Bad things happen.
"Nothing is certain.
"Justice at all costs.
"I need what I want.
"Everything is separate*"

And the list went on and on. For every negative emotion possible within the human heart, there are dozens of memes ready to be a trigger. Memes can self-replicate, mutate, and respond to selective pressures. Memes act very much like viruses. We could even call them mind viruses. Mother Ayahuasca showed me how all the thousands of negative memes can be collapsed into two things – desire and a lack of concern for others. Be aware of these two always.

The goal of negativity, whether consciously engineered or not, is to short-circuit our natural flow to choose intentionally in each of life's situations and replace it with an unconscious reaction to subliminal negative memes to drive a reaction. The resulting negative assumptions and actions turn into belief over time and reprogram our ability to co-create. We start interacting with an artificial world instead of manifesting. As a result, spread over a populace affected by this negative energetic bombardment, society becomes reactive. The creative impulse gets redirected through negative programming and assumptions tied to our conditioned desires and needs instead of being a blooming of positive potential from our best aspirations and capabilities.

Assumptions are the hidden key to the power of our beliefs. Once assumed, our subconscious acts upon it as fact and the energy of this certainty manifests our reality like thought creating the path before a walker who imagines what the next step will be like, and so makes it so. Our natural, aligned state is one of heart consciousness. Doubt is a fear vibration that creeps into thought when belief is not completely aligned with our true self. Doubt is very powerful and damaging. Coherence is bringing things together in a state of logical, orderly, and aesthetic relationship; it sharpens or becomes more focused. Without the focus of heart-centered intention, there is nothing to prevent us from living our lives in reaction to negative memes we aren't even aware are acting as directors.

In the midst of all these examples, an odd thing started to occur. The lessons of recognize and interrupt spun on. All the while I began having crazy visuals of bizarre little creatures. Gobs of them kept popping up and filling my sight. Each time I was caught off guard and could only sum it up as strange, funny, outlandish, abnormal, extraordinary, weird, wacky, oddball, kooky, freaky, off the wall. They were the happiest of creatures but a bit too happy and knowing, if you can imagine that. I got the distinct sense they knew more about what was going on than I did.

Despite their friendly, happy-go-lucky attitude, something else belied more going on. It was something in the way their facial expressions and eyes gave them away. Once they were bicycling in the air. Next they were rowing rowboats vertically up trees. Another time they were riding impossibly-designed roller coasters. "*Weeee!*" they'd laugh with otherworldly glee. They'd always turn to look at me at the high point of their excitement, which after a while got a little creepy.

All of these little creatures looked the same except they were dressed with slight differences. Every place in the world became a wacky amusement park for their antics. When I thought they had crossed the line is when I shifted my lower back to get more comfortable. Little did I know my motion would release one of their rides – a ride inside of me. I looked down and there stretched out inside from pelvic bone up to high under my rib cage was a curved track. It formed a semi-circle resting against my spine.

On the track and held in place, awaiting release, was an equally curved boat with bow and stern as high points. The boat sat transverse to the track at the lower curved end by my pelvis. When I moved my lower back, the boat got released and slid fast, down and then up towards my neck. With the motion came an uproar of Weee's! and cheers and laughter from the little creatures. The chatter and noise erupted from my gut. I watched as their warped boat swung down and up and then back again into original locked position at my pelvis. They were all excited, stamping their feet and waving their arms as they cheered me on to do it again for them. "*Yeah! Yeah! Yeah!*"

The sight was so captivating and bizarre that, of course, I had to do it again. "*Weeee!*" and "*HaHahaha!*" and "Whoopee*!*" rose from my gut. It was the craziest thing imaginable but, like a wreck on the highway, it was hard to pull one's eyes away. It seemed such benign and crazy fun, why not do it again? And so I did it, again and again. Each time they went more berserk with enjoyment.

Then I realized with sudden panic what was happening. And yes, they were tricking me – just as Mother Ayahuasca had warned could happen, even with things we enjoy and love. I discovered their true intent not with any power of mind but simply when my stomach showed signs of needing to purge. But of course! How did I miss it?

The silly warped boat on the track was repeatedly shoving its momentum from pelvis to throat. Each run of the ride was getting me closer to having to purge. I stopped right away and took breaths to try to calm the urge. I felt so tired and jelly-legged that I dreaded having to make my wake into the dark outside. I didn't know if it was worthwhile but I had to give it a try. I appealed directly to Mother Ayahuasca. I assured her I would purge – in fact I wanted to purge, but dawn was only an hour away and I would prefer to purge at the jungle toilet in the light rather than up through the mouth outside now. Surprisingly, she answered me and said that would be all right and the urge immediately subsided. Later, the shaman was amused but incredulous with this episode. He chuckled at the notion of someone bargaining purge conditions with Mother. I didn't care. I had to try.

Several times, when the creatures were showing their widest grins and happiest demeanor, they would stare at me and their faces began to contort in horrific, exaggerated ways. Crazy-happy quickly morphed into frightful-menacing. I soon realized this was yet another, this time graphic example of how the nicest things, left to negative memes, could transform and spin us down into the negative before we knew it. I stayed alert to recognize and interrupt their contortions by diverting my gaze, changing my thoughts, and welcoming them back happy again.

In time, the little creatures scampered here and there but increasingly they fell into the background. Instead, I started asking Mother Ayahuasca questions – questions about what I liked to do, where to put my energies, what more her lessons may mean. She showed me how I had come full circle from my first ceremony with her 18 months before. She took me back to that first ceremony, filled with dark entities running the ceremony. I had felt trapped in another dimension with them and they knew it. I asked her about all the entities had said about getting so much enjoyment out of the pain of our purges. I even watched them shape-shift and collect the purges. Mother was as calm as before in answering:

"You saw dark entities collecting the purge. They liked it, they wanted more – it seemed to be their ceremony to do this, it appeared they were tricking people into anguish for their dark benefit. And all of that is true – but not the whole picture, for what is your truth now? The only thing they were collecting was every by-product of the healing of the medicine, a healing that got rid of things that don't serve you – and those things that don't serve you – all of that purging – they like that, so let them have it! What was really going on? The same thing you saw. But now the perspective is completely different. What you saw before was everything inverted from what it should be. Now you have inverted it back. There is no anguish in being healed. It's another example how you can be led down to the negative.

"Everything here can be an example of that illusion, how you're tricked into going into emotions that don't serve you. Sometimes we do it to ourselves and sometimes others do it do us. But now you know the power of recognize and interrupt, the power to steer clear with intention. Put that same peaceful and tranquil feeling into your days."

I asked more questions but she patiently answered, *"I answered that already. You can ask whatever you like, but the answers are going to be the same."*

I asked her if I should come back for the third ceremony. She gave me an insight, *"If you come back, it will be the same, just like now is the same as the last ceremony."* And then I understood why I heard the "No's" before – simply because for now there was no reason to come back. The answers and main lesson would be the same. I had come full circle from the fear and drama and story of 18 months ago. In that there was a completion – my first completion.

I thought about the illusion of my earlier perspective and how knowing Source was the opposite of that. Mother Ayahuasca bristled at the suggestion.

"*No! Source is not the flip side of anything. They in no way compare, even as opposites! Don't ever compare one to the other – Source just IS. There is nothing else you can say about Source! It exists! It is!*"

She was very adamant about this.
I thought about the Kambo ceremony to come as the first light of day began to show through the top opening in the teepee. Mother spoke once again, "*You've made progress, from there to here. You don't need any more medicine right now.*" I couldn't help but telling her about the shaman's prescription for three ceremonies in a row. There was no pause when she answered, "*You were here last month, then we met again at the San Pedro ceremony, and now these two ceremonies. Four ceremonies. You can keeping repeating if you want to but for right now – you're done.*"
I asked to clarify, "No more medicine?"

She repeated, "*For right now – you're done.*"

The following morning I woke very earlier in my bed back where my wife and I were staying when I was not in ceremony. My wife was still asleep but I felt one of those otherworldly urges to get outside, close to nature. It didn't matter that the sky was totally dark with rain clouds. Outside, the rain came down. It reminded me of the sound of rain on the teepee during the ceremonies. I dressed quickly and made my way down a path to a covered lookout point. I climbed into one of the hammocks and enjoyed the call of the morning birds and the continuing cool shower.
Then it happened. Right before my eyes. Within a minute of me coming to rest in the hammock, brimming with peaceful, tranquil feelings – it was then the clouds parted and a perfect rainbow appeared before me. I felt an overwhelming sense of someone's presence, of someone's caring, of someone's assurance that it is possible to take the lessons and methods for healing into our daily lives.
As a parting gift, Mother Ayahuasca or Source or Spirit or whatever name you give it, took me to a place inside that matched the deepest joy of ceremony space. The message that morning was – such joy is not meant only for ceremonies. It's meant to be with us all the time. Of course the whole episode caused a rush of tears. But that was OK. As I was told, "*Don't wipe those away. Those are healing essential oils. Rub them on you. Take them in.*" And so I did. And so I do.
Days later, while talking to my wife, I mentioned the "*No!*" I had received from the male voice. It was so odd that it was that voice and not

Mother Ayahuasca that answered. My wife's intuition made a suggestion right away – the voice was Grandfather San Pedro. Just as Mother had shown up at his ceremony, he had answered at the end of hers. It's remarkable how the spirits of the medicine complement each other, even if we can only guess the depths of the relationship.

Some time afterwards while still feeling I was in the medicine, the bus I was riding in paused in traffic. I turned to glance outside. There I found my face staring back at me from a rainy block wall. Behind the glasses I saw peace and tranquility and a new sense of connecting with myself and others. It may have taken 18 months and epic travails to reach my first completion – but I wouldn't have missed it for the world. I have the utmost gratitude I can now say that. I wish the same for others. Meanwhile, I can only imagine, with positive intentions, what my second completion will possibly be. Whatever it is, I'm flowing towards it.

THE TRANCE IN THE DANCER

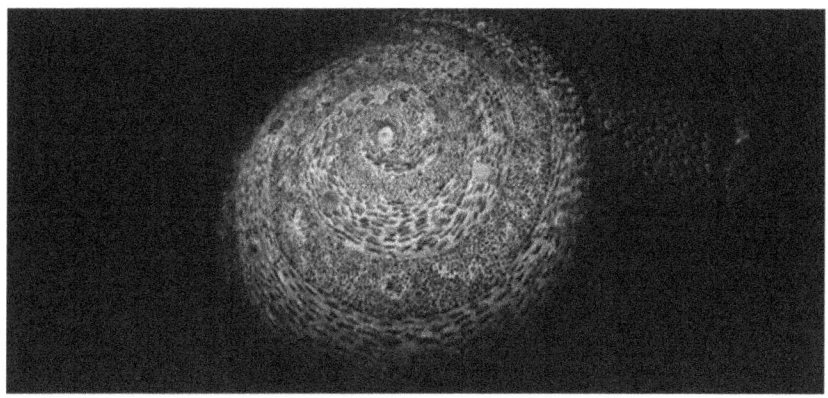

To complete an arrival is to begin an experience.

Eighteen months of travails had changed my life. I had gone so very far only to find myself back at myself. And yet the view afforded by that arrival was different. All journeys have that effect, I suppose. Medicine journeys in particular. Whatever completion had settled within me was unexpectedly open-ended. One assumes a completion is a closed door not an opening one. Increasingly after medicine ceremonies, I started having lucid dreams, dreams of a different character than ever before. They seemed to be guiding me through that open door, but to what?

No doubt I would continue to move forward. But it became clear. The changes steadily expanding within me guaranteed momentum like no other. A new attitude swept inertia from personal action. A new perspective broadened positive impacts from my surroundings. Now there was a promise to blaze trails in ways I never had seen for myself before. I arrived at new potentials with a fresh frame of mind and reliance on heart. I was ready to make the most of it. However, in my naiveté in dealing with the full range of what medicine space offered, I had no idea how much could be contained in "most."

There is an arduous San Pedro ceremony practiced in some parts of South America. After hearing about this way of approaching the medicine, I understand why not many would want to participate. It lasts all night and requires a level of physical commitment and force of will not meant for many. I have not yet had the chance to go to such a ceremony but I see how the intentions behind this ritual highlight the potentials I faced after overcoming my fears and returning to Mother Ayahuasca.

The ceremony begins in the afternoon when participants paint individual flags. On the flags the shaman instructs them to paint two things: what they wish to get rid of and what they wish to achieve or acquire in their future selves. When evening comes, the ceremony begins with the burning of these painted flags in a central fire. Into that fire also goes a fetus of a llama. In some countries, particularly in Peru, including a llama fetus in ceremonies as an offering is considered good mojo leading to positive outcomes. I imagine this originates with the Incas if not cultures before them. The Incas sacrificed llamas to the gods, most dramatically at the Condor Temple at Machu Picchu. To this day, vestiges of the practice survive. In mercados one can find a llama fetus to buy, typically to hang under one's house or building project for luck.

This ritual with the fire is but the beginning of the ceremony. After the participants drink San Pedro, the shaman instructs them to start walking clockwise around the fire. As the darkness of night deepens, the march around the fire continues with drumming and the occasional icaro. In fact, the walking continues half the night, without stopping. Those who must are allowed to pull themselves out of the walking circle briefly to purge or catch their breath but the expectation is such a thing is kept to a minimum. The goal is no interruption. As the shaman explains, walking clockwise winds the energies present into the Earth, sending them to the underworld. The idea is to wind into the underworld all the things we want to get rid of, the same things everyone painted on the now burnt flags.

Halfway through the night, the shaman calls for the walking direction to reverse. Now everyone must walk the rest of the night counter-clockwise. By doing so, the idea is to wind the energies present into the sky, to Viracocha, the great creator deity. This becomes an active meditation to manifest everything the participants wish to achieve or acquire in their future selves. Through this whole process, no matter the direction of motion, it's inescapable some level of trance state will be reached and maintained.

The trance that ensues suffuses normal awareness to the point where the conscious and unconscious, the here and now and everything in between is superseded by a journey, a torment, a rapture. People react many ways to this. Some leave space and time, some leave their bodies, some shape-shift into their spirit animals, some collapse in high-energy, emotional release states that resemble possession. It doesn't matter. The imperative remains: keep the circle moving. For half the night, wind everything we don't want downwards. And now, don't stop winding everything we do want upwards. Everything revolves around the fire, the only thing to stay stationary, the still point, the nexus, prime focus.

Close to morning, just as the sky begins lightening enough to signal night is nearly over, the shaman instructs everyone to dance. Dance freely.

Dance in place or dance away and back. Dance facing the embers of the fading fire. Dance facing east. Dance at the arrival. After spending the entire night in motion, for participants this is the final and most taxing request to be made of them. And yet it's infinitely freeing and transformative at the same time. They discover how a dance before the power of the rising sun not only completes the night, it completes their trance state.

Their completion is an arrival at an experience. It's a revelation, a transcendence born from arduous trials and medicine-induced stamina. It's born from pushing oneself beyond what one never believed could be done. It's the bliss of surviving the otherworldly depths of one's own total release from oneself, from what is no longer needed, and just as importantly and surprisingly, from everything they thought they wanted. In the end, it's knowing why the flags were burned. It's laughter and joy. It's seeing the morning sun sear the night away. It's what they came for. It's personal daylight.

In many ways for eighteen months I trudged clockwise, winding my demons and distorted past down and away from me. That dark night of the soul had deepened along the way but my fire never went out. When I finally returned to Mother Ayahuasca and found in her for the first time a gentle and wise guide amidst the harsh experiences of change, the medicine had me change direction. She let me know I was ready. Now I could wind my energies the other way, to the sky, to open possibilities as wide as creation itself.

There was still a long way to go to get through the night of my metamorphosis. Curiously enough, I continued even though there was no telling if such a thing could ever complete. What if the second half of my night, the winding up, was without end? Was the open-endlessness inherent, by design? We were a journey, not a destination? Only one thing seemed sure – it would never do me any good to concentrate on the goal, that dance before the rising sun until the sky lightened. More than that, perhaps it would do me no good to see it as a goal at all. The medicine reminded me, never get lost in anything before its time, and when it's time, never get lost at all.

Whether or not there really was a chance of getting to my sunrise, that place where the whole trance seemed to be going, I had to keep winding my energies upwards. That wasn't a goal; that was life. And seeing life that way appeared to be a glorious glide, not a pursuit. But as one might suspect, I was about to find that winding up takes the same if not more energy and commitment than winding down. Especially if one attempts it after the trials of winding down. It didn't matter that winding up was all about the positives we wished to discover and manifest. Ultimately, I moved forward not knowing what to call it, and this was just as the medicines would have it.

As the Tao Te Ching says – "*Above, it is not bright. Below, it is not dark. Unraveled, it cannot be given any name.*"

By The River, Spikes Into Elsewhere

Once contacted, plant spirits stay with you. If you are open to the connection. A constant need for the medicine is far from the true, ongoing experience. Altered-state meditative whispers from Grandfather San Pedro and Mother Ayahuasca linger long after the ceremonial fire has become earthen ash. But now and then, the call for a closer dialogue, a deeper heart-to-heart with the plant teachers appears. The sense of it is not unlike the emotive release and wistful reflection given to the anticipation of a visit with distant family members.

The prospect of microdosing the San Pedro medicine as a means to connect with Grandfather was intriguing to me but I was not convinced. The idea of almost connecting, having nearly a journey, a little bit into spirit space, if that's what we're talking about, didn't seem promising. Who wants to call a dear relative and attempt a conversation over a bad connection? Who wants to journey to spectacular-spectacular and be content with a black-and-white 2D view? Would a little bit of medicine be effective? Maybe some things couldn't be phased that way. You don't risk the rocket ride for a sub-orbital flight. Deep experiences are only achieved with escape velocity. Is this true? I wanted to find out.

My first microdose was alongside a river in an urban setting with my wife holding the space for me and not microdosing. In any setting but especially an urban one, it is always advised to have someone in attendance who takes no medicine and is prepared for contingencies. I was told that eight capsules was a full ceremonial dose, so I took two capsules and lay down under a canopy of breeze-blown trees and listened to the rushing waters. Over the next half hour I calmed, became more relaxed, and felt more meditative. Other than that, I felt nothing out of the ordinary. Soon, the reverie expanded to include all the wondrous aspects of nature surrounding me. The trees were not only alive, but conscious. The river was not only flowing, but progressing with a presence and pneuma that was animated beyond the physical.

I turned on my side to daydream on the mesmerizing cascade. My spirit shared the space with mind. And as mind drifted, always busy, forever processing, a slide into a quick thought pulled my focus. I wondered if I was too close to the edge and might, at any moment, lose my sense of balance and fall over the river's bank, down several feet to the water and rocks below. Instantly, a telepathic presence intervened. A past lesson expanded throughout mind – *"Recognize and interrupt. Why go there? Why anticipate the worse and dwell on fears? No fear! No drama!"*

Surrounded by such beauty, there was no need for such thoughts. I was fine. I was safe. Instead of conjuring up dark hypotheticals and worrisome probabilities, I could merge with conscious nature forever all around. This was my first indication that Grandfather was near.

Looking up from the rushing waters, my gaze swept the tall trees. They seemed to wave to me. They appeared playful. They were overjoyed that I now was able to notice them, truly notice them. Like a kindred spirit being welcomed back into a loving fold, I was welcomed by their swaying branches, by the glowing grasses, by the fragrant flowers.

Soon, the grinding of mind faded into the background. I turned onto my back and let my upward gaze flood with motions and colors, all from nature. As I did, I felt heavier once again, more in my body, back to a place of normal. It had been a slight slide into the medicine, a soft overture of what was to come. The sun's position was shifting and would soon leave me without shade. I got up and found another spot to lie down farther along the river bank.

In time, I closed my eyes and concentrated on all the present gratitudes I could express. In and out I pulled deep, slow breaths. It seemed all effects of the medicine had lifted. Now I was simply meditating. Once again I was merely calm, peaceful, relaxed. Once again I noted the passage of time as something that existed. I checked to see what time it was. The fact that I gave any credence to time existing was a sure sign I had left medicine space. But at some low level, the medicine was maintaining an open channel.

With eyes closed, sounds took on new significance. City streets and passing traffic were close by, as was a walking path where locals passed. I was about to encounter my first spike into elsewhere. It began when simultaneously I floated away and city sounds faded into a feathery silence. My senses were vastly augmented and yet they perceived nothing – at first. Then, like a movie fading in, a panorama opened up behind my closed eyes.

I was blazing a trail near the summit of a lofty, rounded peak, somewhere in foreign, resplendent mountains. I was not watching this. I was there. A clear, fresh breeze swept past me as I stepped in view of the summit. Right away, a solitary figure caught my eye. He was a cacao-dark-skinned man, mid-40's, strong and vital with a shock of black hair and a broad smile pointed in my direction.

His clothes were finely crafted but home-made. He worn sandals, pants, and a rough-hewn slip-over shirt with leather-lace ties dangling loose from an open V-neck. His arms were open in welcome. He slowly stepped towards me. He was all warmth, love, and enjoyment of the moment. His eyes sparkled with clear sight and a generous sense of humor. I felt instantly this was Grandfather.

He was as much amused as lovingly delighted with my arrival.

"*You made it!*" he shouted over the wind gusts.

"*You're at the top* –" he swept his hands wider to each side.

"*As you see, there's nothing here. No lessons. No great thing to possess. Nothing to do* –" His gaze favored one side to consider the open spaces and the nearby drops into deep valleys.

His smile widened, "*Nothing to do but fly!*"

I stopped a few feet from him, amazed at the encounter and taking in the expansive 360-view. Nearby were drops of thousands of feet into valleys shrouded in mists and shadow. The sun was halfway down in the west. Across the valleys, other distant peaks rose to our level. The ridge lines and slopes were carpeted in browns and greens. In places, small white lines indicated gigantic waterfalls in the distance.

Grandfather was in the best of humor. He was overjoyed and amused, filled with friendship and love, but strong in what was true in the moment. He tilted his head a little and considered me.

"*Nothing to do up here but fly – but not for you today – you don't have your wings on.*"

He gave his head a little shake and chuckled with high spirits mixed with compassion.

"*What the fuck! A bird that's afraid of heights!? What's with that!?*"

His chuckle erupted into a short laugh. His demeanor was accepting, supportive, encouraging, and non-judgmental. He wanted nothing but the best for me. He knew what I was capable of – what everyone was capable of. It was another healing, the melting away of another layer of fear and self-doubt. He was the coach, the father who knew how to motivate one into their best. He drew closer with invigorated purpose.

"*Today you can't fly – but we can simulate something...*"

Immediately, the scene changed. I was no longer on the mountain top. I was soaring over a meadow of tall grasses, wildflowers, and golden shimmers through the shady branches of nearby tall trees. My POV was that of a bird flying fast and low over a verdant field. If this was only a simulation, I gasped at what the real thing must be like. My initial shock at entering the frame at full speed subsided and I relaxed into the sense of it. And just as the relaxation filled me, the meadow opened up into a straightaway void of trees where maximum speed could be applied. Inches above the waving tall grasses and flowers, I shot forward, picking up speed.

And then it happened. The bottom dropped out. The grassy field ended. I had abruptly reached the edge of a cliff. Suddenly, at top speed, I shot out over the edge. A drop-off thousands of feet lay below me. The great valley depressions sank away into the mists and shadows. I was no longer low over a field. Instantly I was soaring at a great height. The shock of it took my breath away. I froze my wings in place in reflex. Grandfather's simulation had fooled me into confronting great heights. His words echoed back to me – "*What the fuck! A bird that's afraid of heights!? What's with that?!*"

There was no turning back. I was zooming forward through a vast expanse of open sky with the nearest patch of Earth a mile below. I felt the rush of air. I sensed the slight changes in my physical attitude as the horizon line shifted higher to one side, then the other. I maintained a locked, fully open position of my wings.

Then Grandfather's elated whisper was heard.

"*Hold perfectly still and feel how fast you can go!*" He wanted me to entrain the feeling, to make it beyond second nature. It was my nature. All I needed to do was realize what once was, what always was.

He whispered again, "*You can go so fast, so far, and be so still!*" My trajectory was angled slightly down. The distant peaks were gaining in altitude over me. I was heading for the shadows.

Grandfather added, "*The slightest movement changes everything!*" The simulation took over and changed the bend of my wings. I felt slightly greater wind resistance – but now, ever so slowly, I was climbing.

"*Remember – the slightest movement.*" Another slight change was added – one wing curled up at the tip. Immediately, my slight climb began curving ever so slowly to one side.

I felt Grandfather give me total control of the simulation. I returned to the locked and fully open wing position. Again I wanted to be perfectly still yet feel all at once incredible speed. The seeming paradox was not lost on me. The fact that through my experience I was resolving the paradox, in fact seeing how to use the paradox to soar, and in doing so, gaining a widening perspective of all that was possible, it left me in wonder and awe.

I felt there was more to this I needed to grasp. But the rush of it was overpowering. I could not reflect. I simply needed to be.

But the desire to understand got in the way of letting go. The scene quickly faded. I was once again behind closed eyes. The feathery silence faded. City sounds returned from far away. I was back along the river like a kindred spirit being welcomed back into a loving fold by swaying branches, glowing grasses, and waving flowers. I felt heavier once again, more in my body, back to a place of normal. It seemed all effects of the medicine had lifted. Now I was simply meditating. Once again I was merely calm, peaceful, relaxed. Once again I noted the passage of time. I checked the time. The entire spike had lasted ten to twenty minutes even though it felt timeless.

There was a long stretch of deep meditation, then soothing relaxation but little else. I remained quiet and focused on nature and my deep, slow breathing. Nearly a half hour passed before I felt a need to settle back and close my eyes again. This time the spike began with a profound sense of floating. At first I couldn't tell in which direction, then it was clear I was settling down somewhere. The lower I floated, the more the next setting faded into view.

Now a tiny feather from a bird, I floated down and landed in the middle of the rushing river. Right away I was swept along in the current. Up and down and around rocks I surged forward. In time, I felt myself merge with the river in a way that I had become the river and was no longer a feather. There was nothing but the energy, the enthusiasm, the spirit presence of being complete in advancing the flow. The flow was fun, the flow was a dance, the flow was all. The spirit of the waters rushed forward. As it did, a moment of mind poked in, considering the destination of its flow. If I was a river, all rivers come to an end.

Immediately, a telepathic presence intervened. A past lesson expanded throughout mind – recognize and interrupt. I shot straight up, away from the river. I was the bird again. My vantage point was climbing ever higher as I followed the flow of the river. I could immediately see where the river was going. It seemed obvious that all rivers come to an end.

Then Grandfather's voice returned. "*It doesn't end! It becomes so much more!*"

I locked wings and held perfectly still. I felt my speed quicken. I was nearly at the river's delta. There it merged with a gigantic ocean. Without moving a wing, I shot forward, out over the ocean. The endless waters wrapped over the far horizon. I was astounded at the immensity of it all. Around me was endless sky, boundless waters. With such a view, none of my tremendous speed could be detected. It was as if I was in a state of suspended animation, going everywhere at once, without moving.

The scene quickly faded. I was once again behind closed eyes. The feathery silence faded. City sounds returned from far away. I was back along the river like a kindred spirit being welcomed back into a loving fold by swaying branches, glowing grasses, and waving flowers. I was heavier, more in my body, back to a place of normal. I was simply meditating. Once again I was calm, peaceful, relaxed. Once again I noted the passage of time. I checked the time. The entire spike had lasted ten to twenty minutes. It felt timeless.

I relaxed in place for a while afterwards, still feeling a conscious communion with nature around me. It was getting to be mid-afternoon and a chilly wind was blowing out of the east. My wife and I decided to head home. The walk back through city streets seemed to be the real, otherworldly place. I could easily function and navigate crooked sidewalks and dashes across streets in between traffic. We even stopped at a bakery on the way home to purchase some rolls and coffee cake.

I felt I could have stayed a bit longer in the medicine but it was easy to suppress it at that point. The effects were quickly winding down. And so my initial foray into microdosing came to an end. I had wondered if the experience would be short and not very deep. What I encountered was two hours of deep meditation punctuated by deep spikes into journey-space that lasted minutes each time. The duration of the spikes isn't the important thing. It was either the depths or the heights they reached that really took me by surprise.

Who knew I would encounter Grandfather face-to-face. Who could have guessed that such visuals and journeying could happen on a fraction of a full dose. Far from being a mild experience, I found microdosing San Pedro an equally profound way of reaching ceremony space levels. In ceremony, I would be at these spike levels for hours at a time, not minutes – but since the passage of time doesn't exist while you're with Grandfather, it isn't a problem. With the medicine, a long journey can happen in minutes or seconds, just as assuredly as in hours. A change of heart takes no time at all.

"The slightest movement changes everything!"

Bliss Or Amnesia In Aviation Ground School

My first microdosing experience with San Pedro lasted a couple hours instead of the typical eight to ten hours of a full ceremony. And yet, the benefits of my shorter visit with Grandfather had still been profound, surprisingly so. Within the two hours spent lying on a river bank, the microdose produced spikes of deep journeying with unique visualizations. For example, never before had I actually seen San Pedro during an encounter. To finally see him for the first time during any session, full ceremony or microdose, signaled something significant to me.

Two months prior I had gotten the message from Mother Ayahuasca that I was "done for now" and should not participate in a planned third ceremony. For two months I respected that prescription and concentrated on drawing the many lessons received into my daily life. But I did not participate in any more plant medicine ceremonies. After two months, I felt a small whisper, an inkling of something, an overture to so much more.

A San Pedro microdose, I felt, would be a respectful way to go to the edge of full ceremony space to see if I was welcomed back by my plant spirit teachers. The intense visualizations I encountered were a definite, positive sign. I felt my respectful, mild return to the medicine was strongly validated as a good decision. Moreover, something was being initiated in a way that prompted me to seek out a deeper connection to the medicine.

Although the two major spikes during microdosing lasted only ten to twenty minutes, within them were timeless encounters far from the place in nature where I rested. I walked away from that experience with a deep sense that Grandfather had opened a door for me. New realms were there for me to explore, if only I had the will, the presence of grateful intention, and the openness of heart to make it so. To go any farther, though – a full ceremony was in order. To go farther, more work would need to be done. As Grandfather had admonished with a chuckle – "*A bird that's afraid of heights?! What's with that?!*"

On a bright morning I boarded a bus for an hour-long trip south of where I live. I entered a beautiful valley and joined others for a ceremony that started at 10am. All of us had a dose of the medicine large enough to keep us in sacred medicine space until a bright moon shined overhead around 8pm. Seven of us drank the medicine that morning while the warm equatorial sun beat down and a soft breeze chased puffs of clouds over the distant panoply of colorful mountains. We each found our individual places on the property when the silent call to journey became strong enough to silence the group into meditation.

As is customary with my visits with Grandfather, my expanding instinct was to find a most uncomfortable spot to lie down on. A sign that my journey was about to deeply begin was when the uncomfortable spot melted into something cozy and most pleasant. Since I'd done ceremonies at this retreat center before, I presumed I already knew my favorite uncomfortable spot. It was a slab of rough textured concrete bordering a shady side of the house. And so I laid down, closed my eyes, started my usual deep, slow breathing, then focused on all the gratitudes that filled my life. I was ready to float away into the space where Grandfather had appeared to me the last time we spoke.

But Grandfather, as is often the case, surprised with something new, something discerning in revelation into oneself. One of my gratitudes involved all of the beautiful nature around me. As is usual in medicine space, one of my intentions was to connect with nature, become one with nature and encounter the individual trees and flowers around me as conscious expressions of Source energy. Grandfather shook up my reverie on this and instructed me to stand up. I did so only to find I was being directed to a whole different section of the property, a place where I had not spent time in the medicine before.

I knew right away I needed to go among the citrus trees and thin grasses. There I should lie down – there where hot filtered sunlight danced with shadows. There where the intermittent roar and bumping of trucks and buses and their gasping air brakes could not be avoided. There were the pulse of Latin beats from passing car windows mixed with the crow of roosters and the plaintive cries of the Pacific Hornero and shouts of neighboring farmers far off in their fields.

I laid down without blanket or padding, without consideration for insects or the rocks or rotting fruit scattered around. None of it mattered. I would be all right. I was certain of it in a way only Grandfather could convey. I needed to lie flat and touch the earth, touch it fully, as much as I could. I needed to be close enough to the grasses that my face could turn into them. I needed to be surrounded by the raw nature I said I wanted to connect to.

And I fully intended to connect in the way I usually did. But that was not meant to be. Grandfather made sure of it. He was about to bring it home in an overpowering lesson that shook me to my core while it unfolded upon so much more. It was to be an intense initiation, one I would struggle to cope with. One that would overwhelm me for the next four hours – and lingers in my soul even now.

Always in the past when experiencing plant medicines, I would see nature around me transform. It would glow, become iridescent, awaken with a consciousness that communicated directly with me. Tall trees by the river bank would joyously wave hello. The individual blades of grass would wiggle in delight as they turned their attention to me. Bushes and flowers and plants galore would acknowledge me, even speak to me and send loving feelings my way. It was a standard practice, a ritualistic truism that nature would transform like this once I was in the medicine space.

But down among the citrus trees, lying flat with my head turned sideways for a gaze into the sunlit grasses, I was about to embark on the most disturbing, challenging, the most terrifyingly energetic experience of my life. It started with all the trappings of nature around me transforming as I expected. The grasses at eye-level glowed iridescent and the dance of shadows from the trees above me conveyed a conscious joy at me noticing them noticing me. As always, it was as if a veil was lifting to reveal a stage full of happy actors, all playing their part in the grand cosmic wonderment called creation. But then, just as feeling gelled in place, Grandfather interrupted the reverie. He was frank, succinct, powerfully serious but with loving concern.

He whispered, "*You think this is connecting with nature?*"

He let me consider the question for a minute before adding, "*This is not connection.*"

Another minute lengthened into eternity. Like a drip of hesitant honey falling into fire, all sense of time faded away, leaving behind a hypnotic now. I felt a strange sensation, a lightness of spirit all the while my senses sharpened. I was hyper-aware of every aspect of the ground, the grasses, the buzz of insects, the rock pressing against my shoulder blade, the shifting leaves above me.

Finally, Grandfather's voice returned. It was no longer in whisper. Loud and clear he announced with the firm gravitas of the ages, "*I'll show you connection...!*"

What happened next began with full-on awe. It was most disorientating. Then it dialed-up an intensity that took me out of body while at the same time I was amazingly present with hyper-aware senses. It surpassed any concept of overwhelming. Another veil lifted, but this was nothing like and nowhere near the stage and actors of nature's creation I had imagined before. This was above the whole theater. This had left the sky even as a zillion impressions of life coalesced on my awareness. Blindingly clear, I was primal feeling as much as Source action. I was completion as much as infinite process. I was soul death as much as ongoing birth. I was forever disappearing as much as becoming infinitely more. Everything was the same and everything was different. My eyes locked open in total amazement.

I entered a fugue state of rapturous disbelief – a total disbelief that I knew all of this so well, even as I shuddered and shook with an overload of energy received, an energy that needed no belief to exist in the truth. Incredibly, I was no longer looking at nature around me. I was no longer feeling its presence. The dawning truth shined golden everywhere and the light of it was the light of me. I looked out but was feeling myself in what I saw.

Looking at myself, sensing myself in every motion around me reverberated through me as joy. I was the nature I had tried to connect to. There was nothing but me even as the me I knew melted away in the heat of golden bliss. By being myself, by awakening to it, I was the many and the one, the always was. But it didn't end there. The most startling part, the experience I couldn't cope with – was yet to come.

Time made no sense. I don't know how long I shook and shivered on the ground, staring into unity, falling into Source, shaking uncontrollably as the feeling of total joy bathed me in my awakening essence. The knowledge crystallized at my core – how utterly, stupidly foolish to think that saying hello to trees and talking to flowers constituted a connection to nature! The difference of that with true connection was not even orders of magnitude greater – there was and could be no measurement for how dissimilar the two really were.

Awakening to being one with all around me, to feeling it, to being it, wasn't the worst part of not being able to cope. The worse part was trying to handle the energy-rush of rapt soul-pleasure vibrating in that pool of beatific wholeness. I couldn't handle it. It was too much. I was drowning in ecstasy. I was buzzing with infinite volts. It was too much joy, too much love, too much sense of home, family, belonging, completion.

Grandfather let me shiver and shake with the overload for quite a while.

Then he whispered, "*If you want to fly with me – you're going to have to learn how to accept ecstasy.*"

He paused and the feeling intensified even more as he added, "*You're going to have to learn how to accept love. Ecstasy and love – they're the same.*" The odyssey of the four-hour lesson had just begun.

I had hoped that the simulation of flight shown to me in the microdosing experience might be extended and enhanced into real flight in a full ceremony. But there was no way I was flying today. It was certain as I shivered and shook in place, lying on my back and twisting onto my side – flight with Grandfather was not possible until I completed his ground school. And the hardest lesson was the first lesson – be comfortable with the ecstasy that waking up to all oneself entails. Once you wake up, all of it becomes you and energetic limiters are gone. It was made clear – I couldn't be overwhelmed and fly.

Grandfather kept me in that space – that extreme flow of energy, that ultimate intensity of ecstasy. He wouldn't let me shut down. Far from it, he coaxed me to open up more, to let go and allow more in. He repeatedly implored me with his whispers to, "*Wake Up!*" A lucent understanding expanded as shimmering awareness – I was in a self-imposed coma and was dreaming my limitations.

"*WAKE UP! You've been in a place where it's possible to disinvent love. You have the amnesia of the belief and ideas of that place. Wake up and return to who you are!*"

I was beside myself in astonishment and perplexing perspectives. I was stunned with ecstasy and couldn't imagine why there would ever be a place where disinventing love was even a possibility. Grandfather spun my perceptions so fast that all their boundaries flew off and disintegrated. I merged with an infinite creation that included all infinities of possible options – one being a place where love could be disinvented.

In the oneness, the ecstasy, the love, was an intelligence I couldn't fathom because I hadn't fully let go and woken up. But as far as I was able to manage, I was becoming one with an infinite creation containing all possibilities. Resplendent in that view was the understanding that infinite creation explores the fractal depths of all of it, every single probability in its fullest expression. In doing so, it finds even more ecstasy in the playful adventure, the joyful journey, the surprising discovery of even more infinities contained within itself.

But creation cannot truly explore a possibility where love can be disinvented unless it goes there with a solid amnesia of its true nature. Otherwise it wouldn't work. Whatever possibilities it explores has to be totally real in order to explore it. And so, one can only explore and understand some realms by going into the game of amnesia where one truly believes and the rules of those realms exist for all creation, even if they don't. They exist for real and don't exist for real simultaneously. It's the ultimate suspension of disbelief, the grand game within the cosmic play, all in order to have the experience.

Grandfather was adamant and very insistent – part of the infinity of possibilities of creation was making the game so real that it became possible for one to get lost in it and couldn't get out. Some infinities resulted in realms where one could go down the rabbit hole and never escape the game, never wake up from the journey, never reunite with the overarching Source energy of love. Since creation contains all possibilities, these realms will always exist and Source energy will always flow in and through them.

But Grandfather made it absolutely clear – the only way one escaped from those realms of amnesia necessary for proper exploration was to hang onto love – love was the only lifeline, the only thing real in these realms, the one thing we could trust to lead us back out of the rabbit hole to the full measure of who we are. Again he shot me through-and-through with more ecstasy, like an EMT applying electrically-charged paddles to an emergency room patient whose heart had stopped beating.

Again and again the charge of ecstasy jolted me into flashes of soul-Source consciousness, "*WAKE UP! You've been in a place where it's possible to disinvent love. You have the amnesia of the belief and ideas of that place. Wake up and return to who you are!*"

The machinations of my mind raced with all that was happening. A million questions flooded my mental space, even if that mental space seemed now separate from who and where I was. The questions wouldn't stop – why would anyone want to play such a game – what was the point to all of it? Grandfather gathered up the totality of my mind, my mental space and showed it to me, away from me, as just another part of the rabbit hole, another part of what kept me in the amnesia.

"*Let that go!*" he ordered. "*All your questions, all need for what you think is meaning and purpose and a final explanation for the universe – let it go! All of it is just another way the amnesia keeps you spinning within the drama of forgetfulness. When you wake up, you take none of that with you!*"

In that moment, I felt a state of being where all our thoughts, our questions, our philosophies, our need for answers and purpose spiral down from reality and evaporate. All of it is a symptom of the amnesia we can choose to awaken from. But it's our choice. For those who want to stay within the experience of the realms where love can be disinvented, that energy can cycle in there forever if we wish. The key is – we don't have to. It's as easy as waking up. But to wake up fully, we need to be able to exist in the state of completeness, of unity, of unbounded ecstasy – the other name for love, and realize that everything real is contained there.

It's as easy as waking up – but easy can be the hardest option when the snares of experience have one convinced it must be another way. This place convinces us – nothing is that simple. Nothing is that complete and joyful. After all, what is the dream and what is wakefulness? When both are equally real, there can be no difference. No way is it possible to simply become the ecstasy we always were and always will be. Perhaps that happy place is the dream, the coma, the snare of forgetfulness. The place where love disappears is so real. There can be no way to conceive there's a way it's not.

But what if it had to be that way to experience it – to experience everything in ourselves, an infinity of creative options forever finding the expanding depths of itself. One of those options is the one and the many. Yes, maybe everything is one, but another possibility of creation is the one separating into an infinity of individuals. Each one of the infinite-many explores all the possible options individually, eternally unfolding onto more. The creative possibilities of infinite perspectives from the Source also had to be explored. Explored in their separate reality, even if the many is still the one. Until I got a glimpse and feeling of the infinity and creation I was, unless I knew to my core the ultimate understanding possible to be had there, there could be no answers.

But I felt these *were* the answers. Grandfather had laid it all out so completely, so beautifully – the reasons for the game, the suspension of disbelief to have the experience, the joy at the unending range of possibilities to find, the necessary reasons why we lose ourselves in places it seems we shouldn't be. Grandfather had made it all so clear – but then he came back at me with a smile in his voice and proceeded to blow all of it away.

"This too is only a thought, a philosophy, an aphorism pretending to be enlightenment. The true purpose, the real meaning, the final wisdom – it's not something to figure out. Trying to explain it is to get lost in it." Grandfather implored me again, *"Let it go! When you wake up, you take none of that with you!"*

Suddenly, he showed me a native boy who had been kidnapped by a neighboring tribe and severely mistreated during his formative years. The boy had experienced no love growing up, never felt he belonged or had a sense of family. The boy gave no thought to any other way of being. As far as he was concerned, anything else for him didn't exist. And then one day his tribe rescued him. Joyously, he was returned to his home space, surrounded by jubilant members of his tribe. They hugged him and gave him food and a blanket and tried to care for him. But their loving attention was so foreign to him, he recoiled at all of it, overwhelmed.

The trauma of the place he had been imprinted on him. He suffered from strong amnesia of his proper place within the tribe. The love and caring that was normal behavior for his true family and friends did nothing but overwhelm him at first. It took time for him to let go of the past place he had been in and embrace his true heritage and nature. Grandfather showed me how I was like that boy in that I too had been to a place that falsely imprinted an identity and a presumed way of life. He made me feel how my tribe was now gathered around me with joyful hope and delightful promise that I'd be waking up soon and returning to the unity of them, the unity of myself.

But the lesson didn't end there. As the ecstasy flowed through me and I sent love back into the unity, Grandfather expanded my assumptions about what Nature was. He took me beyond the citrus trees and grasses and flowers to the sky and stars and surprises beyond the stars. They too were Nature – the Nature that was me, the unity of ecstasy and love. Finally, he impressed upon me how communion with other people was also part of this Nature – the Nature of life in general. In reality, all things are contained in Nature and the ecstatic energy of me, of what I was feeling. In fact, the more I extended my ecstatic energy throughout all of Nature, especially to the nature of being with other people, the more I united with myself in blissful wakefulness.

It was then he roused me from four hours under the trees and implored me to go mingle with people, go see if there was anyone at a proper place in their journey to want to enjoy some together time and conversation. It was unlike me to do such a thing in the middle of my journey but Grandfather made it an imperative.

And so I got up and strolled out from the trees to the house's wide front porch. Two other ceremony participants were there. For one of them, this day was his first experience with San Pedro. It was a blessing, an example of all Grandfather was teaching, when this newbie participant stood in awe of the colors and moving shadows on the mountains in the distance. Repeatedly he gasped an incredulous "Wow!" He too was feeling the zap of ecstasy at encountering the self-aligned beauty of love contained in all.

He mumbled under his breath an almost silent "Thank You!" I couldn't help but add, "Gratitude is the key – gratitude will always bring out more Wow!" What ensued next was good conversation and laughter until the medicine once again took each of us our separate ways. In this, Grandfather was showing me how to extend the ecstatic energy felt under the trees into my interactions with people. Once again he implored me to take note – "*It's all a part of waking up...expand your communion with Nature to everything!*"

I shed my shoes and socks and returned to lie down in the grasses under the citrus trees, the place where my ecstatic wake-up call had begun many hours before. I stayed there, blissfully floating until after sunset. By 7pm, the medicine was still strong within me. The intense buzz of ecstatic energy still floated me from place to place in my strolls about the property. At one point I stood on the front porch and listened to the joy of the locals playing futbol in the distance.

A bit later, with twilight still warm and orangey-golden in the west, I found a slab of concrete out back and laid down. High above me, a 3/4 moon shone as the glow of fading sunlight let darker blues deepen. Magically it seemed, patches of stars shined bright at me then alternately receded into the blue. In playful dalliance it continued, stars taking turns shining bright. A silent dance of starlight and moonlight ensued, feeding my reverie and guiding my re-entry back to Earth until dinner was served.

After dinner, we all had a divination reading. As is my custom, I only wanted one card to be an overall comment on my day. The card I drew prompted me to be gentle in any process going forward. Opting to go for other message regarding the future, the reading pointed to many avenues of plenty. I had definitely experienced a cornucopia of ecstasy and love pouring over and through me during the day. I could certainly see how I was rich in the blessings of where I had been and the awakening bliss I had encountered. As Grandfather had told me, "*If you want to fly with me – you're going to have to learn how to accept ecstasy.*"

Afterwards, a friend and I shared some Yopo Rapé, which only sharpened my senses again and pulled me solidly into the moment. Expansive lessons continued unfolding, enlarging my heart-space with crystal clarity. Some of us stayed on the patio until 4am sharing stories and music. It was quite a day, an incredible ceremony, and of course it ended with me going to sleep.

But going to sleep now holds a special significance for me, each time I do it. It reminds me how through my energy, my actions, my awareness and love – I can find the lifeline of love, and in doing so, grasp the only way to be a success at ground school. It is up to me to wake up and embrace the ecstasy and love of who we are. Once I manage that, what a wondrous thing it will be to finally fly with Grandfather.

An Opening

In my lucid dream I was in an outdoor space with others. We were gathered around but working independently, all of us quite serious about the fun we were engrossed in. The fun consisted of encountering normal objects in our environment. It could be anything – a rock, a cup and saucer, a potted plant, a jewelry box. The object of our pursuit was to find out how to open each object – for in each object, we had been instructed, was a game. We were assured every object could be opened, whether a rock, an ordinary brick, or an elaborate piece of macrame.

And every object contained its own game with no two games alike. And no two objects contained the same game. Even similar objects, such as identical cups and saucers, had hidden inside them unique games. Our first challenge, somewhat like completing first level of an overarching game of exploration, was to discover how to open an object. Only by opening an object could the game inside be released. It didn't matter which object we found or set our intention upon. No one object contained any better game than any other object. All objects, all games were equally wondrous.

Over time, in many ways, each of us discovered the right combination of experience and intuition to interpret what it took to open objects. Some objects were more difficult to open than others. A few remained elusive and were passed around to see if anyone might have some luck with them. When an object finally opened, it was greater than a surprise, more than a sense of accomplishment. An experiential depth unfolded that went far beyond a reward. It felt as a fulfillment had been reached, a reconnection established. Of course, this was but the first level of what was expected of us.

To open an object was the reveal the hidden game inside. But now it was incumbent upon us to figure out what the game was and how to play it. Naturally, the level beyond that was attempting to play the game. Once we reached a victory in the game we had uncovered, only then could we move on to another object to open. The wonder and joy of discovering each game was intense motivation to win each game. There was so much delightful variety and creativity in each hidden game that it was obvious that the real game was seeing how many objects could one open – how much original wonder could be experienced.

At one point, I encountered a group of six or seven cylindrical objects, only about three inches long and as narrow around as a pencil with rounded ends. There seemed no way to tell just what the objects were or what they possibly could be used for. Even the material they were made out of seemed mysterious. They weren't wood or ceramic or metal but were non-pliable even though their surfaces were smooth, even soft. At first I wondered if I needed to concern myself with what the objects were or what they did. All I had to do was open them to reveal the game inside.

None of the other objects I had managed to open required special knowledge of the object itself to find the opening method. One small wooden tray had opened merely by holding it a certain way and tilting it forward while applying light pressure laterally. Nothing about the tray's function informed that method. And when the tray opened, individual sections of wood grain had flared out to become separate, rising sections in a tall, multilevel stack of interconnected carvings. Certainly, the six or seven cylindrical objects only needed to be handled properly, tilted just so, given the proper pressure, and they would open up. I didn't need to know what they were to access the game inside them.

I set about handling the six or seven objects, feeling their weight, their texture. I began experimenting with ways to hold them. Then a most curious impulse overtook me. I picked all of them up and, gathering them together, began inserting the small bunch in my mouth in preparation to swallow. Someone not far from me saw what I was attempting and raced to my side. He was incredulous at what I was about to do, in fact, he expressed concerned that I might injure myself – especially if I didn't know what the objects were or what they did. But I continued as before, intuitively certain – of what I began to wonder. And the more I wondered, the dawning realization hit me.

I was certain this was the correct method for getting the objects to open and reveal their game. Something about internalizing the bunch of them would prove to be the winning method. But the winning method for what? What would happen if these things opened up inside of me? However would I access the game if it was inside of me? And how could I be so certain that I wouldn't be affected or injured? I had already seen many objects open around me. Some upon opening had grown quite large or extended. If such a thing were to occur in my gut, things could get serious. But like an intuitive slide of gravity pulling fate downhill, I continued pushing them into my mouth and ignored the warnings coming at me.

I knew – and I knew I knew with certainty that this was the only workable method to open the objects. And once they opened, they were intended to open something else. That something else was me. I was the object that ultimately would reveal the game. And once revealed, I would be in the game that needed to be played. But to win the game of me would be the next level – a level beyond the playing field. As I committed to the next level and felt myself swallow – I woke up, and realized, being awake in my life was the hidden game finally revealed. Only two things remained – how to win the game, and what would be the level beyond.

Be the dream or be the game or be the one who's all. For it doesn't end but in the end it may not be about any one thing at all, not if games and dreams are only here to awaken us. We're left forever finding it's nothing else than something more in ourselves that ultimately enthralls.

Ecstasy needs no reason when its name is love. Love needs no name when its feeling is joy. The endpoint is wonder that's beyond apprehension and the dream that's not a dream will always be the next beginning, our wakeful dream, our endless surprise.

Out Of The Fog

The explosive experience can be profound. But so can the subtle. The difference lies not in the overt manifestation of the event, rather upon one's approach and ultimate expectations bearing witness to what is offered. Both may offer the same level of intensity and meaning to be found. It can be argued, in many ways, what one takes away from many experiences is what one brings to them. This is especially true with sacred plant medicines.

This may be one of the reasons why experiencing them is so personal. Two people at the same ceremony, taking equal amounts of the same plant medicine, nonetheless come away with far different tales to tell. Oftentimes, radically so. One participant may hardly feel anything while someone else is transported and transformed. Both people in the same place, same time, same ceremony, with the same medicine inside of them.

This is especially true of Rapé, the shamanic snuff with pre-Colombian roots, shared in ritual as a prayer and connection with nature and oneself (the distinction between which being purely cultural as the plants teach so well). For starters, Rapé is not one thing. Although it may contain similar tobacco and ash bases, the exact formula of plants and their number comprising a selection of Rapés varies greatly, not only between but within Amazonian tribes.

Rapés are created for different purposes. And different Rapés not only contain wide varieties of formulaic blends, but methods by which they're prepared also differ. For example, some shamanic snuffs can only be prepared by women, while other blends must be fashioned under strict ritualistic practices, both external and energetic, that are equally prescriptive or restrictive.

As a result, there is a tendency among Rapé enthusiasts to begin rating one blend against another. Which in many ways is understandable. Why rely on a placebo effect for an experience or invest in substandard medicine that produces minimal results. But there is a danger in the way these informal rating systems progress. In an ongoing race to find the singular Rapé that gives the "biggest bang for the buck," perhaps a whole type of profundity is being glossed over, a whole range of subtle but significant lessons are being missed. In a typical Western-mentality competitive drive to always acquire the next better explosive thing, perhaps an entire spectrum of the subtle-profound in these varied medicines gets lost. Metamorphic pinnacles are just as likely to occur from whispers as from overly dramatic shouts.

Case in point. I had the opportunity to try a Rapé blend I had heard was not powerful and produced minimal effects. Others were curious if I would rate it the same. My experience with it turned out quite different than other snuffs I had tried, to be sure, but I found in its subtleness a doorway into a uniquely profound space unlike any other. Far from saying this snuff was not profound, I had to conclude it offered its magic with an introductory whisper. If that whisper was missed or ignored, it would not yield the sought-after treasures that awaited. Like a firefly in the night so easily overlooked but coaxing one to follow, I approached with no expectations and caught enough of its light to follow.

So, was I preloaded with a need to find profound magic as a reverse-psychology response to hearing the snuff was a dud? Did I need to prove the naysayers wrong? Perhaps. One can always second-guess what happens in every situation and judge it from constrained angles and relativistic cleverness. I can only comment on the experience itself and the way I approached the process. Preloaded or not, I did have the experience I had. And while the effects progressed, I got a strong sense that what I was going through was not only an experience but more importantly an example to follow.

Right after receiving the Rapé, I felt an energetic tingle – but nothing intense. I concentrated on my deep breathing and the meditation of clearing my thoughts. The idea was to get myself out of the way, to release expectation, forego anticipation. Instead of projecting expectations, I listened. I released into the feeling of listening not only with my ears but with my being. In the listening there soon came the impulse to lie down and cover my eyes with my hands – make it as dark as possible. I did this and as much as the darkness deepened, tiny vortexes of energy throughout my body increased.

I was coaxed to follow that tiny, metaphorical firefly into a state often called "the zone." Many have tried to describe being in "the zone" and often it comes down to existing in an effortless flow where one is there and not there and what happens just works in an elevated confluence of past, present, future such that cause and effect have been mediated by a more complete expression of being.

Without knowing how I did it (which I suspect is the key!), I found consciousness sliding into a flow I can now only describe as "the zone." As this happened, another view faded into view as if a fog was dissipating. It was a view of a starfield. The blackness of space surrounded pinpoints of starlight. The stars were unblinking as if I was in the same blackness of space that contained them. But this view only last a few seconds, then faded away as thoughts of what I was doing intervened and interrupted "the flow."

I returned to listening with my being. I crowded out thoughts and expectations by doing this. Soon, the "zone" returned, as did the starfield. It was like being far out in space and the stars and their distance from each other had a 3D perspective about them. Yet, once again, as soon as I started noticing my reaction to this, the starfield faded again, as did that sense of "the zone." This pattern repeated several times. Each time I was able to find "the flow" the energy in my body would vortex and, as the fog of black dissipated, the starfield returned.

This indeed was an example to follow, an experience of being which contained a lesson if one was open to seeing it that way. Like some biofeedback mechanism, the experience took me into a state where I was shown how it's possible to match something you can't force or try with something you can achieve. I would rate that very highly, even though this Rapé was presented to me as not powerful and producing minimal effects. I guess it all depends on what effects one expects and values. That's why all of these rating systems are so subjective – and why Rapé can't be looked at monolithically. It may be one type of medicine but it comes in many varieties, each of which contains a unique opportunity to discover, or simply come out of the fog.

Unpack A Fractal Maelstrom

I start out fully aware I'm going to fail. But failing is not a defeat in this endeavor, since the core experience stays with me, even if I cannot adequately externalize it now or ever. I relate it here, as much as I can, simply to provide myself some record. Porous memory needs reminders as time passes. Someday I might look back, read this, and perhaps be reminded of details long dissipated or obscured. Those details hopefully will spark an experiential flashback into the state of grace that produced the effect. And that effect will once again show the way. The way to me and what was gained that day in ceremony so long ago.

But for now, that San Pedro ceremony is recent, and near, and still reverberating through me in a way only plant spirit contact can resonate. There is no chance anyone else but me will ever understand or feel what my experience in the medicine that day was like. There are no substitutes for direct experience. And when it comes to ceremony, everyone's journey is unique and profound for them. I share this not to say you should do this, learn from this, or you should do anything. I went somewhere and something happened, that's all. For what it's worth, the reader of this can take away what they will – curiosity, comparative analysis, or simple amusement.

My intentions for the day were simple enough. They usually are since experience with Grandfather San Pedro has shown me how much our true intentions are without words. Those realms of feeling most of interest by the medicine are easily and promptly accessed without Grandfather being given a word roadmap to them. More often than not, our word intentions before the ceremony are for our benefit, to get us into a proper frame of mind and heart – they really aren't for Grandfather because he doesn't need them for what he's about to do.

On this day, I simply wanted to continue my path from the ceremony before. There is a sense of surrender and trust and gratitude to bring into ceremony that I find best suits entry into deep medicine space, the place where the most profound journeys happen. On this day, I drank the medicine and awaited my ten-hour encounter with Grandfather with the same approach.

As soon as I felt myself entering medicine space, I found a secluded place out in nature, someplace conducive to what I thought was about to begin. Immediately, Grandfather presented me with an abrupt question – "*Why are you here?*"

He was compassionate but very serious, as dead serious as if he had asked for my greater purpose or the universe's final equation. My mind raced over my intentions for the day and knew they were lacking; in fact, I instantly knew that anything that came from mind would be lacking. A frozen panic chilled me from head to toe.

I had no answer for Grandfather. None.

It was like finally getting your one-time audience before the supreme being and finding out you had nothing to say. This went beyond embarrassment, this was existential crisis territory. Because there is always something, something more going on within us. With all of creation unlocked before you, within you, how could anyone stand there with nothing to say?

I may have been at a loss for words, but Grandfather is never at a loss for action. He swept right past my stymied mind, threw open the lid on the cedar chest of my feelings, dug deeper, and explored what all those feelings were connected to. Right on top, forefront in my feelings, was my mild sadness and disappointment that my wife was not able to join me at the ceremony location. Spending quality time together is one of the primary aspects of our relationship I enjoy. To miss out on such a wonderful chance to share the day went deeper than I ever suspected. As I was about to experience.

With the uncovering of deeper feelings, I began to see visuals, fractals, colors, a maelstrom of movement tunneling ever deeper. I realized I was seeing myself, where I placed my energies, my concerns, my priorities. The unending kaleidoscope of roiling shapes and tunnels and colors reflected me. I was staring into my own cedar chest of heart. I may not know why I was there but Grandfather could easily access what was next for me. In doing so, he was about to spend the next five hours answering his own question ("*Why are you here?*") by opening me up.

Like a thread once pulled, brings forth a scarf, and that once tugged, produces a tapestry, and that once unfolded, drags open a mural – feelings about missing out on sharing the day with my wife opened up feelings about needing connection to feminine energy…

…and that opened up the duality of male/female…

…and that opened up the counterbalance necessary in my need for female influence…

…and that took me back to reliving being a child with my mother, feeling her unconditional love and caring…

…and that took me deep into the desire for the comfort and trust and caring so unquestioned with a mother's love…

...and that drove me into a sense of loss at missing that feeling of total trust and comfort and caring felt as a baby in my mother's arms...

...and that soared me beyond into the arms of Pachamama, the matriarch of planet Earth and the natural world...

...and that expanded into a sense of the female energy in the universe, beyond the Earth, then beyond the universe into the creative force itself...

...and that exploded open into my sense of being separate from the union with Source, and therein a perfect union with the female principle and energies on the other side the duality I was subject to in life.

At the deepest root of my feelings unveiled in my cedar chest of heart was a longing to once again experience the connection, the caring, the total trust and comfort of being back in a state of unconditional, perfected love.

I was, in essence, homesick.

The hours to get through this journey rippled through endlessly layered feeling and ongoing kaleidoscopes revealing ever more overlapping stratums within myself. Everything was shown to twist and spiral into the next thing. Wife, male/female duality, mother, Pachamama, and ultimate Source unity. All things were related. All was cause and effect of everything else.

The journey shuttered and tumbled into so much more. The prime mover of me was nowhere to be found as a point of existential origin. There never could be a point of origin for the vastly interconnected fractals of infinite potentials erupting from unending creativity and loving, even playful expression. In my energy was the fractal pattern of everything else, even Source. Thus, to unpack me would entail unpacking everything – and thus, the hours of falling into tunneling kaleidoscopes I recognized as me.

In that Source potential anything was possible. In the game of play and discovery and creativity and possibilities, even the One as many was a creative probability that had to be explored. Infinite individual expressions of Source all forever finding new ways of being the unending creative discovery from unique points of view. The magic of being was so strong and the need for total adventure so inherent in the unlimited process, that creating things we got lost in was also one of the possibilities that infinite creation needed to explore.

Even the idea that one could be on one's own, separate from Source, might happen in these spaces. If so, actions could stem from the ego of this separateness instead of the fundamental Source love. Time meant nothing to the infinity of this process, so Source energy could forever flow through spaces that were trapped by their own cleverness, their own creativity.

Grandfather made it clear, there were even spaces that creation explored where it was possible to disinvent love. Counterintuitively, only love was the lifeline back out where the Source energy in these spaces could find reconnection with true love. The way back out was simply dependent on the magic of one giving one's energy to love to reinvent it, to keep it alive in the space until one woke up to the realization that love was never gone, never far away, for indeed one is made of love, so the idea of being separate from love is the false ego's way of separating us from our true selves.

Grandfather tumbled me through interlocking feelings and states of being. All action, all intent, was to be measured by whether it was rooted in false ego or in love. Every time one based an action or intent in ego, a fractal tunnel into infinite trapped spaces opened up. Every time an action was rooted in love, one connected back with unrestricted, unlimited Source where anything is possible again. In that connection was the feeling of home I was seeking at my core. So much happened over the five hours, but at one point, Grandfather took me to a mansion in the hills and then a tropical island estate.

These were opulent places, filled with objects and potentials for maximum joy and pleasure. In the expression of these, I was thrust into unimaginable ecstasies, enjoying every possible thing available, and anything I wanted was available. As I started to sink into this ecstasy, believing such a joyful thing could only serve me and signal connection with Source, Grandfather questioned me – "*Is this joy from ego or from love?*"

It was instantly clear that joy and even love itself could be motivated by the false ego. Once you went into that feeling all the way, you could get lost there and lock yourself out of experiencing love for its own sake, the true love that powered the universe. Immersed in the joys and ecstasies of the places I had been taken to, I felt myself slipping into total relaxation, total acceptance of the joy and love offered. As I sank deeper into the angelic pleasure of it, I saw a twisting gear-like-tunnel fractal open before me. Swirling red and white opalescence hypnotically drew me forward, making me ready to release myself into the feeling.

Then, in my peripheral vision, I saw a figure. It stood a few yards away, looking out at the scenery. I only could see the side of it. But, like flipping a switch, the figure popped closer in an instant, then a bit back. It seemed to be waiting for me to release totally into the fractal maelstrom of ecstasy. I was being offered total infinite pleasure and joy. The only catch was –

this was all from ego. There was no other motivation, even though the joy and pleasure and ecstasy and love were completely real. I could explore this, explore it as long as I wanted, if that's what I really wanted. But how long would I want it?

The feeling of Grandfather came near. He reminded me what was happening, where all of this led. A breath before succumbing to the tunnel of love centered in ego, I pulled back my psyche. Instantly, the joy and pleasure and ecstasy left me. Once again I felt separate, homesick for the love, the caring, the comfort of being with Source. As much as the disconnection didn't feel right, it was. I was left longing for the feeling of being with my mother as a child, or the feeling of letting myself go in the arms of Pachamama. Both had approximated what Source love truly entailed.

The lesson was clear and chilling. Even joy and love itself could be a soul-wrenching trap set by oneself. Anything done from ego and not unconditional love, even love itself, took one to the place where in reality, true love had been disinvented. There was nothing inherently wrong with experiencing these realms, since creation contained and explored all possibilities. The catch was, don't get trapped there – and the easiest one to fool and trap you would always be yourself. You could trick yourself into these realms better than anything else could. Never think that joy and ecstasy and love were always weighted only one way, the way that served you.

How they got expressed would always be up to us. We could make them the Source of creation itself or the snare that would encapsulate us in a self-serving box. It was a box of infinite pleasure and joy that folded back upon itself in limitation. It was a box that would always seem designed with no escape. And the idea that there was no escape from these realms was the biggest trick of all. Such a trick was typical of false ego. But who we really are would always be the key to get us out. To lose oneself to find oneself is a cliche but one that applies. To accomplish such a feat would always entail unpacking oneself and the fractal maelstrom the ego had trapped within.

Many odd and terrific things happened during this five-hour journey, too many to relate or even remember as distinct events. For example of one brief interlude, at one point during my flight from Pachamama to an even more expansive expression of universal feminine energy, I found myself in a space where I could encounter and speak to anyone who had died. In my state, the concept was not even questioned. I knew this was possible because I was where they were.

Having recently watched a movie about Steve Jobs and discussed it afterwards at length with my wife, Steve was the first one who came to mind, strangely enough. And instantly, he was there with me. I could ask him anything. Given his personality and beliefs in life, I gravitated instantly to a snappy leading question I'd thought would evoke something pithy from him. I asked simply, "So what do you have to say for yourself now?"

His eyes smiled as his thin lips pursed to hold back the full measure of the eruptive amusement he held within. His whole demeanor was relaxed, breezy, content. He took the question in for only a few moments before answering with a self-effacing humor intent upon having satirical fun with the false ego of his own in-life persona. He chuckled and delivered his reply with soft-spoken incredulity – "Why didn't *I* think of this?" With bemused accent on the "I." The visit continued with other crossed-over souls coming by. Jobs got a bit more serious at one point when he said to me before fading off, "Never put down any part of yourself. It's all you. It's all good."

Later, while spinning through far-flung spaces while lying on the grass under some citrus trees, I opened my eyes to find energy forms swirling around me clockwise in a dance circle. They had humanoid forms but the forms were only clear lines of energy with no solid surface. They were playful, highly energetic, and driven with ceremonial purpose. Repeatedly they coaxed me to get up and join them. I didn't for two reasons. I didn't know who they were and I physically couldn't get up if I wanted to. Instead, I asked Grandfather about them. Who exactly were they? He answered right away – "*The ancestors.*"

[In putting together this book, I was surprised upon re-reading this journal entry. I wrote this entry long before I ever heard anything about the San Pedro walking ceremony and the process of winding energies up and down. And yet, here it is, in the journal, on the day when I was dealing with fractalling energies of homesickness for connection to unconditional love. The ancestors, as Grandfather called them, danced around me, repeatedly coaxing me to get up and dance with them. At the time I didn't. But now, with time and more information, I see what they were trying to get me to do. They didn't just want me to dance. They wanted me to dance in a circle with them – clockwise. They were trying to help me wind those sad feelings and energies down and away.]

Even later, I turned over onto my back and opened my eyes once again. The instant view I was greeted with shook me with stunned amazement. I was staring straight up into the sky. Low and fast-moving, puffy white clouds were gliding left-to-right before a deep blue sky. But that wasn't the startling part. The dimensional view I had was impossible – impossibly beautiful and intense.

Every feathery fragment of moving cloud-mass was receding to an infinite vanishing point. My perspective was not just where I lay on the grass but at every point along the way to that vanishing point somewhere lost in the background blue. I watched as an unending third-dimension depth of feathery clouds moved around and by me. It was as if the clouds had been stretched as far as the third dimension could reach and I had my focal point along the entire length of them.

Before I could recover from this augmented sight ability, the blue sky behind it all suddenly showed its underlying superstructure, an energy grid of cathedral-like stained-glass girders that made up the otherwise hidden framework of the sky itself. This clear structure appeared to be moving to the left as the clouds slid right. I was seeing with a multidimensional ability to sight, one that included not only perspectives unknown to regular sight but also gave access to the hidden energy fields underlying reality itself. This was not something flaring behind closed eyes. This was being seen with open eyes.

How the day's many departures and inward spirals coalesced from hour to hour cannot be described with words or in time. They all unpacked and unfolded in multiple dimensions only to fractally interconnect and intertwine with emotion and energetic transport through experiences that impressed lasting lessons on the heart.

Feminine energy was strong. Source unity and ecstatic bursts of consciousness dominated.

Temptations into rabbit holes of false ego seduced over and over with joy and pleasure. Flights into deep aspects of my true nature co-located me with my mother and Pachamama. I was tested and taxed to limits of comprehension and thresholds of emotional acceptance.

I started the day not knowing how to answer the simple question, "*Why are you here?*" I ended the day wondering if I could ever integrate all of what I had been through. It had all been inside of me. The one left speechless in the morning was once again left speechless in the evening. One was the silence of a vessel closed up. The other was the silence of the ocean emptied. After dinner I had a divination reading to comment on my day. The message that returned pointed to energies of insightfulness and sensitivity.

We are the choice, the magic, or the trap we set for ourselves.
We are and always have been more than we know or could know.
The one is the many. There's nothing to seek. There's everything to be.
The dream and the game are one.
You can't find it. It never ends. There's always more.
It has no explanation. It needs no reason.
Any purpose would be a limitation.

Everywhere is the vanishing point.
So let that go. Let it go. And wake up.
    – (unspoken San Pedro, paraphrased of course)

Three Dreams / Three Nights / Three Words

One would expect much to tell coming away from a significant lucid dream. And yet I had three lucid dreams on consecutive nights that left me amazed – but here I am, with only three words to take away from all of it. The only thing I remember from each lucid dream is a single word, even though the impression I get is that so much more went on within the dreams.

Each time in the dream, a word was impressed upon me three times. Each of the three dreams contained a different word. Each time I was told to remember the word and take it outside the dream. This was very important. I'm not sure who was telling me this. As far as I know now, I never saw them. But the feeling of them was very near, being intensely serious while lovingly compassionate.

1st Dream

The first dream occurred after receiving a blend of Rapé called "Goddess." This was also only two days after a very intense San Pedro ceremony in which feminine energy predominated, including transport back to being a child with my mother, who passed away fourteen years ago, and a powerful passage into the arms of Pachamama. This first dream yielded a word I never heard before and didn't know the meaning of. At first it sounded to me like something in Italian but for the heck of it I put it in a translation app as Spanish – the word "cuido" translated as "I care."

This was interesting, for in a dream I knew was a dream, someone told me to remember this word when I left the dream. How could I have dreamed up an insistence to find importance in an unknown word from a foreign language, a word I didn't know and didn't know the meaning of? Since it was the only thing that survived my lucid dream, it was easy to conclude that someone or something wanted to impress upon me a simple but powerful message. "I care."

That was all, but it was enough to get my attention. The fact that I had to decipher it seemed to be an extra layer of non-deniability to get me to listen to it, to sit up and take notice. If I had simply heard "I care" in English in my dream, it could have been easily dismissed as something coming from myself. But the way this message came to me was saying something more than the word itself. I took this in as wonderfully suggestive and then let it go and didn't think much more about it.

2nd Dream

But then, the second night brought a second lucid dream, and a second word. Once again this word was the only thing that survived the dream. I don't know what else went on in the dream except I feel all sorts of stuff transpired that I don't remember. And again, I was implored three times not to forget one word – and to take this word outside the dream.

This was a new word, not a repeat of the first word. Again, it was a word I didn't recognize, never have used, and didn't know what it meant, if indeed it meant anything. The experience was so strange, having happened once again on a second consecutive night, that I actually woke up in the dark about 5:30am, startled at what was happening. Intensely curious at what any second message might be, I jumped up and scrambled in the dark to find my iPhone so I could plug the new word into my translation app as Spanish.

Standing in the dark, my surroundings lit only by my phone, I entered the word – "camelo." Immediately, the app responded with "baloney." WTF?! Baloney? Seriously? This was too bizarre. Someone or something was having fun with me. Either that or any lofty, esoteric explanation for what was going had just been skewered. This had to be some joke. Or the app was seriously off in its translation, which wouldn't be the first time. I had no patience to research the matter further. I set the phone down and found my way through the dark back into bed. And that was that, end of story as far as I was concerned. Some things are strange in a good way, others in just a weird way. No sense chasing down the simply weird – or so I thought.

Once morning came and I got up, I poured some coffee and checked email as I'm accustomed to do. There in my inbox was a spam email in Spanish. It promised me lots of money if I responded. If I believed the email, a woman with cancer had been prayerfully promised a cure if she gave her money away – so she wanted to give me $100,000. How nice.

This email was funny to me – the first time I had gotten a scam email in Spanish. It was so obviously an attempt to prey upon people's greed in an effort to somehow rip them off – but I noticed that the email was sent to several people, one of which was an acquaintance of mine. I was writing this acquaintance an email anyway, so I thought I'd mention the scam email to them – and a strange thing happened as soon as I typed the word "scam" in the new email – the word "baloney" came to mind. Nah, it couldn't be, could it? I set about researching the lucid dream word from the night before – the word "camelo." Here's what I found:

Definition of "camelo" – hoax, con, lie, swindle, fool with praise, baloney, humbug, to cajole, to con, to snow, to sweet-talk, cock-and-bull story, jest, joke, deceit, rip-off; also, secondarily – flirtation, instant or excessive praise; flattery, gallantry (especially towards women); conquer, seduce, gain trust by flattery. As in, "me huele a camelo" – there's something fishy going on

But even freakier, this word is rare, extremely rare, in fact, last used in the late 1700's. The word origin is from old Portuguese for camel, the Spanish word is Castilian and derives originally from vulgar Latin camellus.

Whew! Not only was I implored to take a foreign word I didn't know outside my lucid dream, but the translation turned out to be an apt warning about the strange scam email I then received. To top it off, this word was nearly obsolete in the foreign language, the word not used for 300 years. The scam email entered my inbox, you guessed it, around 5:30am, the same time the word "camelo" woke me up and I translated it in the dark. Who or whatever was giving me these words had definitely gotten my attention. What it meant or what I could do with it was anyone's guess. At least I could see the warning as a practical example that someone or something "cared."

For fun, I answered the scam email and they answered me – to which I sent one last message, a message they never replied to. In that exchange, I thanked the woman for the offer but suggested she give the money to an orphanage instead. She wrote back suggesting I could do whatever good I wanted with the cash. I wrote back with this – "God told me you will receive many more blessings if you give the money to the children directly. I trust you will do the right thing. Blessings to you."

All of which was great fun. After which, my thoughts returned more seriously to the two words in two days from the lucid dreams. For this to happen once was strange enough, but on back-to-back nights? It made me wonder but there was little I could do other than note that possibly some sort of communication had been established. With whom or why was anyone's guess.

3rd Dream

Then came the third night. This sleep followed receiving a different blend of Rapé; I'm not sure the name. Different Rapés produce such varied results, from the subtle to the intense, from the outgoing to the "in-going." The "Goddess" variety had opened my feelings intensely even as I felt my "floaty" condition was still too much "in the body" for such an opening to take place. As a result, I became sound and light sensitive and wanted nothing else but to float away into the exploration of feeling in a place completely silent and dark. Such a place being impossible at the time, there resulted a discordant edge to what otherwise was a quite remarkable, energetic "in-going" among feelings.

Having the second Rapé on the third night, the effects were starkly different. I was overcome with a strength of being in the body, of being centered, of being focused and aware in the moment. Senses were heightened as was an aura of strength for whatever needed to be done. I could definitely see why tribal people might take such a blend before going out on a grueling hunt that lasted the day or days traversing the jungle. The energy felt was very concentrated in the body, unlike some Rapé that conveys supercharged energy but the energy is used to float one out of body.

That night I had the third lucid dream, out of which I awoke with a third foreign word. Once again, it was a word I didn't know the translation for. The third word was "fuerza" – which I discovered upon waking means "force, strength, or power."

Since then, no more words have come. There were three words in three lucid dreams and for now the pattern has stopped. But then, the number three has its own significance, if one digs deep enough. On the surface, there is the common "the rule of three" (Latin-"omne trium perfectum") principle, which suggests things that come in threes are inherently more humorous, satisfying, or effective than any other number of things.

Beyond that, one can get submerged into all sorts of Biblical references that equate significance to the number three in the Jewish and Christian traditions. In Islam too, the number three holds significance.

Other world religions contain triple deities or concepts of trinity.

Suffice to say, three lucid dreams on three consecutive nights, yielding three foreign words I didn't understand (one of which is rare and obscure even in the native language), seems significant somehow. I just need to determine how. At best, so far, all of this seems to suggest at least some rudimentary contact with something that wants to communicate – and says they care. Which is nice, but I have a feeling I need to keep looking up, looking out for more.

Solo With Sapo

Native Amazonians brew a tea made from the Guayusa leaf. This unimposing, green leaf is filled with caffeine and who knows what else. A Kichwa elder once claimed that drinking the Guayusa tea, "...brings the nature and force of the jungle inside of you, so you basically become part of the nature. So if you're in the jungle, if there's a venomous snake or wasp, it doesn't bite you or attack you because it recognizes you as part of the jungle."

Such claims are easily dismissed as myth, native elder hype, or a placebo effect reinforced by backward tribal superstitions run amuck. Does anyone really believe the jungle is an interconnected conscious entity with the wherewithal to make this kind of assessment then somehow form a consensus with all the living components over a massive ecosystem like a rainforest? Well, yes, people do believe this. Just like some people also believe the whole universe exploded out of nothing about 14 billion Earth-years ago for no good reason and is entropically winding back down to nothing, once again for no good reason – end of story.

Also note, a lot of tribal people have been running around the jungle for an awful long time and they don't get bit or stung the same as tourists who just dropped in to snap a few selfies with the wildlife. There must be another reason for this, most will say. It can't be a simple-minded, mystical, or steeped in fairy tale explanation. I hear the laughter now. The various plants and animals within the jungle are alive, of course, whatever that means, but the jungle itself isn't alive. Not like that. And it certainly doesn't communicate that way. I should know. I live in a cul-de-sac with DirectTV. Hashtag looney.

And yet, occasionally a mercado near where I live has Guayusa. I get some sometimes and chew it. The taste is bright, citrusy, and bitter. I don't know if the jungle sees me as its own or not. Maybe I should be making a tea out of it instead of chewing it raw. But then many people chew coca leaves raw for stamina and to ward off the effects of high altitude, so raw can't be all bad.

It's surprising how so many things in the jungle that are good for us are bitter. Perhaps this is true because they contain a concoction of alkaloids and peptides. The beneficial nature of alkaloidal substances might be counterintuitive after we're told most alkaloids not only have a bitter taste but are poisonous when ingested. Poisons and human health have an interesting history together and it's a complex subject, I know. I'm not a pharmacologist so I can't prescribe. But I know my experience.

There's Kambo, for instance, the venom of the rainforest frog found in Bolivia, Brazil, Colombia, Peru, Venezuela, and Guyana. Here's a poison a sensible person would have no problem concluding is looney to put in the human body. And yet, once again, native peoples have used it successfully for a long while. After French missionary Constantin Tastevin told the non-native world about Kambo in 1925, the jungle medicine didn't spark any interest from medical researchers until the 1950's. Even so, it wasn't until the 1980's that patents first appeared on the peptides found in the venom.

Science must have found something of interest since by now, there's over 70 patents on Kambo. As more research is done, more is being found. The National Center for Biotechnology Information lists a 1993 research study (PMID: 8266343) that concluded, "All the peripheral and most of the central effects of 'sapo' can be ascribed to the exceptionally high content of the drug (up to 7% of its weight) in potently active peptides, easily absorbed through the burned, inflamed areas of the skin." But what are all of those peptides, and just as important, what is the combined effect of them together?

Science says peptides play an important role in molecular biology. They allow for the creation of peptide antibodies. Inhibitory peptides are studied for their effects on the inhibition of cancer proteins and other diseases. There is a whole group of peptides known for their antimicrobial properties. And the list goes on. If you're a scientist or fancy yourself more sophisticated than a Kichwa elder spouting superstitions, there is enough serious research on Kambo to at least raise a few eyebrows beyond skepticism. All the while, the native elder remains in the background, still claiming Kambo as a powerful medicine, not only against snake bites, malaria, yellow fever and other epidemic diseases, but also against the "panema" of negative energies we carry around with us.

Kambo is known as a "fire medicine." When combined with all of the water that one must drink during a ceremony, I like to think of the mixture of fire and water "steam cleaning" my physical, energetic, and emotional systems. Some think of the sapo medicina as only a strong detox, a jungle cleanse, a tune-up for the immune system. For whatever reason, it's harder for some to think of communing with the Sapo spirit in the same way one connects with the spirit of the plant medicines Ayahuasca and San Pedro. The process of receiving the medicine is different. Maybe that's the reason. It's not a plant but a toxin-goo scraped off the back of a frog that goes into the body. How can there be any spirit connection with a toxin-goo? Perhaps because among all the interesting peptides packed into that goo, there are other things, some of which are claimed to be psychoactive.

My relationship with Kambo has evolved over time. The same is true with the sacred plant medicines. I know it sounds odd to claim one has developed a "relationship" with a plant spirit, even stranger with a frog venom, but something beyond a mere altered state takes place. I can't claim I understand it. It might be the plants or peptide toxins allow us access to brain or energetic functions usually turned off, ignored, or obscured by the meme-chatter of consumer-centric life.

Maybe we're not put in touch with spirits per se but our higher self instead. If so, my higher self appears distinct from me. It can give me answers new to me. I can have a discussion with it that's nothing like the predictable boredom of playing chess with myself. Whatever it is, this connection feels like a conversation, a relationship, a telepathic channel that's established. It's a relationship that grows, evolves, deepens over time, just as with any relationship. This is as true with Kambo as with anything. At least for me.

Before taking a trip to Peru, I felt a calling to Kambo. So what is a "calling?" A calling is more pervasive than impulse, more like an altered state than intuition, more aligned with this other relationship dimension than mere feeling can describe. I sensed a calling to do three Kambo ceremonies again in one lunar cycle and to complete this before my trip to Peru. In Peru I was going to a San Pedro ceremony and the sense of it was this cleanse, this purge of building panema should be done in order to clear the way so I'd get the most out of the Peru experience. To travel four hours from my home to the place where I'd done Kambo before and stay close to a week to accomplish this wasn't practical at the time. But none of that mattered to the "calling." The message was clear, if I couldn't get to the faraway location to do this, then I needed to do it myself where I was at.

Do it myself? Was I crazy? Perhaps. Well, to some, certainly. But who would ever administer Kambo to themselves? How could that ever be safe? But none of my protective reservations seem to apply. The feeling of my connection with Kambo made the prospect not only safe, but natural. But who would facilitate? Who'd be the shaman? Who'd be my guide through the ceremony? Kambo would. Simple as that. As with any Kambo communication, the message was powerful, forceful, and confident enough to take no prisoners. The medicine was already in me. I was already with the medicine in ways that forged a mutual understanding. If nothing else, Kambo demands respect and best intentions. If I maintained that posture, Kambo would be my guide. And so I ordered a stick of Kambo and waited.

Until the Kambo arrived, I had time to listen to how it should be done. Kambo cuts to the chase, minces no words, assumes no debate. The method to follow was simple do's and don'ts. None of it mattered if Kambo wasn't on your side. It was clear – no one should do this unless the connection with Kambo was already established and Kambo was the one to prescribe it. No one should ever decide to do this on their own. Which, I know, sounds looney again. What was I saying? I could do this by myself because a frog spirit told me to? And how was I sure the frog spirit was communicating with me? Well, isn't that obvious? It's one of those things that you know when you know. Couldn't be clearer. But anyone could claim such a thing. Yeah, just because I hear voices doesn't mean the voices don't have something worthwhile to listen to.

The day of my first solo Kambo experience, I went about my preparations very seriously. I drank at least two liters of water before burning the holes in my upper arm. I positioned at least five more liters of water by the opening to my walk-in shower. I stripped down to underwear and arranged for my wife to check in on me occasionally in the bathroom. Carefully, I prepared the medicine and placed individual points of it into the small burn holes. Immediately after, I went into the shower as the rushing hot medicine began to take effect.

For the next 90 minutes I drank water and purged. A couple times my wife checked to see if I was okay. The sickness, the hot-headedness, the flush of heat and palpitations raced through me. All the while, I felt guided through the process. I felt something reassure me, give me strength, nudge me on to drink more and purge harder. In time, the worst of the effects settled down. All of the water had been ingested and most of that had come back out. In total, over two gallons. I felt a direction to get up, get naked, and take a shower, not all the way cold but as cold as I could stand it. Afterwards, I felt wiped out but wonderful.

A few days later, I set about to repeat the process. It turned out to be the same process but not with the same results. This time, midway through the worse of the purge phase, I ran out of water near to me. Absentmindedly, I had filled my liter jugs with water but neglected to position all of them close to the shower door opening. And now Kambo was demanding water, more water, always more. I realized what had happened but I lacked the energy to move to help myself.

Kambo didn't care. It needed what it needed. It demanded more water. A cement-mixer of sickness revolved in my guts. Something needed to come out. Kambo wanted it out now. But I was so sick, so tired, so unable to move, I didn't know what else to do but call out to my wife. If she heard me and came, she could bring me the water jugs. I could see them from where I slumped in the shower but they might as well be in the next timezone. I called out but couldn't tell how strongly I was calling. Perhaps I was only thinking I was calling. I tried calling out again. Was that louder? I wasn't sure. Did I have the strength to call out louder? Did it matter? Regardless if she heard me, I needed water now.

It may not seem like such a predicament. So I needed water. I could see my water jugs across the bathroom. For whatever reason, my wife hadn't heard me. All I needed to do was get up and get the water. That's all. Easy for everyone else to say. If you've ever experienced the maximum Kambo can throw at you, you know how impossible the idea of getting up and doing that can be. But Kambo, if nothing else, is persistent. It comes at you with a power of will for what it wants and what it wants you to do for yourself that is relentless. If you ignore its call for water, your sickness won't subside like it could and you definitely won't get the benefits possible from the experience.

Believe me, there is no point in putting yourself through the Kambo experience if you're not prepared to do what it takes to get the help it offers. Of course, some people can suffer the sickness and wait it out until the effects subside. They'll shrug and say they didn't purge much, that it "didn't seem to do much for me." And they're right. I wasn't about to be one of those people and Kambo knew it. Knowing it, Kambo got that much harder on me. Like a coach pushing for a personal best you didn't know you had in you, the intensity ramped up. Like a drill instructor violently getting in the face of a tired recruit and shouting him over the wall, Kambo was all over me.

I felt myself push through the death-grip exhaustion, the debilitating sickness, the physical weakness, the wooziness of a hot head. I managed to reach up and turn on the shower's cold water. A chilling cascade rained down and shuddered over me. I gasped at the shock of it. I shook at the contrast to my hot head. But then it happened. From depths I didn't know existed, a strength from within welled up. From a place beyond all my doubts and presumed certaintics about myself, a force of will that couldn't be negotiated with took a grip, infusing me with a determination I had never felt before.

I struggled to shaky feet only moments before I thought wouldn't hold me, left the shower, and got the water I needed. Kneeling back in the shower, I guzzled it down. And soon it came back up. I repeated the process once, twice, until the rest of the water was gone. At that moment, Kambo took its knee off my chest, it released its vice from my head, it drained the sickness from my spirit. In the place of that sickness I discovered new depths of what I was capable of. In those depths was a most transcendent healing. I not only felt better, I was more of me. And that's an incomparable gift to reccive.

Several days later, I repeated my solo shower ceremony to complete the three needed before the lunar cycle ended. Everything went well the third time. Somehow, I knew it would. I knew I had within me the energy, the force of will, the resourcefulness of spirit, whatever it took. I knew it like I never knew it before. I knew this because Kambo had given me the opportunity to find it. Find it in a way I had never experienced so profoundly, so clearly. There is much gratitude in that.

Some will always naysay any idea of communing with plant or animal spirits. They even naysay any notion of us having a higher self or there being any spiritual dimension to life at all. That's all right. They exist where they exist and it's fine for them. But for me, I can say confidently I know and enjoy the relationships I've made in these other realms. Let the naysayers talk all they want. As the native American saying goes, "It is better to have less thunder in the mouth and more lightning in the hand."

BEYOND RECOGNITION

Where else should you go when you've been to places beyond recognition?

What else can you discover about yourself when what you've experienced of yourself, fully dimensioned, is so far beyond recognition?

What more can you ask for when what you've already received is beyond recognition?

Why should you stay in normal conscious time and space when altered states have demonstrated so well that normal space, compared to the truth of what one's being truly entails, is beyond recognition?

Lessons and messages, healings and shamanic journeys, spiritual quests and ongoing explorations beyond recognition abound. At some point, a person continuing with sacred plant medicines no longer goes to them solely to heal distortions or clear the self-image. At some point, one is drawn to brief flashes of insight and momentary ascendencies that explain so much, contain everything, and feel like the home that was and always will be. One can debate forever whether this is an escape from reality or an expansion of consciousness into reality. Usually, though, debate doesn't cut it.

For those who have experienced what sacred plant medicine space offers, the debate cannot be anchored in mundane formulas and concerns. For those who have not lived, however briefly, in that reality more real than the one so intent upon claiming exclusive domain over your consciousness – no words will ever persuade. No description will ever convince detractors that going to a place beyond the recognition of here can be fundamental to not only understanding oneself better, but understanding our relationship to here.

Yes, maybe Odysseus shouldn't have traveled so very far to get home after the Trojan War. It would have been much easier on him and eliminated a lot of complications – and experience. That's one way he could have done it. But then, the richness of his story and the fullness of his life might have been restricted beyond recognition.

"Not all those who wander are lost." – J.R.R. Tolkien

So I guess for some the question will always remain – why should we ever go to this place beyond recognition more than once? We've been there once so what's the point of going back? Maybe because...

"No man ever steps in the same river twice, for it's not the same river and he's not the same man." – Heraclitus

How can one ever be sure they are following the right path? Claircognizance – when information comes to mind suddenly without logic, without prior knowing, without reasons or even memory. It is just a certain and strong knowing. There is no room for doubt. It just is what it is.

It reminds me of all the people who have had similar experiences and how it affected them.

For example, William S. Burroughs once wrote to Allen Ginsberg about his Ayahuasca experience in Panama in 1953 and said, "I experienced first a feeling of serene wisdom so that I was quite content to sit there indefinitely."

Recording artist Sting wrote in his autobiography that his experience with Ayahuasca was the only religious experience he ever had. For 60 pages he describes how he and his wife traveled to the Amazon in Brazil to do Ayahuasca. He summed it up, "There is definitely a higher intelligence at work in you during this experience."

Terence McKenna related a transformative episode when he was nineteen years old in which a twelve-hour LSD trip was like ten years of psychotherapy transpiring within an hour. It not only gave him a unique perspective on himself and made him a better person, it also healed so much of his relationship with his parents. So much so that he said he never had to go back and revisit those troubling things. The critical aspect was how real it all was. And that was worth everything to him.

Cary Grant (famous film star from last century for those under the age of 50) underwent 100 LSD treatment sessions with a Beverly Hills psychiatrist during the years 1958-1961. These just so happen to be the same years of Grant's greatest box office successes. He said of that time, "During my LSD sessions I would learn a great deal. And the result was a rebirth. I finally got where I wanted to go – not completely, because you cut back the barnacles and find more barnacles, and you have to get these off. In life there is no end to getting well..." But ultimately, his breakthrough did come. "After weeks of treatment came a day when I saw the light. When I broke through, I felt an immeasurably beneficial cleansing of so many needless fears and guilts. I lost all the tension that I'd been crippling myself with."

Cary Grant found peace with much of his problems with intimacy and relationships and how it all intertwined with what happened between him and his mother. He also came to terms with the dichotomy between the stage name Cary Grant and his given name, Archibald Leach. As he described it, "For many years I have cautiously peered from behind the face of a man known as Cary Grant. The protection of that facade was both an advantage and a disadvantage. If I couldn't see out, how could anybody see in?"

Cary was very private and it was rare for him to give an interview. But he reached out to Good Housekeeping magazine and told them, "I want to tell the world about this. It has changed my life. Everyone's got to take it." It has been rumored that Timothy Leary heard about the interview and this catalyzed his own interest in LSD. Then in 1966, LSD was made illegal. That was the same year Cary announced his retirement from acting. The same year his daughter was born. He wanted to focus on being a father and providing permanency and stability for her.

Roberta Haynes, an actress who went for similar treatments from the same psychiatrist beginning in 1959, described her experiences, "I was not happy with my life before the LSD. Afterward I was able to be happy. I really think I came out of it knowing what was important in life...In regular Freudian therapy you get an intellectual change, but it doesn't really change anything. What you get from LSD is an emotional change." The treatment psychiatrist, Dr. Mortimer Hartman, described LSD as "...a psychic energizer which empties the subconscious and intensifies emotion and memory a hundred times."

Others have attributed their breakthroughs, both personal and professional, either directly or indirectly, to "mind-opening" altered states. Francis Crick, who discovered DNA's structure, told a friend how he "perceived the double-helix shape while on LSD." A friend of Crick described in an interview how many researchers at Cambridge University saw a microdose as "a thinking tool." Steve Jobs said LSD was "one of the two of three most important things he had done in his life." Kary Mullis, the Nobel Price winner who revolutionized biomedical research with PCR, the polymerase chain reaction technique, seriously doubted he would have come up with such a thing if it were not because he "took plenty of LSD" in the '60's and 70's. John C. Lilly, LSD user, pioneered the field of electronic brain stimulation and founded the branch of science to explore interspecies communication between humans, dolphins and whales. He also invented the first sensory deprivation changer. He was friends with Richard Feynman, the theoretical physicist who jointly received the Nobel Prize for development of quantum electrodynamics and who, with Lilly, experimented with deprivation tanks, LSD, and cannabis. Carl Sagan, astrophysicist and cosmologist, was a regular cannabis user and advocate for its use to enhance intellectual pursuits, though his support was not public. He did add an essay to a book in 1971 titled "Marijuana Reconsidered." The essay was under the assumed name "Mr. X" but the identity of its true author was only revealed after Sagan's death.

Of course, LSD is not a plant medicine, but it is an effective means to a transformative altered state. It reminds me of a sentiment often expressed by Graham Hancock. If we as individuals don't have sovereignty over our own consciousness and what we do with it, something so fundamental to being an individual, then what freedom do any of us have?

Science journalist and researcher Graham Hancock has sold over 5 million books, primarily delving into the human past and trying to reconstruct our origins and lost histories. His research led him to the conclusion that most of humanity's history on this planet is very boring, dull, uninteresting, non-creative. At least until around 40,000 years ago when changes started showing up. The birth of art exploded around the world. Innovation with tools and language took off. Human history began a trajectory that would change things beyond recognition.

To explain this, some point to the strange case of the HAR1F gene, studied at the University of California at Santa Cruz. Their research raised the possibility that something with the HAR1F gene was responsible in whole or part with how the human brain rapidly evolved to be so different from our chimp ancestors. HAR1F didn't exist until 300 million ago then it stayed constant for an awful long time. Scientists say humans and chimps fully diverged from a common ancestor about 7 million years ago. So that must be when some dramatic change came to fruition.

In a relative blink of an eye, 18 nucleotides in HAR1F suddenly (in evolutionary terms) mutated in humans while the gene remained constant in chimps, gorillas, orangutans, and macaques. Scholarly genetic research can't determine the exact cause of such an accelerated change, even after studying those parts of the entire human genome that changed extensively in the last 5 million years. But somehow human brains did triple in size rather rapidly over those of the chimps.

Even today, for reasons that aren't totally clear, the HAR1F gene "turns on" in the human fetus 7 weeks after conception then shuts back down at 19 weeks. Interestingly enough, at 7-1/2 weeks the fetal cerebral hemispheres cover more than half of the diencephalon. The diencephalon is the region of the embryonic vertebrate neural tube that gives rise to anterior forebrain structures including the thalamus, hypothalamus, posterior portion of the pituitary gland, and pineal gland. Meanwhile, brain science is changing beyond recognition.

Agreeing with Graham Hancock, Terence McKenna came up with his Stoned Ape Theory to explain this rapid progress after so many eons of not much going on. Perhaps climate change forced certain primate groups out of the trees and into greener pastures. In those pastures they searched for food and found psilocybin mushrooms. They found other things too, many of which contained DMT. Over time, perhaps this had a cumulative effect, one that through neural genesis gave rise to brighter imaginations, symbolic language, and a communal tribal sense that not only helped the species survive, but thrive.

A consummate researcher, Graham Hancock became curious upon discovering stories from all over the world of widely disparate shamanic cultures experiencing the same landscapes, visions, creatures, dimensions through plant medicine use. These people had no contact with each other and yet were having remarkably similar experiences. When he asked the shaman why, he was summarily told because these others realms are real. It makes sense, if two people who don't know each other go to the same real place, they'll see the same things. But science called these experiences hallucinations. They were non-real or illusory experiences. Hancock's curiosity piqued when he discovered that even test subjects in research labs who were given these same shamanic substances were experiencing the same things. Half-human half-animal intelligences showed up, complex sacred geometry fractalled around and through them, passages into dimensions appeared where the rules of time, space, matter no longer applied. This alien landscape was so beyond recognition to anything here and now and yet it was a common experience. How could this be?

Of course, there was the quantum physics explanation where simultaneous probabilities of parallel dimensions and alternate universes bounced up and down on the string-theory yo-yo. Hadn't quantum physics blown away many conceptions of reality to the point where final answers to where it all came from and where it went was now relegated to a place beyond recognition?

Hancock wanted to find out for himself. He traveled to Brazil for 5 weeks and had 11 experiences with the Vine of the Soul, Ayahuasca. He says he had an absolutely convincing encounter with another reality, one in which he was getting genuine communication from intelligences unlike anything in the here and now. He was taken on a serious life review where he needed to clearly confront the true motives in his life. He couldn't hide from it. It was made clear to him – his past couldn't be changed but he was being given an opportunity to move forward in a clear way that wasn't like that anymore.

The only thing that interrupted the visions, the contact, the communication was his own fear. It was made known to him, he would have to overcome his fear if he wanted to understand. That was the fundamental rule of moving forward. Once free of fear, he would be able to get maximum benefit from where he went in these realms. Since that first experience, Graham has since explored ibogaine, psilocybin mushrooms, DMT, and more Ayahuasca. He is convinced not only in the reality of the realms made available by these substances, but also the benefits going there can serve those who approach them correctly.

Aldous Huxley had an altered state experience in 1955 he considered most profound, more so than any other. It overwhelmed him so much so that he said everything previous were nothing but "entertaining sideshows." In a letter to Humphry Osmond, he summed it up by asserting his experience was "the direct, total awareness, from the inside, so to say, of Love as the primary and fundamental cosmic fact. ...I was this fact; or perhaps it would be more accurate to say that this fact occupied the place where I had been. ...And the things which had entirely filled my attention on that first occasion, I now perceived to be temptations – temptations to escape from the central reality into a false, or at least imperfect and partial Nirvanas of beauty and mere knowledge."

Ultimately, it comes down to one's personal choice, how one wants life to unfold.

"Don't ask yourself what the world needs. Ask yourself what makes you come alive and go and do that. Because what the world needs is more people who have come alive." – Howard Thurman

"Since things neither exist nor do not exist, are neither real nor unreal, are utterly beyond adopting and rejecting – one might as well burst out laughing." Tibetan Nyingmapa master – Longchenpa Rabjampa

"All thoughts vanish into emptiness, like the imprint of a bird in the sky." From the "Sadhana of Mahamudra," by Chögyam Trungpa

"Small enlightenments have to succeed each other. And they have to be fed all the time, in order for a great enlightenment to be possible. So a moment of living in mindfulness is already a moment of enlightenment. If you train yourself to live in such a way, happiness and enlightenment will continue to grow." – Thich Nhat Hanh

"When it comes time to die, be not like those whose hearts are filled with the fear of death, so when their time comes they weep and pray for little more time to live over again in a different way. Sing your death song, and die like a hero going home." – Chief Aupumut Mohican, 1725

"In shamanic cultures, synchronicities are recognized as signs that you are on the right path." – Daniel Pinchbeck

"Psychedelics are illegal not because a loving government is concerned that you might jump out of a third story window. Psychedelics are illegal because they dissolve opinion structures and culturally laid down models of behavior and information processing. They open you up to the possibility that everything you know is wrong." – Terence McKenna

"It is no measure of health to be well adjusted to a profoundly sick society." – Jiddu Krishnamurti

"Hold on to what is good, even if it's a handful of earth. Hold on to what you believe, even if it's a tree that stands by itself. Hold on to what you must do, even if it's a long way from here. Hold on to your life, even if it's easier to let go. Hold on to my hand, even if someday I'll be gone away from you." – A Pueblo Indian Prayer

The Q'ero shaman of Peru released their teachings to the West when events signaled to them the beginning fulfillment of a prophecy that went back 500 years. They needed to do this in preparation for the day the Eagle of the North and the Condor of the South fly together again. Their word for love and compassion is "munay." The prophecy says munay will guide the great gathering of separate peoples. As Don Antonio Morales, a master Q'ero shaman summed it up, "The new caretakers of the Earth will come from the West, and those that have made the greatest impact on Mother Earth now have the moral responsibility to remake their relationship with Her, after remaking themselves."

The prophecy spells out clearly: North America will contribute the physical strength, or body of the transformation. Europe will supply the mental aspect, or head. And South America will supply the heart. This coalition of strength, head, and heart will allow order to emerge out of chaos.

"Looking behind I am filled with gratitude. Looking forward I am filled with vision. Looking upwards I am filled with strength. Looking within I discover peace." – Q'ero shaman

Or…one can be content with the impression of reality that philosophers, scientists, and mathematicians present as the sane and balanced answer to what and where we are and what this all does or doesn't mean. If you want to go that way, then the question you face is – can we understand our own minds?

Godel's Incompleteness Theorem, Church's Undecidability Theorem, Turning's Halting Theorem, Tarski's Truth Theorem all warn… like some ancient fairy tale, to seek self-knowledge is to embark on a journey which will always be incomplete, cannot be charted on any map, will never halt, cannot be described.

In other words, it's a journey into everything that's beyond recognition.

There is still a way there that satisfies, a way that expands one's consciousness to envelop the possibilities that exist. But no philosopher, scientist, or mathematician can take you there.

You go alone. You go by surrendering to the process in humility and gratitude.

But as Harry Callahan aka Dirty Harry so succinctly summed it up – "I know what you're thinking…You've gotta ask yourself one question – Do I feel lucky? Well, do ya, punk?"

Kawsaypacha Beyond the Puzzle

Re-remembering is illuminating. Only recently have I re-remembered a moment from a Huachuma ceremony a year ago. It was mid-ceremony. Grandfather interrupted me, short-circuiting my streaming mindforms, logical constructs, and imagined pithy questions. He interjected a simple revelation that is stunning only in retrospect. It was a statement of future-fact that appeared as a non sequitur at the time. He whispered matter-of-factly, confidently, *"There will come a time when you'll arrive at a place beyond lessons and messages."*

As his words melted into shimmering nature so alive around me, a swirl of emotional energies swept me deeper into thoughtless meditation. Looking back, that swirl into only energy and emotion was as much prophetic as prescriptive. I feel now this comes to mind as the only thing that makes emotional sense to explain my reflections after two recent ceremonies in Peru – one ceremony at the Temple of the Moon and another in Valle Sagrado, the Incan Sacred Valley. It goes a long way to explain the world of living energy I was connected to, both past and present – the living energy from where all things arise – the living energy the Incas called Kawsaypacha.

Temple of the Moon Ceremony

Words fail. Images give impressions. Feelings stretch their limits. Expectations collide with the coincidence of belief. I arrived in Cusco on the afternoon of gigantic clouds, penetrating sun, and living cobblestones. Three days later I awoke early for the climb through narrow passageways squeezed between walls whose foundation stones were laid in place by hands put to rest five centuries ago. To the meeting place, a gathering of ceremony participants. From there a taxi ride found a place in the mountains high above the scenic overlooks. The weather would be anything as changes overhead loomed. At an altitude topping 12k-feet the door of the maloca opened to welcome all. It was mid-morning.

There were greetings, brief explanations, prayers by a Q'ero Paq'o (shaman) and Wisdomkeeper, the pouring of the medicine, then silent intentions all around. We were free to stay in the maloca or find a place in either of two gardens. I laid down on a rock slab in the garden farthest from the maloca. Underneath the rocks was a tunnel the Incas had used for passage into the Temple of the Moon nearby. A hummingbird, patches of flowers, and scruffs of grass impinged on an awareness that expanded beyond the visible. With the glide into medicine space came a sense of purpose lingering as my original intention. Before I could collect my thoughts, Grandfather scattered them.

"You can have one question. But that's all today. There will be no other words..."

I had no thought of discussing this proclamation. I knew the certainty of it in a telepathic way that left all boundaries of logic ebbing somewhere behind in a timeless silence. I had spoken to Grandfather enough before to know I didn't know until I let go of that kind of presumed knowing. I got right to the point and asked my question. It was something that had been pestering me for quite some time. I never could gauge if the question was minor or major, but I felt it went to the heart of ceremony space itself.

"Is the medicine only for healing oneself and correcting problems within – or is it also for expanded learning and exploration?"

The sky rearranged in the expectant silence that followed. The air electrified with an energy I had never felt before. The rock underneath me felt more and more like an extension of myself. And then Grandfather's answer came. As he said, it would be the last words spoken that day. To deliver them, he drew close, very close, so close that his passionate whisper reverberated through me:

"WHAT'S THE DIFFERENCE?"

With that, he proceeded to unwrap the day like opening his Misaq'epe, the ceremonial bundle containing the shaman's sacred objects. First revealed was a condensed perspective of my question, answered. To need more learning and seek more exploration in medicine space implied something needed to be healed, or a problem or negative energy needed to be cleared.

Conversely, to seek healing and freedom from a problem implied more learning and exploration was required. To be free of one meant liberation from the need for the other. If I was coming to the medicine because I thought I needed to learn and explore more, then there was more to heal. It could be no other way. Extending what he had said a year before, *"There will come a time when you'll arrive at a place beyond lessons and messages, beyond healing, beyond studied exploration."*

Next out of the Misaq'epe was his day-long revelation. Without words he immersed me in an experience of a kind only possible beyond learning and exploration. It was simply being, if being were so simple. But true being is never a static thing. It's exactly the opposite. There would always be something more, but that more is not contained in the something else we usually concerned ourselves with.

It's the more you didn't have to go exploring after or learn about. It's the more of being All, the All that was always you. It's a connection to unity, to ancestors, to a heartfelt energy of certainty, an infinite vibration of joyful expression. It's the unending, creative unfolding of Kawsaypacha itself. In essence, it's home.

Anything else is a temporary puzzle of mind and matter and ego mischief that shifts what one only believes is being learned or explored back upon phantom problems and conditioned impulses for healing and deliverance made falsely urgent by pervasive delusions of supposed purpose, forced explanation, and willful intent, even identity. It's nothing you need to redefine. It's an experience you can't define. The notion of experience itself is too limiting, too time-bound, too sequential, too localized, too constrained by concepts of something being added by process. There is no process. You can't make it happen. It IS happening.

On one hand, life is the puzzle we try to step back from to see the big picture. All the while, we earnestly attempt to actualize the genuine, single puzzle piece we believe we are. If the puzzle were put together as our simple logic and anticipation expected – and we actually were that single cut-out piece – the answers we seek might appear clear. Yet, pursued that way, satisfying answers never emerge. To placate ourselves, we fill our senses and sensibilities with convoluted "-ism's" in a vain attempt to explain the dilemma away.

But the puzzle's picture doesn't emerge after being put together the way we expect. And beyond our imagined problems and their often agonized healing, beyond trans-versing insatiable need for more learning or exploring, there is a More, the All that remains elusive due to our methods to perceive it. The colors and shapes we strain to make sense out of don't have to show the picture we expect. The worldly canvass we believe our single puzzle piece must fit into doesn't have to be three-dimensional. The experience of not being in the puzzle, but the puzzle being in us, brought this out so clearly. That clarity settled in the heart – and only in the heart is it understood.

Bathed in this experience, this unfolding, I felt the steady rise of vibration around and through me, extending into and from the rock I was lying on. Then I heard words, but not from Grandfather. It was the ceremony's facilitator stopping to offer a second glass of Huachuma. "Do you want to go deeper?" I nodded to him, found my legs, then rose up to receive a second glass of the medicine. It was thick, almost gelatin as it glopped from the bottom of a tall green bottle. It went down easy, without taste, and I laid back down, once again joined with the Earth.

I stayed on that flat slate rock until the feel of something more organic attracted me. Under a small tree I found more connection until rain fell too vigorously to ignore. Nearby was an outdoor, covered sitting area with seats grouped around a fireplace. Somehow I moved to it then sat there feeling the fire's warmth for a few moments before I noticed I wasn't alone. Nearby, silent in a seat across the way, the same Q'ero Wisdomkeeper who had opened the ceremony with prayers spoken in the Quechua language now silently meditated. As I looked over to him, he had one hand working delicately in the Ch'uspa on his lap. A Ch'uspa is a small, rectangular, tightly woven bag used to carry coca leaves.

When he looked up it was right at me, with a slight smile, as if he already knew I was looking at him. His eyes smiled back then his head bowed in meditation. We sat there together for quite a while, just the two of us. Once or twice he got up briefly to add more wood to the fire. Otherwise, he was in meditation with his fingers working his hidden coca leaves as if using them in prayer. Sounds of fire crackling, the rain's patter, the soft wind of the brief storm blowing through with occasional thunder was the soundtrack to the puzzle dissolving away.

There was no need to measure time, even if it existed. The two of us shared a silent meditation for quite a while with growing energy of communion between us. As more medicine opened and deepened within me, I felt an energetic link, a telepathic conduit with him. I wanted to connect with him, to understand him beyond the superficial evidence of the five senses. I expected to contact and see something with the joining, but what I saw was like looking through a window. He was a window. I could look through him to see more but not see him other than a window. It was most bizarre and yet clearly so right in the moment. That window was so clear.

He got up and set to work on the ground before me, placing a golden metal vessel and chunks of Palo Santo wood in it. He bent low and set the wood afire, tending the small flame until great plumes of aromatic smoke arose over us both. Then he stood and motioned me forward, towards him. At first I thought he meant for me to get down next to the Palo Santo container but no. He hastened me to stand up facing him.

What followed was a prayer and smudging ritual. Shaking condor feathers near me, he quickly recited in Quechua while intermittently adding the Phukuyr'tti, the ritual blowing used for healing and cleansing. As he blew quick bursts of air through the feathers in between prayer, he moved over and around me, all the while coaxing more Palo Santo smoke to envelop us both.

I discovered later what he was actually doing during his cleansing. In essence, he was cleaning the hucha (heavy energy) from me and introducing sami (light energy) into the aura. The hucha is moved down to the base of the spine and out through the root chakra and into Pachamama to be recycled. Through the crown chakra sami is then introduced to complete the cleansing. Afterwards, he smiled with a quick bow of his head and lightly stepped away. Somehow he anticipated the rain would stop just then and I'd be called to recline on the slab of rock again.

Hours melted, enveloped in a strengthening energy of the place and the people who had lived there so long before. A sense of vibration from ancestors added to the mix of connections to spirit beyond the puzzle. I floated deeper into a tranquility of being joy even as a raw edge and intensity of stories to be told gathered around me. There was something to be told, to be carried forward, not to be forgotten, to make come to pass, to behold and take to heart in a future we were birthing.

It was the effect of the cause, the there of the now, the here of the then, the way to be set among gathering balances long overdue. Amidst the ecstasy of being were stacked, polished stones of events past in a continuum where everything was equally present. Among the humming energies of voices long ago silenced were promises of fulfillment in becoming the prophecy to come. No words were communicated. It was all feeling and intention and compassionate journeying with the essence of who they were – and are.

Out of the sky above me I finally heard a voice inserting itself in the glide and pulsation of the soulful resonance between past, present, and future. It was the ceremony facilitator again, this time gently suggesting I should get up and drink some water. I didn't know it but the rain clouds had long since past by and for awhile now an intense sun at high altitude was baking me into the rock. I had no idea just how hot it was until I returned to my body and felt it. I thanked him for the reminder and did what he said. In the other garden was water and shade. I took in some of both before returning to the second garden and a new spot on the grass under a tree.

There my vibration lowered and I rejoined with Pachamama and the world of the puma. The sights and smells and sounds of nature engulfed my restored senses. The bright sun set all colors aflame with life. A hummingbird's wings quivered nearby like notes from a ceremonial flute. The swaying of branches and leaves over me danced in cadence with ceremonial passion. Nature itself was in the medicine circle, providing a sixth-sense icaro I heard so well. Tears came to my eyes at the thought of nature singing and dancing its own icaro. More tears came on the renewed realization sent through me – there was no difference – the icaro was my own for I was Nature.

Soon, a bowl of cut-up fruit was given to me at the place under the tree.

I found I had to eat so slowly. Each bite approached the limits of ecstasy I could absorb. Afterwards, I closed my eyes and floated back to realms above the garden. I stayed there until the facilitator came by after a timeless lapse of the afternoon to notify me that those who wanted to and were able could soon go to the Temple of the Moon. I thanked him and let him know I would be joining those who went.

In a short while, a small group of us took a hike into the high wilderness beyond the property. Along the way we were told the history and meaning of several sections of the temple area. There was condor rock, where one could sit on either the right (feminine) or left (masculine) wing to balance those energies within us. There was a large, "magnetic" rock, with a huge polished cut-out into which one stood to feel a magnetic, flowing connection to Earth. There was the cool pool of a cleansing stream where ceremonies with the water washed away anything that didn't serve temple participants.

And then there was the temple itself, a gigantic split in the highest point of the mountain complex, where the Incas believed entry into Pachamama herself was possible. This was done for offerings of thanks and wishes for what was wanted in life. I took a photo of part of the temple but only realized when I got home that I had captured someone on top, it appears in the middle of their own ceremony. I did not see this person up there when I was at the temple, but I assume this can be explained away by the fact that I was so deep into the medicine at the time. Finding this in the photo was spooky to say the least.

Each of us were given three coca leaves as our offering to Pachamama, then one by one we climbed the large stones guarding what was symbolically assumed to be the opening of Pachamama's legs.

Each of us had our own private time within the temple to give thanks and make our wishes known only to the temple, only to Pachamama. The

Wisdomkeeper sat respectfully silent by the opening.

There was more than one altar within the temple. The first one was immediately on the left, gouged and polished smooth and flat in solid rock. The light from outside quickly fell off as I stepped back into the temple. The height and width of the space also diminished gradually until I had to stoop down and crouch to go any farther. There was no abrupt end, no way of knowing when you've arrived at where you needed to be. I felt impelled to keep going, to bend and crouch lower into a squat to continue on.

Just when I thought maybe I should not attempt to venture any deeper into what had become a small tunnel, a light came into view. It was quite stark and intensely focused on a spot even further on. It was clear very quickly that the light source was from above, but how was this possible? I had tunneled deep into the dark in the side of a mountain face. To see such an intense spot of light descending from above meant there must be a narrow opening in the mountain that extended all the way down to this exact point.

Strategically enough, this spot of light focused on where it was too narrow and small to go. It was as if I had passed through the legs and arrived at the very cervix of Pachamama herself. Nothing less than the portal to creation lay before me. And before it, I saw in the light, small groups of coca leaves set out on a low layer of polished dark stone. I crawled forward, made my thanks, then placed my coca leaves there too. There I made my wish known and remained in silence to take in the energy coming back at me. Appropriately enough, the offering space was in the light. And interestingly enough, one could physically approach it only on bended knee.

After I exited the temple, all of us sat near its opening and let the feeling of the place and what we had done seep within. It was late afternoon, over eight hours since our first taste of the medicine. For those who had heeded the call to "go deeper" and had the second glassful halfway through, we would be in the medicine space for some time yet. On the hike back to the maloca, we passed by a local woman tending her sheep. The sheep casually grazed and kept moving over rocks it was obvious had been shaped and polished by ancient hands to be part of temple rituals. And life still flowed over them, just as the Incas would have wanted.

I had not planned on staying in the mountains overnight. Likewise, I had not expected a second full glass of medicine. When it came time to be taken into town, the sun was disappearing fast but the effects of medicine space were not. Walking the streets of Cusco back to my hotel ramped the energetic connections to a different level. Modern Cusco seemed to be in varying degrees an elaborate but transitory CGI overlay of another energetic reality quite different and more permanent – one that had been there far longer than the buildings now rising above ancient foundation stones. I walked in two worlds, two times. The earlier time overwhelmed me with its strength and creativity, but also its horror and heartache. Ultimately, it held out to me its promise and unity with cosmic forces that knew that balance would once again be established – one way or another.

There was no end to my Temple of the Moon ceremony until much later in the evening. Looking back on it, I'm glad I had the opportunity to see Cusco this way. At the time it was jarring, energetically disruptive, and sometimes confusing. Lingering impulses and stories from those no longer present passed through me. Overlapping time-frames inhabited the spaces between the spaces. It was obvious the medicine wanted to do more with me – but it wouldn't all occur that evening. I'd have to find a way to continue the connection to this place, this energy and the ancestors on another day.

Sacred Valley Ceremony

Images fail. Words give impressions. Expectations stretch their limits. Feelings collide with the coincidence of lingering experience.

I arrived in the Sacred Valley in the afternoon, a few days after my journey at the Temple of the Moon. I had just climbed through the elevated ruins at Pisac then driven on towards Ollantaytambo.

The following day was filled with a train ride to Agua Calientes, then an afternoon exploration of Machu Picchu. A guide brought the site back to life with details and history, culture and tradition. This came as the culmination of ruin visits on previous days that spanned Saqsaywaman, Q'enqo, Chinchero, Tipon, Puka Pukara, and Pikillacta.

The collective effect of all of this, added to the Temple of the Moon ceremony, was to widen the opening to energies and essences of those once in flesh yet remained in spirit in these places. Never before had time felt so malleable, space so dimensional beyond the perception of regular senses.

It was nearly 10pm by the time the return train ride got me back to the hotel in the Sacred Valley. As before, lingering impulses and stories from those no longer present passed through me from those inhabiting the spaces between the spaces. It was obvious the medicine wanted to do more with me but it couldn't occur that evening. I'd have to find a way to continue the connection to this place, this energy and the ancestors on another day.

A strong impulse was there to take the next day and carry on what the Temple of the Moon ceremony had started. I needed to dedicate a day to a ceremony of my own making. With medicine I had with me, I would find a place out in nature to extend the journey into wherever Grandfather was suggesting. As it turned out, the following day had beautiful weather and a site down by the Urubamba River was perfect.

I took the medicine, had a swim in the pool, then found a place to ease into the onset of medicine space. What followed was a day-long passage into the energy and connection I had felt before. Only this time there was no process getting through and beyond the puzzle of it all. There were no big lessons, no great messages from beyond, no roller coaster ride through past-life reviews, no convoluted constructs of any kind. Only Kawsaypacha. I simply melted into a simplicity that contained all, a loving embrace that was an infinite creative unfolding, a sense of unity with the spirits of those who had gone before, whose truth couldn't die with the stroke of a conqueror's sword for it's a truth intrinsic to our being. And in the great cycle of things, it was a truth that would find transformative power in the new world of Pachacuti.

The day was certainly a fulfillment of what Grandfather had whispered to me over a year before – *"There will come a time when you'll arrive at a place beyond lessons and messages."*

Only after visiting these sites and returning home did I research the connection between the Inca civilization and the Q'ero people. I soon discovered they are believed to be the last of the Incas. They are descendents of a tribe of 600 who fled above altitudes of 14,000 feet to escape the conquistadors. The invaders wouldn't chase them to such heights. And so for 500 years the Q'eros have lived in near solitude and preserved the old sacred ways, including the prophecy of a "pachacuti" or great change to come to restore harmony and order to the world. In that role, the Q'eros are the caretakers of the rites and prophecies of the Incas uncorrupted by Spanish or Christian influences.

Q'ero prophecies are positive in outcome but anticipate tumultuous changes in the earth and in the human psyche. These must come first. These will be profound enough to redefine our spirituality and relationships. They call this tumult before another golden age a "pachacuti." Pachacuti was one of the great Incan rulers. But his name derives from a more general sense of Pacha meaning "earth" or "time," and "cuti" meaning "to set things right." For some, he is the luminous one who stepped outside of time and promises to return to be a transformer. But most believe this interpretation is too literal. Instead of referring to a single individual, they see the prophecy invoking the power of all people to embody this coming transformation.

Signs that this process has already begun were set off in 1949 when, in fulfillment of prophecy, a previously unknown but ancient Incan temple of gold was exposed by an earthquake at a monastery near Cusco. This was a strong sign that Q'eros should now share their prophecies and wisdom with the modern world, even take in outsiders to be initiates with them and help the integration of Eagle and Condor in combined sacred purpose to come to pass.

Unwise and negative paradigms will fade as the sacred ways of old return. Q'ero shamans even speak of a tear in time itself to occur. Critical to this unfoldment are Star Rites, or "Mosoq Karpay," the Rites of the Time to Come. Included in these ceremonial rites is the end of one's relationship to time. This is mediated by one's heart. This is the beginning to plant the seed of knowledge or Pachacuti in one's own luminous body. It then becomes each person's responsibility to nurture that seed and follow through until it blossoms. It is an offering of a destiny of sacred transformation for the earth and for all who live on it.

But the Q'ero believe the complete, ancient knowledge cannot be manifested again by an individual; it's only accessed by a tribe. This will be a tribe of those who took the leap into the body of an Inca, a luminous one. With that commitment one connects to the stars, to the opening doorway between worlds and possibilities. Only then can the prophesied tribe explore the healing range of human capabilities. Only then do we regain our rightful, luminous nature overall and begin the golden age.

But we must dare to take the leap.

The Interrupted Conversation

One beautiful afternoon I took a microdose of San Pedro while relaxing by the river. Before long, I got into a continuing discussion with my wife, some of which was contentious. In a good way. The way that works through opposing sides of an argument.

The conversation continued a topic we had tossed around back home over coffee. It regarded people who say they've received a message from beyond and need to share it. Oftentimes portrayed most dramatically, the claim is made that their directive or calling is to share this message with the world. Also included in this group are people who say they're simply relating their experiences from beyond with no other agenda, but in doing so, they manage to pull towards them a growing group of followers. Not wanting to disappoint, be misunderstood, or leave anything out, the followers are fed more and more of the same until simple sharing starts to walk and talk like a prophetic calling with prescriptions and embellishments galore to please an audience egged-on to keep returning wide-eyed and expectant.

It's an old question – what are the motivations of these people with messages for the world? Do they make a cottage industry out of their calling in order to support their lifestyle, oftentimes a lifestyle of success they hadn't enjoyed before? Do their efforts, even for the best-intentioned ones, eventually morph to be as much about ego and profit as about fulfilling their original calling? For that matter, when is such a calling ever fulfilled? As long as there exists one person in the world who hasn't heard and understood this message from beyond, must the process by necessity continue? How does one in such a position keep their head in the mystical, prosperous clouds while maintaining an earthly existence based in honest intentions?

If someone comes back from a near-death experience with a strong, otherworldly impulse to share the profundity they've learned, that may be completely valid. So they write a book to share their message. But then they write a second and third book. They sell tickets to conferences for people to hear them relate more details about the message. Over time, given the need for more material to speak or write about, maybe their original message evolves into an increasingly elaborate methodology for living.

Out of this emerging, systematic philosophy comes cult-like nomenclatures and reinforcing practices for devotees to study and habitualize. How much of this "mystical branding" is done because it is required by the original message and how much is manufactured and packaged to distinguish this particular good news from the rest of the available messages from beyond clammering for attention?

Since, as they say, there's nothing new under the sun, a case can be made to suspect that much of these new methods and their related jargons are in whole or part borrowed from other, more ancient traditions. This is explained away by the excuse (or valid point) that such ancient wisdom must be "updated" for current cultural consumption. Maybe a modern translation of ancient, esoteric concepts is good for reconnecting new generations with universal truths. Yes. Or perhaps it's intellectual plagiarism when the original format of the concepts is clear enough and approachable but the ancient material is in the public domain and thus there's no profit in it.

So many so-called universal truths are quite simple and straightforward. Does anyone really need a weekend conference and practice workbook to get the concept of "loving others as yourself" or "do no harm?" But if people need to change the world by reaching the billions of needy people with these important messages, is there anything wrong with making a living by it at the same time? People have to live and if they flourish as they grow a way to spread the good news to more and more people, how can that not be a good thing?

My wife recently read a book by Anita Moorjani called, "What if This is Heaven?" This is a more recent, follow-up book to Moorjani's earlier, very successful and engaging near-death memoir, "Dying to Be Me." Both books, it can be argued, have powerful messages that can inspire people and in so doing improve their lives. In the discussion between my wife and me before we took the river walk, I had raised the general curiosity about people with a mystical message turning the process into an ongoing business.

Greatly liking the books, my wife questioned my implicit questioning of Moorjani's motives in producing her latest literary effort and the paid talks she describes in same book. In all fairness, Moorjani herself describes her challenges and processes in staying true to her message, in spite of encountering influences that could pull her back in the worldly influences of being a guru, needing approval, fear, and more.

Rightfully so, when we got to the river, my wife drew parallels between Moorjani and others, such as Terence McKenna, someone I had directed her to in the past. Perhaps his notoriety and numerous talks were motivated by ego and/or making money. Who's to say? What's the difference between what he did and what Moorjani is doing now? If fame results from spreading a message, how does one ever manage to keep the fame and lifestyle issues in check so the message doesn't get lost or blown into something the great beyond never intended?

All of this holds valid points. The answer to it may or may not be as simple and clear as those mystical messages from beyond. It seems one can never tell. It all comes down to intention, motivation, what exists in a person's heart and mind. If something improves peoples' lives, helps them get through problems, inspires them to be their best selves and treat other people better, then more power to the process that brought it about. Isn't that reasonable?

The main caveat I see is the convoluted dross that inevitably gets embellished over the simple, pure messages in an effort to keep the gravy trains running. There's a danger that people will be so flooded with methods and practices and jargon and workshop exercises ad nauseum that the symbols will be mistaken for the meaning. When that happens, it is all too easy for the intent of the original message to get lost or be distorted beyond recognition.

Sitting by the riverbank, steeped in this very interesting conversation, I quickly became aware of a building energy coalescing within and around me in a rush. San Pedro was showing up in a big way. In a fractured instant, my will to speak was shut off. At the same time, I saw an aura of energy in a sphere that extended out from me nearly nine feet in all directions. As soon as I saw this energy, it imploded into my chest with concussive force.

Simultaneously, another form of energy blasted forth from the same place, and in doing so lit up my surroundings, the river, the trees, the clouds, even the sky more intensely. A strong connection to that shimmering glow overpowered me with an immediacy both gentle and nonnegotiable. In that split moment, a moment of implosion/explosion, a mantra started and softly repeated from everywhere. Its repetition returned for the next hour. It was my mystical message from beyond. Ultimately, as the meditation persisted, I felt it was a call to focus, to center on what was real and what was important, to not be distracted.

Over and over I heard – *"Stay grounded in core energies / core energies are ascendant."*

It was a paradox made sensible, a union of earth and sky, a surge of true-self energy that allowed a magnificent grounding, a grounding that counterintuitively enabled transcendence. But this was an incomparability that didn't dissolve here and now. This transcendence looked a lot like being in the present moment. Except those moments expanded in the core of significance and potential. Far from dissolving the here and now, both became more real, more approachable.

Grounding in a fully-dimensioned reality eliminates the drift towards so much distraction, so much banter, so much wonder over the outliers of our presumed cleverness, so much wise doubt chasing the code-hacks of ultimate meaning, so much anxious consciousness finding the nuanced voids in ourselves. I laid back and took it in. I laid back and let it out. I laid back and found a grounding in the ascendant. Far from journeying away, I sank into a state of being more there. In many ways it was a there constrained by a now in order to have form. In other ways, it was a now to be experienced in its totality, a completeness outside time.

As the mantra faded away, an infused sense of potential energy swelled within. The possible wanted release as an expression of here and now. I contained the zero-point probability that joins that potential at the nexus of what I did, what I created. Awakening to a grounding in the ascendant empowers expressions of being, it drives fully kinetic the essence of us.

For those few moments out of time, I was more in my skin, truly inhabiting the space I took up. It was a glimpse at a state of balance of opposites I rarely if ever manage. Like most people, most of the time if not all of the time I exist in varying degrees shifted from such a profoundly resonant equilibrium. But simply feeling it is possible while we breathe on this planet is tremendous.

And so I guess I've rejoined the conversation in a new way – for I've gotten my own mystic message from beyond. One could say I now face the dilemma of what to do with it. As with most of my plant medicine experiences, I'll write it down so the vagaries of fading or rearranged memory don't rob me of knowing critical details of what happened last year or last decade. Granted, I could write this in a private document and keep it to myself.

Or I could make it available for others to read. The same old questions about ego and profit motive (not all profit is financial) could be spun around my efforts here, just like with Anita Moorjani or Terence McKenna. For now, I leave it at this – if someone reads any of their work, or the work of others with a message from beyond, or if they read this, and if any of it has a positive effect, then I defer to the unanswered question: what's the harm?

Raki-Raki Yanantin Time

My trip to Peru affected me more than expected. Climbing Inca ruins and feeling the energy of Cusco became a connection with people who once lived there long ago. Adding power to this were the San Pedro ceremonies, one at the Temple of the Moon and another in the Sacred Valley. They only reinforced the fervent energy of the place and especially the people long past whose essence still permeates the area.

I remembered standing in Plaza de Armas in Cusco, the place where in 1572 the last Sapa Inca, Túpac Amaru, spoke his last words to quiet a saddened but tumultuous crowd before being beheaded – "Ccollanan Pachacamac ricuy auccacunac yawarniy hichascancuta" ("Pacha Kamaq, witness how my enemies shed my blood").

This was the same plaza, in Cusco, where 209 years later in 1781, Túpac Amaru's great-great-great-grandson, José Gabriel Túpac Amaru, was publicly executed by the invader Christians. As one historian described the execution – "Amaru II was sentenced to be executed. He was forced to bear witness to the execution of his wife Micaela Bastidas, his eldest son Hipólito, his uncle Francisco Tupa Amaru, his brother-in-law Antonio Bastidas, and some of his captains before his own death.

The following is an extract from the official judicial death issued by the Spanish authorities which condemns Túpac Amaru II to torture and death. It was ordered in sentence that Túpac Amaru II was condemned to have his tongue cut out, after watching the executions of his family, and to have his hands and feet tied...

"...to four horses who will then be driven at once toward the four corners of the plaza, pulling the arms and legs from his body. The torso will then be taken to the hill overlooking the city... where it will be burned in a bonfire... Tupac Amaru's head will be sent to Tinta to be displayed for three days in the place of public execution and then placed upon a pike at the principal entrance to the city. One of his arms will be sent to Tungasuca, where he was the cacique, and the other arm to the capital province of Carabaya, to be similarly displayed in those locations. His legs will be sent to Livitica and Santa Rosas in the provinces of Chumbivilcas and Lampa, respectively."

So much for Christian love and compassion, loving your enemies, turning the other cheek, and emulating the Prince of Peace. History has amply shown all over the world – all of that faux piety only gets lip service after the blessed clergy mercilessly wipes out anyone who doesn't agree with them, forbids their culture and language, steals their gold, and brainwashes their children to deny and forget their heritage. Just about every town in South America has a Catholic Church in the center of it and yet the genocide this represents somehow gets a pass. It's sadly instructive to see how the descendants of the original victims of this outrage even today stoically cling to the language, religion, and customs of the invaders.

I came back home feeling pulled by unfinished business. It was hard to tell what any of it meant. Was this merely a spiritual connection to members of a civilization long gone or a calling to be part of something now? The past and present felt intertwined in something important, a destiny of potential unfolding. If nothing else, I felt certain I needed to return to those places, if not to do something, then to receive. Receive what, who knows?

I anticipated all this to subside. I expected the passing days to see the churning feeling wane. When it didn't, I sought a day surrounded by nature. Possibly being in a clear space with so many natural things to commune with might coax the answers to come. And so I reached out to a friend. We had talked about a hike to the highest point in the Cajas Mountains, a national park west of Cuenca. Neither of us had been to this peak before but it was always a goal. Weather was a critical factor. Conditions change rapidly in those mountains, particularly at those altitudes. One does not want to be caught on a narrow ridge-line above 14k feet when stiff icy winds or rain clouds and blinding fog overtake the place.

Long story short, we made the trek on what turned out to be a beautiful day. It took us 2-1/2 hours driving on dodgy dirt roads to get to the trailhead, arriving at 7:30am. Nearly five hours later, we were nearing the peak. From afar we could clearly see that some kind of official marker post adorned the top. It appeared to be a white concrete obelisk chopped off flat on top.

Before our last push to the summit, we rested. My friend turned around and was startled at what he saw. Right above us, in clear view, was the marker obelisk. And on it, regally perched with determined eyes scanning the lowlands all around, was a massive bird. We didn't know what kind, but on first sight one might guess it was an adult eagle. It obviously could see us but was not perturbed in the least.

Given my plant medicine history with bird and flight symbolism, it seemed that nature was trying to tell me something. I had gone into nature, deep and high, surrounding myself with nothing but nature, and here I was, within feet of the highest point in the Cajas. And what should be waiting for me at my goal but this massive, beautiful bird. The next day I discovered the bird was actually a Mountain Caracara, also known locally as Curiquingue. A bit more digging uncovered another connection beyond the bird symbolism from medicine space. It turns out this was the same type of bird from which the Incas collected feathers to decorate the crown of the Sapa Inca, their king.

I imagine all of us tend to stretch the meaning and significance of "signs" we receive, but this seemed pretty obvious. Whatever I was feeling had substance and I needed to pursue it. Sure, but how? More importantly, did I know why? There was only one teacher I knew that could blast through this level of confusion and anxious curiosity and help me read the signs correctly, if indeed that's what they were. There was one teacher I trusted to help me find my own answers at this level. And so I headed south for a night with Mother Ayahuasca.

Mother Ayahuasca may be the teacher I trust but more trust is required for a successful journey. One must also trust the shaman who makes the medicine and holds the ceremony space. In that regard, I had no doubts. I had been in ceremony with this shaman multiple times before. I knew his competence and compassion all too well. But I also knew he has a subtle, almost quiet way of pre-staging the energies before ceremony.

One of his techniques is to be coy but magically suggestive about the medicine itself. Many times he will admit to new wrinkles to the night's brew. It'll be a slightly different kind or prepared a whole different way than before. This night I was surprised and interested at his answer when I asked him about the medicine. With understated gravitas he calmly dropped the bomb that this medicine was not brewed like any before – this brew had been buried for two months until it fermented. Other things happened in the preparation after that. He wouldn't go into the whole preparation method, but his manner and expressions implied the result was something special.

Four participants shared their intentions around the fire in the teepee. Mine were vague but swirled around the energies gathered from my trip to Peru and the subsequent nudges from elsewhere that hadn't abated since I returned. Surprisingly, the shaman shared his own intentions for the night, which were quite personal. I was quite impressed by his honesty, humility, connection to us, and lack of ego-need to present himself as the all-wise guru with no work to do anymore on himself.

Far from suggesting I should question his abilities, the personal way in which he shared what was going on with him only confirmed how confident I was in him. I admired how he kept things in perspective. He was not the medicine, nor was he the spirit teacher, although he understood it and the realms it gave access to far better than any of us did or probably ever would.

He was simply a knowledgeable, insightful guide into the intensely personal and infinitely beyond. He did not control those mystic realms any more than a Sherpa controls the steep slopes of Everest. But if you were going to the mountain, he was the best one by your side. Beware of any shaman who feels he or she needs to play the role of shaman as expected by ceremony participants.

My journey started with subtle visuals that grew more intense as I focused on them. Elaborate and colorful geometric patterns corkscrewed and fractalled with intent and design to a seductive vanishing point. At first there was gold movement on black, then bursts and patterns of colors got woven in. The rounded gears of perfectly-meshed movement grew ever more complex, composed of fine webbing and morphing filigree. I watched and meditated on what feelings were coming up but mostly I noticed something else. I saw how, as my interest increased, so did the complexity of the visuals, as did my desire to see where the evolving movement went.

Although the pattern and color of the movement never repeated itself, there developed a feedback loop. Drawn to be interested, I watched the movement get more complex, at which I got more interested, thereby spawning more intricate movement and color patterns, which only drew more interest. There was no end to how involved the movement and patterns became. Just when I thought the dizzying multiplex couldn't get more surprising and interesting, it effortlessly slid to the next level. If I intended to wait for the ultimate movement, the final shape, the best color combination, the most significant revelation within the patterns, I'd be waiting in perpetual awe. One thing was certain – it was terribly difficult to pull my attention away.

Up until then, I hadn't heard Mother Ayahuasca's voice. So I called out to her. I let her know, while the visuals were wondrous and captivating, I didn't want to spend my entire ceremony enthralled in multi-various morphs of sacred geometry kaleidoscopes. I needed to go deeper and explore the things I had brought to ceremony on my heart and mind. No sooner had I put out this intention than the chaotically perfect visuals diffused into darkness.

Not only was I a bit surprised that I could direct my journey so immediately, I felt Mother approved of me being aware enough not to get stuck in low-level dazzle. If anything, the visuals had been a test of sorts. She was testing if I had integrated her message about avoidance of going down rabbit holes that were ultimately negative or didn't serve me, no matter how entertaining or distracting they might be. It was the lesson from a previous ceremony months before – *"Recognize and interrupt."*

Freed from this roller coaster dazzle ride, I floated through a rich blackness, an energized abyss that began pulling thought and feeling out of me like inter-soulular dust and gas amassing from its own gravity arising in the subconscious void. Before long, Mother and I were in conversation. Her voice was soft, almost whispery, and yet her awareness and the impact she intended was hyper-vigilant. It started with my concentration on the energies from Peru. It swirled and gathered mass with the feeling that something needed to be done or received. It achieved critical density when stories of Eagle and Condor flying together met Q'ero tribal prophecies and questions if any of us had a role to play to help with anything needing to be done.

Some say it's wise to take pause before getting too wrapped up in seemingly worthy causes. The common adage from Carl Jung would have us believe "what we resist, persists." This would have us believe it is much better to affect change only by our example than by fighting against anything. The energy of opposition only increases what you fight and oftentimes makes you become what you are trying to eliminate. One does not erase hate by hating hate. One does not stop war by battling those who would wage it.

But does the same hold true for communications? If we try to reach the world with messages from spirit about our need to reconnect with the Earth and ourselves, are we not fighting, resisting other ideas? Ideas resist other ideas, so if we try to communicate what we've gotten from spirit, are we not resisting something else, thereby encouraging it to persist? Metaphorically, can the spirit wisdom of the condor ever help balance the greed and technocratic, planetary destructiveness of the eagle? What if the messages held in ancient wisdom from spirit are never communicated for new generations?

Without diligent communication of the message to reconnect to spirit, any example set by those who try to integrate these healing messages are easily overwhelmed. The influential juggernaut of scientifically-manipulative media and mesmerizing, ego-and-greed based memes continue to drive consumption culture. Resisting this maelstrom by example alone doesn't seem enough to heal the planet and steer us away from self-destruction.

Worse yet, even the messages from spirit, in many ways, have been co-opted by the profit-motive machinery of ego. Whole industries have grown up around New Age, old religion, and spiritual concerns in general, with the result that many in the masses gloss over or ignore the messages because they assume they're being communicated merely for financial gain with little import or genuineness.

It's nothing but the latest hyped production from some self-proclaimed guru living in their eco-friendly mansion. Far from being altruistic, the true motive is assumed to be a gathering of followers who are coaxed to be self-help addicts desperate to feel better about their lives and stave off pangs of repressed fears about their mortality.

This "enlightened" collective will gladly purchase the latest twist in the ever-complicated good news and thus feel good about themselves, maybe even spiritually superior. In such a toxic environment, how can one's good example or healing communications ever hope to counterbalance the scientific materialism of an ever-encroaching global corporatocracy that has no qualms destroying the planet or crushing people's souls if it means a fatter bottom line?

I suddenly noticed that the conversation had become one-sided. I was spinning off, gathering more into my concerns and arguments but Mother Ayahuasca had gone silent. It became obvious – my flurry of questions and conjecture was only the tip of a "gneiss-berg" extending below the surface into shifting tidal forces of emotion that ebbed and flowed in a vast sea of energy within me but emanated from everywhere. This "gneiss-berg" was a rock of hardening patterns of mind, not a simple iceberg that floated before me.

My perspective slowly telescoped back until I was no longer in and of that rock but beyond it, watching it float in a sea of displaced spacetime. The "gneiss-berg" was not me but something my energies had created. Once manifested, I had allowed myself to go into it, trying to find the far reaches of its hidden depths. It was definitely a hazard to soulular navigation. Layers and striations and moving bands of intent and shades of meaning snaked around and through the rock. In an instant I saw it for what it was. It was the condensation of where I had let my energies go.

Now that this rock existed, I could involve myself with it as long as I wanted. In all likelihood, it would enlarge. As it did, the layers and striations and moving bands would intensify and grow more complex. The realization hit me with a flash of concern – my "gneiss-berg" could endlessly fascinate and engage with me – just like the multi-various morphs of sacred-geometry kaleidoscopes I saw at start of ceremony. What had I done? Only replaced one non-serving distraction for another?

Mother's voice was near. If I didn't want to spend my entire ceremony enthralled by endless fascinating visuals, then why had I turned around and created the same thing in a different way with my own energies? My perspective widened to see my "gneiss-berg" as a self-reinforcing, paradoxical double bind. Having accepted that I'm subject to these influences and concerns and there needed to be something done about them, I could never be sure of the validity of any doubts or reservations about one course of action or another. Were they simply the product of my own unconscious limitation to see the whole picture more thoroughly? And so, ever more energy needed to be pumped into the equation.

To simply walk away from it was out of the question because obviously it was tangible in my heart and mind. Where that tangibility came from was a moot point once it was there requiring attention. To deny its importance flew in the face of what all the layers and striations and moving bands kept reinforcing. If anything, the more I went into it, the more important it became. Even the method of "*Recognize and interrupt*" would be hard pressed to penetrate the cult-of-self conditions I was gathering into solidity with my own energies. While there may be real matters to consider very near to me, the way I was going about it would only have me endlessly chasing the far horizon.

I could not believe how effortlessly, unconsciously I had substituted my questions and concerns for the engaging visuals at start of ceremony. But the sinking feeling was there – both were taking me towards a no-convergence point, one I would never reach and gained nothing by the attempt. As soon as I absorbed the full import of what she showed me, I felt such a release of dismay at what I had done. I felt I needed to apologize to myself and Mother for where I had allowed things to go, not only in ceremony but in the weeks leading up to it.

As soon as this understanding mixed with repentance and relief, everything changed. Unlike the chaotic visuals from before, the "gneissberg" didn't just fade like a bespeckled fog. The floating rock simply winked out of existence, leaving behind a living void. The suddenness of its disappearance was felt as heat, an ache welling up from my feet and rushing to my head. I had to purge and the urge was strong. But this purge wasn't going to be through the mouth. I struggled to my feet in the dark, hurried from the teepee, then followed the path through cool blackness to the jungle toilet.

Does it really matter where you have your transcendent experience? If it's truly transcendent, I don't think so. As humorous as it might seem now, that night I had mine sitting out in the open, darkness all around, while purging into a hole in the ground. In those moments I released my "gneissberg" so to speak. For quite a while after, still wavering in energetic excess and high frequency fluctuations, I sat not knowing if I could maintain control over a body I had left. It was all I could do not to release fully into the experience and simply let my body flop off the toilet and roll away on the ground.

In time, I managed to stand and walk back to the teepee. I wobbled outside and attempted to maintain a spacetime presence. Spatial relationships and movement of my muscles altered in alien ways. The ground appeared so far away. My legs were jellied noodles of sparking energy. My feet were frequency patterns interfacing with Pachamama. My inner sight received only a fraction of what was being perceived from my eyes. Nature was all around and I knew I couldn't leave it and duck back into the teepee. With some effort I sat on the ground and felt everything settle around me in welcome.

I felt too good to be in my skin. I felt too expansive to be in one place. I felt too cleansed to have a thought. The night cradled me as I birthed new feelings of peaceful contentment. After timeless release into it, I began to settle more into my body. As I did, I began to feel chilled. I changed position to hug my knees to retain heat. As I did, the heat gathered at my feet and intensified up my body.

When the heat reached my head, another purge gathered within. This time it was through the mouth. It came from deep within, below my stomach, beyond any physical part of me. When it was over, a rush of peaceful contentment rippled through me until I floated away again. This time, I floated among fireflies that flitted all around. They were real fireflies, not hallucinations, and yet the way they looked to me in my condition might as well been an inspired flight-of-fancy masterpiece by Vincent Van Gogh.

Over the next two hours, I went through three cycles of peace, then cold, then heat, then purge. Each time a deeper level of peace was gained and a more intense purge was required. After the last purge, Mother gave me a vision fully-formed, something I can only describe as the four offerings. It was a thought-form, complete in the instant, explaining the four stages of help Mother was willing to offer anyone who approached her with right body, right heart, right intentions, and with gratitude and a willingness to surrender to what was needed and then do the work to move through it. The vision was so complete, I've described it elsewhere in the chapter, Ayavision – The Four Offerings.

During all of this, the shaman played music and sang icaros. More than once he came out of the teepee to ask me if I was all right, how I was doing. In time, he relit the central fire and I returned to my blanket by it. Much later, the shaman would remark on my night's journey. His eyes showed he had felt its significance. He noted, given my past experience at ceremonies with him, I was the last one he expected to spend so much time by myself outside the teepee in middle of ceremony.

After the fire burned out, all of us rested until dawn. The shaman brought out liquid tobacco snuff to sharpen our awareness and focus at the close of ceremony. Soon after, we took turns receiving Kambo. For the next two hours the jungle frog venom worked through us, completing the cleansing and chasing away leftover errant energies from the night before.

I walked from the shaman's house. All the while along the mountain path back into town I felt more than rejuvenated. A healing was taking place, one I would need to complete by integrating the essence of it into daily life. Some healings act on the sores and maladies we possess. Other healings, as I found out, act on the maladies and patterns that possess us. Possession by bad energies does take place, but it's not done to us by some external demon. We do it to ourselves which, as it turns out, is much more insidious.

We create the ride that's fun or interesting or so important – at first. But then it becomes something we can't get off. No longer are we riding the ride. The ride is riding us, then it becomes us. At that point, the question on how to get off doesn't make any sense. Of course, someone could simply explain this to me and I'd accept or reject it. But even if I accepted it, how far would I take it in and act on it? How easy would it be to fall back into old patterns? Those are very comfortable patterns, even if we can't see they're nothing but self-reinforcing paradoxical double-binds. Mother wasn't going to tell me this. With a one-two punch, using pretty visuals and then my own juggernaut of a mind, she took me there instead. For that, I'm forever grateful.

Walking down into town, Mother's spirit was with me, as was her lesson. And what had become of all my concerns about our possible role in resolving the issues of our time? Mother assured me – nothing she had put me through ever said we should do nothing or turn our backs on communicating what our heart has received. The difference is in the way we approach it. Realize that forces and cycles and balances have and always will work themselves out according to the natural flows and infinite designs of Source.

We can help it along but it doesn't serve anyone or anything to lose ourselves in the attempt. Now may indeed be a time when the balance needs to swing back towards a reconnection to spirit. But we shouldn't underestimate spirit or the cosmic-scale cycles in play. She reminded that the forces and powers of the eagle also had many positives. It should never be about which was correct, which would win, condor or eagle – it was about the coming together of the best elements of both.

We may think that the massive greed-monster of corporate materialism is about to swallow the planet and yet she reminded me – every monster already contains the seeds of its own demise, otherwise it wouldn't be a monster. Gigantic edifices that can't be scaled by lowly peasants eventually crumble from within. The greatest darkness is penetrated by a single torch. The action of water eventually brings down the highest mountain. The metaphors are endless. As should be our belief in what we claim to represent. Go forward, but calmly, confidently, at peace in the knowledge that the balance is inescapable.

Yes, what I've called Raki-Raki Yanantin Time will come. But it's not something to fight for. It's inevitable. When we know that, we help to manifest it, possibly sooner than it would otherwise come. How would you act if you knew with certainty that a healed planet and a reconnection with spirit will happen by moving ahead in resolute peace? That's the way to place energies that draw all of us into that future. Don't fight for a future you fear won't happen.

Fear will only delay the inevitable for that is the nature of fear. Be peaceful in knowing that's where it's all going. It's in the design. There's no other way. Communicate it, yes. Point out where things are going wrong and in doing so wake up anyone lost and conditioned not to see. But above all, pass on the peace of knowing. Maybe not in my lifetime or yours, but eyes will someday open and a new synthesis as an expression of balance will be established. Rest assured, Spirit is not going away.

In the Quechua language:
Raki-Raki ~ when two things are separate that should be together
Yanantin ~ harmonious relationship between two different things

Shaman Schwaman, Yeah Whatever, Really?

What difference does a shaman make? It's easy for someone to call themselves a shaman, so does the word mean anything anymore? From my experience, there's only one way to know. It would be easy to say it's one of those things where you had to be there, there's no way else to understand. But it's worth the attempt to convey nonetheless.

Case in point. Once upon a time there was an Ayahuasca ceremony somewhere in South America. It had lasted over ten hours. As the cliche goes, it was intense. Dawn had just come and the shaman closed out the ceremony by passing around the talking stick and then liquid tobacco for us to snuff; he spoke to us in low, compassionate tones about all that transpired, he then allowed us one-by-one to say our own silent words over the central fire as we dropped a pinch of incense into it and made it crackle.

So far so good. Anyone calling themselves a shaman could have done this.

We had reached a point of completion and yet expectancy. Expectancy for what? That's never certain. Even at end of ceremony, the medicine is still present within, still doing its thing.

The shaman made the end of ceremony official by respectfully tending to the glowing embers of the fire until they were snuffed out. As the final wisps of smoke headed upwards to find the opening at the top of the teepee, he paused a few moments to look at the ashes in reflection. Then he was gone. He quickly turned and exited, leaving all of us floating in our experience, very attentive, but silent. And we remained silent. There was too much to say and nothing all at once. Either way, words would never do. Communication had become something else.

Enter the shaman.

A few minutes had passed. He had left us alone with our feelings, letting them swizzle and expand and swirl us into a mood, a mood that can't be described.

He stepped back through the teepee flap and quickly squatted down. He said nothing. He looked around at all of us, one at a time. He made serious, I'm-in-you and you're-in-me kind of eye contact. His face blended intensity, seriousness, and love with an ever-present but slight grin. When he had finished reaching all of us individually with his eyes, he looked down to the ground before him. In an instant, he dropped into meditation.

A little while later he picked up a small rock and rubbed it between his fingers for a minute. Everyone was silent, entrained on him. His mood and energy told us something was coming. In silence he made us wait. Then he reached forward and struck the little rock on a bigger rock lying in the dirt.

Tap. Tap-Tap.

The single sound of rock on rock filled the teepee. Then the tap pattern repeated, and repeated until the rock strikes tapped a simple, repetitive beat, a tribal beat. Over and over he tapped out this beat. What did it signify? It could be anything, Earth's heartbeat, some kind of Morse code to the spirits in the sky, a comment on all that had happened in the ceremonial night still so near to all of us.

The shaman's eyes fixated, unblinking, on the two rocks. One striking the other, both forming the beat. The beat contained its own immediacy, its own push and pull to awareness, its own command of being what it was.

Soon, someone else in the teepee began tapping on their leg, keeping the same rhythm. Then someone else began clapping to the beat. In time, more in the teepee added their versions of the same beat. A piece of wood was struck to another to make the beat.

Then a woman, moved by the beat, began singing a song of spirit and love and communion. She sang in Spanish. She sang to the beat. Before long, everyone in the teepee had joined in somehow, some more than others depending on how much they were still floating, but all were in time and tempo with the shaman's first taps. The beat stayed the same as the intensity rose.

After reaching a crescendo of song and beats, now filling the teepee and spilling out into the cool air of dawn, the singing stopped and the beats from all of us, one by one, faded and stopped. It all stopped except for the shaman. He kept his two rocks tapping for a while, and then he too ended the beat with a final, definitive tap. When he did, he kept his eyes on the ground and rocks before him. He let silence flood back into the teepee. He lifted back out of his meditation and took a few quiet moments to drink it in. Then he looked up and scanned all of our eyes once more. His knowing grin was a little wider now.

He made eye connection with all of individually, then stood abruptly and swept out of the teepee once again. We were left smiling and laughing and rolling back into the dirt in joy. The whole musical performance couldn't have been more perfectly orchestrated. It was all in the moment, spontaneous, unexpected, unrehearsed. And yet it had transitioned through beginning, middle, and end as if the best sound recording producers and engineers had sweated over it long and hard. For us, it had just happened, it had flowed from us, from where we were. We had discovered where our expectancy was going.

The shaman had taken us there, without a word spoken, without prompts or methods or scheduled exercises. We were not only back in the medicine, we were fully in what we needed. We were present, we were united, we were blessed and lifted beyond the effort and struggle of the night before into our individual healings.

Powerful integration had begun. We were in ecstasy.

No doubt about it. This was a shaman.

Serious Adjustments in How After What

Ayahuasca and Huachuma (San Pedro) work very well together – either blended in the same cup or experienced in separate ceremonies close in time. They are quite different but complementary. I was reminded of this after a recent journey with Mother Ayahuasca. Much was explored during the night, not the least of which was my questions about how we communicate with others and the world. I've heard an expert in the field of shamanism assert that a common message from shamans all over the world is simply – the experience is not the thing, the knowledge from the experience is the thing.

If this is true, should we be content on integrating this knowledge for ourselves and leave it at that? Are any of our attempts to communicate this knowledge to others a sign we don't understand on a fundamental level? Such things need to be experienced, not heard as hearsay, end of story. One person cannot tell another this knowledge. In finding a block within myself regarding this, maybe I'm channeling the Zen tradition too much.

Zen is replete with koans that encapsulate the presumed paradoxes and dilemmas of living. To paraphrase one such koan – If a person says they know about this stuff and want to tell you all about it, that's a sure sign they don't in fact know, for if they did, they'd know better than assume they could.

This goes much deeper than mere reverse logic. This drives to the heart of what experience and communication is and all it can possibly be. Mother dissolved this logical rock and its hidden depths in her inimitable way. I guess my block and this rock would say I feel I need to share what happened and yet I can't adequately describe how she did what she did because if I thought I could, I'd certainly be broadcasting to everyone I didn't understand the process. It would be firm evidence that I'm either woefully deluded or else steeped in my own ego desire to somehow know it all. And if I can't do a good job of explaining it due to the subject matter, then what's the point of attempting communication at all? Ah, so much for the double-binds of mind.

There are ample signs that whole philosophies and religions have grown into influential monoliths planted in the human mind in order to deal with counterfactuals like this. They deal with it as if all of it has substance and actually needs to be dealt with.

Curious. Mother Ayahuasca didn't go there.

Instead, she took me to a realm beyond my rock where a single, simple directive flooded my heart – "*The most important one to communicate with is oneself. When you can do that, do that completely, all the rest falls into* place. Find yourself there and you'll discover there is no rock. If you want to communicate with others, do so by experiencing full communication with yourself first. Let them see that. That's all you need do."

Forty-eight hours later, I brought this message to Grandfather Huachuma. The sacred cactus medicine took this message and ran with it. Unlike the usual conversations I have with Grandfather, this time what started as a conversation transformed into an experience. By the end of the day, it was one of the most dramatic demonstrations I've ever endured of learning by living the example.

When I say "endured" I don't mean to imply it was unpleasant, not entirely. But medicine space shows us how some intensities shatter limits and test our ability to absorb what is being offered. Stretching limits, dissolving limits, redefining limits, call it what you will, medicine space seems to be all about finding new, personal ways of doing this.

Grandfather saw I had Mother's message on my mind. He understood better than I – she had told me *what* needed to be done. Whether I expected it or not, by coming to him I had now bought a ticket to experience *how to do it*. Since I seemed clueless about her intention in telling me to communicate with myself, Grandfather took me to task. My conception of communication needed some serious adjustment.

I was lounging on a patio overlooking a verdant valley ringed by majestic mountains. The patio was up in the trees, near the sound of water flowing and flocks of birds sporadic in their dalliance, including bird calls from the Pacific Hornero. The sky was a manic-expressive display of sun and rainclouds chasing each other in a slow-motion ballet. Micro-stormbursts confined to a single far valley or ridgeline came and went. The breeze was cool but undecided which direction it wanted to come from. It reversed direction with gusts that rippled through the leaves around me.

Over the next three hours, I was shown by example how communicating with oneself, the way Mother Ayahuasca meant, was dependent upon opening up all channels of input. Opening them all the way.

Life is Being. Experience is Being. Being is life. Experience is life. Experience is the raw material. Being is the energy. Life is the raw material of the experience. Say it in any combination you like. Laugh at its simplicity, its self-referencing redundancy, its childishness. It didn't matter. Words weren't the way to experience it anyway. The fact is – the more you open up to all that's possible to receive, the more you have to communicate with yourself – and ultimately others if that be your choice.

Grandfather swept forward with examples as experiences as gusts of wind rocked the trees nearby. Blow away all the crap prescriptions and explanations and limitations. So many devotees are steeped in method and practice. Some are all intent to raise their energy to their crown chakra. Grandfather had no patience with such preoccupations. Who the hell ever said one chakra was better than another? What kind of limiting, ego-goal is that? Grandfather was adamant – *you have all of those energy points for a reason, and the importance of each cannot be compared, ranked in specialness, or rationalized away by a voodoo desire for transcendence.* It was an oxymoron anyway – desiring transcendence – when greed, desire, and illusion was loathed bugaboos of that kind of guru-voodoo.

Even the limitation of saying there are a certain number of chakras – seven, twelve, how many now? Should we form a weekend conference and argue the point? He swept me past all of that. The subtle body contains a vast array of energy states and moving, intersecting points that one could spend the rest of eternity sub-dividing without end.

Why get stuck on a certain number? What's the point – to isolate a particular attribute of our being? To say – this is the sexual spot, this is the heart spot, this is the third eye spot, and on and on. "*Don't miss the point,*" implored Grandfather. "*What Mother Ayahuasca wanted was all of those energy points and more turned completely on simultaneously and receiving fully – being fully in one's being, being fully in one's experience, being fully in the energy of union with life.*"

What some called Kundalini energy was a sense of what this full open experience could be. Most devotees were chasing it to achieve some transcendent experience, often envisioned as a blissful state beyond the here and now. Grandfather made clear, the total communication with self really was a transcendence but one that intrinsically included the here and now in all its lowly, normal attributes.

When fully activated, our experience could include this so-called lowly place we live and see it as part of the complete transcendence. Nothing in creation was to be "transcended" to experience "transcendence." Anything that transcendence could reveal to one there could be revealed here. The here and now was not seen as a transcendent place precisely because we weren't communicating to ourselves properly.

While some try to raise energy to their crown, others proclaimed that primal energy was located at the base of the spine. Many got lost in the metaphor of rousing, then raising this base, serpent energy to the "thousand-petaled lotus" at the crown.

Grandfather swept it all away. Never mistake the state for the metaphor reminded Grandfather. Never assume the metaphor conveys the state. Metaphors are impressions and sometimes convenient guides in light of the limitations of mind. The reality of anything, by definition of that limitation, would always be so much more and most times bear little resemblance to the metaphor. One can follow a map to a scenic spot but the scenic spot will always be more than the map. No one takes a photo of the map once they reach their scenic spot. Stay focused on the experience and the knowledge to be gained from it.

Grandfather took me into the metaphor of transcendence and blew through the wireframe oversimplications of it, replacing the convoluted tinker-toys with an expanding experience of here and now. I felt myself receiving in every which way, through every physical sense and the states of mind and intuition beyond the physical. Colors, sights, sounds, touches of minute particles of a breeze on single hairs on my arm, impressions, insights, the taste of smells wafting in subtle patterns from the trees and bushes and flowers, all intermixing and unfolding upon combined sensory groupings and emotional feedback from it all.

As sensory input expanded, so did awareness of what I could be aware of. New depths in 3D sight pulled me into foggy clouds skirting a far mountain top. The sound of flapping wings divided into component parts of individual control feathers sending a group of birds zipping through nearby branches. Water cascading over rocks in the distance amplified to reveal a pattern in the rocks that coaxed the water to fall a certain way.

There was no limit to how much I could do into the experience of everything around if I remained fully open to it. Being had no limitations although we could certainly put all sorts of elaborate constraints on it. Even with my breathing, I was implored to take in more, to always take in deep, slow breaths. As the experience intensified, a gentle rain began to fall and take me with it on its ride. Moist breezes whipped around. Small animals scattered in the trees. Hot spots of key light from lighting grid father-sky burst forth here and there. Being was a non-stop show with everyone and everything in starring roles.

Even the feel of being settled in my body, lying back on a bench seat on the patio broadened in dimensionality. The sampling rate of everything coming to me changed all perception of time. How I could be speeding through input while the impression of it passed in near slow-motion was unfathomable. A sense of being overwhelmed and yet capable of so much more gave me a sort of motion sickness.

I couldn't decide if all of this was way too much to handle or if the potential of more needed to be explored and now that the process had started, it couldn't be stopped. Had the dam broke? Was the flood upon me? On other days at various times, prompted by other medicine journeys or emotional heights, I had thought I was so into the moment, so present, so grounded in the here and now. This was an order of magnitude over and above.

As I reeled back, max-permeated and saturated by experience all the while taken to a place where one couldn't help ever-expand into more, I felt a unified jolt through my body. For an instant, it was as if I had become a lightning rod for my own communication with myself. The energy pulsed through me, leaving me a soft mass of sensations and feeling without comment or examination, without reflection or interpretation. Only inputs now flowing through me unrestrained. In a few minutes, to my surprise, I discovered that among my heightened inputs during that lightning rod moment, I had experienced an orgasm. It wasn't so much noticed at the time it happened since every area of being was also at an equally elevated orgasmic state at the same time.

Over the next couple of hours, the experience relaxed and settling down. A peaceful sense of connection blended with the heightened inputs from my surroundings. There was a deep sense of appreciation for all there was to experience. Grandfather made it clear – this was not all there was to communicate with myself. This was only an example of how to do it. This was the wide-open, extreme example, the one that defined the space. I should carry the feeling of this complete input state with me always, let it inform the way I approach anything in my day. Not everything would be an extreme, full-open input overload, nor should it. That wasn't the point. I had been shown the final state, the ideal, the total deal so the feeling of it would stay with me.

No matter how I now decided to direct my energies, no matter which things I decided to do, I should always approach them intent upon a communication with myself that took in as much of the experience as I could. As I had seen, it was possible to take in so very very much. So many people close themselves down to all there exists to experience. The result is stunted potential, misunderstandings of purpose and potential, and states where people confined themselves in an unconscious prison of limitation or reduced expectations. Such warped perspectives and partial viewpoints would never be affected in knowing oneself, in knowing others, or succeeding in one's passion or purpose in the world.

No matter what I wanted to do with people or in the world, it would be much better served if first I opened to the depths and ranges of experience, and then communicated to myself by this action. My cause or project in the world might succeed or fail, my efforts to bond with others or share whatever I thought important might fall flat – but none of that mattered if one completed a full communication to oneself. As the shamans say – the experience is not the thing, the knowledge from the experience is the thing. So give yourself the knowledge. This is as true in living as in a plant medicine ceremony, for after all, what's the difference?

Too Much Swag

Too much swag. Simply too much. It doesn't matter if it's "something we all get." It's too much.

Maybe I should look upon it as my booty, loot, spoil, plunder, haul – a bonus experience from my medicine journey. Perhaps I need to look at any positives from it – find self-growth takeaways to learn from. OK, maybe someday I will. But for now, I'm going to conclude there are some things I'm not ready for. They're just too much to handle in full-on medicine space. It's way too hard absorbing, carrying away so much emotional, energetic swag. By writing this, I'm dealing with it. I'll explain.

Over two years ago, Grandfather San Pedro told me flatly – *"Don't come visit me unless you stay two days for back-to-back ceremonies."* It had been a prescription I didn't understand then but in trusting the process, I subsequently found great rewards in following the advice more than once. Now here I was, so long after, being presented with another opportunity for back-to-back San Pedro ceremonies.

It should have been an easy decision but far from it. I hesitated, concluding definitely not to, then reconsidering. My indecision swirled around circumstances so different, so charged, so volatile, so emotional. It was unlike anything I had contemplated as part of a ceremony before, much less back-to-back journeys with San Pedro.

The core issue centered on a good friend. After months of staying out of this friend's personal matters, things that were none of my business, circumstances made it my business. A second friend, troubled by what they knew, confided in me information they were afraid to share with my friend. This second friend feared once they shared the news, it wouldn't be believed and yet the act of sharing might blow up their friendship with my friend.

Two months passed. It had gotten to the point where there was real danger if I didn't reveal to my friend what I knew. Others were involved. Triangles and histories among relationships intertwined. Where once as a friend I stayed out of it, now as a friend I needed to at least convey the information so my friend could make their own decisions fully aware.

I sat with my friend by a river one night and we had the talk. It was obvious and certain the news would be hard to take. And it was. There was danger, betrayal, manipulation, uncertainties on the table. We both were supposed to travel the next day to back-to-back San Pedro ceremonies. We had been in many ceremonies together before. But the timing of this couldn't have been worse. Although my friend was grateful enough that I came forward with the information, there was no way he was OK with what it had done to his world.

Everything was upside-down, in flux, permeated with pain and indecision. Worse yet, none of it could be absolutely verified in the moment, maybe not for days, if ever. But now there was doubt. Trust was at stake. Never before had either of us imagined going into sacred plant medicine ceremonies steeped in so much emotion and upheaval. And of course for him, so much more than me. I had my mirror-neurons firing away, feeling bad for him, exuding compassion for what he must be going through. But it was he who stoically held back the full measure of the sadness and pain he was going through. It was not a good night by the river.

But the next day came and we both headed south out of town as scheduled. He got delayed and had to take a later bus but by mid-morning we were both drinking San Pedro at the start of what would be two-days of ceremonial turmoil. Alone on the bus for over an hour with his thoughts, my friend couldn't help but be emotionally primed for a wild ride. We all stated our intentions for the day, he was subdued, referring to all on his mind and heart in the most general of terms. Then we broke circle and went our separate ways to private spots on the property to hear Grandfather's voice.

I spent the first half of the day lying under citrus trees, reeling while the medicine took apart all of my thoughts and concerns. Questions about what I was doing with my days, what I thought I might do, what was important and why, where to take myself in moving into the future, all of it I handed over to the medicine. In turn, all of it was summarily dissolved away. Grandfather didn't want to address it. He wouldn't pay attention to it in any guise. Repeatedly he brought me back to experiencing everything that was going on around me in the present moment.

"Pay attention, go into it, enjoy, expand, be aware, feel it fully – that is the imperative."

The here and now was the answer but not to any of my questions. Those things were long gone. Dissolved. Faded in forgotten mists and immaterial fogs that never should have existed. There was no point asking the wrong question. Wrong questions never brought forth correct answers.

The sun beat down. The UV rays were intense. After a few hours of this, I managed to stumble to my feet in search of water. I couldn't believe how hot it was. But not in degrees, not in the usual way. This was hot like being cooked by invisible rays in a microwave oven, from inside out. I staggered around in search of relief.

I got water from the kitchen. The baking rays seem to emanate from everything, reflect off everything. I found a seat on the covered patio and settled myself down. I wasn't quite, as they say "trippin' balls" but the medicine was strong, so strong I felt like a wave-front, not wholly physical. The only reason I was moving around at all was to find relief. The heat I was feeling flowed inside out after being agitated from something invisible outside in. At least that's the way it felt at the time.

As soon as I sat down, I noticed him. My friend was sitting across the way in another chair on the patio. He looked glued to emotions that stretched him on a medieval torture rack. Instinctively, my wave-front locked in on his, scanning it like a sensor array splayed out from the saucer section of the USS Enterprise lost somewhere in the gamma quadrant. Turbulence and contortions in a slipstream of pain, anger, and confusion were immediately clear.

We started the only conversation we could manage. We checked in with each other in fits and starts. We made observations that were obvious. We floated suggestions that were impossible. It didn't matter. Speech was only the surface layer anyway. Underneath we were negotiating transmission rates, interchange protocols for how two energy forms could reach each other on a deeper level.

The next three hours cannot be described in any mundane detail that conveys meaning needed for comprehension. Except to say it was one of the most difficult times I've ever gone through in my life. We stayed there together and went into it. We were both full blown in the medicine. I felt we were linked energetically. Our emotional quotients were off the charts. To try to console a friend while blasted wide open was nothing compared to a friend trying to find anywhere to be within himself to escape what he couldn't avoid.

I could feel it all. It wasn't so much anything we said to each other. To read a transcript of that afternoon would probably seem disordered, halting, trivial, even incoherent. It wasn't. A different order of communication was occurring. A different way of being empathetic had become all consuming. A level of compassion that stemmed from all of us being one took over. It was like not being in the body that needed to take its hand from the stove, but feeling it all nonetheless. There was only so much one could do and yet that didn't stop it all from flowing over you.

The night waned away with dinner and conversation then retiring to bed when exhaustion caught up with us. It would be so good to lose ourselves in sleep. Sleep might be healing. If not, at least it was a respite, a brief amnesia from the state we were in. The only thing was – sleep would bring tomorrow. And tomorrow there was another ceremony.

On the second day I resolved to give everyone their private space and time. Including me. Especially me. I couldn't go through the same thing again. That interlocked afternoon of churning heart-space on the patio had been too much. Yes, emotion was something we all get. It's the swag of life. But experiencing emotion that way for so long was too much. Especially emotion that wasn't mine and yet in medicine space it was.

Maybe the medicine was opening up to me new avenues of communication and compassion, new depths of relating to other people, but still it was too much. I needed a day alone with Grandfather to recover, hopefully soar into an understanding of what had happened. If medicine space had put me there, perhaps it could console me into a peaceful state again.

I was far from peaceful starting the day. I was unsettled, hyper, on edge, raw. We drank again knowing that another ten-hour ride was at the bottom of the glass. I found a different spot away from the citrus trees this time. The day before I had been oblivious to some ant bites but now they were itching. At least the sky was threatening rain. Rain was good. I wouldn't be microwaved from inside out like before. I laid down and tried the impossible task of letting go while concentrating on something I should be doing with Grandfather.

I closed my eyes and tried a meditation on what was next. Since I was still unsettled, the natural thing was to go into what I needed to work on. So I meditated on that. What work did I want to do in medicine space that day. I had ten hours to do it. I should be able to get a lot done. As carryover from the day before, lingering feelings presented a mixed bag. No one feeling predominated but what floated to the top was a sense of sadness. Probably sadness for my friend. But was that all? Did I have other sadness I needed to explore, to root out, to be done with?

I asked Grandfather. I needed to know where these thoughts and pangs of sadness were coming from. The more I thought about it, the more substance the topic gathered to itself, the more I felt I had hit upon something real. But instead of taking me into the feeling, Grandfather presented his doubts. He wondered why I should own such a thing and immediately think work had to be done on it? If I wanted to go into sadness, it was certainly possible. But it was just as likely I was creating something to work on when nothing was there.

He grabbed me by the emotional energy and thrust me into myself. So where was it? Where was all of this sadness I needed to work on? I could certainly create some if I dwelled on it long enough. But in truth, nothing was there. I had almost sucked myself into doing a day's work on a sadness issue that didn't exist until I set about as a do-gooder to remedy it. It was almost laughable and almost scary. I was almost beside myself with where it all went next.

Grandfather took me back into the present moment. He brought me back to experiencing everything that was going on around me.

"Pay attention, go into it, enjoy, expand, be aware, feel it fully – that is the imperative."

The here and now was the answer but not to any of my questions, not to any of my impulses to "do work" on myself. Those things were long gone. Dissolved. Faded in forgotten mists and immaterial fogs that never should have existed. There was no point asking the wrong question. Wrong questions never brought forth correct answers.

"Get out of your mind and into the moment. Let go."

The day was deeply emotional and heartfelt once again. Only this time, it was anchored in the present moment. I was enthralled and laughed while watching two puppies and three chickens play together in a farmer's field. I laid on the grass as the rain fell and cooled me. The ceremony facilitator's dog came and snuggled by my side. This dog had recently been hit by a car. Now it ran by hobbling sideways and it struggled to get around and find a way to lie down, it was slow and a bit addled, but I could tell it was the same spirit, the same personality, the same dog I had known for over two years. The physical condition was not the spirit.

In the distance, a farmer was playing music. Beautiful birds swung by and chirped near me. A grandmother came out of her hut a farm-field away to check her garden. A lamb in a distant shack sounded like it was giving birth. Life was in motion all around. And the more I let myself go into it, feel the present moment, the less I was concerned about me. The farther into it I went, the more I slipped away.

At one point I was staring at wisps of fog rolling over a ridge-line as the sound of raindrops fell from leaves on a nearby tree, and Grandfather whispered to me – *"There are many ways to ego death; you can commit to it by being swallowed by a gigantic anaconda during a medicine journey, or you can release into it by watching the rolling fog – both and more will get you there if you let go."*

Releasing into it gave me the opportunity to experience it without fear. This stayed true to Mother Ayahuasca's mandate to me – *"No fear, no drama, no story!"* No anaconda was eating me. This was a glide, a letting go, a clearing of the mind, an opening of the soul so that the edges of one's essence could no longer be discerned. It was so peaceful, so comforting, I forgot myself and the process proceeded in the direction it was going. And where was that?

Grandfather no longer used words. He let me know directly. The letting go never completed in a way I would understand but it eventually included the crossing over of spirit. Some called it death. The momentum of my glide carried on with a penetrating tranquility. I had no desire to stop my movement towards and through it. Being fully in the moment allowed letting go of myself, which allowed me to glide into ego dead. If one continued the glide, the process led to death itself and beyond.

My clearing and opening took me to the crossing point and beyond. And beyond was beyond recognition. But it was so final, so serious, a type of serious of great import and substance of purpose. It was so strange to know there was no going back. This was it. This was something that could never be undone. But it was not an arrival at a destination.

It was like stepping across a border and knowing a whole country was behind you. But another one and more continents beyond that lie ahead. Everything else that concerned me the day before and today, it all dissolved as a fog that didn't exist and in many important ways, never did. That was the feeling, the crossing, the final expansion. Everything I thought I knew, that made me me, was dissolved. What was left couldn't be placed in terms of me or more. This was serious. This was final.

Then Grandfather snapped me back. He had the rain pelt me awake in normal deep medicine consciousness. I was still watching, unblinking as the clouds moved over the far ridgeline. But now my crossing journey was over. Was it an actual journey or a dream? It couldn't have been real or there would be no way back from where I went. Could it?

Grandfather only asked – *"Did it feel real?"*
"Yes," I answered.
"There's your answer," he said without hesitation.

For the next hour I sat in dazed and amazed silence, leaning against a wall, watching present moments pass by in living color. I felt otherworldly, as if back from the dead, with one foot in both worlds. Whether or not that was true could not be a topic of debate. The feeling was all consuming. It was odd to be immersed in everything sensory and tangible again. For all of it was the everything I experienced dissolving away. It was the everything that didn't exist and in so many important ways, never did.

And that included me. My ego death showed me that. I was part of the dissipating fog represented by the glide of letting go. But Grandfather would not let me wallow in thought. Immediately, he thrust me forward. I was also part of the rain, the birds, the trees, the dog limping in a circle nearby to find a more comfortable spot to lie down. Whatever I was thinking about my experience also had to dissolve with the rest of it. Back to the moment.

In time, I met up with my friend as we both settled down from medicine space. It had been a significant day in positive ways for both of us, which was good to hear. This was only possible because we stayed for back-to-back ceremonies and not allowed ourselves to be chased away by too much swag in the first one. I still contend it was too much. But now I have to wonder – can too much be just enough sometimes in medicine space?

If we fully go into the moments of medicine space, those moments can sure feel like too much. But too much loot may be a blessing in disguise. Too much swag is only an estimation crafted by our limitations, even our ego. For real, what are we fully capable of? How much communication and compassion is possible? Do we ever scratch the surface of going into this in what we call normal consciousness? What is our capacity for such things as communication and compassion? How much transformation would be possible in ourselves and the world if too much swag was just enough for everyone? Grandfather's words came back to me – *"Pay attention, go into it, enjoy, expand, be aware, feel it fully – that is the imperative."*

As before, the night waned away with dinner and conversation then retiring to bed when exhaustion caught up with us. The two days in ceremony had been taxing in many ways. It would be good to sleep. Not to lose myself or invoke amnesia this time but to restore myself for all tomorrow was about to bring to me. Tomorrow I would return home to see my beautiful wife. Tomorrow would be more all-consuming present moments passing by in living color. All of it would be more to go into, enjoy, be aware of and feel fully.

"After all," nudged Grandfather with playful seriousness, *"If that isn't our imperative, then what is?"*

The Ride

Sometimes sacred plant medicines take you on a shamanic journey. Sometimes they take you on a shamanic ride. This is the story of a ride that became a transport, a reality, a cipher, and ultimately an enigma. I had never mixed Yopo Rapé and San Pedro together before. I had never used San Pedro powder in a kuripe pipe as snuff.

Yopo contains DMT and would normally need a matching MAOI if ingested. But the kuripe pipe bypasses the stomach, avoiding the nullifying effect of digestion.

Ceremony Ingredients:
Anadenanthera Peregrina –Yopo Rapé
Echinopsis Pachanoi – San Pedro cactus, Huachuma
A kuripe pipe

Set and Setting:
Evening at home
Yopo Rapé and San Pedro powder in 50/50 mixture
Self-administered using the kuripe pipe

The first thing I noticed was there wasn't much to notice. This was odd. All other Rapé experiences, especially with Yopo, started strong right after snuff got blown through the pipe. I had time, on impulse, to quickly change into something more comfortable and return to my seat. I settled back and closed my eyes. It took a few more minutes before high-energy vibrations, first in my extremities, cycled inward to warm my core. When terahertz juddering filled me from head to toe, a projection of inner sight lit up a scene – a living set I was swept into. I wasn't watching myself or watching the scene. I was there.

How peculiar. Surrounding me was a large, empty parking lot far out somewhere in a flat landscape. It appeared to be on the edge of a city. Obviously, it was a parking lot once used by a substantial business or factory now all but shuttered and abandoned. Large, warehouse type buildings sprouted skyward in the distance. The vast parking lot swallowed a lot of space and the buildings got lost in the open flatness around me. There were no cars in the parking lot. Plenty of space for me to ride my unicycle. Yes, my unicycle. Which, apparently, I was quite good at. Nothing around and nothing to do but zigzag and zip my one wheel on the hot tarmac. Not quite pointless fun is the way I looked at it. Quite an opportunity to ride as much as I wanted, where I wanted. No interruptions, no obstacles, no goal beyond the moment.

Sensory input was rich, not dreamlike at all. I lost myself in the blast of midday sun, the shifting traction of shoes on bike pedals, the grab of gravity this-way-that as my balance wavered on quick turns, the jerk of my arms and the smell of air laced with traces of city busyness chattering on without me somewhere in the distance. As soon as I merged fully congruent with being in the scene, I heard a voice – "*Come with me.*" In a flash followed by a blur I got snatched out of the scene and inserted into another. The ride continued but it was oh so different.

It was night, not day. It was warm, not hot. I was riding but the unicycle was gone. Underneath me was a powerful motorcycle spinning serious RPMs. The gauge in front of me wavered at 70mph. An arrow straight road stretched into the moonless darkness before me. I knew I had been riding awhile. Firmly settled into the contoured seat with bare hands in confident grip of the handlebars, I could smell the warm desert on either side of the road.

Blasting through cool then warmer patches of midnight air, I knew right away I was heading due east. I was relaxed but far from complacent. There was something serious about this. Not serious in a bad way. Serious in importance. I was channeling a sense of determination. Was it from the voice who brought me here or from myself – I couldn't tell. I didn't even consider a destination. That's how important was the ride itself.

In time, the lights of a city came into view up ahead on the right. The desert darkness sloped down just enough on that side, revealing a roughly circular sprawl of self-contained lights. It wasn't a large city since I could see the dark edges where the sprawl hadn't yet penetrated the blank desert sands. The road ahead forked in two directions. The straight direction continued east. The other path curved off to span the darkness between me and those city lights. My channeled determination already knew my course. East it was, into more blackness, racing across more open flatness, intent upon the undeniable uncertainty that I needed to make all of this inevitable.

In time, the endless straight road separated from the sky. Still an hour away, the pale glow from approaching morning light made itself known in patchy grays edging into pastels. The horizon was now distinguishable. I varied my speed, sometimes peaking at 85mph, sometimes easing back to 60mph to take in studied side glances at the surrounding terrain. Morning colors were awakening in the desert. Mostly my inner governor was set at 70mph. There was no other traffic, no cross streets or stoplights so why not. It was then that the voice returned. It was strong. It was matter-of-fact. "*Ride until first light breaks the horizon, then turn south.*"

A timer had been set. My race into the unknown was about to shift with first light of day. How it would all coincide didn't seem to matter. Not when it seemed obvious that whatever was supposed to happen would. I was controlling it and there wasn't anything to control simultaneously. Some call it the flow. It seemed indicative of the ride. And sure enough, when the first tip of a rising sun broke over the horizon in glaring glory, I eased back on the throttle. It was time to turn right, turn south, no matter where I was. First like a mirage, then as a revelation, I rolled up on a dusty gas station and coffee shop off to my right side.

Over a thousand CC's of power idled back as I scoped out the lay of the land. On the far eastern side of the coffee shop I spotted it. A dirt road. Heading straight south. I rolled the bike off the tarmac and leaned into the right turn. There was no activity outside the gas station or coffee shop and no traffic on the dirt road. But it was smooth. More important, it was right where I needed it to be. I accelerated and found 50-55mph a decent speed for the conditions. There lay nothing and everything behind me, nothing and everything before me. Already the desert sun was advertising the coming heat of the day. The left side of me warmed up quick. Scrub brush and the occasional abandoned fence post cast long shadows into the west. And the ride continued.

I rode into the middle of nowhere. The sun climbed to a position overhead. It climbed until it was in the same position as before when I was in the parking lot with the unicycle. It was midday. There was something to note about being midday but what? As I considered it, a body of water came into view up ahead on my left. It was a lake of substantial size. The flat landscape and lack of surrounding structures made it hard to gauge just how big the lake was. The water was seriously calm, calm enough to be a perfect mirror for the empty sky. I knew right away this is where I needed to stop.

I braked, lowered my speed, and turned off into the dirt for a roll to the water's edge. I switched off the engine and felt the silence of the immense emptiness all around overtake my awareness. Stepping off the bike, I shuffled to the point where the toes of my shoes touched the motionless water. I looked around in every direction. This was serious and yet it seemed directionless. Directionless until now. Now I was at the lake. Whatever that meant. I waited for something to change, something to impinge upon my senses as a sign, a signal of intent.

Nothing came. Nothing moved. Nothing disturbed the scene. So what was I supposed to do here? Was somebody coming? Was something going to happen? Was the next part of this only found on foot by walking? At first light I had turned as instructed. Now it was midday and my intuition told me to pull off here. Now what? I walked back and forth. I walked back to the dirt road and looked both ways. I sat on my motionless bike for awhile. I got back up and followed the edge of the lake a bit. I looked around in the dirt for something, anything. Was there something I was supposed to find half-buried and pick up?

Mystified by it all, I finally called out in a loud voice, aiming it at the sky as much as the desert. My shout fell flat without resonance or echo – "So what now? What am I supposed to do here? What's going to happen?" It had been a long while since I heard the voice but now it returned. Its words weren't a direction this time. It felt like an observation. The voice was softer than before, in more of a whisper. It seemed to come from everywhere and nowhere – *"That's what you need to find out."*

I was left standing. The sun beat down. The water tempted me to jump in and cool off. The desert invited me to see what was on the other side of the lake. The bike invited me to jump back on and tear away with a red-lined tachometer. The road invited me to go forward, go back. The coffee shop invited me to come back and laugh it off with a cold brew. Memories of city lights from the night before tempted me to find out what that little town was like. The east-west interstate tempted me to leave the desert entirely. None of it was a resolution. Not when the feeling of being at this lake was strong. But there was nothing there. Or so it seemed.

In time, I telescoped out of the desert, out of the scene, out of the vision, out of my senses into a blackness of being. I felt myself lifting away from the ride, released from the setting but not liberated from my question or the voice's answer. As I floated there, all-consumed by question and answer, the voice returned one last time. Out the blackness I heard it clearly. It spoke in exclamation – *"You are the metaphor!"*

Sometimes sacred plant medicines take you on a shamanic journey. Sometimes they take you on a shamanic ride. A shamanic journey is an experience that is happening to you, even if you sense you have a part in directing it. While you definitely direct a ride, even if given instructions, my ride wasn't something that just happened to me. I knew all along I made it happen. I had to since the landscape was so real. Such a ride can be more tangible than a lucid dream. Such a ride can fill the senses in ways that most visions don't need to. Maybe it's fallout from integrating a message from Ayahuasca to communicate fully with myself. Perhaps is a crazy word to use in medicine space.

This is a story of a ride that was a transport, a reality, a symbol, and ultimately an enigma. Sure, it seems easy to find all kinds of symbolism in it – riding until one sees the light, then changing course until one finds their oasis in the desert. After revelations given to me two years ago by Mother Ayahuasca, I left North America for South America. Was that my turning south?

There's much more I won't go into. Because it would be easier if I hadn't got the distinct impression at the end of the ride such symbolism was not the way to go. The channeled feeling that surfaced from the medicine as I floated back out of the experience preempted any preoccupation with that. Don't go into symbols was the directive. There are no symbols here. No way. There's only you – and "*You are the metaphor.*"

If that is so, then what did I represent during the ride? Well, I guess like the voice said, that's something I need to find out.

Blinded By The Light

Many sacred plant medicines are experienced in total darkness – no light, no fire, no moon. Opinions differ about this practice along with reasons why it's necessary or unfounded. Ayahuasca is traditionally experienced at night and many San Pedro shamans only practice in the dark. And yet I've experienced a Ayahuasca-San Pedro blend out in nature during the day and found it remarkable.

I've heard it said that restricting ceremonies to the night may not be traditional but arose in reaction to the invader Christians. European colonists ran riot over South American culture, forbidding most traditional practices that were religious, spiritual, or mystical in any sense that wasn't Catholic. Some native people tried to appease their new masters by renaming things – thus Huachuma became San Pedro since both seemed to have the keys to heaven.

In an effort to try to maintain traditional ways, some indigenous people started holding plant medicine ceremonies under the cover of darkness in hopes of hiding what they were doing. If this is true, then maybe having plant medicine experiences only at night is a vestige of colonization and not tradition. And yet many shamans swear by the dark. They say there is something to recommend it.

The dark restricts distractions. The dark is evocative of a blank slate with which the medicine can work its magic. The dark is primal, often connected to our earliest fears, the very thing plant medicines like to explore and get out of the way first. The dark frees our awareness to explore the possible and go within instead of fixating on the trappings of the present.

And yet, I wonder – how much dark does one really need? How many kinds of dark are there? What are the ways we can access the dark that makes dark darker? Odd questions to have and not something I had given thought to until one evening that included an experience with Rapé. This was a blend I hadn't tried before but right away it made its energy known. Laying down on the floor to let the energy amplify, I felt encouraged to seek dark and quiet. No sound, no light. I intuitively sensed that darkness and silence would yield the deepest journey. And so in went the ear plugs and I closed my eyes.

Immediately, I felt myself drift deeper. Body energy ramped up its frequency. Even with eyes closed, the impulse was to go darker. The lights in the room could still be detected through my eyelids. And so I covered my eyes with my hands. Even better.

I transitioned my breathing. Deep and slow but more than that, I meditated on how the breath was not only falling out of me – it was falling into me. In and out the breath was a fall. A black-on-black moving mandala faded into view. I let go of thought and went into the darkness. As I did, more detail showed in the improbable black-on-black mandala.

And a voice said, "*Now close your inner eye.*"
Right away, without thinking about it, I felt myself close my inner eye.
Immediately, the voice said and reverberated again and again without end – "*Now close that eye...now close that eye...now close that eye...now close that eye...*"

Like a mirror-reflecting-mirror regression to a vanishing point, I felt eyes closing one after another. This produced an energetic rush and a letting go that startled me, so much so that I experienced a flash of anxiety that drew me back. I was letting go in such a way that was releasing me with infinite speed into something else, a more complete state. Not expecting this and overcome with the rush and energy of it, I was jolted by an instant of fear which pulled me back at once. Afterwards, I lay there stunned. I was very warm and chilled at the same time.

I'm left to wonder. One can wait for night to have their sacred plant medicine ceremony. Once it gets dark and the fire is out, one can close their eyes to intensify the darkness. But is that as far as one can go? Are there other eyes to close to go deeper? If so, does such a progression ever end? In attempting to go into that, where is one headed? I experienced a terrific acceleration once the process began and only a moment of anxiety prevented me from...what? I haven't found out. But I'll always remember that voice echoing to the vanishing point – "*Now close that eye...now close that eye...now close that eye...*"

Yes, I know – it seems counterintuitive to close eyes to experience more. And yet, if the whole purpose of the dark is to block out distractions, like closing our physical eyes, is there sense to be found in going deeper into it? Most devotees to a spiritual or mystical path work hard to open what is called "the third eye." It's all about opening. But is there something to be said for darkness and quiet at every level of our being? If we think too hard about it, paradoxes pile up. According to many shamans, we experience sacred plant medicines by going into the dark for a reason. And that reason is good, evidenced by the healing that comes out of it. But it's up to us to see just how dark it can get.

How deep is the darkness where we finally find the answers that all our distractions of sight, of mind, of intuition, of every kind of sight keeps us from discovering? Are there ultimate answers to find once we know – how deep is dark?

The Sanctuary of Some Special Things

In this lucid dream, I was working with other people on an unknown but significant project. The project needed something and I was asked to go to another location to bring back a special thing. I knew not what it was but nonetheless it was certain this thing would be key and helpful for the work to be done.

As soon as I left the project site I found myself far away. I was approaching a revered object. It resembled a large doll house or tabernacle made of precious wood and draped with an ornate silk and satin cloth. The cloth hung in two sections with an opening seam in the middle of the space. I pulled aside the two pieces of cloth to reveal venerable wooden doors which I also opened with great care.

Inside the cabinet were various small shelves going back to a depth of about six inches. On each of the shelves were small boxes of differing shapes arranged in no particular order, each with a lid that could be easily pulled off and pushed back on. Each lid was covered in a fine cloth decorated with a subtle but intricate floral pattern. I knew right away that this was a sanctuary of special things. I also knew intuitively which small box to reach for.

I never opened the chosen box nor was I tempted to open any of the other boxes that filled the shelves. I merely held the box I needed in one hand while closing the doors and pulling the ornate cloth sections back in place. I returned to the project location at once and handed over the special box. As soon as I did, my location changed.

I was now walking in a dense and beautiful forest. Up ahead along the path was a brief opening in the canopy where sunlight bathed the ferns and grasses in a bright, shimmering glow. Telepathic communication from somewhere made it clear – I was headed to the sunlit spot to find my eight special things. I felt right away that my connection to nature, to the natural world, must be one of these things. But as soon as I felt this, I was given more information.

The message assured me – yes, connection to the natural world was indeed one of the things – but it was one of my eight common things, not one of my special things. Both sets of eight could be realized and understood, used and combined in wondrous ways to explore the possibilities in potential, to thrive and enjoy the fruits of creation, to manifest all that was me.

The following night, I dreamed another lucid dream. In this one I was meditating. In my dream of meditation, I started with the one thing I knew – that connection to the natural world was one of my common things. As I now came to understand it in meditation, the common things were fundamental to the nature of my being in life.

In my dream's self-guided meditation, I visualized myself once again walking along the same forest path. Strangely, as I walked towards the small clearing where the sunlight shimmered on the ferns and grasses, I got no closer to them. Instead, my focus shifted. In my growing appreciation of the denseness and many aspects of the delightful forest around me came, one by one, realizations that detailed the rest of my eight common things:

8 Common Things
- connection (to the natural world / connection to nature)
- health (sustainable physical functionality / self-healing attributes)
- instinct (physical / genetics / autonomic responses that serve)
- input (sensory input / perception of all received / sensibility from inputs)
- output (conveyance from inside out / ability to communicate out to the world)
- intuition (energetic telepathy / emotional intelligence)
- relationship (tribal / community / association impulses)
- self-awareness (consciousness)

And there my meditation ended. I surfaced out of my dream meditation and knew I would soon wake up. And once awake, I was left to wonder. If these are my eight common things, then what are my eight special things? And if my common things are fundamental to being in life – then what purpose do my special things serve? Do I already have them and just need to realize it or are they something only gained by a directed quest?

One thing my intuition was certain of – I wouldn't find any of my special things in the same sanctuary cabinet where I found the little box to bring back to the project. My special things were someplace else. And they weren't in boxes. No one had collected them or put them away for safe keeping or cloistered adulation. Ironically, finding my special things might not be as simple and easy as going to the sanctuary cabinet to fetch the exact thing needed for project work.

And that left me with more wonder – what does that say about my special things? And what does it say about how I need to find them? It doesn't seem at all certain it's possible to discover my special things if my common things are the only tools I have to find them with. It's tempting to conclude I won't get there from here. By why be tempted in that direction? Why not look to possibilities instead?

In fact, I do have a hint that it's possible. I have seen the shimmering sunlit spot up ahead in the forest. I have sensed that at least one of my special things might be found there. But walking on that path didn't get me any closer to that sunlit glow. That seems paradoxical if the sunlit spot exists in the middle of that beautiful forest. Shouldn't traveling the forest path be the way there? Could there be another way to it?

I have to imagine I'll find out. At least I'm going to try. And I sense more every day that imagination will play its part. And who knows, maybe it'll turn out that what I crudely call imagination is actually one of my special things. With that key piece in place, perhaps the rest will follow – as sure as sunlight is only part of the reason grasses and ferns shimmer and glow.

Then again, perhaps the desire to arrive at that sunlit spot is showing me something more fundamental. That sunlit glow exists up ahead like a rainbow one might see. It's tempting to react as if one can race there and find the end of that rainbow. Such a preoccupation is ultimately futile and foolish for the rainbow keeps moving as we move. Its very existence is predicated on knife-edge angles of reflectance that are shifted in the ways we move. Finding joy in the rainbow right where we are is what it's about, not chasing after special things in sunlit spots, like so many pots of gold just waiting at some phantom place up ahead.

The lesson comes into focus. Simply walking the forest path is what it's about. Finding that walk special seems to be the key. Once that is realized and internalized, then all the common things don't seem so common anymore.

Ayavision / The Four Offerings

One never knows what Mother Ayahuasca may show you. The possible spectrum of one's sight within a journey with yagé is wide. Accessing multiple manifestations all at once occurs naturally. Time as we know it becomes a memory, replaced with a new type of spacetime one might call UIT, Universal Infinite Time. When the fire of the ceremonial circle burns out and deepening night beckons Mother to appear, there's suddenly no difference among physical, emotional, energetic, spiritual, and mystical sight.

First comes your surrender to the plant medicine process with good intentions. If this happens, then all your ways to see join together. Your powers of perception augment throughout outer and inner space. All sight focuses into a single but collectively distinct force. It is then the real work begins deciphering the soul-clenching cavalcade called you. Where that healing work goes fills the endless night and expands in revealing ways. Often, it continues to a resplendent dawn. Hopefully, it progresses for life as the healing effects are integrated. If approached correctly, it scares your fears out from hiding places deep within your psyche and lights the way forward with new attitude and energy.

But something else may happen during the night. During that eternity of being fully opened and rearranged by the medicine, flash-visions from Mother may burn as insights into your essential core. Some of these nuggets of meta-intuition are easy to see as applying to you personally. But others at first don't appear personal at all. They're more general, with a wide sweep and universal understanding that transcends the you you think you are.

I had an insight like this recently. Although in general it wasn't personal to my process in the ceremony that night, it was an unavoidable rush of light I absorbed in my own self-revealing dark. Now I see how it applies to me. Now I see how it applies to all of us.

It was the middle of the night, midway through a recent Ayahuasca ceremony. I found myself deeply preoccupied by my journey while sitting on the ground outside a teepee. The sky was heavily overcast. The only light around me was the ever-startling, on-and-off zips of fireflies flitting in the black bushes and trees. Earlier in the night, the ceremony had begun with claps of booming thunder that produced no rain. Finally, now an occasional quiet drizzle found the spot where I sat. Each drop of water was felt individually and communicated with. Such a meditation after repeated purges was refreshment for my soul. But refreshment was about to be interrupted.

The flash of inter-cloud lightning was too quick and bright to take me by surprise. The burst of blue-white light arced above me from what seemed horizon to horizon beyond the trees. All of the heavy overcast hanging low lit up. Tree branches everywhere shock-silhouetted black in a stunning sight crescendo. The lightning was long over but I still reacted to it. After many hours of pitch blackness, being thrust into the opposite conditions made a statement I couldn't ignore.

As added exclamation, a few minutes later, the sky flash repeated. When it did, my journey was interrupted. My concentration reset. My awareness was cleared. And into the void came a thought-form fully expressed. It expanded without having to explain itself. Right away I knew it completely. It was showing me all that Mother made available for those who came to her. It was clear – all she could do was present the opportunity to the willing. If one approached her the right way, then four stages of progress were possible. I was being shown the path of help Mother offered to anyone who came to her with right mind, right heart, right body. I was being shown the four stages of Ayahuasca. I was being shown the four offerings.

First Offering – Fun-House Mirror

The first help I saw Mother present is what I interpret with a fun-house mirror analogy. She shows us the distorted image we have of ourselves, everything that warps the truth about who we are, what we are capable of, what is important, the hurts and resentments and guilt we carry forward as part of our identity. She makes us experience this distortion in all of its ramifications. This distortion contains all of our fears, even those we hide from ourselves. All is laid bare and obvious before us.

It is up to us to step up and accept what we see, confront it, understand it for what it is, realize where it all came from, and most importantly, how we don't have to maintain such a deluded existence as this illusion to be our life.

This stage can be terrifying, too painful to endure. Many flee the medicine and never come back after being forced to confront their demons, the vapors of negativity and self-fallacy, the baggage of past self-deception, and all the wounds the ego likes to wear as a coat of many sad colors.

But for others, it often leads, if approached correctly, to what is called ego-death. In truth, it is the death of the distorted image. It is a massive purge of what doesn't serve the real being we are. Mother gives us the opportunity to see the way things are being played out. But it's up to us to step up, look deeply at the distortion, and feel our way through it to the other side.

Only if this is done can we progress to the Second Offering.

Second Offering – Clear Mirror

The second help I saw Mother present is what I interpret with a perfectly clear mirror analogy. She shows us nothing less than who we really are.

Probably for the first time in our lives, we finally get to see ourselves without the distortions our past and our fearful and hurtful habits have put upon us. We come to a sense of resolved paradoxes, of being a loved, unique soul and yet one with All. We feel the priorities that stem from unconditional love. We know what it's like to be heart-centered. Previous explanations and convoluted processes fall away.

The truth of Being is experienced as simple but profound, personal and yet infinite, creative and adventurous with ecstasies of self-fulfillment available in any direction we choose. But we must choose. And we must not be distracted by fear.

If we stay clear, we can access the magic of Being. But we must look long and hard into the clear mirror.

Many can't accept what they see (after all, who do they think they are to be that magnificent, that at-one-with the ultimate quintessence). Many are overwhelmed and flee back to the illusion of comfort in the old distortions. The old habits and wounds almost feel comfortable in comparison for they have identified too long and hard with their presumed pain and existential angst.

And yet, only if one can stand and stare and accept what is shown to them in the clear mirror, only then is the Third Offering made available.

Third Offering – Window Beyond

The third help I saw Mother present is what I interpret with a perfectly clear window analogy. With this offering she allows us to see beyond ourselves into the mysteries of the universe. If we accept what we see in the clear mirror, if we become one with our true selves, then the clear mirror turns translucent. As it does, our image disappears, but in its place all of creation appears before us.

Finally freed of our distortions and now accepting of who we really are, we are ready to look at the wonders possible. Depending on our powers of intuitive sight and understanding, higher orders of knowledge and heart-sense is available. But the window view only stays clear without the limitations of what doesn't serve us.

If we fall back into old ways or try to interpret what we see through the window with old beliefs and limited by ego-based feelings, then the window fogs over and turns opaque. We make our view clear by clearing ourselves. When really clear, amazing details about ourselves and all of creation come into focus.

Only when we can gaze through the window offered and be at peace and one with all we encounter are we allowed access to the fourth offering.

Fourth Offering – Portal Beyond

The fourth help I saw Mother present is what I interpret with an open portal analogy. Now the window disappears, leaving in its place an opening to pass through.

Once we choose to move forward, Mother guides us on journeys into the cosmos, into the universe of ourselves, and eventually beyond the universe into higher realms that infinite creation manifests without end. These are the shamanic journeys that offer the most and require the most. These are the places of the heart beyond lessons and messages and explanations. This is the magic that is always in plain sight, which says much about the kind of sight that's common.

The most difficult thing sometimes is to arrive at the quiet and the simple and the already perfectly-complete – and know it as ourselves.

Mother made it clear. These were offerings. Everyone who comes to her has to choose to accept what is offered and do what's required. She can't make us accept or move forward. And the four stages don't happen automatically. And they aren't final once we reach any one of them.

We may spike in intensity on our journey and manage to eliminate our distortion and in doing so see our true selves – only to fall back into the fun-house mirror once again when we're back in the old routines of life. Someone else might have a flash insight to accept their true self and their mirror transforms into the window on the universe. But a moment later, resurfacing self-doubt or conditioned fears make the window fog over and return to being a mirror. If the true self is also doubted, the mirror image morphs with distortions.

Magic or delusion is up to us. The fear or transcendence we get reflected back upon us is always our own. But Mother is always there with her special offerings. She will always show up for those who approached her with gratitude, humility, preparation, and a heart-based attitude.

Ayahuasca isn't a cure-all pill one pops and the pill does all the work. In love, Mother offers the way, the tools, the self-reflections that often come to us as wild, even terrifying experiences, but it's always up to us to show up and, as shaman say, "stand in your own footprint." If we surrender our old selves to what's possible, the magic of the four offerings can take us as far as we want to go – as far as we are willing to accept the help offered.

In Both Worlds

When is re-entry?
Has it happened?
What are these mixed signals?
Where do I land?
How do I know it's stable underneath me?
Do I just step out and act normal?
What *IS* normal?
Why do I feel different?
Everything seems the same but it's not.
I can't explain it. I just know. I feel it in my bones.
All indicators say I'm coming back to my world.
But if that's so, why is everything so off? I'm so out-of-sync.
Like I've got a foot in both worlds...

Welcome to life after returning from sacred plant medicine space.

For some, for many, for most in varying degrees, the world we return to is less real or approachable than the extraordinarily improbable one that swirled us away in ceremony. Much will be different, at least for a while. If opening of wounds and cleansings took place, perhaps for a long while. If we've experienced healing, one hopes that difference lasts a lifetime.

Reality is transmuted. Priorities are shuffled. The very passage of time may play tricks with conscious awareness. Everyone confronts individual expressions of how integration into regular life plays out. But integration is key. Integration allows us to use what we learn from medicine space in our lives. That sounds like a good thing, and it is. But it can be a process that marks a difficult transition. There is no formula for how long this takes or even what's involved. So much depends on the individual and their circumstances. It may be hard to fathom at the time it's happening, but so much good occurs all the while we're passing through it, even the difficult parts.

Some of that difficulty stems from the fact that many of us erroneously believe that the sacred medicines do all the work, like instant coffee or a breath mint. In reality, it's more like a partnership. And just like when we were kids, no one can learn how to ride a bike for you. Likewise, no one but you can learn how to apply medicine space lessons. The spirit of the medicines stay with you, like a disembodied guide hovering by while you teeter on your training wheels, but their interceding is in a support role.

They know your satisfaction at zipping around on that bike will only come when you do it yourself, all the way.

Depending on circumstances, integration can be more or less disorientating. Avoiding the worse effects would be nice of course. That's why it's good to be aware how certain factors increase the likelihood that re-entry will confront us with challenges. For example...

The quicker one rushes back into old routines, the worse it can be, especially if those routines somehow reinforce the very things the medicines were attempting to get us to shed. We may rush back into these old habits simply because our life schedules demand it. Or we rush back because unconsciously these habits give us a level of comfort. It's probably a mixture of both. And the path of least resistance is to settle for any modicum of comfort, in any guise. That can feel preferable to the challenge of forging something new in ourselves.

The more family and friends you have who expect you to be your same old self – in fact, may be highly codependent on you staying that old self – the worse it can be. Our connections to special people are important. Strong yet tacit fear of jeopardizing those bonds in any way can possibly undo the progress gained in medicine space. Needless to say, to have the people around you on board with your transformative process is huge. The best thing loved ones can do for someone undergoing integration is 1) not pressure them into old behaviors or comment negatively because those old behaviors are not as they were, and 2) not recoil or act strangely at the new behaviors one is developing or feels drawn to.

The more immediate and noticeable some changes in you take effect, the worse it can be. For example, if suddenly the thought of bingeing on alcohol is repugnant, that may not play well with relatives and friends who team up to get you to join in with them. New questions may arise and force one to confront new facts of life. Can you be with these people and have fun if you don't participate in the alcohol part? Will they accept you under those conditions? This may raise follow-on issues in which you wonder what the get-together is really about anyway, bingeing or being together? New perspectives play out many ways.

Certain foods may not be as pleasing as before, especially during the first couple of weeks after ceremony when the medicine is still strong within you and the special dieta that prepped you for ceremony should still be followed. How comfortable are those comfort foods anymore? Actually, I think if it was up to the medicine, one would remain on some form of the dieta permanently.

If you uncharacteristically need more "quiet time" to meditate and process your feelings, that could be misunderstood by loved ones as signaling a pulling away or retreat into isolation. This is especially true for gregarious types who weren't that prone to fits of meditation before. Know that a lot of processing continues after the ceremony. Much of this is non-verbal, emotional, energetic. Give this process the time and space it needs. Make sure friends and loved ones understand and are onboard with the reason for it.

You might find you're "off your game" at work. Abruptly, the thought of what passes as productive time and meaningful interchanges leave you in stunned silence. A sense of other passions, other pursuits may cause a fair share of daydreaming. Don't neglect these flights of fancy. These daydreams, either rare or dismissed for so long, could now be awakening a reconnection with your deep passions long neglected. Inherent in the renewed interests are alternate possible directions to take moving forward into a happier way of living.

Mass-produced or addictive entertainments and uber-hype of the 24/7 news cycle may now appear vapid or as obvious mind viruses or programming. It's something like the drifter in the old 1988 film "They Live" who discovers a pair of sunglasses that allow him to wake up to the fact that aliens have taken over the Earth. I'm not suggesting you'll see aliens but the feeling could be similar given how separate and disjointed the entertainment bombardment has become. It may appear so strange that you wouldn't be surprised to see hidden messages like "Stay Asleep," "No Imagination," or "Submit to Authority" sewn into the lining of the scantily-clad dancer trying to sell you a new flavor of toothpaste on a pop-up web advertisement. Like Piper in "They Live," in reaction to this onslaught you might lash out in ways you don't understand and shout at somebody, "I come here to chew bubble gum and kick ass but I'm all out of bubble gum!"

The outlook and quality of your dreams may change. Some of these can be quite lucid, even if you've rarely if ever experienced a lucid dream before. These flights and tableaus can be so engaging, so real, so mystifying and compelling as to disturb, confuse, or cause puzzling or emotional preoccupations during one's wide-awake time. If stressed upon or reacted to negatively, these dreams can make the process of integration worse. While they shouldn't be ignored, neither should these dreams be over-analyzed. Be aware of them, be open to impressions and feelings that come out of them, then let them go to do their thing. They are but the fireworks above the celebration your spirit is having. Some dream content may in no way appear to be a celebration, quite the contrary. But after being tied down by fears and distortions, hurts and guilts, insecurities and illusions of ego, one's spirit is simply exercising the increased ability to move about and take you with it. That's a good thing.

If one attends multiple plant medicine ceremonies, especially if some time elapses between them, integration can complicate itself. The ceremonies may have had wildly differing results and our post-ceremony outlook and feelings will hinge on that. No one can see the whole medicine process out-of-time and so there's no way for us to apply an overall perspective to something we haven't completed. And yet the medicine spirits do seem to exist out-of-time.

In retrospect, they always seem to have a plan for us. One that will not be evident. And individual ceremony parts may not even seem consistent while we're in the thick of it. Add to this the confusion of switching back and forth between ceremonies and "real life" and you have a recipe for a goulash that can be hard to swallow. But there's a good reason for what the medicine does. We have to believe that. If we can manage that, a series of ceremonies over time has the potential to deliver some of the deepest insights and healings.

Wouldn't it be nice if, in hindsight, we could take our own advice? All of this I say now would have been interesting to hear a couple years ago when I set out on my own tumbling soul-fest. But would I have listened? Would any of it have mattered if I ignored it all? Most likely ignoring it is what I would have done. It reminds me of the message I got the day after my first ceremony – "*If we had given you the answers you needed directly, you only would have argued with us. So we had to take you there. It was the only way. You couldn't be told. You had to go through the worst to get the best insight.*"

Looking back on it now, I can see that, see it in a way I understand. Even the fact that I came to the medicines in the first place could be seen as a roundabout tactic by the medicines. Initially, I came to Ayahuasca with my wife to support her. My approach was, no way was the ceremony work about me. And most likely the medicine knew in advance this would be so. If the medicine had given me a calling like it had done for my wife, I would have argued with that calling.

If they were going to get me to drink medicine at all, my calling had to be passive and roundabout. The medicine had to hook me with a ploy, then shoot me through-and-through with a psychological imperative. The ploy was being there to support my wife. Then it made me face the urgency of casting out my demons. It seems the medicine had been after me all the while. Or at least it was the yearning of my higher self. And it got to me the only way it could. This is not to say I had no choice in working with these medicines. But perhaps my higher self had already made the choice, and didn't percolate down to the more human reality I live in right away.

After the initial shock of that first ceremony, there were plenty of people who attempted to set me straight during the year plus I spent in agonized integration. I had an answer, a rebuttal, a debate team tactic to escape all of it. It's questionable to even call what I went through during the first year an integration. It was more like watching reruns of "The Night of the Living Dead" in slow motion on a virtual reality headset implanted on a chip in my cerebellum. The fact was, I knew what I knew, or at least I thought I did, and all the advice on Earth and from realms beyond wasn't about to penetrate my certainty about the predicament I was in. It took time, more medicine, and a caring and insightful shaman to snap me out of that. Once that happened, only then could the rest of my integration begin.

That's not to say I hadn't absorbed anything in the beginning. Far from it. After I returned home from those initial ceremonies, I did experience major changes, as described in detail previously. But as significant as all of this was, it was superficial to what was going on inside. I was like a prisoner who had found religion early on in his life-without-parole sentence. Chalk up whatever transformation you want, my basic condition was the same regardless what I found.

As far as I was concerned, all of the magnificent changes were confined within a box made on a foundation of dilemmas and paradoxes that supported walls of fearful certainties. Sure, I might be able to lose 40 pounds in four months, quit my profession, sell all my belongings, and move thousands of miles to another continent – all of which was unthinkable before, but don't ask me to imagine myself on the other side of that feared barbed wire.

Did I rush back into old routines? Sure I did. Were some of the changes in me sudden and noticeable? You bet. Were once favorite foods and beverages off-putting? Yep. Did I need more meditative time? Quite a lot. Was the corporate workday a soulless thing that left me slumped in stunned silence? Oh, yeah. Was the world news cycle an addiction to drama? Hell, yes. Were popular entertainments suddenly as fulfilling and believable as a 1950's laugh track? No doubt. Did friends expect me to play the part scripted for me by the matrix? Is the blue pill blue?

There seemed to be nowhere to turn to find elements supportive of the kind of integration I needed. My wife had gone to Hawaii for three months to work out what the medicine had shown her. It was a necessary part of her process and I was fully supportive of it. If anything, her absence gave me the solid alone-time that I needed to go deep into my meditations. Those contemplations made it possible for me to outline new habits. With no one else around, I had the benefit of not getting push-back regardless of what I tried.

The medicine was wise like that. My wife got exactly what she needed and so did I. But that meant we would be apart for three months. When she returned, we sold our belongings and moved out of the country within a month. Big changes were afoot. But had we integrated everything well? It's hard to say. It's obvious now, we had integrated what we needed at the time to move forward. After getting settled in our new country, I believe another phase of integration began. Like Odysseus, having sailed through the Pillars of Heracles, there were times when we were blown by winds to within sight of home and then back for more. It was a hell of a ride but one we wouldn't have missed – for the world.

In many respects, the wonders and challenges of sacred plant medicine space invites us to become our own hero, our own savior, our own best friend and confidant. And the hero, of course, is a pervasive archetype, well entrenched within us. In some way or another, we all get that call in life – the call to set out on our hero's journey – a quest to ourselves and all it entails – even if we must paradoxically, leave our image of ourselves behind in the process. To be one's own iconoclast in the face of our false image of ourselves, our life, our future, it's the call to be one's own luminary.

The stages of the hero's journey have been well documented:

- The Departure – The call to adventure, although one is reluctant to accept it.
- The Initiation – The crossing of a threshold into new, more dangerous worlds, and in doing so, gaining a more mature perspective.
- The Road of Trials – The presence of supernatural aid while enduring tests of strength, resourcefulness, and endurance.
- The Innermost Cave – The descent into the innermost cave, an underworld, or some other place of great trial. Sometimes this exists within the hero's own mind. Through this trial the hero is reborn in some way– physically, emotionally, or spiritually. Through this experience, the hero changes internally.
- Return and Reintegration with Society – The use of new wisdom to restore fertility and order to the land.

All of these stages exist in sacred plant medicine space. But with any true, heroic journey, none of it is automatic, assured, or blessed with guaranteed outcomes. That is up to the hero. It's up to us to make it so. And that's why there are so many different stories about medicine space. Everyone's hero journey, their profound effort navigating these stages, is different.

The key will always be getting out of one's head and into the experience. The knowledge comes from the experience, not from speculation or endless analysis and hypothesizing. As Taisen Deshimaru said so succinctly, "If you have a glass full of liquid you can discourse forever on its qualities, discuss whether it is cold, warm, whether it is really and truly composed of H-2-O, or even mineral water, or sake. Meditation is drinking it!"

Likewise, sacred plant medicine space is the act of drinking life, drinking yourself fully instead of forever holding them apart as paralyzing or limiting thought-streams. It is the only hero's journey I can think of where the act of surrender catalyzes the most rewarding victories.

Terence McKenna also summed it up nicely – "Plotinus, the great neo-Platonic philosopher, he spoke of the mystical experience as the flight of going it alone, to be alone. And in the psychedelic experience there is this issue of surrender because a lot of people want to diddle with it. They want to say they did it but they don't want to have to face an actual moment where they put it all on the line. And yet the whole issue with this stuff is to let it lead, to let it show what it wants to show. So, somehow individually, we have to reclaim our experience. The real message, more important than even the psychedelic experience, the real message I try to leave with people…is the primacy of direct experience. That as people, the real universe is within your reach. Always. Everything not within your reach is basically unconfirmed rumor."

Differing personality types and the mixing of conflicting inner intentions on why the journey is necessary will always come to bear. In the end, the individual's make-up and history contribute greatly in determining the route one takes through medicine space. No one's journey can be predicted and each of us will react differently to similar trials along the way. Each hero is unique. Each faces unique challenges. Each can achieve uniquely spectacular rewards.

Heroic Intentions

The quest for IDENTITY (finding oneself)

The EPIC journey to find the promised land, the good city (is heaven real?)

The journey in search of KNOWLEDGE (what's it all about?)

The search for LOVE (or rescue the loved one in distress – oneself, or ultimately a quest to bond)

The WARRIOR'S journey to save his people (we won't get there until everyone gets there)

The TRAGIC quest, spurred by penance or self-denial (this is my last stab at an answer, rock bottom)

The quest to RID the land of danger (cast out the demons)

The GRAIL quest (the quest for human perfection)

The quest for VENGEANCE (living well and being well is the best revenge, a dish served cold)

The FOOL'S errand (plant medicine as a bucket list item or mere recreational high)

What you integrate is what you've taken away from ceremony. What you take away is what you've put in your intentions. What you put in is what comes out from inner need. What comes out is what is revealed by medicine experience. What is revealed is what's hidden from the conscious self. What is hidden is what is reactive to layered illusion. What is reactive is what is based in what doesn't serve. What doesn't serve is formed around us by us. What is formed contains maladaptive energy. What is energy but the stuff of creation. What is creation but the action of Source. What is Source? It all leads back to the same place. In both worlds, which is one world, it's you.

The question remains: how does integration after a plant ceremony ever come about? The experience did so much but often much more of what's new needs to be done. Is there anything, one core concept behind getting it accomplished? For that answer, I defer to a shaman…

A shaman told me a story once about two friends who lived far apart. One day their paths crossed. Both were busy but they had time to quickly say hello and catch up…

"What are you doing now?" asked one friend of the other.

"I heal people," came the proud answer.

"Really!"

"Yes, I lay my hands on them and concentrate and they are healed."

"How wonderful! I'm so glad for you. It's good to see you but I have to run."

Quite some time later, their paths crossed again.

"What are you doing now?" asked one friend of the other. "Are you still healing people?"

"Yes," came the answer. "Only now, I heal without touching; I just hover my hands over them."

"Really! What a wonder! How marvelous! I'm so glad for you. It's good to see you but I have to run."

More time passed and eventually their paths crossed once more.

"Hello! So what are you doing now?" asked the friend. "Are you still healing people?"

"Oh yes," his friend replied with obvious satisfaction. "Only now, I heal at great distances. I don't even have to see them."

"Really! That's spectacular! I'm happy for you. It's good to see you but I have to run."

A long time passed but finally their paths crossed again.

"And what are you doing now?" asked the friend. "Are you still healing people?"

"Oh no, I don't do that anymore," the friend waved off the suggestion.

The friend was shocked, "Really? But that was amazing. You were doing so well."

"I thought so," admitted the friend. "But then I discovered the real power."

The friend was wide-eyed, "What's that?"

"I discovered people could heal themselves."

The Lesson

Once upon a time in a galaxy near near away there lived a most ordinary psychonaut with a peculiar intention. He wanted to know La Medicina so he could receive his lesson.

And so he attended a plant spirit ceremony and sprung forth afterwards overflowing with immense joy and fulfillment. The lesson had been received and he was blessed with a most profound message to guide his life.

The lesson was – *square*.

He shared his lesson with everyone so they too would have the benefit of it. Everywhere he went, he recognized squares, and at night he dreamed of squares. When he meditated, he saw visions of squares. He was happy and content with how well he had integrated the message from the medicine. So in tune was he with his lesson that he even wore a T-shirt with his square emblazoned there for all to see.

But then someone dared to ask him – "You got all you ever need from one lesson?"

This was highly rude since it implied that his lesson wasn't complete, wasn't good enough to satisfy everything in him for ever more. He didn't answer rude comments – but it planted a seed of doubt. Was the medicine calling to him? Could it be possible there was more to receive? How could there be more than what he had already experienced? How could there possibly be more than square?

In time, he needed to find out. And so he returned to the ceremony space, for an enhanced lesson. He expected to receive a deeper understanding of his square. But that's not what he got at all. This time he was shown so much more...

And so he sprung forth afterwards with immense joy and fulfillment. The lesson had been received. He was shown where the square went. He rejoiced to finally know the secret of life.

The lesson was – *cube*.

He excitedly shared his lesson with everyone so they would have the benefit of it. Everywhere he went, he recognized cubes, and at night he dreamed of cubes. When he meditated, he saw visions of cubes. He was happy and content with how well he had integrated the message from the medicine. So in tune was he with his lesson that he even wore a T-shirt with his cube emblazoned there for all to see.

But then someone dared to ask him – "You really got all you ever need from this lesson?"

This was highly rude since it implied that his lesson wasn't complete, wasn't good enough to satisfy everything in him for ever more. He didn't answer rude comments – but it planted another seed of doubt. Was the medicine calling to him? Could it be possible there was more to receive? How could there be more than what he had already experienced? How could there possibly be more than cube?

In time, he needed to find out. And so he returned to the ceremony space, in search of more. He expected to receive a deeper understanding of his cube. But that's not what he got at all. This time he was shown so much more...

And so he sprung forth afterwards with immense joy and fulfillment. The lesson had been received. He was shown where the cube went. He rejoiced to finally know the secret of life.

The lesson was – *tesseract*.

He excitedly shared his lesson with everyone so they would have the benefit of it. Everywhere he went, he recognized tesseracts, and at night he dreamed of tesseracts. When he meditated, he saw visions of tesseracts. He was happy and content with how well he had integrated the message from the medicine. So in tune was he with his lesson that he even wore a T-shirt with his tesseract emblazoned there for all to see.

But then someone dared to ask him – "How do you know this message is all you'll ever need?"

This was highly rude since it implied that his lesson wasn't complete, wasn't good enough to satisfy everything in him for ever more. He didn't answer rude comments – but it planted another seed of doubt. Was the medicine calling to him? Could it be possible there was more to receive? How could there be more than what he had already experienced? How could there possibly be more than tesseract?

In time, he needed to find out. And so he returned to the ceremony space, in search of more. He expected to receive a deeper understanding of his tesseract. But that's not what he got at all. This time he was shown so much more...

And so he sprung forth afterwards with immense joy and fulfillment. The lesson had been received. He was shown where the tesseract went. He rejoiced to finally know the secret of life.

The lesson was – *metacube.*

He excitedly shared his lesson with everyone so they would have the benefit of it. Everywhere he went, he recognized metacubes, and at night he dreamed of metacubes. When he meditated, he saw visions of metacubes. He was happy and content with how well he had integrated the message from the medicine. So in tune was he with his lesson that he even wore a T-shirt with his metacube emblazoned there for all to see.

But then someone dared to ask him – "How do you know this message is all you'll ever need?"

This was highly rude since it implied that his lesson wasn't complete, wasn't good enough to satisfy everything in him for ever more. He didn't answer rude comments – but it planted another seed of doubt. Was the medicine calling to him? Could it be possible there was more to receive? How could there be more than what he had already experienced? How could there possibly be more than metacube?

In time, he needed to find out. And so he returned to the ceremony space, in search of more. He expected to receive a deeper understanding of his metacube. But that's not what he got at all. This time he was shown so much more...

And so he sprung forth afterwards with immense joy and fulfillment. The lesson had been received. He was shown where the metacube went. He rejoiced to finally know the secret of life.

The lesson was – *metatron's tree of life.*

He excitedly shared his lesson with everyone so they would have the benefit of it. Everywhere he went, he recognized trees of life, and at night he dreamed of trees of life. When he meditated, he saw visions of trees of life. He was happy and content with how well he had integrated the message from the medicine. So in tune was he with his lesson that he even wore a T-shirt with his tree of life emblazoned there for all to see.

But then someone dared to ask him – "How do you know this message is all you'll ever need?"

This was highly rude since it implied that his lesson wasn't complete, wasn't good enough to satisfy everything in him for ever more. He didn't answer rude comments – but it planted another seed of doubt. Was the medicine calling to him? Could it be possible there was more to receive? How could there be more than what he had already experienced? How could there possibly be more than the tree of life?

In time, he needed to find out. And so he returned to the ceremony space, in search of more. He expected to receive a deeper understanding of his tree of life. But that's not what he got at all. This time he was shown so much more...

And so he sprung forth afterwards with immense joy and fulfillment. The lesson had been received. He was shown where the tree of life went. He rejoiced to finally know the secret of life.

The lesson was –

Panic and awe shot through his whole being. He had no words for what he had experienced. He could not describe it much less understand it.

He wanted to excitedly share his lesson with everyone so they would have the benefit of it. Everywhere he went, he recognized his experience around him in ways he couldn't fathom, and at night he dreamed of his experience in ways he couldn't interpret. When he meditated, he saw visions of his experience becoming much more than he thought it could be. He was unhappy and discontent with how he was integrating the message from the medicine.

He was so frustrated with not understanding its lesson and not being able to share it with others. With overflowing emotion he threw all of his other T-shirts away – away with the square, the cube, the tesseract, the metacube, and metatron's tree of life. He was left with nothing to show anyone of what his experiences meant to him because he himself did not know what had happened to him.

But then someone dared to ask him – "How do you know if these messages are all you'll ever need?"

Suddenly he found this question highly insightful, not rude at all. He realized it implied much more about him than merely being commentary on the message. It implied he was something ever unfolding, ever emergent into more, with more to receive.

He had no answer for this insightful comment – but it planted another seed of doubt. Was the medicine calling to him? Wasn't it forever possible there was more to receive? In the infinity of creation, could there always be more than what he had already experienced? Did the lessons never end?

In time, he needed to be sure. And so he returned to the ceremony space, in search of more. He didn't know what to expect but he knew it would be a deeper understanding of what he needed. He was ready to continue his boundless journey into himself as a way to explore life and creation itself.

But that's not what he got at all. This time he was shown so much more...

And so he sat in the ceremony space infused with immense joy and fulfillment. The lesson had been received. He was shown where it all went. He rejoiced to finally know he was the secret of life.

The lesson was – *square*.

He was back to square one. He now knew his first lesson had been complete. He only needed to see beyond himself to himself. It was not square but what he put into square that mattered.

He had no words for what he experienced. He could not describe it but that was all right. He felt it. And that made all the difference.

He wanted to share this feeling with everyone he met. Everywhere he went, he recognized it was what he put into the experience that mattered. He was happy and content to feel that he was the message – he was the lesson. With overflowing emotion he threw himself into life. No T-shirt was needed to express it all. His actions would say everything.

But then someone dared to ask him – "How do you know if these messages are all you'll ever need?"

He answered back – you ask about messages, why not ask about need? What do you need? More importantly, why do you need? Is need the only reason to explore yourself and creation? Is that why creation does it? Feelings from deep inside said no. There was no need, only joy and exuberance. There will always be another question and in the question is need. In the question and the need will always be another seed of doubt.

Was the medicine calling to him? – That was the question. Was there more to receive? – That was the need. There would never be any completeness there, only doubt.

In time, he returned to the ceremony space. But not to search for more – this time, he returned to make the question less, his need less.

But that's not what he got at all. This time he was shown so much more...

Smiling Tiger Wobbly Horse

In my lucid dream it's a sunny afternoon. I'm traveling in a taxi with a family I don't know but am spending time with. I'm sitting in between the taxi driver and one of the adults of the family in the front seat. On the adult's lap is a boy about six years old. The boy is turned away from me, enjoying the breeze and view out the open passenger side window. The rest of the family fills out the back seat.

The taxi slows at a four-way stop sign. Alongside us is a park. Down the cross street a little ways are diagonal lines, parking spaces for those visiting the park. The parking places are empty of cars but my attention is drawn to the space closest to us. In that space stands a most unusual horse.

It's a misshapen horse, wobbly on its feet. It's large and lumpy, pasty white in front and emaciated and fragile in back. I'm positive this horse is unable to run. Just walking around would present problems. The horse manages to move in slow counter-balancing steps while staying in place. In this way it avoids falling down. Its bushy head is turned away from us, attracted to sights and movement in the park. I can't take my eyes off this animal. It certainly is a most unusual horse.

Out loud I comment, "That's really an unusual horse!"

The little boy, sitting on the lap of the adult next to me, leans towards the window and tilts his head in consideration. Next moment he answers me with a joyful lilt to his voice, "I like it anyway!"

There is no way this horse can hear the little boy. And even if it had, horses don't understand such language. Nevertheless, no sooner has the boy's words hit the air, but the horse's head turns to face us. To everyone's amazement, the head is that of a tiger! And no sooner have we realized this, but the tiger's expression changes dramatically. A great big Cheshire cat type of smile erupts on the tiger's face.

"Look at that!" I cxclaim to the boy, "He likes what you said!"

Just then, the little boy turns his head around for the first time to look at me. This motion and his widening smile of appreciation and glee erupts just like the horse's smile had moments before. The movement and the smiles of both follow in kind like some self-referencing reflection. But my amazement is not on this. I'm shocked to find this boy, this face – this is my face; it's me as a boy! I'm talking to myself at a much younger age. Why he is with this family I don't recognize I have no idea.

My attention draws back to the horse with the tiger's head. The tiger's smile continues to widen. It widens so much that it starts to appear warped. If it continues, the effect might even seem mischievous or menacing. And just then, the dream ends.

After I awake, this dream returns to me during the day, prompting me to come to terms with the symbols it provided. I have no idea where to start. The most obvious place is the strange horse. Why was it a horse with a tiger's head? Is there such a thing in any folklore or mythology? I have never heard of such a thing. And yet I soon find out to my amazement that "Mǎ mǎ hǔ hǔ" is a well known Chinese chengyu, a proverbial idiom. As with all such tales with sources shrouded in time, the details of the story differ slightly to quite a bit depending on which version you hear.

For some people, "Mǎ mǎ hǔ hǔ" or Horse-Horse Tiger-Tiger as it's known in English, is an old story about a horse and a tiger that get into a fight. Neither animal is able to defeat the other. This came to mean a fight with no definite winner, a result that was just 'so so.'

Another version says a long time ago an artist drew an animal and asked other people to guess what animal he had drawn. Some said it a horse and others said it was a tiger. Seeing this difference, the people said the picture was 'Mǎ mǎ hǔ hǔ' or just 'so-so', meaning average or carelessly done.

All stories about this Chinese chengyu are popularly understood to refer to something done hastily, carelessly, not taken seriously, with mediocre results. But there's a more elaborate version of "Horse-Tiger," 馬虎 (mǎhū) or 馬馬虎虎 (mǎmǎhūhū). It's said to come from a tragic story about an eccentric artist from the Song dynasty.

According to the story, soon after the artist started to paint a tiger, a man came by offering the artist money to paint a horse. Instead of starting the horse on another canvas, the artist simply added a horse's body to the tiger's head already started on a first canvas. Seeing this, the man refused to pay, saying the whole thing was ridiculous and not what he asked for.

Left with no buyer, the artist hung the odd picture in his living room, where his eldest son saw it and asked about it. The father was angered that the son questioned it and snapped back that it was obviously a tiger. The father explained how a tiger is a fierce animal that eats men and if the son should ever see one he should defend himself at once. Set correct by his father's outburst, the eldest son went for a walk in the woods where he encountered a horse. He immediately killed the horse and hurried back to exclaim what a hero he was because he had killed a tiger. Before the father could respond, the owner of the horse ran up and demanded compensation for the dead horse. The artist was angry and frustrated at what trouble the painting had caused.

While the father was still angry, his younger son saw the painting and he too asked about it. Flying into a rage, the father yelled that the younger son must be dumber than his older brother. The older brother was told it's a painting of a tiger and he went out and killed a horse. The painting is obviously of a horse! Set correct by his father's outburst, the younger son went about his journey to the mountains, where he came upon a tiger. Believing such a thing was a horse, he went towards it and tried to ride it. The tiger killed and ate him at once. Learning of his younger son's death, the artist cried every day. He blamed the painting for his troubles. He burned it and told everyone not to be as careless as he.

All right. So how to sort it out? My lucid dream included the horse-tiger symbolism of an ancient Chinese chengyu, something I previously knew absolutely nothing about. The dream also had myself as a young boy talking to me and liking this odd combination even though the animal was obviously misshapen. When the animal's tiger head smiled in response to the boy's joyful approval, despite how I called the combo odd, the boy had then turned and smiled at me in a similar way as what the horse-tiger had done.

It seems pleasant enough except for the fact that horse-tiger means something that is mediocre or executed in a careless or sloppy way. Why should the boy or I ever be content and pleasantly accepting of that? Especially if, as I suspect, given the fact this comes in the form of a lucid dream, the misshapen horse-tiger is standing there to represent something, certainly something personal to me.

In shamanic tradition, combining humans and animals or animals with other animals is a common recipe for spirit animal messages and power symbols. It can suggest a combination of attributes that either benefit each other in a symbiotic way or conversely create tension as each try to express themselves but cannot quite do it for each expression cancels the other out.

It's easy to see this horse-tiger animal referring to me or my life. For one thing, the Chinese animal that matches the year of my birth is a horse. Added to this, my astrological sun sign is Sagittarius so it's not a leap to look at Greek mythology associating Sagittarius with the centaur Chiron, who mentored Achilles in archery. As such, Sagittarius is half human, the head portion, and half horse, the body portion. To have a lucid dream replace the human half of the centaur with a tiger's head points to a transformation of the human, possibly an augmenting the human with tiger's attributes.

What are these attributes? Plenty of sources claim to know. A little research yields what one would expect to find about tiger. Raw feelings and emotions are emphasized along with primal instincts, spontaneity, and fast action when needed. Of course there's strength, willpower, and overcoming obstacles. Other items are not so obvious, such as trusting oneself, living up to one's greatest potential, patience, and a strong intuition. Within China, tiger is looked upon as the king of all beasts and represents powerful energy. There are many places to go with all of this but I have little except my feelings as a guide to know which interpretation is correct.

If the horse-tiger combo represents me or my life, invoked by the Sagittarius half-human half-horse centaur, then perhaps it means even though the horse was misshapen and turned out to be quite unusual, what some might call just so-so or mediocre, an infusion of the tiger attributes into the human half of the centaur presented different and powerful possibilities. It's true if taken literally, one can claim that even if this tiger wanted to run into the hunt, those legs under the horse wouldn't be up to the task. This could be saying that all the positives associated with the transformation into tiger connect to a bedraggled horse, meaning the transformation can't help but produce what many would call a carelessly done, so-so result.

And yet the core sense of the dream, the feeling of it, leaves me wondering about a critical component. That being me as a young boy. That young boy was in the dream and talking to me. That's never happened before in any of my dreams. That interchange with my younger self was the highlight point and is what lingers and resonates. That feeling of connection to myself goes beyond the question of why is my younger self finding such satisfaction in such a hodgepodge result. The crucial element falls into place when he says he likes it anyway and the tiger smiles. This is doubly reinforced when the tiger's motion and smile is immediately repeated in sequence by my younger self and his turning to me and smiling.

It's obvious my younger self is trying to tell me something – is literally telling me that it's all right, be at peace with how everything turned out. The dream may ultimately be showing me it's all good, don't sweat how I got here, no matter how many might-of could-of should-of's make the whole thing appear misshapen. Despite all the ways it looks odd, it's really working out for the best. In this sentiment the tiger and myself as a young boy wind up simpatico.

The lesson I'm left with is a healing of my inner self, the inner child. I can see he is not only at peace with what he sees, he appreciates it.

The message I'm left with is one the dream coaxes me to say to myself always when I think of my life – *"I like it anyway!"*

A Jungle Beyond Limits

It seems so long ago. Much longer than two and a half years. A time when my wife and I planned a vacation from our corporate jobs. It was to be a getaway unlike anything we had ever done. We were in the mood for an adventure, something to shake things up. In hindsight, we certainly succeeded in ways we couldn't have foreseen. At the time she felt a strong need to participate in Ayahuasca ceremonies while we visited South America. I had no such calling but I did have a lifelong fascination with the big questions, the kind of questions I heard these plant medicine spirits sometimes answer, even if the answers couldn't be put into words. With that as the principle lure, I considered tagging along to share the experience.

When she told me about the retreat center in the jungle she was planning on going to, I told her all well and good for her but, given those terms, I'd be opting out of that part of the trip after all. The jungle was not for me. That was certain. Too many unknowns. Too many obvious discomforts. Too many wild possibilities. If nothing else, too much exposure to things that might trigger my serious ant and bee venom allergies.

There had to be an easier way to cleanse one's soul and get right with oneself than being subjected to that extreme order of difficulty. As it turned out serendipitously, she found a more "civilized" setting for the ceremonies and I was persuaded to participate anyway. So much happened as a result of that decision as the saga in the journals in this book attest.

Fast forward to now. Two and a half years later. Little did I suspect, what should come back around to confront me again was the prospect of facing the jungle. The jungle had never given up on me, even if I had written it off with what I thought was solid reasoning and fervent certainty. And why not. Going there was so unnecessary. So many other options for participating in sacred plant medicine ceremonies existed without having to enter the jungle. Why would anyone ever go there? I couldn't see the point.

But the jungle stood firm in its silent challenge to come and encounter it. It knew there was something I was missing, some order of magnitude of understanding that only expressed itself by going to the home of the plant medicines and experiencing them there.

I realize it may sound strange to speak of the jungle as a conscious thing, something one communicates with and receives messages from. That kind of anthropomorphism for many smacks of the presumed backward voodoo mythology that often gets traditional or indigenous methods rejected out of hand. But actually the act of attributing human traits, emotions, or intentions to non-human entities is more universal than most think. In science it's seen as an innate tendency of human psychology anywhere at any time, even in our modern or, to be more accurate, postmodern times.

One only has to search our cultural past for examples. From a personified wind in Aesop's Fables to classic 15th-century European paintings depicting music taking the form of a woman, from the rabbit who's late for a very important date in Alice's Adventures in Wonderland to popular movie and television characters and sport's mascots, we humans have no issue with projecting personality and human-like characteristics on all sorts of things to reinforce the archetypes that motivate us. I'm reminded of the brooms and buckets coming to life in the classic cartoon movie Fantasia.

Given this simmering but repressed allure of the jungle, it became convenient enough that a shaman I know is part of a project to establish sections of the rainforest as a preserve. The goal of the project foresees how once a large parcel is bought and appended to the enlarging preserve, hopefully the natural treasures therein can be spared from the avarice of gold miners, ranchers, oil men, loggers, developers, and carbon-exchanger soybean conglomerates, to name a few. In association with this shaman, I found myself invited to come to the jungle for two days of Ayahuasca ceremonies. I had to take a step back. How had that happened to me, someone who had long ago sworn off the jungle?

When first offered the invitation, I didn't know if such a thing was tempting or not. My knee-jerk reaction echoed my conviction that such a thing was out of the question. I knew where I stood on the prospect of trips into the jungle. Hadn't I rejected that very same thing two and half years ago for good reasons? Weren't those reasons still valid. Why, yes, they were. So no problem, right?

And yet, I hesitated. I couldn't quite say no right away. A little voice reminded me that problems with ant and bee venom allergies had abated after several Kambo treatments. No sign of that remained. It was a minor point in the current scope of all that could happen out in the wild, but it put a crack in my certainties. Doubting my own doubts came into focus. Could I actually do this?

Something about this invitation had undercurrents of feeling that presented itself as more than an offer. Could it actually be, as they say, a "calling?" Even so, why ever would I need such a calling? What possibly could the jungle offer that was missing in myself? More obscurely, what possibly could there be in me that needed fixing that the jungle offered a remedy for? Perhaps it was more than a calling. I sensed maybe it was a challenge.

Did I feel somehow incomplete because I had never gone to the jungle? No. In two and a half years, I had never once regretted my decision to bypass that option. Yet here it was again, staring me in the face like some crazed puma on the hunt, circling around, determined to make the kill. The tug to take that next step grew in strength. It was as if the jungle would not accept my rejection from years ago. It was relentless. It knew how to get under my skin. It whispered to me about the thing I had left undone. It tugged at my curiosity. Somehow it knew I would ultimately say yes. Despite my better judgment. Despite my concerns. Despite not even being certain why I was heeding the call. When the time came, I packed up my stuff and headed out.

It was a unique time to head out. The shaman had timed these ceremonies to maximize their power. The two days in the jungle would coincide with a most extraordinary celestial event. One that hadn't happened in over 150 years. It was the time of a blue moon, the second full moon in the same month. It would also be a supermoon, actually the second supermoon of the month, the first having been a "wolf moon." Supermoons occur when a full moon closely coincides with the moon's perigee, or the point in its orbit closest to Earth. This makes the moon appear nearly 14 percent larger and 30 percent brighter than usual.

If that wasn't enough, this moon was also to be a blood moon. A blood moon happens when there's a lunar eclipse and the darkened surface of the moon appears deep red. All totaled in effects, this moon would be a *super blue blood moon.* Needless to say, the energies to be infused into Ayahuasca ceremonies by such a moon promised to be significant. Especially in the jungle. Again and again I heard the whisper from the plant spirit, coaxing me forward – *"Come visit me where I live and grow..."*

The trip to get there was not incidental. A four hour drive east over mountains topping out over 11,000 feet started the trek. As we wound through foggy switchbacks, I considered the things stowed in my backpack. Would they be adequate? Were they the right things to bring? As far as I knew, the all-night ceremonies would be out in the open, under the moon. Without cover, the night air temperature might drop unbearably cold. If I could help it, I wanted to avoid being deep in the medicine, out in the open, freezing cold and unable to do anything about it.

The first indication that things weren't going to go as I had envisioned was when we started down the eastern side of the mountains. The air suddenly turned humid and warm. Of course, a whole other weather pattern existed where I was going. What was I thinking? This was going to be the jungle. Weren't jungles humid and warm? How had I missed that? Did I really need all the warm stuff I packed away? The shaman had merely said to be sure to bring a poncho and tall rain boots. It was a rainforest after all. Expect rain. Expect mud. Possibly deep mud. I pushed the oversight aside. It was all right. Much better to have more warm stuff than was needed than get caught with not enough. So I told myself.

The trek continued. Once I arrived at a small village, I met up with the shaman and others who were coming along. They had traveled for seven hours by bus from the place where the shaman lived. Then we had to hire a driver to take us another hour to an even smaller, more remote village, one that didn't appear on the maps. Bypassing that village, the driver drove off-road onto a dirt path up into the mountains. Along the narrow path we bumped along for another half hour. Finally, we arrived. Not at the place we needed to be but at an opening in the jungle where our hike could now begin.

Now, I have hiked in many places. Even in South America I have hiked in remote natural parks, sometimes at elevations topping 14,000 feet. The shaman said our hike into the jungle preserve to the ceremonial space would take about an hour. No reason to think such a thing wasn't doable. Obviously, he and others had done it before. But I had no idea what I was about to encounter. What we headed into was not a path, not a trail, not anything but jungle. There was no way of knowing where you were stepping. The shaman led the way with a machete. With vegetation everywhere, there were rocks, uneven ground, even small streams cutting through tall grasses and ferns underfoot. And this area wasn't flat, anywhere. The whole hike would be an arduous climb up through jungle and back down through slippery mudflows and who knows what else. And this I needed to do with a backpack stuffed with things I merely might need? The pack weighed about 35 pounds. So much for thinking it was a good idea having more warm stuff than was needed.

I quickly found myself fighting to maintain balance, stepping knee deep in mud, grabbing onto vines and small tree trunks to stay upright. The shaman had warned about grabbing at just anything. Some vines had sharp stickers on them. And some "vines" could be hanging snakes as far as I knew. The darkening canopy of tall trees thickly interwoven above didn't let in much light. I quickly lost my breath and fought to maintain any pace at all. I felt like sitting down, collapsing with a task that was simply too much for me. But the troop pushed on. I had to go with them. There was nothing else to do. No other option. The jungle had slapped me with the first lesson – *some things are an uncompromising imperative no matter how you feel about them.*

A member of the troop tried to encourage me and keep my spirits up. He'd say, "We're almost there..." as we descended into another morass of leaves and vines and trees and rocks and mud. Always at the bottom of these slippery descents would be a rocky, rushing stream to cross. Once on the other side, we'd face another laborious climb back up. One dense valley after another needed to be traversed. As I climbed I slowed down even more. I'd hear a voice behind me once again, "We're almost there..." It got to be a cry of false hope. We kept going and going and yet it felt like we were never getting anywhere.

Finally, I stopped and gulped in air to avoid fainting. I wavered woozy and tried to steady my failing balance. The encouraging member of the troop saw my condition and suggested he could carry my pack for me. I told him I didn't want him to have to do that and tried to keep going. In time though, it was inevitable. I could not make it with these conditions. He took my pack and another member of the troop gave me a walking stick plucked from the jungle to help keep my balance. I noticed a couple others were also having difficulty continuing. A friend of mine was on the verge of fainting. But the shaman reminded us that night was not far away. We had to keep going. We shouldn't get caught attempting this hike in the dark. The uncompromising imperative reared its head again and growled. We had no choice. No other option. This was it. Keep going or get stuck in a worse condition.

The last ascent was grueling. We made it to an elevated camp with the last bit of afterglow from sunset fading in the west. We had been robbed of guiding light when dark clouds in the west had dimmed sunset prematurely. Luckily we made it but just barely. Upon arrival, I thanked the other member of our troop for carrying my pack then I collapsed with all confidence about what I was doing in shatters. I felt totally drained and powerless, exhausted and all shook up. I had never expected the hike in to kick my ass so thoroughly. It was not exactly the condition to be in just before drinking Ayahuasca.

And yet the shaman announced the ceremony would begin soon. He worked to set up his mesa and position tree stumps and boards for us to sit on. This was happening regardless if I felt I needed time to recover or not. Once again, the forward flow of events became an uncompromising imperative. This is what I had come for. There was no way I was not participating. Even if I couldn't fathom how. That contrast was stark and shook me again just as the hike to get there had rocked me off balance.

All of us needed to set up a space to go to during the night of journeying with the medicine. I was practically zombiefied in my exhaustion. I began to unpack sleeping bag and blanket and the shaman quickly told me the place I had picked was not good. There was a crude house at this location, built on site with materials gathered from the jungle. We learned later that the bugs did not infest the wood of this house or eat it because they saw it as part of the forest and left it alone. The house was designed in two sections, both up on stilts with flights of wooden stairs leading up from ground level. The shaman suggested I set up my place somewhere on the structure above, off the damp ground and more away from creatures that might come in the night. The kitchen area was built above what he was turning into our ceremonial circle space. So I set about finding my area by heading up one of the stairs.

Now these were the most unusual stairs. Someone had designed these tapering, thick blocks of wood to slant down at an angle toward you as you climbed. This might be somewhat of an aid in climbing up but I immediately saw how treacherous such a thing was going to be when trying to come back down. Have you ever gone down a flight of stairs with each step sloped down, away from you, at a 20-degree angle? Worse yet, I could only imagine how challenging it would be to negotiate such steps in the dark while on the medicine. And yet, the uncompromising imperative presented itself once again – this was happening, there was no other space. I had to make it work.

A friend of mine set up his hammock in the room designated as the kitchen. In fact, it was far from a kitchen; rather, it was no more than an undifferentiated room defined by uninsulated wood walls. It was totally bare except for a couple rough-hewn shelves and a few plastic and metal pots scattered about the floor. I found my space out on the open balcony behind the door to the kitchen. It was up off the ground as the shaman suggested but still gave me a full view of the jungle and rising supermoon. I didn't want to be cooped up in the windowless kitchen. Besides, we were soon told that the kitchen side of the house was a prime place for rats and mice to search for food. It was best to stay off the floor in there.

Down below me I could see the faint glow of the candle the shaman had lit on his mesa. Its light penetrated not far into the tall grasses nearby. I took a moment to sit on my sleeping bag and stare out into the jungle. I had never encountered any stretch of woods or forests before that was this alive, this vibrant, this noisy. The whole place chirped and buzzed and throbbed constantly with hidden activity and jostling life. The earlier darker clouds had continued to move west and now the eastern sky was beginning to glow bright with the enlarged moon. It was some comfort that I was finally here, in my place, where I would stay for the next two days. The shaman had said he would be fasting for the event and I had determined to do the same. The last food I had eaten was an early breakfast before leaving home that morning. My plan was to take no other food until I returned home after the event two days later. I drank some water from my pack and then heeded the shaman's call for everyone to gather for the ceremonial circle.

Including the shaman, there were ten of us in the circle underneath the house. The one candle was barely enough to light what needed to be done and yet the shaman moved around as if it was more than adequate. He talked to us awhile about the night, about the power of the space around us, about our intentions, and about the remarkable energies added to us by the extraordinary lunar cycle. Then he motioned to his mesa to inform us that four different medicines were being offered and we were to choose which one we wanted. I looked at the four, different sized bottles standing next to the candle. One contained an Ayahuasca called "the parrot." Another was an Ayahuasca called "the jaguar."

The third was a mixture of three Ayahuascas in one bottle. Two of the Ayahuascas were contributed by the Shipibo and Shuar tribes of Peru and the last ingredient was the shaman's own Ayahuasca brew. These were mixed half-and-half, half shaman's brew and half from the tribes in Peru. The fourth and last medicine we could choose from was in the smallest bottle and contained only enough medicine for two doses. One of those doses was already spoken for, so there was only one dose left. This medicine was not named but the shaman and another participant warned us that the fourth medicine was extremely strong and not recommended except for those most experienced in journeying.

The shaman sat cross-legged in a hammock close to the mesa and made a most unusual announcement. He said simply, "There is no shaman tonight. You will be your own shaman. I will be here if you need anything, if you need help, but this night is all about you."

We had time to decide which medicine to take. The shaman began the ceremony with liquid tobacco. He came around to all of us, one by one, and poured the brown liquid into the well of our palms. After a prayer, we snuffed the tobacco up both nostrils. I had done liquid tobacco many times at other ceremonies, but this time it struck me very energetically. Immediately my whole body vibrated and buzzed. I felt light and floating. It was an unexpected, strong reaction and took me a couple minutes to recover.

By then, it was time to choose my medicine. I chose the three Ayahuascas in one bottle mixture from the Peru tribes and the shaman's own brew. The shaman poured the thick brown liquid into a slender metal vessel and offered it to me. I drank it down and waited while everyone else decided and received theirs. Afterwards, we sat silently for a while, meditating on the candle flame and the process to come. Night was definitely entrenched around us. The strong moonlight would come and go as fast-moving clouds swept over the ridge where we had camped. Then one-by-one, each in his or her own time, we stood and made our way silently to our journeying spaces. None of us were newbies at this. But none of us had any doubts that this experience would be an order of magnitude beyond.

I climbed back upstairs and got settled in with hoodie and sleeping bag. For a while I watched the spotlight of the moon flood the jungle with bluish light then disappear with the passing of a cloud. All around flew lightning bugs, their luminous trails marking the changing angle of flight. The pulse of insect and animal noises didn't let up. If anything, it intensified under the influence of the unusual moon. In time, I felt I needed to ease back, recline, and close my eyes. When I did, I heard the approach and scattered movements of tiny mosquitoes.

For what seemed hours I felt a presence, a probing, a curiosity, and a determination. Something was checking me out, scrutinizing my approach and intent. Its scouts had been the mosquitoes, who never left me, but soon the presence made itself more directly known. It revealed itself with an attitude of strength, power, determination, interest, variety, and passion. It was raw instinct and primal energy. It became obvious after a while that this presence was the jungle itself. I sensed myself holding back, standoffish, anxious of the unknown.

The moon was now in a far different section of sky. During one stretch of time a quick but powerful downpour of rain filled the air and blanketed the jungle. Then it stopped as quick as it began. It had been hours since the ceremony began and I had heard many things going on around me. Others in the troop had gone through violent bouts of purging. Some had gone to where the shaman sat in his hammock to ask for help and had icaros and cleansings performed. Some had sung prayerful songs. Others had requested more liquid tobacco. Still others had raced into the darkness to find the jungle toilet. Through all of it, I had reclined and endured the probing, the curiosity, the interest of the all-encompassing presence. Beyond that, not much had happened.

But now the medicine was swift and came on strong. The presence of the jungle began to speak to me. It asked me why I was not letting it in. It seemed perplexed at my anxious holding back. My self-imposed limits were artificial to it. It wanted in but I knew not what that meant. And so my doubts floated to the surface. It saw them and questioned my actions. It asked me why I came to visit it if I was not going to be friendly, to engage with it. It said finally, frankly, that it was not respectful to come to it and not engage, not let it in. It had its own ways. It was wild, unrelenting, chaotic but governed by the rules of craft and power and unapologetic passion. It didn't understand my attitude. It didn't approach in anger or with malice. It was simply raw power and no-holds-barred instinct and unaccustomed to what it was seeing in me.

In that moment, when it revealed its thought, its feeling about the way I was acting as a guest in its house, I found myself agreeing with it. It had a point. I was not being friendly or respectful to come visit and then hold back so suspiciously. In that instant I let myself go. I opened up to it. In fact, the act of doing so became another uncompromising imperative, one I needed to find the strength of will and character to see through to completion.

With that release came a rush of warmth from within. It was more than that; I was effusing heat and sweat. I ripped off my hoodie, exposing more of myself to the jungle air. Immediately, I had to purge several times through the slats of the balcony railing. The shaman had said that purging from the second story like that, over the railing, was all right to do.

As soon as the purges were out, it happened. I was hit by a most intense golden flash. It blasted me back from the railing. In the next instant I saw and felt the surge of a cream-colored anaconda with red spots leap through the golden flash and shoot at bullet-train speed inside my chest. It took all breath away. It cleared all thoughts. It was explosive and colored with soul-centered fireworks of varied emotion and continued to expand through profound depths of revelation.

I crumpled back flat on my sleeping bag and swirled away. To where continues to stump me even now. It was a final beyond that can only be described as the ultimate state of Being. I didn't exist there and yet I had some kind of consciousness to perceive it. I couldn't see anything but a most magnificent living crystalline fog. Since nothing else existed there except everything contained in Being, it must have been the consciousness of Being itself. It was self-contained but All, all at once. It simply was and had no explanation. It existed in a way that knew no duality of non-existence. It was not the other side of non-being. There was no such thing. It was power and energy, creative force and infinite intent. It was beyond concepts, beyond process, beyond needs and measures. The most stark feeling was realizing I didn't exist. There was no person, no separations, no reason to be anything but Being. Everything that used to be the world I came from was known as an unreality. There was nothing else. End of story in a state of expression that never ended.

Just then, as if from another universe, I heard a sound. It was my name. Someone had called my name. It was so far away, so alien. It took quite a while to even recognize the sound as being language and then knowing that language was expressing a word, then realizing the word was somehow connected to me, and in making this sound, someone or something was trying to get my attention.

In the presence of Being, I was stunned, flooded with overpowering feeling and completeness. I had no capacity to answer or find out where my name was coming from. I drifted back into the crystalline fog. A most ecstatic release flowed through me. Everywhere was a joyful glide into peace and contentment and effortless expressions of what felt like divine purpose. I had left the limp rag of flesh in one unreality and united with a boundless consciousness of Being somewhere else that was more than real.

Then my name was heard again. This time it was followed by more words. This time I recognized the voice as that of the shaman. His voice was far off. I realized now he was downstairs at his mesa. I heard him call me and say it was time to come down and join the circle. Everyone was going to close out the ceremony. I grappled to feel myself in my body enough to shift in place to aim my eyes at where the sky had been. It was still dark but, given the position of the moon, it must have been between four and five in the morning. I couldn't believe it was so late. Where had the night gone? Why was I so deeply blasted away in the medicine if the ceremony was now closing? I reeled in confusion as I slipped back deeper into the place of Being. It continued to overpower me and leave me limp. There was no way I could respond, much less attempt to get up and join the group. I could understand that language, those words now but there was no way I could communicate like that. And if anyone thought I was in any condition to attempt to go down those slanted stairs, they were crazy. I couldn't do it. It was impossible. Simply impossible.

As soon as I thought that, the shaman's voice sounded again. But this time he was close. In fact, he had come up the stairs and was kneeling close at my side. "Come on, Mike. We're closing the ceremony. We all need to be there."

I tried to mumble something but knew it was babble. The shaman said more but I haven't the foggiest idea what it was or how long he tried to say it. Finally, I heard him very close. "Come on. Give me your hand."

This was incredible. He wasn't going to take no for an answer. Why he was so determined to get me up and downstairs at the closing circle, given my condition, was beyond me. But then, so much was beyond me at that point. Namely, myself. Only a fragment of any notion that I existed at all was present anymore. And even that fragment of existence was known as being unreal. But I had to use this unreality to interface with the shaman who wouldn't go away. Again he implored me, "Give me your hand!"

I couldn't feel my body so the best I could do was try to set the intention, make a willful suggestion of mind to lift my hand. I didn't know where to lift it anyway since I couldn't see anything but the crystalline fog. I knew the attempt to raise the hand had succeeded only because I felt the shaman's hand grab it and grip it firmly. The touch of his hand reverberated. I was not the only unreality. There was something real, as fake as it was, in contacting another person, another bit of unreality. It was very strange. But I was thankful that was over. I had done what he asked. So much for that. The ecstatic beyond pulled me back farther into it.

But then, incredibly, impossibly, more words came from the shaman. They were the most ridiculous things I had ever experienced. He simply said, "Now, get up!"

I don't know how I answered him. I know I expelled a huge sigh of disbelief. Perhaps I tried to explain. Maybe I told him I wasn't there. Really not there. None of it was real. Not even me. I was in the place of Being. Whatever I said, he didn't want to discuss it. He answered back, "Keep holding my hand." Then he added, "Raise up."

Most of me was gone. But a part of me still trusted him. I knew him as the one best equipped to navigate these spaces. That trusting part of me had to consider what he was saying and how he was saying it. That part of me had to notice the seriousness and forcefulness in his voice. I may not know the reason why he kept pursuing me this way but one thing was sure – I knew he wouldn't be doing this if he didn't think there was a damned good reason for it. If all was well and I could be left alone to drift away, I had no doubt he would do that. So my curiosity with him not taking no for an answer kept me from merging completely with the crystalline fog.

"Come on," he came at me again. "One leg up."

The next stretch of time is fuzzy as fog. I did try to pull myself up onto all fours. I did try to lift one leg to get a solid foot under me. Several attempts at this resulted in me collapsing like a bag of jelly without a bone for support. Eventually, the shaman got me to a standing position. I only knew this because he was now standing and I was somewhat eye-to-eye with him. It wasn't because I felt any of my body in a standing position under me – I didn't. As if to prove it, once or twice my standing position crumpled back to the sleeping bag.

It didn't matter. The shaman was immediately after me again to get up. Once again I heard from nowhere, "Give me your hand." Once again, "Now raise up!" There came a point when I finally stood, holding onto the balcony railing with one hand, and somewhat stabilized in place. Holding in place was good. Holding in place I could somehow manage. My grip on the banister railing was my lifeline. But there were no congratulations or sense of accomplishment for this coming from the shaman. He merely waited until my eyes met his in the strong moonlight and he let loose with a final directive, "Now, come!" With that, he turned and hurried down the stairs and back to the closing circle in the dark under the house below.

This was my existential moment, the apex of criticality, my spiritual apotheosis. I had become my own uncompromising imperative. What now? My body stood at the top of the flight of stairs at the point of greatest vulnerability, the maximum test of my force of will. Would I succumb to the thought that I couldn't do it? The question was odd. Did I even exist to entertain such introspections? Even if I did exist, didn't I have to be in my body to attempt such a thing? The shaman had gotten me to my feet. But he strategically left the rest for me to do – or not do. It was no longer a test of will or competency. This was a test to see if I existed at all. And if I did, would I be constrained by any limits on what I thought I could do? How I answered that told the story where my existence or non-existence meant anything at all. He had gotten me to the point of decision. Now I needed to face it alone.

I wavered, a gnawing indecision stealing away time. But in a timeless space, what did that matter? Something stirred within me. It was the only thing that could shift me out of complete immobilization. It was an echo of a feeling, but what a feeling. It was the feeling of letting the jungle in. It was the sense of personification of the jungle as a beast, an animal, a thing, a consciousness all wild and raw and relentless and uncompromising. Yes, uncompromising. It was the passion of that animal that forever lived in the urgency of survival. It was the immediacy of being eaten alive or eating another alive. It was a way of being that didn't understand hesitation in the face of opportunity. It was the persistent probing of a life force that couldn't conceive of defining oneself by thoughts of limitation.

The jungle moved me forward. The animal moved me down the stairs. It took, I am told, over five minutes for me to descend nine steps. Nine slanted steps in the dark. It didn't matter much even if there had been light for I couldn't see much. Once I set feet on dirt at the bottom of the stairs, I turned to my right. I knew the closing circle would be in that direction. Only when I looked there, I was blind. The shock of it hit me. The only thing I could see was the crystalline fog. The fog was so clear, so inviting, so much so I began to engage with it. I don't know how long I just stood there but long enough for another participant to come to my aid.

I heard a woman's voice on the right side of me. Her whisper was soft through the fog. Then I felt someone take a hold of my right arm and lift it. She pulled me gently in the direction she wanted me to move. "It's all right," she whispered. "Come this way." I followed her lead and shuffled to the right. After a while she said, "OK, that's good. Now down." She applied light pressure to my arm, prompting me to sit down. Lost in the shimmering fog, I went down to the ground. She hurriedly pulled me back up, "No, no, no!" she corrected. "Down...and back." In a minute, she had me seated. Now I sat in a vortex of energetic fog. I still couldn't see anything or anyone. I tried to murmur a "thank you" to her but who knows what came out.

Finally, the shaman was able to close out the ceremony. He spoke to us about the powerful things that had transpired during the night. He spoke to the necessity of letting the medicine do what it needed to do. He commented on the beauty of the night, the power and beauty of the jungle, and the strong intercession of spirits who were helping us along our paths. Then he passed the talking stick for all of us, one by one, to share what we wanted to share. This whole closing ceremony was surreal to me. It was as if I had holographically beamed from far beyond into an alien ritual to sample the energies present. Outlines of people and objects faded into view and then back out again as I merged once more with the living fog.

When the woman next to me, who had helped me sit down, shared her story for the night, I found it very moving and interesting and full of heart energy. When she in turn gave me the talking stick, I don't remember what I said. It seemed to be short phrases and long pauses delivered with unblinking eyes. I think I said something like, "...it's very powerful...and it continues..." The following day, the woman told me she really liked what I had said as she smiled and giggled in a way that suggested it was somehow over the top in a good way. I didn't ask her to tell me more about it. I'm not sure I even want to know. Being there was enough. Being there was more than enough.

The sharing circle finally ended with another round of liquid tobacco from the shaman. I remember receiving it in my palm and snuffing it up. Then I remember climbing back up the flight of stairs and collapsing on my sleeping bag. And yet, even with all that had gone on, I could not fall asleep. Awareness was strong. The lesson of surpassing limitations and any thoughts of limitation was hot within me. I watched the last of the moon edge west. I listened to the jungle get ready for dawn. The feeling of the jungle was different now. It was no longer probing me. I was simply in it, among it, carried away by it. It carried me into a sunrise that echoed the glory of the golden flash from the night before. The first ceremony was done. A most important lesson had been offered and received.

Three or four hours later, people began to stir from their sleeping spaces. I went downstairs for a visit to the jungle toilet. When I returned, I discovered the shaman up and about and putting on his mud boots. He was laughing as he announced something had bit him on his foot. He explained how he had put a foot in a boot and got bit. So he shook out the boot and put his foot back in, only to get bit again. He shook out the boot harder and out this time dropped a big spider. "He wasn't poisonous," the shaman explained. Then he smiled, "And he lived."

Several of the participants planned on a long hike up to a waterfall that was quite far away. They said it would take them at least three hours to get there. I knew I was not up for a six or seven hour hike in jungle conditions, especially after the hour-plus hike in the day before had kicked my ass. So I bowed out of going with them, as did my friend. I'd stay and meditate with the jungle back at camp. The shaman really wanted everyone to go but was all right with our individual wishes. But he did approach me. He said, "If you are going to meditate with the jungle today, you want to drink some medicine first?" I said yes. And so, the shaman poured me another dose of the same triple brew I had drunk the night before. At 10am I drank it and a half hour later the hiking group left for their day's journey to the waterfall and back.

Soon after I drank the second dose of medicine, a bumblebee came around me and wouldn't leave. It kept buzzing around and when I moved it followed me. This is somewhat odd since bumblebees usually avoid contact with animals and humans. It's interesting to note that it's often said the bumblebee does the impossible simply by flying. Its large size, small wings, and the physical dynamics of what is required for flight should definitely mean an insect like the bumblebee wouldn't be able to fly. And yet it does. As such, the bumblebee is often looked upon as a symbol that anything is possible. The bumblebee simply does not give in to what should be its limitations. It has found a way to resolve its uncompromising imperative. In that, it was a visible reminder of what I had gone through the night before. A message by example from the jungle to start the day.

The day progressed in peaceful communion with the jungle. My meditation was enhanced by the sights and sounds of all somehow in motion around me. There seemed to be infinite variety, endless fascination, an undercurrent of power and presence to my meditation. Time passed not as time but as a cavalcade of raw expressions of the animal that was the jungle. It knew I was there. I knew it knew but now I also knew it knew me. The feeling of it like that was different than how I had seen it the day before. Then it was alien, an unknown. Now it was a recognized life force I interacted with and was getting to know.

The waterfall hike group didn't get back to camp until late, after 6pm. They had just made it back before sunset robbed their path of light. They were joyful but rightfully exhausted. Didn't matter. It was time once again for the shaman to prepare the circle for another ceremony. I was just coming out of my day's ceremony meditation. Now it was time to drink again. Now it was time to face the night again. Once again we had a choice of medicines – the parrot, the jaguar, or the Peruvian blend of three. I chose to stick with the Peruvian blend. It had been beautiful during the day. Now it was time to see what it would show me through the night. After liquid tobacco, we drank, then retired once again to our individual spaces. I climbed the stairs to my sleeping bag. There were more clouds at the start of night and so the beginning of the journey was in more darkness than before. As the night progressed, the sky cleared and the powerful super blue blood moon hovered overhead, brilliantly so.

The feeling of being in the medicine was powerful, edgy, but comfortable, like lying down with resting wild animals who, for now, accepted you. Once again I couldn't sleep. The medicine made me very alert. I heard the familiar Ayahuasca buzzing and saw the fractal-spiraling creatures that made the sound coming at me. It was a sign that the door to deeper medicine space had opened wide and I was floating through it. I had to purge right away. Once through, I saw incredible miniature scenes, dancers beautifully choreographed, impossibly staged with morphing set tableaus and fabrics becoming colors becoming tunnels becoming other scenes where the dances continued ever on. It was incredible, wondrous, gorgeous in detail and design but ever fractalling away, nothing ever remained the same, as if none of it was real, only the movement forward possibly a constant.

All of this was but the entry hallway into a more profound personal space where the medicine took me into my thoughts and feelings about limitation. Where did the idea of such a thing comes from? How did I ever decide to latch onto a restrictive boundary point to define my limitations? What can be done? What can't be done? The medicine wouldn't entertain questions about what couldn't be done. It was as if such a thing as "can't" was the most certain unreality of all. It took me into how, over and over, in so many little ways, assumptions and thoughts tossed aside become prime markers that define one's limitation space. My mind would be taken through situations simple to complex, and in all of them, my instant reaction to those situations would be questioned. Why did I relate to them in the way I did, expecting a limitation at some point? Why had I placed the limitation – *there*?

This flew deeper into the idea of the impossible. I was simultaneously in jungle space and Being space, where ideas of impossible played out far differently than the way it did in my approach to situations, in my approach to life. As the hours went by, I couldn't escape going into the concept of limitation and seeing it for the unreal thing is was. Every time I tried to refocus on something else, the medicine would bring limitation in front of me and stick it in my face. It did this repeatedly until the feeling of limitation, not the idea of it, returned incessantly as something to be challenged. The night in the jungle was so calm and peaceful and powerful and yet it was the emotional stage for the medicine to upset all of my inner limits and concepts about personal limitation.

By about 2am, with the moon high in the sky, I felt as if I didn't know myself in some ways. I had no conception what exactly I was capable of. If the medicine wanted me to dispense with all belief in limitation, then where did that leave me? There were no barriers, no parameters, no way of defining the edges of what one was or could be. The enormity of this realization left me rootless in a primal instinct of Being, an instinct that melded well with the animal of the jungle that was also with me. This powerful but uncomfortable feeling seemed to be precisely where the medicine wanted me to settle into. I meditated on that awhile and then I noticed someone down on the boards, at my side. It was the shaman.

He asked me how I was doing and read my energies as I answered. He settled in and stayed to talk with me for the next half hour. It was a most personal conversation. It was a beautiful exchange of thoughts and feelings and what was going on with both of us. At one point, he told me that spirit was synonymous with breath. Then he sang me a song in Spanish. It was about a dragonfly and the breath it possessed that carried it aloft. It was most powerful to have this shaman sing a song just to me, directed towards the energies I needed at the moment. I could feel the love and understanding of possibilities that it intended.

Then the shaman leaned in closer. He knew that all of us were expected to hike back out of the jungle at 7am. That was only four hours away. Most of us wouldn't be totally out of the medicine by then. But it was a departure time that had to be kept to make our transport connections. He noted the trouble I had hiking into the jungle. Someone even had to carry my pack halfway in. He assured me that I would need to carry my own pack out. I explained how I had messed up and brought too much stuff. The pack was heavy for the conditions. He was unfazed. He said our mistakes carry no lesson if we avoid the consequences of our actions. If it was my mistake, then carrying it out was the consequence of that. It would also be the lesson. Because of this, he wanted me to leave with another member of the group a full half hour before the rest. With a half hour head start, that would help make up for my slow pace because everyone needed to leave the jungle together.

I needed to begin what he was telling me to do in a little over three hours. It hit me as daunting. The thought of it had loomed ever since the first day when I had trouble hiking in. The very thing I couldn't do two days ago I was now going to have to do with medicine still in me and with no backup person to carry my pack. It was up to me. No one else could get me out of the jungle. No one else could confront my uncompromising imperative. Once again, it hit me in the face. This was exactly the lesson of the medicine again, the lesson of the night before finding a way to come down the stairs to the closing circle. This was also the lesson of what I had just gone through all night – confronting one's concept of personal limitation. This would be the perfect, final demonstration to the jungle and the medicine that I had absorbed their messages – the message of power and raw presence of the jungle combined with the disbelief in limitations shown me by Mother Ayahuasca.

There were a few moments of silence as I let it sink in what needed to happen. It needed to happen regardless if I thought it was impossible. That was quite a thought. More than than, for the jungle and medicine's sake, it needed to happen precisely *because* I thought it was impossible.

In that moment, the shaman leaned forward. He pointed an index finger at my nose for emphasis as he spoke. He locked eyes with me. His voice deepened as he proclaimed, "In the morning, remember – focus on the path...focus on your breath!" He repeated it as a deeply felt mantra, "Focus on the path...focus on your breath...focus on the path...focus on your breath!" He held my gaze for a few moments in silence, then he stood and moved off into the night.

Everyone expected him to form the closing circle for the night's ceremony, as he had insisted the night before. But the sky lightened in the east, the birds and animals made their morning sounds, and I was worried about the time. The shaman said he wanted me to leave a full half hour before anyone else. That meant I should be ready to go by 6:30am. I reached into my pack, turned on my phone, and checked the time. It was 6:10am and no one was up and ready. There had been no closing circle, no gathering to finish out the ceremony. I jumped up and furiously began packing up. I had a lot to do to get my overstuffed pack put back together. Plus I seriously needed the jungle toilet for what the medicine wanted me to purge. By the time I got everything ready, it was obvious I wouldn't be leaving a half hour early. The person that was supposed to guide me out was just waking up. Everyone had to scramble just to leave on time at 7am.

I sat on a bench and considered the added wrinkle now added to my task. There could be no accommodation now for my slower pace. I would need to keep up with everyone, with my full pack. There was no other option. The uncompromising imperative had just become a bit more uncompromising.

I found a walking stick and at 7am we all set out from camp. It took only a dozen yards to get into the thick of the jungle. This was it. I had to do this. There could be no limitation now. This had to be possible, otherwise I wasn't getting out of there. I took one deep breath through my nose after another. As I did, I recited the shaman's mantra in my head.

"Focus on the path...focus on your breath...focus on the path...focus on your breath!"

Not long after we entered the jungle, storm clouds swept over the tall canopy and it began to rain, a jungle rain, swift and strong. Before long, the path we needed to follow became crisscrossed with instant rivulets and streams from the sudden runoff of water. Mud became mud pools. Loose rocks became slip-stones into the weeds. The morning light dimmed and half the light under the canopy went away. I wasn't the only one struggling with the conditions. But it seemed the medicine kept clearing my mind. When it cleared, the jungle animal came up in me with the mantra again.

"Focus on the path...focus on your breath...focus on the path...focus on your breath!"

I don't remember most of the journey out. I remember being helped out of a pocket of mud up to my knee. I remember a helping hand climbing over a fallen log. I even remember lending a helping hand when someone needed to get across a rushing stream. The clearest memory I have is coming up a slope and seeing the shaman and others standing at the top. I thought they were waiting for the slow ones bringing up the rear. But no – they were standing at the end of the trail. We had somehow made it. The impossible was proven not so impossible. I had demonstrated it to myself thanks to the power of the jungle within me, the wisdom of Mother Ayahuasca, and the guidance of a knowledgeable shaman.

The shaman was not done with us, though. As we all staggered out of the jungle onto the dirt road, we had barely begun to catch our breath when one of the participants announced that we were late arriving and our ride had decided not to wait for us. This left us with no way back to the main road. We were going to have to hike out on the road. That would take a least another hour. It was a crushing blow to everyone who had just survived the exit to the road and thought the hard trekking part was over.

Without hesitation, the shaman turned and started hiking up the road. And yes, the road at that point was a steep incline. Most people were standing in a daze or sitting on their packs. The prospect of another hour of hiking on this uneven, rocky dirt road had to sink in before anyone could move. I too was sitting on my pack and yet I felt exultation at having accomplished what I believed was personally impossible for me to do. In the moment, the dirt road looked not so challenging compared to what I had just exited from. Plus I wanted to show the shaman how I was integrating my lessons. And so I stood, shouldered my pack, and followed the shaman up the road.

I hiked for only about five minutes when I noticed that the road curved left ahead. As I neared that curve, I was struck by an odd sight. There stood the shaman sporting a big grin. As he saw my incredulous face, that grin erupted in a laugh. A few more steps revealed something else around the curve. Could it be? Oh, wow, yes! It was our transportation, parked and waiting for us. In his playful but teaching way, the shaman had gotten to the road first and told the driver to hide around the curve. The wiping away of the manufactured problem gave us intense relief and a good laugh. The extra hour hike out to the road was summarily canceled. But in playing this little trick on us, the shaman had gotten us to dig even deeper, realizing what we could do. But this time he didn't make us do it.

We all said our goodbyes back in the little village. We went our separate ways. I hugged the shaman and thanked him. I threw my pack into the trunk of the car and settled in. I was spent during the four hour drive back home. When I got there, the place was totally surreal. My wife was a sweetheart getting me fruit juice and anything else I obviously needed. I couldn't say too much right away. I was staggered. What was real? What was unreal? What was possible, or more correctly, what wasn't possible? What was left behind? What was taken inside? The daze of the journey kept me in medicine space for several days afterwards. I had not slept or eaten anything for those two days. I had lost nine pounds. I drank the medicine three times within 24 hours. I had been forced to face myself and where I thought the boundaries of who I was and what I could do began and ended. I had gone somewhere complete, somewhere magnificent, somewhere that lives and is the One reality. Over and over I had been thrust across the edges of my uncompromising imperatives. Now only one imperative remained. Integrate what I had learned.

The song the shaman sang to me that last night in the jungle reverberates even now. It contained a clear and gentle call to be in touch fully with one's spirit, with one's breath, the substantial yet ineffable essence within us that gives our wings the impulse to soar.

The jungle and Mother Ayahuasca showed me how so much of who we are is beyond the possible. I experienced how we have the power, like the power of the jungle, to let everything beyond the possible inside us, to motivate us, to pull us forth into all we can be.

But in the meantime, right off, there is one thing I can apply, one thing I can take away and use in my daily life no matter what I'm doing or what is going on, no matter what I want to accomplish. It's a simple prescription when faced with anything new, or bewildering, or puzzling, or daunting, or difficult, or yes, even impossible. Now I know a method for facing such things.

It is simply this – "*Focus on the path...focus on your breath...focus on the path...focus on your breath!*"

The Why, The Fear, and the Exploration of the Curious Curios Presumed Inside
The Why – Letting Go

At the end I ask why. For the end connects to the beginning. It joins in a way I couldn't have anticipated before. Fused to it now are changes in me that modify the need and meaning of asking the question at all. Before I could ever face my fears, there was always the "why." Why drink Ayahuasca? What was the real reason? I used to think the beginning of this process would be the proper place for a "why." But now I see how in the end one more fully pursues the answer to such things.

This obvious question of "why" and equally apparent answer are counterintuitive traps. It's tempting to sidestep the issue by saying the full answer only appears on the other side of one's experience. At the end of the journey, we assume we'll be able to reflect on it and reason or feel why. But in such a mystical space, cause and effect probably don't operate as we anticipate.

The real reason may be too difficult to know up front. We tell ourselves we know, but do we? How confident can we be in what we tell ourselves? Especially when the solution to the "why" implies knowing oneself. If we knew ourselves to any full extent, would any of this be necessary? It's too easy avoiding how it becomes a "situational irony." It's like someone asking us to take a photo of the reason our camera doesn't work so they can diagnose the problem.

In an attempt to answer "why," participants in a plant medicine ceremony are encouraged to meditate on their needs. The act of centering on them, we are told, forms intentions to help guide our trajectory into the momentous beyond-o-sphere. We think our needs are obvious or non-existent but does any of that really inform us?

When the journey is finally underway, so the story goes, these intentions provides a gravitating still point, an anchor to our energies, a roadmap for the spirit world to follow in approaching us. More simply, our intentions form our shopping list, the things we want to pick up from the experience. We're also told our intentions supply a centering place of solace when we feel lost. And it's comforting when going into the experience to feel one has a refocus point, a go-to trick to pull out of the hat when little or nothing else can be held onto. Needing to believe in such comforts, few of us question the logic of such a thing possibly existing while the swirl of one's self undergoes dissolution and rebirth.

People are encouraged to establish serious intentions for the Ayahuasca experience, encouraged to the point of stressing it as a procedural necessity. The need for an intention gets reinforced with much cross-legged sharing of personal stories in safe-space confessional group encounters. And yet, among the heartening stories and the anguished needs arising from these stories, there may be whispers of something else. What usually goes unsaid or is alluded to only in the briefest of hushed commentary is the terrifying, pushed-aside, but suspected fact that absolutely no guarantee comes with any approach or related hocus-pocus. Cue the paranormal grin-of-knowing from the shaman who's blowing smoke in your face.

If you are searching for truth about the process, the unwritten fine print disclaimer says there's only so much preparation one can be given or acquire when launching this deep into the personal unknown. Especially, if during the journey of knowing, the all-pervasive unknown leaves one without a solid person to know. Any understanding of why at that point, beyond words as it invariably will be, must remain mystically implicit but fading, like the dissipating shamanic smoke wafting over your head.

Lacking final insight, we still think we must admit to an answer to "why." So we stretch an answer into shape from our this-world preoccupations. Answers may swing from the curiosity of the recreational drug dabbler to the sublime aspirations of the devotee of everything smacking of enlightenment of spirit. Some believe the brew calls to those needing the mystical medicine and so, believing they are in need, they tell themselves they heard that call. Others add a ceremony as a tourist line-item to their bucket-list. And there will always be those who merely want to score trendy one-upmanship points with their altered-state friends back home as the experience is dropped pridefully into conversations as another badge of being a certified dare-devil.

We have to tell ourselves something about the "why" and yet, despite the diversity of yagé psychonauts, once anyone arrives on the other side of awareness, regardless how trivial or profound the intention of their sought-after experiences may seem at the outset, an intensely personal unchartered realm is unveiled. Oftentimes, stunned beyond calculation, that becomes enough reason on its own. Then we see why it was prophetically tempting to claim the full answer to "why" only appears on the other side of one's experience. It seems to follow – the unknown dictates it.

But something else may happen. Steeped in the experience and soon after, our "why" may no longer be as sensible a question as it appeared at the outset, at least not in terms that satisfy. Somehow the bar gets raised on what is fulfilling or perhaps the need to measure such things simply evaporates with the smoke from the smudging of the sage or Palo Santo. Excuses one gave oneself for "why" become faded preoccupations of a different state of mind, a mind not merely rearranged but left behind and replaced with something woken up with dazzling clarity. As many can attest, not all arrive at this clarity – and tellingly, only the medicine knows "why."

Night envelops the energy forms of a willing nature and a shaman, who's oddly way-too-normal to be putting off such a chakra-shaking vibe, commences purification rites with shaken leaves and the hypnotic drone of an icaro. Sitting near you in the maloca's circle is the full range of why's. Some are merely psychoactive adventurists while others are deeply troubled and in desperate need of cathartic answers and transformative relief.

The brew has passed your lips. The central fire draws your gaze into a dancing point beyond the space, It's a timeless place that defies even chaotic subatomics – all such concepts as rendered simplistic to the point of being unnecessary. Night sounds in nature sharpen and stretch an abiding but pinpointed awareness. Panicked recognition rubs deep into all self-referencing attempts to hang on. An emotive overture erupts. And it begins.

Everything you hold as so important is mocked by a queasy chorus self-consciously orchestrated just for you by a looming but unseen presence. A dizzying rush envelops body and soul with a fainting flush from the alternating slaps of heat and cold and gut-wrenching nausea. Flying into the feeling, you're hit with the ego-glare of a terrifying realization.

Suddenly you realize the true measure of all of your well-crafted intentions doted on for days. It's startling clear that Mother Ayahuasca doesn't care the slightest tinker's cuss what you think about indulging in her entheogenic brew. She stares right through your best-crafted intentions, unimpressed and unpersuaded. She only cares what you feel, that buried time capsule festering from the matted hairball thing that grows out of the "who" you've made of yourself.

As night becomes eternity, for better or worse, her unfolding discoveries of you overtake the dwindling self that's dissolves into questions and messages and life review out of thin air. It becomes abundantly unavoidable – she's not only interested in exposing everything swept under the experience-illusion mask called you (you'll never ever hide it from her) – she's going to the heart of what it would take to clean it out, even if it means a wild ride and there's nothing left behind.

For those who try to hold their space with excuses, a rapid descent into Dante's difficult detours await. Resistance will only feed energy into the divine comedy of Purge-atory. Mother's Medicine also doesn't abide experience dabblers or life grifters. She returns to them either a disappointing nothing or swings to the other extreme by summarily kicking their asses with a self-revealing reality horror show so epic in proportions that they helplessly scramble onto the next flight back to mindless distractions and packaged comforts.

On the other hand, many if not most of the truly deeply troubled do find relief or release. The "how" of her help is often by surprise, if not shock. Shuddering rearrangements of the notions of self appear. The intensity is at the level of having one's soul shot through a cosmic car wash of visuals and reconditioned in an emotional Vitamix. Stripped of the costume of distorted self, one impacts nether regions of wonder more real than our dualistic spacetime, that place some dramatists suspect was long ago inverted in purpose by the dark legions of the Demiurge's energy-sucking Archons.

I look back on my intention from my first ceremony with a far different perspective. It's obvious the Ayahuasca experience is unique for each person, even if look-alike patterns emerge. If iconic symbols or elements are shared among differing people, it is likely because they came to the ceremony with common issues, related emotions, a similar need for a type of healing that evoked the medicine in kind. The entheogenic roller coaster may swing this way or that and rise and dip with archetypal patterns all can agree upon, but one should never confuse the well-worn tracks of sensory archetypes with the singular experience they evoke. Many people may similarly describe how they reached for the sky as the clackity car reached the apex of the climb, but the near-death intensity of their descent and the screams heard on the rush inward through the fall are singular and remarkably exceptional.

The journey Mother Ayahuasca provides doesn't seem as much inward or outward as somewhere else. That somewhere else is more real than here, more intense than can be imagined, and more apt to leave one grappling with intermediary issues of message integration upon one's return. For many, like me, such a journey required confronting and clearing away my fearful debris and programmed identity before anything new could manifest in its place.

But as the shaman's paranormal grin suggests, there is no guarantee. The rabbit doesn't come out of everyone's hat. Sometimes, despite the fear, one has to go down the rabbit hole. Perhaps only then will having the hat and the magic make sense. Only then might we let go of "the why" in exultant abandon and become one with the exploration of what it means to exist, how it feels to really BE.

Memo By Deb

When Michael first related his Ayahuasca ceremony experience to me, it was apparent that this was his worst nightmare come true, a thousand times over. His emotions were raw and elevated to precipitous levels. His sense of what was real and not real had been totally discombobulated and slashed to smithereens. His ability to reason through to a sensible resolution was practically non-existent, although he was valiantly employing some tried and true ways to calm and soothe.

I'm Deb, Michael's wife. I witnessed his first Ayahuasca experience firsthand and supported him during the aftermath over the next two years. It is an understatement to say that Michael is the love of my life, and my cherished life partner in whom I constantly delight. So it is another understatement to say it was a huge challenge for me to see him experience the horrors and traumas of his first ceremony and the following years, especially when I was also going through my own integration and changes.

Typically when someone seeks out sacred plant medicines, they are seeking healing. And healing comes in many ways and doesn't always look like healing up front. When you clean out wounds, it's not a pretty sight; when you detox, you can feel sicker before you feel better. And when your not-so-healthy worldview and self-view have been upended as part of a rigorous healing process, simply applying these new ideas to your life back in the "real" world is not so simple and can take some time.

When someone does Ayahuasca and/or San Pedro ceremonies, it is an essential part of their healing process to integrate the often powerful and disrupting experiences and messages they received. Hopefully they have family and friends back in the real world that will witness their ongoing process and be a constructive part of their needed integration.

Michael did not have an easy process, and it was excruciating for me to see him go through his unending emotional upheavals and then to figure out how best to support him. In these last two years, I've learned a lot.

What follows comes from my perspective about what I experienced, and how I learned to effectively listen, support and heal with the man I love. I'm not a trained counselor or shaman and have no formal qualifications so I'm not suggesting or recommending what you might do. My hope, by sharing my story with you, is that you will find some helpful ideas on how to work best with your loved one's healing process.

Initially I was the one who was "called" to the South American plant medicines. For years, seriously and for fun, we'd been fascinated by and enjoyed researching unique conspiracy theories and metaphysical concepts through books, YouTube videos and candid discussions. We'd gotten to be quite the armchair experts on various topics. We were especially opening our eyes to how the world really worked and the illusions of the "matrix." We were "waking up." So it should be no surprise that we came across the South American sacred plant medicines.

Both of us had experienced the too-many trials and tribulations of family issues, past relationships, financial situations, job and career about-faces and challenges, and well, you name it. I had focused for many years (actually decades) on healing from the wounds and traumas of my life and while I had made some progress, as I turned to various religions, workshops, retreats, and countless therapies for guidance, none of them lived up to their promises. My issues were like a mile-high stack of rice paper that was being reduced by one or two pieces of rice paper, and sometimes added to. I was getting frustrated.

Sometimes it seemed I would forget I'm an unlimited creative conscious being that is strong, capable and resilient. Regardless whether I remembered or forgot that, one thing I know for sure: that IS who I am (and who we ALL are) and that essence does come through and gets expressed, one way or another.

There comes a time when, whether you realize it consciously or not, that you say, "Enough!" and move unerringly in the direction that will resolve the persistent problems once and for all. In looking back, I see that happened to me. I was at my wit's end with my never-ending emotional processing that wasn't resulting in healing but I kept going, tenaciously seeking healing and peace. Energetically that must have been a huge clarion call to the universe.

Once the Universe sensed my unrelenting commitment, it conspired to send me everything I needed for that resolution. It had actually been doing this all along. It had been sending me tools, opportunities, insights, people, synchronicities and serendipities. Since that hadn't been enough, I got "called" to Ayahuasca.

Over the years, the Universe had placed challenges squarely in front of me that needed to be cleared for me to heal my problems. Sometimes, I welcomed those challenges as opportunities, and sometimes I resisted those challenges as they appeared formidable and unsolvable and not connected to my ultimate healing path but contrary to it. Lately as I was being sucked more and more into compulsive overwork and drowning in a sea of futility, my whole being was crying out to simply "be" me and relax in peace and love. I couldn't see then but I've realized that my hopes, desires, prayer and intentions were being answered all along.

Ayahuasca's "call" was strong. Every time I watched online videos or read books and articles on sacred plant medicines, my response was *undeniable – I was immensely interested and felt my heart "sing." There was no question in my heart or mind – I was going to follow an unerring and powerful urge to work with Ayahuasca.*

Initially it was only going to be me, going to South America and participating in some Ayahuasca ceremonies. Michael had opted out, as it was going to be in the Amazonian jungle and the known and unknown discomforts of that, along with his severe allergy to ant and bee venom played heavily into his decision. One day at work, at lunch (I rarely take lunch), I sat with a gal (she rarely takes lunch too) and 5-10 minutes later, as we had finished our quick eats and were crossing through the kitchen, probably not to see each other again for a few months. I happened to mention I was going to South America to do Ayahuasca. This was the first time I'd ever said the word, "Ayahuasca" to a friend, and at work, no less. Surprised, she told me about a past co-worker who had worked at a center. I contacted her and voila, ended up choosing that retreat center instead.

Serendipity. Synchronicity. Perfect alignment.

Since it wasn't in the jungle, now Michael said he would join me. While I was surprised at his choice, I was happy for his support and hoped he would get something out of it too. I was so looking forward to being on vacation together, exploring a new country, and experiencing the unknown psychedelic healing space together. With innocent anticipation, we stepped forward into our initiations with the sacred plant medicines.

Little did I know this two-week exploration and "journey" would obsessively engulf us in trials, tribulations, major life changes and ultimately healing over the next two years of our lives; and it is still ongoing.

Michael and I sat far apart during that first Ayahuasca ceremony, to give each other the space for our individual journeys. For me, this first ceremony was uber-intense. In my entire life, I'd never smoked, never drank alcohol, never did any drugs, never. I'd focused on preparing with the recommended diet and had my intentions mapped out. I was determined. In spite of all that, I was completely unprepared for what happened with me.

My journey was exceptionally emotional, long and ultimately rewarding but I also went through 5-6 hours of constant purging and processing. The shaman even gave me something to soothe my sore throat, which persisted for a few days. Little did I know at the time but those hours of severe purging were extra torment for Michael, who sat catatonic watching the dark entities swirl around me, as if they were causing or at least feeding on my suffering. Feeling paralyzed and not able to get them *away from me added to his misery.*

Although my experience had been extreme, it was manageable. I knew my next steps were to rest and integrate the powerful experience and messages. I hadn't anticipate what had happened to Michael, and how much he would need my loving support as he struggled with the aftermath.

After the ceremony concluded and people gathered to have some food and drink at another building close to the maloca, I couldn't find Michael. Finally I started to walk back to our room with a friend and came upon Michael coming back the other way. Everything looked strange to me too; apparently we were still "in the medicine." I felt like I was walking in a different world and didn't recognize the alien surroundings. It took all of us to find our way successfully to our rooms.

The next morning, I was shocked to hear of his journey. I was still recovering from my extraordinarily emotional experience and dealing with my own integration back into the real world. So to hear about his horrific experience in detail was shocking and overwhelming to me.

I could hardly believe what Michael was saying. I didn't know what to believe. I was brand-new to the sacred medicine space and was completely out of my element. I didn't know what could possibly be true or not, even after hearing confirmations from another participant and that the shaman was repairing the "rift" and clearing the space. In fact, it was said this rift needed to be fixed before any other ceremony happened there. It was an incredulous story, and one that I had NOT experienced even though I'd been in the same physical space, though apparently not the same dimension.

More importantly, I had no idea how to support Michael. Both our efforts to get support from the shaman or the retreat personnel failed miserably. All I could do was listen to him, and see if there was anything that I could offer him to solve his situation. I quickly found out that I couldn't solve it for him.

I realize now that Mother Ayahuasca had a plan, and that the best thing I could do was love him unconditionally, manage my emotions and worry, and be true to what was right for me. Not an easy undertaking. But having also been "in the medicine," and integrating my own process, the ability to receive guidance from Ayahuasca was still strong and that helped me in my attempts to support him.

Part of me was MAD – I was mad at Michael for not following the directions to eat after the ceremony. And why hadn't he waited for me so we could walk back together. He hadn't even followed these simple directions designed to support our reentry from psychedelic space. It was difficult for me to realize that he simply couldn't function in this world normally, while still experiencing the trauma.

I was also upset that Michael and I were there to experience this sacred space together and that wasn't happening – our journey together with the medicines had been aborted. The biggest part of our vacation was a bust. And nothing I tried or said to him or to the retreat personnel worked – I couldn't make it better.

Part of me was SCARED – I had no idea what was real or not real, and what powerful otherworldly forces could be at play. Were there really demon and evil entities present or was this all a hallucination? I saw other participants leave the retreat immediately after their one experience, and they were not in good mental spaces – they had experienced some serious traumas and who knows what was next for them. I was scared for Michael – regardless whether his experience was "real" or a powerful hallucination, it was real for him and it was affecting him in a huge way. And he wasn't getting help.

Part of me was CONFUSED – I didn't understand this other-dimensional space at all. I couldn't get traction on what to do and not do, to support Michael in his nightmare. Typically I have the knowledge, intelligence, experiences and resources to work out the proper solution, especially when it is fueled by my love and caring focus. In this case, my best efforts to help him seemed to be ineffective. For example, I didn't know if encouraging him to continue with the upcoming ceremonies was the right thing – would doing so result in more trauma which would be horrible, or would it result in healing?

Part of me was DETERMINED to complete what I came to do. I knew I had to focus on my process, even if I continued without Michael in ceremony with me, and it was vital for me to prepare for my next ceremonies. At times, this felt like abandonment – Michael abandoning me, me abandoning Michael, me being selfish for myself – but I realized that it was essential for me to focus on my work during the two week retreat period. So I continued, but had to manage the extra weight of worry and resentment.

Part of me was able to TRUST that Michael would work out whatever he needed to. I knew him well. He is a no-nonsense type of guy and doesn't let anything or anyone walk over him. He has a strong intuitive sense that has served him well before. I trusted implicitly that he could handle himself as he had done with serious situations in the past. I believe that some of this trust came from my own association with Mother Ayahuasca. As little as I knew this mother's process at that time, in looking back, I see that I was being guided as well, in an unerring manner.

In looking back, there were several key insights, most of which I gleaned after the fact.

First, I see how important it was for me to have compassion and understanding when Michael simply couldn't function in the real world right after ceremony – with what he had just experienced, regular worldly procedures truly didn't make sense to him.

Second, I had to drop my image of how his process should be. I couldn't do his work for him, no matter how much I tried to make it better, I couldn't. I was in a position where I had to simply allow his integration process to unfold without imposing my expectations on it. Even though I fought it mightily, I ended up flowing with what was, rather than my idealized version of what I wished it to be. Because I couldn't do anything else.

Third, I had to realize that all the love and knowledge in the world was not going to necessarily result in an immediate and good solution. Sometimes, things take time.

Fourth, even when I was struggling to support him, it was best for me to be sure to focus on and do what is right for me. Even if it meant going my path alone, or abandoning him to his process or feeling abandoned as well.

Fifth, I felt myself trusting, and fighting against trusting because this didn't feel like the trust I knew from before. Now I see how the plant medicines have their process, perhaps even out of time, not easily discerned by those of us in time, and I learned that it was OK to open up to a new level of trusting.

Lastly – Perhaps most important, I sure didn't understand all this at the time, and it was OK. What I intuitively did to support him and my deep love for him seemed to be enough.

And so the retreat continued. I was so grateful that even though he skipped the next ceremony, that he did the one after that – the messages he received were powerful and positive. We sat next to each other, outside in nature. Partway through the ceremony, as part of my process, the plant medicine spirit (I'm not sure if it was Mother Ayahuasca or Grandfather San Pedro as the medicine had been combined) encouraged me to ask Michael a question.

I resisted for about 30 minutes, and the request came again and again. I did not want to disrupt Michael's ceremony but finally I gave in and turned to Michael (who was somewhat "back" and "present"). I asked him, "Would you take care of me?" He looked at me so sweetly, and told me, "Yes, I'll take care of you." He told me later that I looked and acted like an oh-so-sincerely hopeful three-year old. This was a very healing and powerful interchange for me and I'm so grateful for this intimate connection with each other.

I have found that it's OK for support to be a back-and-forth thing. I can support him, and when I need it, he can support me. In fact, it is very healing to receive love and to give love. In spite of all Michael was going through, he was always able to be lovingly and fully supportive of me.

After that ceremony, he didn't participate further. Which was hugely disappointing to me at the time as I wanted to partake with him, and I had hoped that he might get some completion for himself. Without question, I know now that if he had done the last two ceremonies it would not have been helpful to him, given the situation at the time. There were interchanges that happened with other participants (and perhaps would have happened with him) that would have pissed him off thoroughly and further distanced himself from any future healing. Now, I'm so grateful that he did not participate, as I see the full process that needed to unfold, in a unique time frame and pattern.

I continued my ceremony process and he was truly supportive of me and listened intently as I related my experiences. And I continued to be supportive of him. In spite of the good vibes from his second ceremony, the trauma of the first one was still powerfully present with him. I struggled with how best to be there for myself, when I was embroiled in my own healing processes, my disappointments regarding him missing the other ceremonies, and my frustrations in not being to get him the needed help from the staff, and even the futility of it all as he would have rejected that help as being co-opted by the dark entities.

It was vital that I recognized that my emotions were mine and it was important that I didn't vomit those emotions all over him – it would hurt rather than help. I knew enough, at the time, to reign in my disappointment, to resist the urge to control or coerce him to "go along" with the prescribed process, or to make him feel guilty. Mostly because it had never worked in the past, and I knew that it wouldn't work well now.

And in the afterglow of my own ceremonies and some internal guidance from the plant medicines, I seemed to be able to grasp how best to "be" with myself and how best to "be" with him and then actually "be" that way. I believe that those who have not experienced the medicine, but are supporting someone who is integrating after their medicine experience, will also have intuitive access to the wisdom of the sacred plant medicines.

What do I mean by that? Isn't that rather high-woo-foo-foo? Let me explain – Mother Ayahuasca "called" me to work with her BEFORE I had taken part in any ceremony. Both Mother Ayahuasca and Grandfather San Pedro continue to "speak" with me, in the weeks, months and even years after being in that ceremony space and obviously no longer under any medicina effects. In fact, during one ceremony, Mother Ayahuasca told me specifically that she would always be with me when I was out of ceremony, and always had been with me. I was told that I simply had to ask my question, and then listen for the answer.

In some ways, it seems that we are all "One". I have seen in my experience how whether we are "in" the medicine or not, that we all have access to the same intuitive, spiritual insights that are vital for us in living our lives and supporting others. So yes, I do believe that each of us does have that intuitive access. When a person is working in the medicine, and committed to their healing path (which they are, regardless of how obvious that may seem to the onlooker), synchronicities do occur that support that ongoing healing process. So when supporting someone who is integrating, we are guided, sometimes unknowingly, to do, say, or be in a way that helps them in a good way. And sometimes that "good way" is not realized until well after the fact.

But coming back down to earth and dealing with what is happening in the moment...

It was still important for me to manage myself, and own that my feelings and my emotions were MINE. My joys, my disappointments, my frustrations, my fears were all MINE. And his were HIS. When I was spinning in frustration or fear or disappointment, I wasn't able to be there for him and actively listen for what was up for him. Yet it was vital that I owned my feelings, since they were valid for me. And then, I could be there for him (and myself) fully.

Over the next year especially, there were times that I fell short. Plenty of times. There were times that I couldn't listen any more. There were times I was impatient, or was tired of hearing the same story with the same ending, told with fervent drama and passionate pathos, and seemingly no healing resolution. There were times when I wished he could focus on the beautiful messages from his second ceremony but I could see how entrenched the trauma from the first ceremony was. There were times when I doubted that healing would ever occur, and wondered if Michael had opened up his Pandora's Box of traumas that would never be closed.

In looking back, I see that the best thing I could do in supporting Michael and myself was to love him and myself. And that is NOT contradictory even though at times it seems what he needed and what I was able to provide for him and not over-extend myself in the process were at odds with each other. For me, I learned more about coming from unconditional love, not a love that says his situation is more or less important than mine, not a love that says he is right or I am right, but simply a love that allows the process to unfold in an atmosphere of unconditional acceptance of where we both are. And a love that cares for all concerned. And trust!

It was an important act of unconditional love to take care of myself, first and foremost, as I listened to my inner voice as I integrated my messages, and navigated all our upcoming life changes. And also importantly, to be there listening and caring and loving Michael every step of his way.

A year after that first ceremony, we had made major changes in our lives, as Michael has described. It was a whirlwind of alterations and adjustments, to say the least. It was obvious that Mother Ayahuasca and Grandfather San Pedro were still behind the scenes taking excellent care of Michael and myself.

Spurred on by my inspired ceremony with Grandfather San Pedro, shortly after we returned home from our vacation, I finally heeded my inner voice that had been speaking for 5 years – I went by myself to Hawaii to snorkel for 3 months and was "Auntie Deb" to a precious family with two young children; both were enormously healing to me. It seems amazing to me now, but the serendipitous way this unfolded dissolved any concerns I had about leaving Michael alone at home while I followed my healing path.

Also, before my Hawaii trip, I retired early from my career, it turns out, permanently. I believe that the plant medicines had melted away many layers of fear and paralyzing inaction enabling us to see what our possibilities truly were. We easily made the decision and moved out of the country, irresistibly propelled by some inside guidance that helped us finalize our multi-year research and quell our fears to become expats.

Our lives were taking massive new turns, with huge adjustments required, and we had no idea what was in store for us in the future. Yet we had eagerly shed our old lives and started down our new paths. Normal reasoning processes had mostly been shelved and we were operating from an elevated perspective, initiated by our inner higher selves and nurtured into massive expansion by our Ayahuasca and San Pedro ceremonies. Any fears, put in our new and proper perspective, naturally dissolved. We were claiming our aliveness. There was a lot to be very grateful for.

Even though Michael was still embroiled in his post-ceremony trauma with no resolution on the horizon, he had made some huge changes. So had I. In spite of ourselves, Ayahuasca and San Pedro seemed to still be working, behind the scenes, at the core, and we were witnessing the surprising and welcomed evidence in our improved lives. It's easier to see this looking back, rather than at the time, of course.

I did notice that the "light" was back in his eyes, and this is something I continue to notice every day, many times a day, even now. I was very encouraged and so grateful for this tangible sign of progress.

After our big move, initially Michael did not want to continue working with any sacred plant medicines, and I was thrilled to be in the South American world where I could explore that sacred space frequently and fully. It is so tempting to be judgmental about this. And so important NOT to be.

Even though I was more open at the time to working with the medicines, and Michael was not at first, both of us were following our paths. I had to realize whether slow or fast, burdened or expansive, easy or hard, I had my path and he had his path, and it was vital for both of us to relate with each other without judgment. Especially since I saw how all of that shifted so quickly for us. I learned quickly to honor wherever we both were, without any right or wrong about it. Being "on the path" is a perception thing and the medicine had shown Michael and me how woefully inaccurate perceptions could be – and had been.

When Michael was supporting me at this point, which he did in spite of his own challenges, he did so out of respect for my life course, concerns for potential pitfalls, love for me, and a willingness to "allow" whatever was necessary for me to grow. Sometimes, I think when he "allowed", that it was simply knowing that my desires were so strong that he couldn't make me change my mind in spite of his fears about that ceremony space.

And I'll have to say that for a while I thought I had the upper hand in navigating the medicine space since he was not participating. Talk about my ego being in play. When I'm tempted to go in that direction, it's been helpful to take a healthy dose of reality. He's not better or worse than me; he's not further along nor am I. All that is simply judgment on the human level that has no bearing on the beings we truly are.

We are all on our own individual path, and one path is not better or worse than another's. After all, red, yellow, purple, green and blue (and more) are all beautiful colors in our landscape of life and who's to say which color is more evolved. My egotistical assessment has often gotten challenged and I realize how ridiculous it is to judge, when we simply don't have the higher "sight" to make proper judgments.

In our new home in our new country, almost immediately I participated in another Ayahuasca ceremony. Afterwards, my direction with Mother

Ayahuasca took a sudden detour – what I thought my course was initially got halted abruptly. I had a beautiful and insightful journey, however the interactions with some staff at the retreat center demonstrated clearly to me that loving integration support was horribly missing there, and needed to be essential in any future ceremony space. I had suppressed my initial intuitive "nudges" and concerns previously, and it quickly became apparent that indiscretions, viciousness, and runaway egos had no place in sacred plant medicine space. While I was grateful for the huge insights that caused this, and was glad for the redirection, for a while I had no idea what was next. My integration was continuing, albeit roughly, vigorously, and solidly in an excellent direction though it didn't seem like it at the time. In fact, for a while I thought Michael had been right all along and that the plant medicine space was more treacherous than desired, especially if you chose the wrong retreat center or shaman or facilitator who didn't walk their loving talk, etc.

Never underestimate the value of powerful intentions and synchronicity. What we had both asked for initially, was being realized and manifested in our lives. We were NOT going to go just partway and then stall. Small steps were being taken; huge strides had already happened and were continuing. We were so close to the situation that it was hard to see it all at the time, yet it WAS happening, in an undeniably ongoing process. We were amazed with how our lives were already unfolding.

We heard some recommendations from a friend about working with Kambo and San Pedro. We were impressed by this friend's energy, the light in his eyes, and his life-changing story. Our ears perked up and we really heard and felt the "call." If you ever wonder if someone or you have been "called" to the medicine, just hear / feel the undeniable resonance with that idea. It's like a loud clear bell ringing. Both of us were "called" this time, and it felt good that we were both completely aligned with the same process at the same time. I was gung ho, and so was Michael.

Once again though, I completely underestimated and unanticipated what would happen.

After those three Kambo ceremonies and two San Pedro ceremonies, which answered Michael's big question, and then two San Pedro ceremonies the following month, I can only say that I'm in awe. And filled with gratitude. And completely in awe.

What a transformation in Michael, and I had witnessed it firsthand. He had turned the corner in his healing process. I had seen a beautiful shaman work in a quiet and effective way with Michael and with myself. What a difference!

It was surprising to me how our relationship had taken leaps and bounds in that past year, culminating with these ceremonies. While we had always been "simpatico" and finely tuned in with each other, doing Kambo and then San Pedro together were magical ways to unite deeply with each other. We had reached new levels of intimacy and vulnerability. We were next to each other, as we both projectile vomited during Kambo. For three days. On each of the days, we were in sync as we slept and recovered after the sessions.

On the second day of Kambo, I had a very difficult time, which Michael witnessed. And he shared how I'd looked at him and how I interacted with the shaman who was helping; I was once again that hurt but hopeful three-year old. That gave me insights into my process for which I was grateful. And we both experienced the spot-on intuition and instincts of the shaman as he guided us through each of the three days of Kambo.

Michael shared his revelation about the "CGI ants" and "They exist – and they don't exist" with me, and my heart leapt with incredible joy! At last – he had his answer. And one that he could accept, completely understand, and take in fully. I breathed such sighs of relief when I saw the emotional weight lift from him. And his messages became my messages as these were also very helpful to me.

In the past, there had been times that I wished he'd never gone down that path. After all, his primary focus had been to support me, although he was participating also out of curiosity and honest questioning about his future. There were times that I blamed the retreat center, especially the head person and the shaman, for not "holding the space" and for not providing the necessary integration support.

While all that is valid, and shame on them for not doing so, it has only been recently that I have seen the intricate way that Mother Ayahuasca and Grandfather San Pedro work. For Michael, this was the only way – Michael needed the ceremony to unfold the way it did, because he would have rejected the message any other way. And in fact he probably would have rejected any "calling" too, so the path to the medicine and to healing was through my "calling" and his loving support for me.

And all that means that spiritual growth, emotional healing, regaining aliveness will happen in response to our innate "calling" to heal and experience life in healthy and vibrant ways. It's who we are; it's what is natural to us.

After the third day of Kambo concluded we both felt "complete" and light and free. We walked into town, and enjoyed a delicious lunch. Imagine, after all those Kambo sessions, we felt so good we could enjoy a lovely meal right after projectile vomiting for a couple hours. The next day we continued our work with San Pedro. Again, we were so tightly connected and in sync with each other as we drank the medicine, shared our intentions, and experienced our days. Sharing our divination readings later that evening was a treat. Our journeys couldn't have been more different, yet we couldn't have been more "together."

It was great serendipity that we participated in two more ceremonies one month later. In every one of these seven ceremonies, I also experienced for myself miraculous and deep healing, along with powerful insights. Doing it together, our intimate and vulnerable connection was getting deeper and more powerful.

Supporting Michael at this point was pretty easy. He was on fire. And making leaps and bounds in his learning and healings. It was like watching a snowball roll downhill picking up speed, momentum and it couldn't be stopped. I saw how he was learning how to be in the medicine space in the most effective way, and I was able to truly trust that Grandfather was expertly guiding him on his path. Because I SAW it happening. I stopped worrying. Finally. At least for a while. Even though it would be another six months before he would be ready to work with Mother Ayahuasca.

After these ceremonies, I was directed by San Pedro to stop doing ceremonies for the time being. I was alternately happy but disappointed with this recommendation. I'd enjoyed the connectedness with Michael during the ceremonies, and this wouldn't be continuing, at least for the time being. Both of us were again on different paths. We accepted this direction without hesitation and we did question it. While I could see the path that Michael was on, there were times that he questioned the wisdom of me stopping ceremonies for a while. Finally we were both able to let go.

Now Michael would continue his journeys independently. And I would be with him in ceremony in a much different way, emotionally connected but not physically present in the space. He would be sharing before and afterwards about his next calling, his intentions, and then his experiences and insights. Also he shared his lucid dreams with me. I shared my dreams and continued insights with him. It was good.

One of the keys to navigating this space together, was that we were both witnessing each other's wounds, traumas, patterns, and we were both vulnerable and intimate with each other. We shared completely and neither of us judged the other. Or if we did, we were able to hold it in an accepting way, even laugh at our situations and our judgments. Both of us were owning and loving ourselves more than ever, and therefore we could do the same for the other.

In supporting people who have experienced the medicine, and are integrating the messages, inspirations and lessons into their "real" lives,

I've seen how important it is to not judge people. That's not always easy to pull off. Yet, when I realized that everyone learns in their own way and in their own time, it doesn't make any sense to judge them. It did make sense though to hold my ground about what was right for me. And not be afraid of the fireworks.

As he continued to work with San Pedro and I saw his progress over the months, and heard about every detail of his ceremonies, I still hadn't learned to trust completely. Does that ever go away? Perhaps. I got to be gentle with myself as I worked through that process.

To say that I was nervous about him going back to Mother Ayahuasca is another understatement.

What helped the most was that I hugely respected Michael's desire to complete his process with Mother Ayahuasca. That was one mighty loose end to wrap up. Yet I could go down so many rabbit holes. I had seen what had happened before, and I was afraid for him. Was I projecting my lack of courage and insisting that not working with Ayahuasca was the right path? Was I concerned that he wouldn't be able to handle it, or that the shaman wouldn't hold the space properly?

Or was I jealous of his progress and wished that I was in that mental mindset to work confidently with the plant medicines again. Especially when I'd been directed NOT to. Ultimately, I needed to let go, and trust that he would navigate his process in the best way he could, and that I needed to respect that. Also I needed to respect myself and my path.

And that seems to be so key to supporting well the person on the sacred medicine path – manage yourself and your fears, trust the process, respect all concerned and love unconditionally. In many ways the shaman's story of the healer that Michael has related really made sense to me. This healer initially was healing people, was learning better ways to heal and perhaps inflating his ego along the way, and then ultimately stopping his activity of healing people because he saw that they were healing themselves all along. In supporting Michael, was I coming from ego or love? Did I have his answers and he did not? I felt like I was madly fluctuating between supporting him and trusting that he could find his own way until I was able to see that he was navigating well. Sure he still needed me, but not my ego, just my love.

So he went back to Mother Ayahuasca. He came back, in one piece, not traumatized. It was intense and good. He had survived and thrived. He had ridden the roller coaster through all the phases, and he had emerged victorious. What a huge relief for me!

I have realized that in witnessing his experiences with him, and seeing how it all works out months later, it gave me an enhanced ability to trust more unreservedly and completely when future situations arise.

At this point, it was a pleasure to join him when he continued with the Grandfather San Pedro ceremony, when Mother Ayahuasca showed up instead. That sure gave me a chuckle. Since it was mostly friends that were there for that day, I was going to hang out at the house where the ceremony was being held. Everyone there was going to be in the medicine, and I was not. While I had no idea what Michael was going through during that ceremony, I was happy to connect with him when he needed that tangible expression of love. That evening, it was a treat to hear of everyone's journeys and messages.

I was continuing to see, that for Michael, the medicine was working very powerfully and on purpose with him. He would seize opportunities within the medicine to go deeper, to listen more fully, and he had become proficient at understanding the medicine space and utilizing it adeptly.

Over the next many months, I witnessed him exploring the space in a different way. I had still not been called back to the medicine, and honored that lack of calling. It had become easier to honor my path which was quite different than Michael's, and to honor his path as well, since we were both able to respect each other's perspectives and contributions. Often when Michael did a ceremony and drew a divination card afterwards, he would draw one for me and that card would accurately portray what my process was at the time. Quite fun, actually!

Oftentimes, it seemed as though both of us were speaking and living from more rarefied medicine space territory – in other words, we were consciously accessing and operating from our intuition which was growing in leaps and bounds. We shared our nighttime dreams, our daytime musings and meditations and learned much from each other. We were learning to trust more, live life more spontaneously and without consternation or judgment when things did or did not work out. We were both "feeling" much more intensely, on both ends of the emotional spectrum and learned to flow into an acceptance of those enhanced impressions. Our discussions grew more lively and even contentious and the results were very rewarding as we were both able to accept and allow varied opinions while sharing our own and finding common ground if that was possible. Sometimes it wasn't.

We were still trying to figure out what our new lives in our new country were going to be all about. What was our purpose? Where would our passions be? These were questions that we brought to the medicine space and explored in our daily lives.

When Michael wrote about The Four Offerings, I really got the message that it wasn't about always trying to "fix" the problem, since *there really isn't any problem, simply a healing or unfolding process and going through the four stages. Wherever Ayahuasca or San Pedro wants to take you, it is important to have an attitude of acceptance and allowing. Easier said than done when you are trying to support someone in the aftermath of integration. It is so much easier to love someone when you are able to see their true divine essence and who they really are – a beautiful being who is capable, complete and able to navigate their life adventures and explorations. It helps to "hold on loosely" which is easier when you have that confidence in the underlying love that forms our Universe. And to accept that crap might actually be good, especially when "there is no good, there is no evil."*

So how does all that apply when choosing where to do your ceremonies. Ayahuasca is a tourism industry too and there are plenty of centers ready to take your money, pour some brew, and call it good. While it is vital to choose the proper shaman and retreat center, I finally realized that our best efforts had been good enough for those initial ceremonies – I'm extremely grateful for all the good that came from them, in spite of the challenges. Mother Ayahuasca and Grandfather San Pedro will "work" sometimes in spite of the retreat setup. The important thing is that we got there and we embarked on powerful healing paths! On that note, here's a few things we learned about choosing your ceremony space.

Personally I wouldn't go with written online recommendations alone. People tend to share good experiences; they will rarely share rough experiences as they may feel that it will negatively reflect on them or they will be subject to backlash. I found value in talking with people, one-on-one.

Find out how many people are in each ceremony – I would aim for lower numbers as it is challenging for anyone, even an experienced shaman to properly hold the space for too many people. Twenty or twenty-five may be way too many even with more than one shaman presiding.

Find out what type of integration support is offered during and after the ceremonies, and after you return home. This was sadly missing in our retreat, as other than the two shamans (who were not available enough for after-ceremony support), and the lead facilitator (who was likewise absent for after-care and didn't even show up during the sharing circles), there were only volunteer and/or untrained staff without professional credentials who were not knowledgeable nor experienced in handling after-ceremony emotions and traumas. In fact, the best support person at our retreat was a volunteer, and this was his first retreat in a support function.

Find out if the staff are volunteers and what training is provided. We were on the receiving end of volunteers sharing incorrect and frightening information, with good but misguided intentions. We saw staff being overworked and not available for questions or support. If the support staff are mostly volunteers who are only being compensated with room and board in exchange for work hours, then you will tend to have constant turnover with little focus on enhancing training and support since they'll be gone soon anyways. In South America there are visa restrictions so unless someone has a residency visa, they will typically have to leave the country within 3-6 months.

I really appreciated those volunteers who provided loving help during my ceremonies – I will never forget them! Thank you VERY much! I know there are many who are attracted to these retreat centers who have their hearts and intentions in the right place. Over the last few years, I have talked with many of them who worked at various centers and sadly though, there seems to be a consensus that their biggest challenges were NOT how to support the clients during rough journeys, but how to deal with the top-dogs who owned and ran the centers.

Look for other red flags such as inflated pricing and inflated egos. Some ceremonies with excellent shamans cost very little; others cost a lot more. Sometimes the costs are justified; often they are not. Labor and services in many parts of South America are inexpensive compared with other countries. Regarding the egos, it may be hard to sense this before you get there, but do as much research as you can. Don't be intimidated by what seems to be spiritual advancement, or metaphysical prowess – listen to your instincts here. I loved Michael's sharing of what constitutes a real shaman. I have had the privilege of meeting many shamans, facilitators and retreat owners in the last few years and it is pretty easy to see what is truly valuable for clients doing the sacred plant medicines and what is not. So follow your intuition on this and don't be afraid to call "bullshit" even if it is only to yourself.

We can have a funky view of karma – if we are experiencing something crappy in our lives, we can become resigned to the so-called karmic necessity of it; but who's to say that throwing off that perspective is what is needed instead – perhaps the karmic necessity requires us to say, "No more, I'm done. I deserve better. I deserve happiness, freedom and joy!"

In supporting myself, and supporting Michael, during our journey, in summary this is what I've found to be most helpful:

Active Listen. *I found that simply listening to him was enough. I didn't have to agree or disagree. Just listen. With heart.*

Listen Within. *Listen to your intuition within, and don't be afraid to* *follow it. Without justification. And the other person who's been in the medicine also has some powerful intuitions.*

Don't Sabotage. *Don't encourage the reinstatement of old habits that no longer serve. And don't ridicule, rather encourage the nurturing of new productive habits. Allow the nurturing of new relationships, new pastimes, and new interests.*

Physical and Emotional Habits. *Stay on the dieta as long as you can, and incorporate some of the dieta elements permanently. Support your new-found preferences: for example, if you have found that you have no more desire for alcohol, stay away from environments where that is the norm. Support your physicality by exercising, eating well, and getting plenty of rest. Massages can be nice. Support your emotionality by giving yourself more quiet time in the form of meditation, yoga or some other centering and calming practice.*

Don't Judge. *Some people come to the medicine fully prepared and still have horrific journeys that require healing support afterwards; others come woefully unprepared and have powerful insightful journeys. Everyone has their own path. Be grateful that the person is on the path of healing now, whatever that may look like.*

Get Help. *If reaching out to the shaman or the retreat personnel doesn't work, do know there are plenty of integration counselors that specialize in working with people with post-Ayahuasca ceremony issues. Reach out, get help. They are familiar with the ceremony space and will be able to shed light on the process. We didn't realize there was that support out there, and there's been an increasing awareness of the need for it, so there's even more integration support available now.*

Gratitude. *Search for and recognize the positive changes that have already occurred, and be grateful. Oftentimes, these changes are not apparent at first until you realize how much has actually changed. See these changes as proof that healing is occurring, and have patience as the next healing steps formulate and emerge.*

Trust. *A valuable process is unfolding, and while it can be insightful, beautiful, it can also be arduous, painful and unrelenting. For Michael it took two years; for others it can take more or less time. You can strengthen the process, by knowing that others have been in the same place and they came out the other end in triumph. Read about their stories and be* *inspired. And whatever you can do to replace spiraling negative thoughts that can overwhelm – do it. Replace worry with confidence that it will work out, panic with calm as you listen for the next step, over-thinking with following your intuitive nudges. You truly can TRUST that all is unfolding in good time as the Universe is Love.*

Forgiveness. *When you falter in your support and understanding, and you will, forgive yourself and them. Over and over again. That kindness and gentleness that you embody when forgiving will help you take the next step with grace. I found it helpful to forgive myself and then act as though I truly had forgiven myself.*

Laughter and Lightness. *Don't take it so seriously all the time. Change up the energy; plan something fun and frivolous – it doesn't have to expensive. Appreciate the little things. Laughter is indeed the best medicine. If you can't find something to laugh about, just start laughing and you'll find he'll join in and maybe never wonder why.*

Unconditional Love. *There is a difference between a cloying, controlling love that is fraught with fear, and unconditional Love that loves the person EXACTLY how he is, who he is, and what he is experiencing, with compassionate acceptance and allowing for all the good unfolding.*

The other night I drew a divination card. I asked a comment about our two-plus year journey so far – including our major move to a foreign country, and our ongoing path with Mother Ayahuasca and San Pedro. The card was all about celebrating being victorious!

How appropriate! We have been focused relentlessly on creating our new lives and healing. At times, it was hard to have faith and often we got the needed reinforcement that all was well. We have manifested amazing changes, and beautiful healings. It feels good to bask in savoring our successes and knowing that the future will unfold in an equally astounding and surprising way. I am grateful about where we've been and how far we've come. I love celebrating our victories to date, and eagerly anticipate the next installment.

Deborah Joy Miller

Postscript

"They call it the medicine. We call it the poison."

More than two years after those words were whispered with venomous pleasure, they hold no charge for me. If anything, they've become a phantasm of underlying archetypal fear that once formed the undercurrent of my whole life. It was a life throttled by fear, made risk-adverse to the point of suffocation of so much dream stuff, the very essence of my potential. In the place of all that could be grew fear, drama, story in glossy guises with hidden strings moving my unaware puppet. Incredibly, while I was going through this limitation year after year, I thought I was operating in my best interest.

How could so much go so wrong for so long and be so acceptable as normal? Everything seemed good enough. And "good enough" was part of the amnesiac narrative. How could bad ever come from good? Medicine space showed me anything is possible when creative force is applied to our magical energies. As Pachacutec, the Inca ruler said, "He who envies the good draws evil from them for himself, just as the spider draws poison from flowers." Bad can come from good if we allow ourselves to slip into amnesia and illusion, negating who we are. Action then gets driven by a misunderstanding. As they say, it's an illusion, but a persistent one. And persistence is one of the keys to its power over us.

I heard a story of one woman in another part of the world who commented a day after her Ayahuasca experience, "It was cool but what did it mean?" As the shaman says, it's not the experience that matters but the knowledge that comes from it.

Should we think ultimate meaning comes instantly? Did we expect answers to be literally handed over or were they something one needed to bring out for yourself and feel? Did we think the medicine was a magic pill that works by itself in one sitting? Are we aware of changes yet to rise up in us? Will we be watching for them? With what intention did we enter and exit the space? Did we surrender to the medicine process or fight it as best we could? What thoughts have we given to how we'll integrate and meditate on all that transpired? More than what it meant – how did it feel?

It's significant how primal knowledge from medicine space begins and ends with feeling, not grand philosophies or blueprints. I can start a ceremony with a single question, but how I proceed from there is so important. I have found if I churn with follow-up questions, debate or interview the medicine spirit over what it sends back to me, the day proceeds to interesting but ultimately superficial levels.

On the other hand, if I ask my question then go into how the question makes me feel – if I then surrender to the ride the medicine takes me on from there, it's possible to go deep and see where underlying core issues fester, where new perspectives give illumination, where I accept the offer to move through my stuff.

On the other side of that surrender and journey into feeling, a healing may wash over me, old patterns may dissolve away, new priorities may form out of a better understanding. Or I may feel more work needs to be done but progress has been made. I don't know if knowing this before my very first ceremony would have helped me or not. Would I have listened to it? Could I understand without experiencing it for myself?

In my case, I was facing a fundamental question – were my fears real? Well, as one particular shaman smiled and told me – "They exist – and they don't exist. If you put your awareness there, then they exist. Your fear makes them real." But how is that possible? Fear producing fear, up from its bootstraps? How does that work? How does it ever start? The plant medicine spirits laid it out for me in excruciating detail over many ceremonies, with heart-wrenching emotion, through wild-ride experiences that burned changes into my very core.

I've learned to pay attention to paradoxes and dilemmas, those seemingly unsolvable knots of life. I've been shown it's at those very points, the nexus of anxiety and confusion, where one is closest to a resolution, to a breakthrough, to a transformation. The darkness before the dawn. The shock before the awe. If I had given up at the point of shock, if I had allowed my fears to chase me away, so much potential would have been lost.

On that night so long ago, the night I once called the worst night of my life, I was made to go into those fears, to face them, to move through them, to let them scrape my soul clean of any notion that keeping them at bay was the best course of action. What I truly faced that night was fear itself, not dark interdimensional entities. They were only the best manifestation of fear for me to experience in the context the plant spirits had to work with. As they lamented to me, if they had approached me any other way, I would have argued with them. They needed to approach me in a way tailored to get through to me. Everyone's journey is unique to them, fashioned in response to what the medicines find when they do their scan of the person coming to them.

A shaman told me a story once about a man who had a remarkable ceremony experience and exclaimed to his friend all about it. The friend was so taken and inspired that he too went to a ceremony. But afterwards, the friend berated the shaman, claiming he was cheated, asserting the whole thing was nonsense. The shaman inquired why the man felt this way. Because this ceremony was nothing like what my friend described, shouted the man. The shaman wasn't flustered. He merely informed the man that each ceremony is unique. What one experiences or takes away from it is meant *only for them and only on that day*. It is a communication with what each person brings to ceremony. The man got the exact ceremony meant for him and him alone on that day. No more, no less.

My experience was horrendous and yet, as whacked as it sounds, it was truly the quickest, best way for me to begin to experience that fear held no real power over me.

For I did walk away from that experience. I did survive. I did come back. More than that, I came back with something added to me, even if I wasn't aware or didn't fully understand it at the time.

I moved into the future with a new inner setting, a new resolve, a blossoming perspective that provided in time an opening of possibilities. As a shaman told me once, there are two things one must do to be healthy – move and have no fear. Moving keeps the body healthy and balanced. No fear keeps the soul from falling into rabbit holes with no way out. What the medicines did for me is show me the way to move forward, giving me a way to pull the rabbit hole out of the hat and dispense with it. The rabbit was never there to begin with. Not really. It was nothing but a distraction made earnest by my fear.

Fear is very creative. It'll find devious, even no-fear ways of reinforcing itself in our lives. It'll have us thinking we are acting in our best interest, being perfectly logical, prudent, and wise. That's why so much of what we think of ourselves when we plunge into medicine space can't be trusted. Is it truly us or only our fear and hurt talking? How did we ever get to the point where we believe we are that fearful and hurt? As much as we loathe it, we can't see how we can ever be separated from it. In turn, we silently loathe ourselves. I learned in ceremony we gain the most in medicine space by surrendering – but never surrender in fear. Surrender in trust and gratitude. It makes all the difference.

How unique a gift to be taken to a place where fear had lost its power over me. What would that even be like? I was no longer like the elephant trained since it was very young to believe the chain around its foot was an effective means to hold it in place. For many years the adult version of me had remained in place long after outgrowing that chain. Was the chain ever there? Yes and no. I know now both can be true simultaneously. In that fully-dimensioned paradox there's hope. In that there's a chance of seizing back one's power of self-determination. In that is burgeoning potential, anywhere one decides to direct their energies.

At any time I could have snapped that chain at will. If I chose. But I never tried to choose. There was no point if it didn't matter. No point if the chain was as strong as I always believed it was. Even if what I thought I knew was wrong. I didn't know that. I had no perspective to see that. My lie had become my truth. Once in place, it was no longer a lie. My belief had made it a truth. It governed so many decisions along the way. It assured I'd stay locked in a comfortable routine of diminished expectations. It left me with a false certainty and faux comfort. For so long it was what it was. That's life. As I acquiesced to it, a wider matrix of opportunistic influences swallowed me.

During shock and before awe I heard the last thing said to me by the dark entities. At the time, it hit me hard. It was the ultimate, most self-enclosing trap of despair I could imagine.

"*YOU created this!*" I still hear the way the whispered but guttural exclamation chilled the air.

Now I see how right the entities were. Even though I was in no condition to realize it at the time, I was being given the ultimate message of hope. And yet I took it as soul-crushing despair. I know how crazy that sounds. Working through the paradoxes we've made of ourselves can be crazy at times. That is the power of fear. But if I created this, I could uncreate it. I could take back my power. I could channel my energies through the clear mirror, not the funhouse mirror. And that was what Mother Ayahuasca was trying to get me to see. In time, with the help of Kambo and San Pedro and the help and patience of a remarkable shaman – and eventually with return visits to Mother Ayahuasca, I saw it too. I felt it.

What started with denial and reluctance has broken through to perception and willingness. I've passed through my warped, funhouse mirror. I've burned away so many distortions born of fear. I've stared long and hard into my clear mirror and at times was so overwhelmed I felt I couldn't accept it all. The completeness of it knocked the breath out of me. Gasping, overloaded, I thought at times it was too much to bear. But then the medicine took me deeper, where none of it was about thinking. It's always been about heart and always will be. They showed me how heart can hold so much more than mind.

The plant medicine spirit guides never gave up on me. They never tried to monetize me or enlist me in their cult. They never categorized me with labels from the DSM-5. They helped me wash the mud off. They didn't tell me I was mud-man and try a practice on me to deal with me being little more than mud. They never tried to over-prescribe themselves as an ongoing for-life regimen. At times they even told me flatly, "*You're done for now.*" In their otherworldly way they opened new perspectives then offered experiences into which I could step forward – or not. When I did, I was the one who took myself forward. Not into symptoms. Into causes. Into healing. Into more.

They were there reliably to guide. And in time, my clear mirror opened up into a window on so much more. At times, in timeless flashes, that window has faded to become a portal into wonders and realms of love and joy and ecstasy and creative unfoldment previously unimaginable. And I know now, more assuredly than I know this world exists (and doesn't) – that this complete level of being is our real legacy. Our real home. And it's always near. So near it's part of us. As we are part of it all. But all of us already know that, somewhere inside, even if we don't fathom or feel it. And feeling it made all the difference. It's like feeling a real mother's love. Once felt, nothing can erase or call into question its existence.

I asked Grandfather San Pedro once if visiting medicine space was only for working on issues, correcting one's problems, or finding lasting healing. I wondered if expansive learning and exploration by itself could be valid reasons to enter the space. On that particular day when I asked he allowed me only one question. The rest of the day would be without words. But he did answer with – "*What's the difference?*" His answer came across blunt and perplexing, even when its deeper meaning unwrapped in my head and heart.

His answer became clear. To need more learning and seek more exploration in medicine space implied something needed to be healed, or a problem or negative energy needed to be cleared. Conversely, to seek healing and freedom from a problem implied more learning and exploration was required. To be free of one meant liberation from the need for the other. Both existed hand-in-hand.

If I came to the medicine because I believed I needed to learn and explore more, no doubt there was more to heal. In other words, I was admitting to myself I not "there" yet – which is another way of saying I hadn't woken up to realize I had been and always would be there. It could be no other way. I extended this with what he told me a year before – *"There will come a time when you'll arrive at a place beyond lessons and messages, beyond healing, beyond studied exploration."*

So am I there yet? Will I have more issues to work on, more healing needed, more to learn, more to explore? I might as well ask how is it the universe is infinite? How would the medicine answer me?

I can hear Grandfather chuckling in the background with the latest rising dilemma twirling in 256 dimensions in the palm of his hand, showing me the next iteration of the creative fractal – a perplexed state born of mind that doesn't have to be that way.

I also sense the strength of Kambo providing the resistance to push against the limitation of mind in the void of weightless possible space in order to get things moving.

And right alongside them, I feel Mother Ayahuasca zooming me through empty, expectant drama sets of my mind's endless sound stage.

These plant spirits know what is next for me is inherent in the design. It's a design infinite but emergent, creative but chaotic, definite yet probabilistic. None of it will be pinned down and I wouldn't want it to be. They have made that clear. And yet they have also shown me how the one most likely to pin me down is myself. We create the rabbit holes we jump in. Navigating that landscape will always be wide open with possibilities. Inherent in that is the greatest game creation ever played, but not to win, only for the experience of joy and love.

For myself, I have and will again arrive at places beyond lessons and messages, beyond healing and explorations. Once there, so much more will unfold in and out of me. It can't be described solely as lessons and messages, healings or explorations anymore. It can't be described at all. It would seem self-evident within an infinite creation this would be so. Once on the way, we simply merge with medicine space and such questions of limits won't make sense any more.

The infinite speed of discovery I find there will leave me standing still since anyone going that speed is effectively everywhere at once. In that moment, that paradox will not be an issue. It will be understood. As will so many others. But more wonders will have to unfold in that infinite search space.

So what more is there to me? What more is there to infinity anyway? What more can one see or be in medicine space? Perhaps the answer lies in something I'll always remember, something I feel is the most positive, uplifting thing any of us can hear…

"YOU created this!"

IAM

I am not body
I am not soul
I am the space that forms the bowl

I am not name
I am not eyes
I am the pause between the sighs

I am not emotions
I am not thoughts
I am the other way across

I am not passion
I am not role
I am the peace in place of the goal

I am not future
I am not past
I am the quickening and the vast

I am not beginning
I am not end
I am everything that nothing intends

I am not probability
I am not potential
I am what appears when everything's essential

I am not question
I am not answer
I am the trance in everyone's dancer

I am not pattern
I am not force
I am the reason there can never be a Source

I am everything I am
I am everything I'm not
I am the how in the why of all whatnot

I didn't write this
You didn't read it
I didn't expect it
You won't remember it
It's the abyss of bliss
The way everything fits

www.ingramcontent.com/pod-product-compliance
Lightning Source LLC
LaVergne TN
LVHW041538070426
835507LV00011B/818